Restructuring
Development Theories and Policies

Restructuring
Development Theories and Policies

A Critical Study

M. Shamsul Haque

State University of New York Press

Published by
State University of New York Press, Albany

For information, address State University of New York
Press, State University Plaza, Albany, N.Y., 12246

Production by Diane Ganeles
Marketing by Anne Valentine

Library of Congress Cataloging-in-Publication Data

Haque, M. Shamsul.
    Restructuring development theories and policies : a critical study
  / M. Shamsul Haque.
        p.   cm.
    Includes bibliographical references and index.
    ISBN 0-7914-4257-8 (hc. : alk. paper). — ISBN 0-7914-4258-6 (pbk.
  : alk. paper)
    1. Economic development—Case studies.   I. Title
  HD75.H317   1999
  338.9—dc21   99-17954
                                                                   CIP

10   9   8   7   6   5   4   3   2   1

For My Parents

Contents

Preface   ix

Chapter 1: An Introductory Overview   1

Chapter 2: Practical Crises of Development   13

    Development Crises in Third World Countries   14
    Crises in Capitalist and Socialist Countries   20
    Development Crises at the Global Level   23

Chapter 3: A Taxonomic Prelude to Development Theories   39

    Taxonomic Principles for Development Theories   41
    Major Limitations of the Existing Classifications   44
    Restructured Taxonomy of Development Theories   47

Chapter 4: Conservative Tradition of Development Theories   53

    Theories of Economic Growth   54
    Theories of Modernization   72

Chapter 5: Reformist Tradition of Development Theories   81

    Conservative Reformist Theories   84
    Radical Reformist Theories   89
    Critical Reformist Theories   97

Chapter 6: Radical Tradition of Development Theories   103

    Classical Marxist Theories   105
    Radical Dependency Theories   111
    Neo-Marxist Theories   115

Chapter 7: A Critique of Development Theories   129

    Theoretical Shortcomings in the Development Field   130
    Adverse Implications of Current Development Thinking   144
    Newly Emerging Challenges to the Development Field   153

Chapter 8: Restructuring Concepts and Theories of Development 161

    Redefining Development as a Concept   162
    Restructuring Development Theories   173

Chapter 9: Reforming Development Policies   205

    Reforming Policies to Achieve Natural-Physiological Autonomy 206
    Reforming Policies to Realize Politico-Economic Autonomy   217
    Reforming Policies to Enhance Cultural-Intellectual Autonomy 233
    Summary and Conclusion   243

Notes   249

References   311

Name Index   363

Subject Index   367

Preface

After decades of struggle for development, it is increasingly apparent that there has not been any considerable socioeconomic progress in many Third World countries which continue to suffer from adverse human conditions such as economic poverty, social inequality, political instability, and external dependence. These symptoms of underdevelopment are also becoming permanent features in the former socialist countries, especially after the recent collapse of their statist regimes and adoption of market-centered reforms. On the other hand, the advanced capitalist nations still remain perplexed with fiscal crises, trade deficits, social pathologies, crimes, and violence. At the global level, the problems of unequal world order, ethno-religious conflicts, environmental pollution, and ecological disasters also continue to be serious developmental concerns. These diverse national and international crises of development can be considered, to a great extent, as the manifestations of the failures of the whole development enterprise comprised of various development theories, models, policies, projects, agencies, and experts. In this regard, Sachs makes the following comment: "The idea of development stands like a ruin in the intellectual landscape. Delusion and disappointment, failures and crimes have been the steady companions of development and they tell a common story: it did not work."[1]

The experiences of the development failure, however, have not constrained the expansion of the development field. In fact, the scope of development theories and policies has multiplied and led to continual production and reproduction of development-related literature. Within the conservative tradition, there emerged various economic growth theories (including classical theory, neoclassical theory, new growth theory, Keynesian theory, post-Keynesian theory, unbalanced-growth theory, and stages-of-growth theory) and the theories of modernization (dealing with specific social, political, and cultural factors). The reformist tradition also offered varieties of development theories and models, which covered the basic needs approach, the redistribution-with-growth model, and the theories of underdevelopment and dependent development.

On the other hand, within the radical tradition, there evolved different versions of classical Marxist interpretations, neo-Marxist analyses, and dependency perspectives. Directly or indirectly, these theories, approaches, and models have often functioned as intellectual guidelines for formulating and implementing development policies and programs undertaken by varieties of regimes in capitalist, socialist, and Third World countries. In the process of studying, applying, advocating, and revising these theoretical frameworks, there has been an unprecedented expansion of the development field, especially in terms of the quantitative proliferation of books, journals, reports, seminars, graduate programs, and practical policies related to development.

Thus, there appears to be an incongruity between the continuing condition of underdevelopment on the one hand and the expanding scope of development theories and policies on the other, which implies the inadequacy and ineffectiveness of such development theories and policies themselves. It is because, to a large extent, the actual socioeconomic conditions related to development are products of various development policies, and these policies are usually guided by the prevalent development theories: the aforementioned adverse conditions of development, thus, indicate the ineffectiveness of development policies, which in turn reflects the inadequacy of development theories guiding such policies. With regard to the theoretical shortcomings in the development field, some of the contemporary development scholars suggest that people's confidence in the analytical capacity of the field has declined, that its major theoretical traditions are in crisis, and that its ideological foundation is in doubt.[2] This situation of inadequate development theories and ineffective development policies implies that there is a need for serious rethinking in the field.

In addition, the insufficiency of development theories and policies has become more critical today due to their incapacity to address certain newly emerging national and international events, including the changes in world order after the collapse of various socialist states, the worldwide triumph and expansion of capitalist ideology and market forces, the globalization of culture industry and information networks, the exacerbation of ethnic and religious uprisings, and the consolidation and radicalization of environmental movements. The inadequacy and incapacity of development theories and policies to encounter these unprecedented events also require the reexamination and restructuring of such theories and policies.

Among these current global events requiring a rethinking in development, one of the most crucial phenomena is the worldwide advocacy and dissemination of market ideology, which is not only evident in the endorsement of promarket programs (e.g., structural adjustments) and policies (e.g., privatization, deregulation, and liberalization) by varieties of regimes, it is also implied in the current theoretical shift in development thinking from a state-centered to market-oriented approach. Since the early 1980s, the dominant role of the state in development has come under attack in most Third World countries, and this role is increasingly being assumed by internal and international market forces.[3] The previous state-centered models of development, despite their adverse effects such as bureaucratic rigidity and inefficiency, were not without certain favorable socioeconomic outcomes, including economic growth, employment generation, income redistribution, and improvements in health, housing, and education.[4] However, these statist models are now being abandoned in favor of promarket policies based on rationales such as efficiency, competitiveness, innovation, deficit reduction, and revenue generation.[5]

But in reality, this emerging market-centered approach to development has not only failed to resolve the existing development crises, it has also worsened the situation further in many Third World countries. For instance, compared to the socioeconomic situation under the statist governments during the 1960s and 1970s, under the promarket regimes of the 1980s and 1990s, the condition of poverty has worsened in many African and Latin American countries in terms of an increase in the number of people in poverty, and a decline in economic-growth rate, per capita income, and living standards.[6] In these countries, under the promarket atmosphere created by the so-called structural adjustment programs, there has also been an expansion of socioeconomic inequality, especially in terms of the patterns of income distribution.[7] Some of these countries also experienced a worsening situation of external debt and dependence during the period of market-oriented reforms.[8] The condition of dependence has deteriorated further for most Third World countries due to the increasing penetration of transnational capital into their economies, expanding foreign ownership over their assets, growing external interference in their national economic policies, and diminishing status of their economic sovereignty.[9] These adverse implications of the emerging market-centered development framework, especially for Third World countries, also signifies an immediate need for reexamining and reconstructing the development field.

Theoretically, the dominant trend underlying these promarket development policies is the revival of neoclassical economic model as the primary basis of such policies. More specifically, the contemporary promarket programs, such as stabilization and structural adjustment, have this neoclassical model as the theoretical premise that assumes the superiority of market forces over state institutions, encourages the adoption of market-oriented policies such as deregulation and privatization, and recommends the transformation of the public sector based on market principles.[10] This renewal of neoclassical development model and its globalization represents a form of theoretical regression in the development field. It is because the limitations of the mainstream development theories (especially their indifference toward social inequality, external dependence, unequal exchange, and cultural hegemony) that became serious intellectual concerns in the past, have become increasingly acceptable in this age of promarket reforms guided by the neoclassical model that hardly addresses issues such as inequality, dependence, and hegemony. In line with this intellectual transition, most Third World countries have apparently changed their development priorities from basic needs and social equality to economic growth and efficiency, from equal world order to free international competition, from economic self-reliance to foreign investment, from cultural identity to global culture industry. These changes in development thinking represent a significant setback in the development field, which requires a serious theoretical reexamination and critique.

The above practical and intellectual contexts of development constitute the background and rationale of this book. It aims to offer a critique and reconstruction of the existing development theories and policies. It begins with a systematic account of the major forms of contemporary development crises such as poverty, inequality, external debt, dependence, environmental catastrophe, and unequal world order. The purpose of analyzing these practical development crises is to highlight the fact that the existing theories and policies of development have been relatively ineffective to interpret and overcome these crises, and to stress that there is a need for serious critical study of these theories and policies.

In this regard, the book not only presents an analysis of the prevailing theories and models of development in terms of their taxonomic identity, ideological positions, and main arguments, it also provides a critique of these theories and models in relation to their theoretical problems such as epistemological empiricism, normative indifference, analytical reductionism, and cultural ethnocentrism. In addition to the general assessment of these inherent theoretical shortcomings in the development field, this critique also explores the adverse implications of such theoretical shortcomings for more practical issues such as intellectual hegemony, politico-economic domination, cultural erosion, and environmental disorder. The criticism is extended further to examine the current worsening theoretical situation in the development field under the influence of the global market ideology. Such a critique is an essential prerequisite for any theoretical reconstruction in the development field. As Pieterse mentions, "the deconstruction of development is the prerequisite for its reconstruction."[11]

Following this theoretical critique, the book attempts to restructure development theories and offer a more holistic, multidimensional, and liberating development framework that emphasizes various units (group, class, nation, and international system) of analysis and covers different dimensions (economic, political, social, cultural, and ideological) of development. This reconstructed theoretical framework is subsequently used as an intellectual basis to reformulate the existing development policies into alternative policy measures, which may provide necessary practical guidelines to development managers or practitioners. In this whole process of restructuring development theories and policies, the primary emphasis is on human autonomy—this autonomy is not only from adverse material conditions such as poverty and hunger, but also from various forms of subjugation that exist between classes, between genders, between races or ethnic groups, and between nations.

It is likely that the book will be relevant to a broad range of societies, academic disciplines, and practical professions, especially due to its cross-cultural focus, multidimensional scope, and interdisciplinary perspective. More specifically, it will have considerable relevance to Third World countries and post-socialist nations looking for development alternatives, to the academics and practitioners dealing with development theories and policies, and to various social science disciplines offering courses in development and undertaking research on development issues. The book contains a significant amount of development literature—including the original theoretical works, recent academic studies, and professional reports—which serves to substantiate the analyses and critical arguments made in various chapters. This extensive list of development-related books, articles, and reports itself can be useful to those interested in development studies.

In the process of structuring, writing, and revising the manuscript, in many ways, I received help and cooperation from my friends and colleagues. In this regard, I am grateful to Roshen Kishun, Mohd Ghazali, Subhash Sharma, and Arvind Singhal for their moral support during the completion of the study and their enthusiasm regarding its publication. At the National University of Singapore, I would like to mention some of my colleagues who assisted me in various capacities: N. Ganesan and Zaheer Baber for proofreading certain chapters, Farid Alatas and Habib Khondker for encouragement, and James Jesudason for lending me some of his collections. I must mention also the cooperation I received from Zina Lawrence, Diane Ganeles, and Jennie Doling of the State University of New York Press in the process of publishing this book. Without their cooperation, it would be quite difficult to reach the final stage of publication. Lastly, it is necessary to highlight my indebtedness to the authors whose valuable works are used in this study. I alone am responsible for the entire content, including interpretations, arguments, and errors, of the book.

CHAPTER 1

An Introductory Overview

The need for a serious theoretical discourse in the field of development is paramount today. In recent years, there has been growing dissatisfaction among scholars within the conservative, reformist, and radical traditions with the existing knowledge of development and related studies. Such knowledge is often considered practically irrelevant, conceptually Eurocentric, theoretically impoverished, ideologically prejudiced, paradigmatically bankrupt, and philosophically parochial.[1] This intellectual frustration is evident in the current preoccupation of development thinkers with the analysis of diverse social, political, economic, cultural, and environmental predicaments. Similar to the critique of the earlier "decades of development," the recent decades have been considered by many critics of development as the "lost decades," for the Third World—the decades of poverty and malnutrition, inflation and unemployment, landlessness and marginalization, external debt and technological dependence, environmental and ecological crisis, ethnic and communal violence, and the loss of cultural identity and solidarity.[2] Consequently, some writers have expressed their doubts about the very purpose of the whole development enterprise.[3]

Indeed, while the number of books, periodicals, seminars, and conferences on development continue to multiply, very little has changed in the condition of world poverty.[4] As a result, many contemporary development scholars are no longer engaged in rationalizing and refining the prevalent theories and models of development; they are more concerned with the inadequacies of these theories and models to deal with various development crises.[5] However, the prevalent interpretations of these crises are quite inadequate, especially, because of their reductionist focus on the empirical and quantitative indicators, they rarely go beyond the observable symptoms of these crises. For a comprehensive understanding of the existing development crises, it is necessary to transcend these empiricist analyses and pursue a rigorous critical study of the theoretical underpinnings of such development disorders. It is because, in general, the practical maladies of development are inseparable from various theoretical problems in the development field.[6] Since the nature and forms of these practical and theoretical crises of development will be discussed more extensively in the subsequent chapters, only a brief analysis of these crises is presented below for a preliminary overview of the situation.

At the practical level, there are alarming economic, political, and sociocultural conditions not only in Third World countries but also in advanced capitalist nations and the former socialist states.[7] In *Third World countries,*[8] despite all development policies and programs undertaken by governments, development assistance provided by international agencies, and development theories and models formulated by scholars, it is quite well known that the situation of poverty and hunger has deteriorated in many African, Asian, and Latin American countries. In these Third World countries, the application of the borrowed models and strategies of development, in fact, has increased income inequality, strengthened the centralized power of the civilian and military bureaucracies, and expanded the burden of external debt and dependence.[9] The contextless nature of development policies and programs adopted by Third World regimes has often been detrimental to the well-being of the majority of people. For instance, urban-centered development policies have led to expensive and conspicuous urbanization at the expense of rural impoverishment, export-led agricultural and industrial policies have worsened the conditions of landlessness and food scarcity, and inappropriate education and training policies have led to more international migration and brain-drain.[10]

Moreover, the dominant Western bias inherent in the development field[11] has considerable adverse implication for the erosion of the existing indigenous cultures, values, and norms in Third World societies. Historically, although many of the non-European civilizations made significant achievements in the spheres of culture, science, and technology that equaled, and often surpassed, those in Europe,[12] under the centuries of colonial rule, these achievements of the precolonial civilizations were undermined, supplanted, and forgotten. Such an unequal historical process of cultural formation has been accentuated further by the postcolonial globalization of Western cultural framework and its penetration into Third World societies, especially, through the massive programs of modernization and development undertaken by Third World regimes using the Western benchmark of progress. In addition, through various forms of cross-cultural exchanges and international institutions related to development, the Eurocentric view of progress has affected almost every dimension of individual and social life in Third World countries. As Braun observes, "To speak of development meant in essence projecting the European model of society on to the entire world."[13] Realizing the seriousness of such Eurocentric prejudices in development thinking, Pieterse suggests that since "developmentalism" reflects Western history and culture, it requires a thorough historical and cultural review of the whole Western project or the "deconstruction of the West."[14]

In the case of *advanced capitalist nations*, in addition to the prevalence of some of the aforementioned Third World syndromes of underdevelopment, there are serious sociocultural disorders related to expansive capitalist production and excessive industrialization in these countries.[15] More specifically, the forms of crisis in these affluent societies include the worsening situation of unemployment, homelessness, income inequality, racial discrimination, legitimation crisis, state repression, violent crimes, drug abuse, premarital pregnancy, child abuse, broken family, loneliness, and alienation.[16] However, these internal crises in advanced capitalist nations are often disregarded by the elite intellectuals,[17] including development scholars, who are mostly interested in studying and focusing on Third World problems. The major development-related problems in advanced industrial nations are not often reported by international media that are primarily interested in exposing Third World disorders.

On the other hand, in the former and existing *socialist countries*, there are not only growing problems of poverty, inequality, external debt, inflation, and unemployment, many of them have also come under serious challenges posed by ideological anarchy, ethnic unrest, violent crimes, and political instability.[18] Today these new phenomena represent significant obstacles to the overall social progress, national integrity, and regime legitimacy in these countries. Although the recent procapitalist ideological transformation in the former Soviet-bloc countries has replaced their one-party regimes, and contributed to the end of the Cold War,[19] such procapitalist reforms have also led to the "Third Worldization" of these countries as they have been afflicted with various development problems found in Third World countries. In fact, after the massive promarket reforms, the problems of poverty, inequality, diseases, and crimes have reached such alarming levels that the recent elections have reinstated the reformed communist parties in power in cases such as Poland, Hungary, the Czech Republic, Bulgaria, Rumania, Slovakia, and some of the former Soviet republics.[20]

In terms of the *overall global context*, there are many cross-national issues that also have serious implications for development: such issues include international economic inequality, military dominance, cultural subjugation, and environmental disasters.[21] With regard to this international dimension of development crises, one needs to begin with the historical fact that the colonially inherited structures of international inequality and hegemony still continue to stifle the autonomous economic, political, and cultural development of Third World countries in the postcolonial epoch. Although the recent demise of the Cold War has created certain opportunity for Third World countries to liberate themselves from the ideological hegemony of the superpowers and to introduce a more self-reliant mode of development,[22] such opportunity is being lost, especially due to the recent procapitalist transition in the Third World within the emerging context of a more unequal (capitalist) world order based on greater Western (especially American) dominance over the global economic, political, military, and information structures.[23]

However, in the current era, among the various realms of world order, it is the hegemonic information order maintained by the global media that is playing a critical role in advocating and legitimizing the unequal economic and political orders. Today the massive network of global media not only represents a profit-making "culture industry" that produces cultural products, sells them as commodities, and perpetuates international economic dominance, it also functions as a "consciousness industry" to legitimize the unequal interclass and international structures by creating the public consent in favor of such hegemonic structures.[24] By disseminating cultural and intellectual products worldwide, this network of global media—controlled predominantly by various Western news agencies, radio broadcasts, television networks, film producers, music industry, and book and magazine publishers—has expanded the dominance of Western capitalist culture and the deformation or degradation of the indigenous cultures in Third World countries.[25] Another global-level issue that affects all nations and poses a formidable challenge to the existing mode of progress is related to the question of environment, because the costs of industrial civilization are now appearing in different forms of environmental degradation and ecological catastrophes. It has been pointed out that it is this ecological crisis that has weakened the belief in human progress marked by the mastery of nature.[26]

At the theoretical level, the coexistence of voluminous theories and models of development[27] on the one hand, and the above practical (economic, political, cultural, environmental) crises on the other, reflects the inadequacies of these theories themselves.[28] It is because actual development outcomes result from practical development policies, which in turn are guided by various development theories: the worsening of development conditions implies the ineffectiveness of development policies, and thus, inadequacies of development theories. According to K. Dopfer, the existing paradigm of development is incapable of explaining major developmental problems, such as poverty, inequality, and ecological crisis.[29] Goulet also mentions that the mainstream development models "exported by the West to Africa, Asia and Latin America are flawed in their very roots."[30] In fact, today development theories themselves are being considered as a basic component of the "global problematique," because they constitute an ideological and institutional device to enhance the process of intellectual bureaucratization and to perpetuate domination and exploitation.[31]

Although one should not overgeneralize all development theories and models as equally flawed, there are considerable similarities among these theories and models in terms of their major shortcomings. For instance, various traditions of development thinking, ranging from the most conservative to most radical perspectives, suffer from the common problem related to the rhetoric of "developmentalism,"[32] implying a tendency to reify development into an ideological construct. According to Mathur, beyond the apparent diversity and controversy among development theories and models, they are similar in terms of their Eurocentric civilizational paradigm, overemphasis on industrial production and consumption, and certain deterministic tendencies.[33] Even the theoretical alternatives offered by some scholars have come under attack for not being significantly different from the existing development thinking.[34] For instance, the recent reformulation of development framework to incorporate the cultural dimension has been considered an intellectual tactic to present a more authentic and attainable image of development, so that the credibility of the development field is maintained despite its failures.[35] Due to the major shortcomings of development theories and their alternatives, it is felt that there is a need for a serious rethinking in the existing development field.[36]

In this process of rethinking development, first, it is essential to undertake a rigorous critique of the prevalent development theories in terms of their intellectual limitations and practical problems. In other words, a fundamental restructuring of the development field requires a thorough reexamination of its existing theoretical foundation.[37] This pressing academic task of a theoretical critique has been emphasized in recent years in different modes of expression. For instance, suggestions have been made to question the mainstream ideologies and models of development, to deconstruct their Eurocentric prejudices, to search for alternative worldviews, to identify Third World alternatives, and to construct a more unifying theory of development.[38] With regard to this need for the critique and reconstruction of the development field, Jacob Reuveny made the following comments:

> The only possible solution to the current crisis is to go "down to the fundamentals," through a reexamination of the premises of the leading Western theories of development, a revision of these premises and attempt to deduce new theories from the revised premises.[39]

The significance of this critique and reconstruction has increased in recent years for various reasons. *First*, the inherent limitations of mainstream development theories have not only continued, some of the theoretical shortcomings have worsened further in recent years. For instance, the epistemological dominance of economic empiricism over most development theories, which leads to the exclusion of noneconomic dimensions (e.g., political sovereignty and cultural identity)[40] from the development discourse, has not only continued, it has been perpetuated further due to the renewed dominance of neoclassical economic-growth theory under the contemporary promarket atmosphere. The perpetuation of a reductionist tendency in mainstream development theories has also continued in terms this predilection toward economism or overemphasis on economic dimension[41] while overlooking noneconomic issues. There has not been any considerable improvement in development thinking in terms of its indifference toward indigenous values, norms, and ethics found in Third World countries.[42] In addition, it has been pointed out that the major traditions of development theories (including both conservative and radical theories) still suffer from the Eurocentric bias, which is reflected in their interpretations of progress based on a unilinear and evolutionary worldview, in their strong belief in the metaphor of economic growth, and in their endorsement of development paradigms that are predominantly based on Western assumptions.[43] Furthermore, the aforementioned failures of development theories and models to address practical development crises (e.g., poverty, inequality, external debt, cultural hegemony, and environmental disorders) have not yet been rectified. This continuity, and even worsening, of various theoretical shortcomings in the development field indicates that there is an urgent need for reconstructing development theories and policies.

Second, the growing significance of reconstructing the development field also lies in the fact that during the 1980s and 1990s, the national and international contexts of development have fundamentally changed, especially due to the unprecedented global events related to various dimensions of world order. For the development field, it is necessary to pay special attention to the recent changes in international politico-economic order, which include the following: (a) the demise of the socialist bloc vis-à-vis the expansion of Western economic and military power; (b) the diminishing influence of socialist and postsocialist countries (China and Russia) over the global security structure such as the UN Security Council; (c) the increasing incorporation of Third World countries and transitional (former socialist) economies into the transnational capitalist structure; (d) the weakening solidarity and growing economic competition among Third World countries; (e) the increasing dependence of Third World economies on foreign capital and external markets; (f) the more direct roles of international agencies in advocating and imposing promarket policies that benefit transnational capital; and (g) the emergence of neoconservative political leaders as the dominant forces in the state apparatus. This newly emerging politico-economic order based on more inequality, hegemony, and dependence, has been reinforced further by influencing the world public opinion through the global media dominated by advanced capitalist nations.[44]

Thus, as mentioned before, the perpetuation and legitimation of unequal politico-economic order is being facilitated by an unequal information and cultural order. The point here is that due to the contemporary changes in politico-economic order and cultural configurations within and between nations, the relevance of the previous development theories and models is questionable. In other words, it is likely that the traditional development thinking, which evolved under the postcolonial context and the Cold War atmosphere, is quite inadequate to explain the above new global phenomena. For instance, today an authentic development theory must highlight the critical role of the hegemonic culture and information industry in reinforcing and legitimizing interclass and international inequality and subjugation, which represents a crucial development issue that needs to be adequately addressed.

Third, a critical reexamination and reconstruction of the development field has become imperative also due to the fact that in the current context of market ideology and promarket reforms, there is a growing tendency toward the intellectual hegemony of conservative neoclassical theory that assumes market competition as the panacea for all socioeconomic problems. In such a global context influenced by the fetish of market ideology, the essential dialogue among various theoretical traditions (e.g., economic growth theory, modernization theory, dependency theory, and the neo-Marxist school) has diminished. In line with the marginalization of alternative development perspectives by the promarket development models, most countries have adopted promarket policies in the name of efficiency, competitiveness, innovation, deficit reduction, and so on.[45] Due to this worldwide ideological transition and the influence and pressure of international agencies such as the International Monetary Fund (IMF) and the World Bank, most Third World countries have shifted their development thinking[46] in terms of replacing the state-centered programs by market-oriented strategies, changing development objectives from the overall societal progress and nation-building to economic growth and productivity, and altering development priority from economic sovereignty and self-reliance to free trade and foreign investment. These shifts in government objectives, policies, and programs in Third World countries represent the aforementioned theoretical transition in the development field toward the neoclassical market models, the marginalization of alternative development perspectives, and thus the eclipse of development dialogue. Therefore, it is essential to pursue a serious rethinking in the development field.

Fourth, in relation to this increasing theoretical parochialism perpetuated by the dominance of market-oriented development framework, there is a growing tendency in the development field to exclude critical issues, including income inequality, political repression, external dependence, and cultural hegemony, from development studies and debates.[47] In recent years, the relevance of these issues to development discourse has increased further due to the promarket policy atmosphere created by structural adjustment programs (encompassing policies such as deregulation, privatization, and liberalization) that have worsened adverse human conditions such as poverty, malnutrition, income gap, urban-rural disparity, international dependence, and foreign ownership and control in many developing countries.[48]

These promarket policies have also created the potential for other features of maldevelopment such as corruption, extortion, and cronyism,[49] which constitute a serious obstacle to genuine development in these countries. In addition, the promarket reforms have diminished the self-reliance of Third World economies and exacerbated their subordination to foreign capital: due to these market-centered reforms, the terms of international exchange are being dictated by transnational economic powers, the national control over the local industry and agriculture is being eroded, and the valuable state enterprises are being purchased and owned by transnational corporations.[50] Despite the above negative developmental outcomes of promarket policies and reforms, Third World regimes have adopted such policies and reforms not only due to their own vested interests but also because of external pressures exerted by the global economic powers and international agencies.[51] Since this contemporary global context—characterized by market-centered policies adopted by Third World countries under the influence of both the regime interests and international pressures—has adverse implications for development, there is an immediate need to launch a serious critique and reconstruction of the development field.

Finally, there is a demand for rethinking development also due to the emerging intellectual indeterminacy caused by recent global phenomena such as the collapse of major socialist systems and the apparent eclipse of socialism. The end of socialism as an ideological alternative to capitalism has led to a certain degree of confusion among Third World intelligentsia who used to be guided by either the capitalist or socialist ideological tradition. In most Third World countries, the socialist ideological inclinations are under attack, the capitalist perspective is often suspect, and any new ideological outlook is yet to be formed or articulated. In this situation, the previous development theories and models that largely emerged under different ideological camps, seem to be in intellectual disarray. More particularly, due to the recent disorders in the socialist bloc, the proponents of radical theoretical traditions (dependency theory, classical Marxism, and neo-Marxist analysis) have considerably lost their intellectual credibility, and they are increasingly being portrayed as obsolete and bankrupt by their conservative counterparts. This recent intellectual dislocation in the development field caused by the global ideological transition, has created a certain degree of conceptual and theoretical ambiguity among scholars and experts in the development field. As a result, it has become quite essential to undertake a serious critical study of various development theories and policies, so that a more balanced evaluation of these theories and policies could be made, any strong ideological prejudice in the development field (such as the current fetish for market ideology) could be overcome, and the necessary reconstruction of development thinking could be accomplished.

In short, in this age of unprecedented global transformation—including the aforementioned changes in internal socioeconomic condition, international politico-economic order, cultural and ideological structure, and environmental and ecological situation—there has emerged a new set of development opportunities and constraints that requires a serious reexamination of the whole development enterprise and its reconstruction into an alternative development outlook. In this regard, this book not only offers a critique and reconstruction of the existing development theories and policies, it also explores an alternative development perspective that attempts to address the existing theoretical limitations and practical crises in the development field. It also outlines the macro-policy frameworks needed for the realization of a genuine mode of development.

The book comprises nine chapters. This introductory chapter presents a brief overview of the current practical and theoretical crises of development, provides the rationale for a further critical study of the development field, and sets the agenda for the rest of the study pursued in this book. In chapter 2, based on various empirical sources of information, an attempt has been made to offer a more detailed and systematic analysis of the major practical crises of development experienced by Third World countries, advanced capitalist nations, and the former (and the remaining) socialist states. By highlighting the major forms and degrees of these practical crises, this chapter draws attention to the inadequacies or failures of the existing development theories and models to deal with such crises, and thereby points to the need for a critical reexamination of these theories and models themselves.

With a view to facilitate this theoretical reexamination, chapters 3, 4, 5, and 6 are engaged in classifying and clarifying various theories of development that emerged during the past two centuries in various academic disciplines and were selectively put into practice in different countries. More specifically, chapter 3 presents a critical analysis of the prevailing classifications of development theories, and offers a more integrated and logically sound taxonomy of these theories, so that the analysis of each development theory could be made clearer in terms of its similarities with and differences from other theories. After addressing the taxonomic problem, chapters 4,

5, and 6 are devoted to the discussion of various conservative, reformist, and radical theories of development. In order to overcome the problem of fragmented and oversimplified description of development theories often found in the existing literature, these three chapters attempt to present more comprehensive analyses of these theories before their critique and reconstruction pursued in the subsequent chapters.

Thus, once the basic tenets and arguments of development theories are presented, the remaining chapters of the book have been devoted to the critique and reconstruction of development theories and the articulation of alternative development policies. In particular, chapter 7 explores the major intellectual inadequacies of the existing development theories, especially in terms of their tendencies toward epistemological empiricism, analytical reductionism, normative indifference, ethnocentric outlook, and fabricated universalism. It also explains how these intellectual inadequacies can perpetuate adverse practical outcomes, including the exacerbation of academic hegemony, legitimation of politico-economic inequality, deterioration of environmental problems, and erosion of cultural identity. Following this critique, chapter 8 is engaged in restructuring development theories. In this theoretical restructuring, the emphasis is on the realization of human autonomy from all forms of human subjugation rather than on the affirmation of hegemonic development objectives imposed by the dominant classes, institutions, and nations.

In line with this restructured theory of development, the last chapter (chapter 9) suggests certain fundamental reforms in development policies with a view to enhance human autonomy from the subjugating structures experienced, especially by the common masses in Third World countries. However, it is emphasized that in the current epoch, human autonomy from the global structures of cultural, intellectual, and informational hegemony has become more crucial than the other domains of autonomy, and this emerging historical reality should be recognized by contemporary development thinkers.

CHAPTER 2

Practical Crises of Development

In order to comprehend the significance of a critical development study, it is necessary to examine the major development crises or disorders that challenge the existing development theories and policies, and perplex the overall development field. However, in the existing development literature, various crises of development are usually described in such a localized (country- or region-specific) and fragmented (issue-oriented) manner, that it is quite difficult to have a comprehensive and integrated view of the critical development situation. Although this chapter may not reveal any development problems that have not already been studied or explored, its main objective is to present a more coherent scenario of development disorders by synthesizing the prevailing facts and analyses related to these issues.

Beyond this immediate goal of putting critical developmental facts and analyses together, the chapter aims to draw attention to the magnitude and intensity of the prevailing development crises that require an immediate and thorough reexamination of the current development theories and policies, and thus, make a case for a critical development study as undertaken in this book. However, depending on the scope and contents of various development disorders, in this chapter, they have been classified into three major descriptive categories: (a) crises of development in Third World countries, (b) crises of development in advanced capitalist and socialist (including the former socialist) nations, and (c) crises of development at the global level. As presented below, under each of these categories, various development problems have been classified further into more specific subcategories.

Development Crises in Third World Countries

Many Asian, African, and Latin American countries, in spite of their decades of intensive development efforts, still suffer from diverse forms of development crises. In the past, although a massive amount of government policies and programs were undertaken in these Third World countries to overcome some of the major development problems, in most cases, the results have been quite disappointing. In certain instances, in fact, these policies and programs themselves have worsened and perpetuated such development-related problems. Although the list of such problems is almost endless in Third World countries, this section of the chapter briefly examines some of the major crucial issues reflecting the nature and extent of development disorders in these countries.

POVERTY AND INEQUALITY

In Third World countries, despite the perpetual rhetoric of economic growth, the conditions of poverty, hunger, disease, and illiteracy remain alarming. For instance, of a total Third World population of nearly 4.3 billion, about 1.3 billion people are in absolute poverty, 700 million without enough food, 1 billion without access to health services, 1.3 billion without access to safe water, 1 billion without adequate housing, 900 million adults without literacy, and 12 to 15 million children die every year from hunger and disease.[1] On the other hand, the overall growth rate of per capita production and income in the Third World was almost zero in 1980; and in the decade of the 1980s, there was no appreciable improvement in the living conditions, especially in Latin America and Africa.[2] In fact, during the period between 1965–73 and 1980–87, the overall growth rate declined from 4.2 to 1.3 percent in the "highly indebted countries," from 3.8 to 2.9 percent in Sub-Saharan Africa, and the situation was equally bleak in most Latin American countries.[3]

Over the recent decades, although some economic progress has been made in few small Newly Industrialized Countries (NICs) such as Hong Kong, Singapore, South Korea, and Taiwan, in the overall Third World context, this economic success remains insignificant because these four NICs represent only 1.7 percent (73 million) of the Third World population (4.24 billion).[4] In fact, the larger NICs (both old and new) still suffer from a significant degree of poverty: for instance, the number of people living in absolute poverty is 72.4 million in Brazil, 26.4 million in Mexico, 16.8 million in Thailand,

35.2 million in the Philippines, and 47.8 million in Indonesia.[5] According to the UNDP report of 1991, the percentage of population living below the poverty line is 39 percent in Indonesia, 27 percent in Malaysia, 58 percent in the Philippines, 16 percent in South Korea, and 30 percent in Thailand.[6] In fact, in many Third World countries, the situation of poverty has worsened during the recent period of promarket reforms.[7]

The scenario of Third World poverty becomes even worse if one considers the structure of such poverty in terms of the patterns of property and income distribution, which is extremely unequal in many Third World countries. More specifically, approximately 80 percent of all Third World agricultural land is owned by only 3 percent of landowners; and in the low-income Third World countries (often considered as the Fourth World), the richest 10 percent of the population account for more than 33 percent of income, while the poorest 40 percent receive only 15 percent.[8] At the regional level, 40 percent of all rural households are near-landless in South Asia, three-quarters of the population have no access to even 4 percent of land in Africa, and only 1 percent of landlords own more than 40 percent of arable land in Latin America.[9] This economic inequality in Third World countries is likely to expand further under the contemporary market-centered policies of structural adjustment that lead to the retrenchment of welfare programs for the poor, and the expansion of economic benefits to the affluent industrial and business groups.[10]

EXTERNAL DEBT AND DEPENDENCE

In addition to poverty and inequality, the worsening condition of external debt and dependence also represent a serious development disorder in Third World countries. The total Third World debt increased from $100 billion in 1970 to $800 billion in 1980 to more than $1,500 billion in 1994.[11] In Latin America, the amount of debt has reached $450 billion; and in Africa, the external debt ($175 billion) was more than 45 percent of the region's Gross Domestic Product (GDP) in 1985.[12] In fact, some of the Third World's economic showcases are the largest debtor nations.[13] More specifically, the external debt of Brazil amounts to $121.11 billion, Mexico $113.38 billion, Argentina $67.57 billion, Thailand $39.42 billion, Indonesia $84.39 billion, and South Korea $43 billion.[14] For some countries, the total external debt is almost equal to their total Gross National Products (GNP), and for others it is even higher than GNP. For instance, in 1991, the external debt as a percentage of total GNP was 73 percent for Sri Lanka, 75 percent for Costa Rica, 85 percent for Bolivia, 88 percent for Yemen, 90 percent for Kenya, 114 percent for Honduras, 109 percent for Uganda and Nigeria, 133 percent for Egypt, 135 percent for Jamaica, 251 percent for Tanzania, and 426 percent for Mozambique.[15]

The external debt of Third World countries has expanded due to some major factors, such as the significant increase in their military expenditures,[16] the massive amount of capital flight, the declining terms of trade, the continuous process of debt servicing, and the financing of expatriates.[17] According to Steidlmeier, without capital flight, the situation of external debt in the 1980s could have been much better:

> Argentina would have a debt of $1 billion rather than $50 billion; Mexico $12 billion rather than $97 billion; Malaysia $4 billion rather than $20 billion; Nigeria $7 billion rather than $19 billion; the Philippines $15 billion rather than $27 billion; Brazil $27 billion rather than $106 billion; and Venezuela a surplus of $12 billion rather than a debt of $31 billion.[18]

Unfortunately, due to the above factors contributing to expansive external debt, Third World countries now pay about $160 billion a year in interest, amortization, and profit remittances to the affluent creditor countries.[19] As a result, there is actually a reverse flow of resources from the Third World. For instance, according to the UNDP report of 1991, the net flow of resources from poor countries to rich countries in 1989 was $50 billion to $60 billion.[20] In this regard, Fagen mentions that "the poor countries are, perversely, financing the development of the rich countries."[21] More importantly, the burden of external debt has created various forms of economic and political dependence of Third World countries. The abovementioned hunger and poverty of Third World people are not isolated from such external dependence. According to a Unicef (United Nations Children's Fund) estimate, about half a million children die every year in the Third World because of this external debt, since it takes away a significant part of Third World income through debt servicing.[22]

THE POPULATION PROBLEM

Another burning issue in Third World countries is the issue of population which, for the past few decades, has been identified as one of the most critical obstacles to Third World development. The world population increased from 2.5 billion in 1950 to 5.6 billion in 1994, and at an estimated growth rate of 91 million per year during the 1990s, it may reach 10 billion to 12.5 billion by the year 2050.[23] It is also expected that almost 90–97 percent of this population growth will occur in Third World countries, while in most of the rich Western nations the population will be either stable or declining.[24] However, according to Bradley, with few exceptions, most Third World countries are not overpopulated, and the current analysis and policies offered by international agencies and the core states are inadequate, because they address problems of food consumption, not food production and distribution.[25] Since world food production has been twice as much food as needed to feed the world population, overpopulation is a false concept both in absolute and relative terms.[26]

However, this statistical overview, which blames the fertility pattern of Third World people for their poverty and hunger, does not reflect more crucial sociohistorical factors causing the problem. As Bradley suggests, food crisis and hunger in the Third World is not caused by overpopulation; there are other deep-rooted causes,[27] including the introduction of cash crops and displacement of labor during the colonial rule, the incorporation of rural societies into the world capitalist system reducing peasants' freedom to produce their own food, the pathological effects of various remedial measures such as "green revolution," and the abandonment of the poorest countries by capitalist nations after exhausting their surplus. Almost similar explanations are offered by Bunge, Patterson, and Shrestha.[28] Despite this alternative view on the relationship between poverty and population, what remains a central concern is that the programs for population control have not been very effective in Third World countries, which is evident in the aforementioned expansion of the world population. The ineffectiveness of various measures to control population growth lies in the narrow focus of these measures themselves, which emphasize mostly the birth-control techniques while ignoring the role of socioeconomic issues, such as poverty and inequality, in determining the fertility patterns in these countries. For instance, in poor countries, the low-income families tend to have more children not only because they are illiterate and uninformed, but also because of their tendency to avoid the risk of having very few children who may not survive (especially due to a high rate of infant mortality caused by malnutrition and lack of medical care), and because of their uncertain economic future requiring more income-earning members in the family. In other words, it is not only the population problem which, according to the common interpretation, worsens the situation of poverty, it is also poverty that accentuates the population problem in Third World countries.

MIGRATION AND BRAIN-DRAIN

Another crucial demographic problem that has considerable implications for Third World development is the issue of migration and brain-drain. Migration and brain-drain is caused by different factors, such as the extreme economic gap between advanced capitalist nations and Third World countries and the inappropriate Third World education system more relevant to Western countries. After World War II, millions of Asian, African, and Latin American people migrated to economically advanced Western nations, particularly the U.S.; and recently, millions of them have migrated to the oil-rich Arab countries.[29] This migration has brought foreign exchange to Third World countries and enhanced their international interaction; but due to the "demonstration effects," it has also affected their cultures, diverted their patterns of consumption toward foreign goods, and distorted their indigenous modes of development.

However, a specific form of migration that is crucial for development is the migration of skilled and productive human resource or the so-called "brain-drain" from the Third World to the economically advanced countries. According to an ILO report, the number is between 19.7 to 21.7 million.[30] More recent studies show that at least 35 million people from the Third World have taken up residence in advanced industrial countries during the past three decades and one additional million join them each year: during 1985–90, Africa lost an estimated 60,000 middle- and high-level managers; during 1972–85, four Asian countries (China, India, South Korea, and the Philippines) sent more than 145,000 scientifically trained workers to the U.S.; and today, Latin American countries lose more than 20 percent of their graduates who choose to emigrate.[31] It is observed that in the late 1970s, through this process of brain-drain, the U.S. received almost 80 percent of its migrant skilled workers from Third World countries, which had cost these poor countries more than they received from the U.S. in foreign aid.[32] Similarly, Germany would have to spend $33 billion to rear and educate the number of workers it gained through immigration during the period 1957–73.[33] Brain-drain is detrimental to Third World countries not only because they invest a significant part of their scarce resources in creating skilled human resource, but also because such human resource is essential for their own development. Today, due to this brain-drain, there is an extreme disparity in the distribution of human resource between the poor and rich countries.[34]

THE PROBLEM OF URBANIZATION

In many Third World countries, government initiatives to imitate the NIC-model of development has led to a serious intersectorial economic imbalance or distortion, particularly in the form of over-urbanization and rural impoverishment. In the name of modernization, the recent urbanization in the Third World is mostly initiated and favored by the political, bureaucratic, and business elites residing in modern cities. In most of these countries, urbanization took place without much indigenous industrial development and without any substantive change in the mode of production, as it happened in advanced capitalist nations. Small pockets of modernity and affluence in these artificially grown cities distinctively contradict the backwardness and poverty of agrarian Third World societies. However, the number of the Third World's urban population increased from 287 million in 1950 to 1 billion in 1980, and it might rise to 2 billion by the year 2000.[35] The massive expansion of cities—often caused by urban-biased government policies and the centralization of political power in cities—has caused rural impoverishment, worsened the condition of poverty and unemployment, created the problems of slums and health hazards, and increased the cases of urban crime and violence.[36] Thus, this distorted form of urbanization poses a considerable challenge to a balanced and equitable mode of development in Third World countries.

Before ending this analysis of various Third World crises, it should be mentioned that to overcome the critical problems of poverty and hunger, many poor countries are seriously considering the path of some NICs. However, while the NICs have often been cited as examples or models of development for other Third World countries, there is a significant number of critics. It is mentioned that Latin American NICs have an external debt amounting to more than 60 percent of their GNP, and there were significant signs of economic deceleration in some Asian NICs (Philippines, Malaysia, and Indonesia) in the 1980s.[37] Moreover, for some scholars, there is simply no room in the world market for "new Japans" or a "new Gang of Four" (referring to the four advanced NICs in Asia); and due to the continuing wage increases, the existing NICs themselves may be driven out from some of the commodity markets.[38] The recent market crises in Asian NICs (especially the historical fall in the value of their currencies) show the serious vulnerability of these economies. It was already concluded in the 1980s that the NIC model of development (based on the small-state framework and favorable international conditions) might not be feasible for other Third World countries in the 1990s, and it might also be undesirable because it could lead to external dependency and cultural pathologies.[39]

Crises in Capitalist and Socialist Countries

Many of the advanced capitalist and socialist nations are not altogether free from some of the aforementioned development crises experienced by Third World countries. In addition, there are certain critical problems that are more serious in these countries than in the Third World. Given the space constraint, however, this section briefly examines the major internal disorders that exist predominantly in the leading capitalist and socialist countries such as the U.S., Britain, the former Soviet Union, and China. Although many of the socialist states have collapsed, an analysis of the past and present crises faced by the former and remaining socialist systems is significant for evaluating the practical problems of socialism as a development perspective.

CRISES IN ADVANCED CAPITALIST NATIONS

Among the advanced capitalist nations, in the U.S., more than 38 million people live below the poverty line (20 percent of them are children), 20 million are without adequate nutrition, 3 million are homeless, and 39 million are without health insurance.[40] With regard to economic inequality, the situation in advanced capitalist nations is not very different from that in many Third World countries. For instance, in terms of ownership, in Britain, the wealthiest 10 percent people own 53 percent of total wealth, and in the U.S., the richest 10 percent people own 56 percent of the nation's wealth, and the super-rich 0.5 percent households own 35 percent of such wealth.[41] In terms of income, during the period since World War II, the top 20 percent Americans received more than 40 percent of the country's total income and the poorest 20 percent received less than 5 percent.[42] Thus, Durning concludes that "it will not be too long before there is a Third World within the First World, and a First within the Third."[43] In addition, there has been serious financial crisis in the capitalist world. For instance, during the 1980s, the U.S. experienced an annual $155 billion federal budget deficit, $150 billion to $200 billion trade deficit, and $2.6 trillion in debt.[44] More recently, the conditions have not improved to any significant extent.

In addition, there are concerns for various sociocultural crises in advanced capitalist nations, which include the erosion of family bonds, decline of community, diminishing education standards, racial injustice, stifling ghettos, sex discrimination, crime and violence, aesthetic uncertainty, loneliness and alienation, alcoholism and drug abuse, and ethical and moral confusion.[45] For instance, the U.S. has 14 million reported crimes, 3 million cases of child abuse, 28 million cases of women battering (4.7 million with serious injury), and 150,000 rape cases per year; and it also has 48 percent divorce rate, 27 percent births outside marriage, and one of the highest numbers of prisoners per capita (426 per 100,000 people) in the world.[46] According to the Federal Bureau of Investigation, there is one murder every 28 minutes, one rape every 6 minutes, and one robbery every 63 seconds.[47] Another critical issue is drug and alcohol abuse, which has become a major concern in the leading capitalist countries. In the U.S., although there are tough antinarcotics government policies (including interventionist military measures in foreign countries), about 30 million people are occasional users of cocaine, more than 600,000 people are heroin addicts, the population as a whole consumes nearly 60 percent of the world's illicit drugs, and alcoholism alone costs the nation $80 billion per year in accidents, deaths, and diseases.[48]

In advanced capitalist countries, there are also various forms of political and administrative disorders, which include various degrees of political discontent, suspicion of authority, legislative ineptitude, repression, collapse of the two-party system, police brutality, nuclear proliferation, arms race and arms build-ups, bureaucratic inertia, administrative inefficiency, bribery and corruption, and abuse of power.[49] Although development scholars and experts find these problems mostly in Third World countries, they tend to ignore the existence of such problems in advanced capitalist nations.

CRISES IN SOCIALIST (FORMER AND REMAINING) COUNTRIES

According to some Western sources of information, the former Soviet government spent 15 to 20 percent of its GNP on defense for 40 years (defense expenditure increased from $125 billion in 1975 to $258 billion in 1983), and its ruling Communist Party had cash assets of

4.5 billion rubles, while 20 percent of Soviet citizens lived below the official poverty line of 75 rubles a month in the 1980s and the annual budget deficit amounted to $120 billion during the first half of that decade.[50] To overcome these paradoxical economic realities, Gorbachev introduced a relatively unrealistic synthesis of market economy, political democratization, and socialist governance, which gradually led to ideological confusion, political anarchy, economic catastrophes, external dependence, and finally the collapse and disintegration of the Soviet Union itself. However, under the facade of democratization, the current government of Boris Yeltsin is no less authoritarian than the previous socialist state,[51] not to mention the worsening economic hardship under the recent promarket reforms. Today in the Russian Federation, Boris Yeltsin's procapitalist economic reforms have largely failed: although 5 to 8 percent people have gained fabulously from such reforms, about 50 percent now live below the poverty line, 30–40 percent earn less than $50 a month, industrial production has dropped by 50 percent, the unemployment situation has worsened, and public health and life expectancy have declined significantly.[52]

Such impoverished conditions have become more unbearable due to the unprecedented inflation rate, which reached 1,353 percent per year in the Russian Federation, 1,445 percent in Ukraine, 1,194 percent in Lithuania, 1,057 percent in Moldova, and 1,009 percent in Estonia.[53] Like Third World nations, these emerging postsocialist market economies also have become the victims of external debt. Between 1980 and 1992, external debt increased from $8.89 billion to $48.52 billion in Poland, from $9.76 billion to $21.90 billion in Hungary, from $392 million to $12.15 billion in Bulgaria, and from $2.24 billion to $78.66 billion in the Russian Federation.[54] Today, the valuable assets of these countries are increasingly being owned or controlled by Western transnational corporations.[55] Thus, according to Landau, the resources of Poland and the industries of the former East Germany are enriching the Western economy.[56]

Under the "fables of free market," there are also growing problems of economic stagnation, declining real income, unemployment, and the rebirth of factionalism based on ethnic, religious, and cutural differences in Eastern Europe.[57] The growing economic hardship and international politico-economic dependence of these countries is no less painful and detrimental[58] than their past experiences under the allegedly "totalitarian" regimes. According to the United Nations (UN) report, since the collapse of communism in 1989, there have been unprecedented, alarming conditions of poverty, mortality, and health crises in Eastern European countries.[59]

On the other hand, in China, the promarket reforms have ensured the advantage of cheap labor, raw materials, and tax incentives for Western and Asian investors, but for the majority of its people, such reforms have created various undesirable outcomes such as double digit inflation, official corruption, and income inequality.[60] Despite a high rate of economic growth, the total unemployment in China could soar to 268 million people (over 22% of its 1.2 billion population) by the turn of the century.[61] In addition, in terms of political instability and disintegration, in the postsocialist world, Czechoslovakia has disintegrated into the Czech Republic and Slovakia, and the Soviet Union has collapsed and given birth to independent states from its constituent republics.[62] The above problems of declining living standards, rising inflation, worsening unemployment, expanding external debt, and growing political instability have been described by Petras as the *Latinamericanization* of the communist world.[63]

Development Crises at the Global Level

In addition to the aforementioned development disorders in Third World countries and problems in advanced capitalist and socialist nations, there are serious crises at the global level that affect almost every society. Most of these global crises are often related to the dominant, mainstream perspectives of development that tend to endorse the national-level accumulation of wealth without considering its international economic implications, encourage the maintenance of a state-centered political order without addressing the ethnic and racial differences within and between nations, require massive industrial and technological expansion without much concern for environmental and ecological degradation, and perpetuate an unequal world order that strengthens the hegemony of few global powers over the powerless Third World countries. In this regard, the following discussion will address some of these major global-level crises of development such as international inequality, ethnic and racial conflicts, global defense expenditure, environmental and ecological disasters, and unequal world order.

INTERNATIONAL INEQUALITY

Similar to the abovementioned situation of income disparity within each nation, there is extreme inequality between the richest and poorest nations in terms of their levels of income, ownership, and consumption. In the current global economy, while there are 157 billionaires, there are more than one billion people living on less than one dollar a day; while one billion live in affluence and luxury, another billion live in destitution and 100 million are homeless.[64] Approximately, the advanced industrial countries represent 20 percent of the world's population (5.5 billion) but account for 80 percent of the global GDP ($22 trillion) and consume 80 percent of the world's goods (the U.S. with 5 percent of the world's population consumes more than 35 percent of the world's resources); whereas Third World countries represent almost 80 percent of the world's population but account for only 14 percent of the global GDP.[65]

Between 1960 and 1991, while the share of global income for the richest 20 percent of the world population increased from 70 to 85 percent, the share for the poorest 20 percent declined from 2.3 to 1.4 percent.[66] According to Sivard, "Incomes of the richest fifth of the world population average fifty times the incomes of the poorest fifth."[67] In terms of ownership, the world economy is increasingly dominated by multinational corporations (MNCs). Currently, there are about 2,000 large MNCs worldwide, of which the largest 300 account for 75 percent of the world's GNP; some of these MNCs (e.g., Exxon, General Motors, IBM, Nissan) have each a gross corporate product larger than the GNP of many Third World countries; and of the top 50 MNCs, 42 percent are U.S.-based, 38 percent European, and 14 percent Japanese.[68] This extreme international inequality in wealth, income, consumption, and ownership indicates a serious global disorder in development, because a reasonable degree of economic equality constitutes one of the most essential components of genuine human development. Unfortunately, instead of reducing such inequality, the past development activities seem to have widened the economic gap between nations and perpetuated the economic dependence of the poorer nations further. Thus, although Third World countries have acquired independence from the former colonial rule, there is still continuity in their economic dependence based on the above structure of international inequality. As Brewer mentions, "Formal political independence, with a flag, an airline and a seat at the UN, does not guarantee real equality."[69]

ETHNIC AND RACIAL CONFLICTS

Another issue that transcends the scope of nation-states and poses a challenge to development is the reemergence of worldwide ethnic and racial conflicts.[70] An understanding of such contemporary ethnic and racial problems would require a serious study of colonialism that led to massive international migration, and thus, to demographic restructuring in different nations and regions. While Europeans migrated to other continents with a colonizing mission, millions of non-Europeans were forced to migrate to various parts of the world as slaves or bonded plantation workers.[71] For instance, under British colonialism, about 28 million Indians migrated to other British dominions, 55 million Europeans went to other regions, and within a decade after World War II, some 55 million people migrated to different parts of the world.[72] Thus, the colonial process destabilized the racial and ethnic composition worldwide.

During the postcolonial period, the ethnic problems in many Third World countries worsened further due to the colonially inherited structure of the state and the definition of nationhood based on artificially drawn (imposed) state boundaries.[73] Such colonial inheritance of the problem can be found in the racial struggles in Africa and other continents, in the resistance of Amerindians against their integration into the current nation-states, in the conflict between the Westernized and anti-Western Arabs, and in the destruction of aboriginal societies and their cultural subordination in many advanced industrial countries.[74] It is increasingly becoming evident today that the postcolonial projects related to the formation of the nation-states (both capitalist and socialist) have been quite ineffective in different parts of the world.[75] After the recent demise of the Cold War, the ethnic, religious, and racial uprisings are becoming a serious challenge to the integrity of the existing nation-states and their socioeconomic progress.

In the recent past, the list of these conflicts and uprisings included events such as the violent civil wars in Angola and Mozambique, the separatist movements of Tamils in Sri Lanka and Kurds in Turkey, the everyday struggle of ethnic minorities for equal rights in Western nations, the resurgence of ethnic national identity in the newly independent Soviet republics, the uprising of the Palestinians for an independent Palestine state, and the struggle of blacks for achieving the postapartheid economic justice in South Africa.[76] Although certain progress has been made in some of these situations, it remains piecemeal and incomplete. For instance, in South Africa, the recent voting rights given to blacks has made improvement in the structure of "apartheid democracy," but it has failed to change the "apartheid economic system" that ensures almost monopolistic control over capital, industry, and fertile land by whites who represent only 4.8 percent of the country's population.[77] As Taylor observes, "South Africa today is a place where the white minority of 5 million owns the economy, the 32 million-strong black majority runs the politics and both races have a living memory of three centuries of oppression."[78]

More recently, the most brutal ethnic violence has taken place in Bosnia and Rwanda. In Bosnia (a predominantly Muslim republic of the former Yugoslavia), it was Bosnian Serbs who had control over heavy weapons, and thus, occupied most of the Bosnian land, massacred more than 200,000 Bosnian Muslims, raped and tortured tens of thousands, and forced a million and a half to exile.[79] This is an event in which the double standards of Western nations and international institutions became clear: the so-called contact group countries (the U.S., Germany, Britain, France, and Russia) remained relatively inactive, the UN Secretary General continued to treat both the victims and the aggressors alike, and the UN peace-keeping unit (UNPROFOR) kept the Muslim victims defenseless by imposing an arms embargo on them.[80] In Rwanda, more than 500,000 people were killed in a recent genocide committed by the Hutu-dominated regime against the Tutsi population, several hundred thousands died of hunger and diseases, and four million were displaced within and outside Rwanda.[81] There are potentials for such ethnic violence also in other parts of the world that have ethnic heterogeneity. In the former Soviet territory, for instance, there is a significant number of Russians in various republics (about 30 percent Russians in both Estonia and Latvia, 20 percent in Ukraine, 38 percent in Kazakhstan, 21 percent in Kirgizstan); there are 50 million Muslims in Central Asian republics; and there have already been wars between Azerbaijan and Armenia regarding their control over Nagorno-Karabakh.[82]

Expansive World Defense Expenditure

Another crucial global problem challenging the prospect of a genuine world development is the colossal defense expenditure, which diverts both material and human resources away from programs meant for human well-being. For instance, in 1985, the world military expenditure ($940 billion) was more than the total income of the poorest half of the world's population. During the period 1960–87, the world military expenditure totalled $17 trillion, and it grew faster than the world's per capita economic product.[83] The two superpowers (the U.S. and the former USSR) accounted for the largest global defense expenditures (about $1.5 billion a day): between 1948 and 1988, the U.S. alone spent $8.4 trillion to build its military power.[84] Such colossal defense expenditure is inseparable from the economic interests of the major arms producers such as Rockwell, Northrop, Martin Marietta, Boeing, Propulsion, and Hercules, which have significant influence on the U.S. government policies to build and sell weapons.[85]

Even in Third World countries, military expenditures increased on average by 35 percent between 1980 and 1987,[86] which remain a major obstacle to socioeconomic progress in these countries. In 1992, of the total central government expenditures, the defense sector accounted for 15 percent in India, 30.6 percent in Pakistan, 22.1 percent in South Korea, and 17.2 percent in Thailand.[87] Today, although 800 million people live in absolute poverty in South Asia and Sub-Saharan Africa, the governments in these two regions continue to spend $27 billion on arms (Sub-Saharan Africa $8 billion and South Asia $19 billion).[88] This expansive defense spending has not only led to the waste of scarce resources, it has also worsened the situation of interregional and international tensions and conflicts.

ENVIRONMENTAL AND ECOLOGICAL CATASTROPHES

In recent years, there has been growing worldwide concern for various forms of environmental disaster and ecological imbalance, including the greenhouse effect, ozone layer depletion, deforestation, land degradation, and destruction of plant and animal species.[89] The main source of the greenhouse effect[90] is the emission of carbon in the atmosphere, which has reached a catastrophic level due to the expansive use of electricity, a significant increase in automobiles, and the massive amount of deforestation.[91] For instance, the annual emission of carbon through the combustion of fossil fuel increased from 93 million tons in 1860 to 5.5 billion tons in 1988, and it may reach 10 billion tons in 2010.[92] Deforestation, which also increases the amount of atmospheric carbon by reducing the earth's capacity to absorb it, has become alarming. It has been found that one-fifth of the world's tropical rain forest has already been lost since the middle of this century, and today, there is very little remaining of the original forests in Central America, Southeast Asia, and West Africa.[93]

One concrete evidence of this greenhouse effect is an increase in temperature by 0.6 degrees Celsius during the past hundred years, and this increase may reach 2.5 to 5.5 degrees Celsius in the next century.[94] The implications of this global warming are catastrophic. It will lead to a significant rise of the sea level, which has already caused the erosion of coastlines, endangered countries and cities that are on the low-lying areas, and put one-third of global cropland at risk. On the other hand, according to Brown and Young, global warming also means a hotter summer and drought which, in 1987 and 1988, reduced the world grain stocks to the lowest levels in decades.[95]

Another ecological disaster is the depletion of the earth's ozone layer.[96] Recently, due to an increase in the global production of chlorofluorocarbons (CFCs), the average ozone concentration over the South Pole has declined by 50 percent and in some isolated spots it has disappeared.[97] The depletion of the ozone layer increases detrimental ultraviolet radiation, which in turn leads to skin cancers and cataracts, depresses human immune systems, creates all sorts of lung and heart diseases, depletes marine fisheries, retards the growth of trees and crops, and damages animal species.[98] Before 2075, ozone depletion is expected to increase 3–15 million cancer cases and 0.5–2.8 million cataracts cases in the U.S. alone.[99] Even at the current levels of ozone, according to a 1987 U.S. government report, total crop losses were estimated to be 5 to 10 percent of production.[100]

The major environmental threats to world agricultural production are the various forms of land degradation caused indirectly by the abovementioned global warming and deforestation, and directly by overcultivation, overgrazing, and the depletion of ground water. These factors have led to the problems of soil erosion, land desertification, and salinization. Each year, about 24 billion tons of topsoil are lost globally, which may reduce the grain harvest by 6 percent; and the process of desertification destroys an estimated 6 million hectares per year worldwide, and makes another 20 million hectares unprofitable for cultivation (35 percent of the earth's land surface is already under such threat).[101] Another factor for land degradation is salinization of soil caused mainly by intensive irrigation. This salinization has reduced millions of hectares of crop-yielding land all over the world, which amounts to 24 percent of irrigated land worldwide.[102]

All the abovementioned factors, including global warming, soil erosion, land desertification, flood, and salinity have reduced food production significantly. The rate of increase in grain production declined from 3 percent a year during 1950–84 to 1 percent a year during 1984–90, and the world carryover stocks of grain (as world food security) decreased from 461 million tons in 1987 to 290 million tons in 1990.[103] In addition, due to the worsening ecological and environmental conditions, the frequency and costs of natural disasters have increased. For instance, the number of major global disasters per year increased from 16 in the 1960s to 29 in the 1970s to 70 in the 1980s; and the costs of annual losses caused by these disasters increased from \$10 billion in the 1960s to \$30 billion in the 1970s to \$93 billion in the 1980s.[104]

Although environmental crises have become one of the most widely discussed issues, historically, it is the advanced industrial countries that have largely been responsible for such crises. It is because, in the process of industrializing various economic sectors, producing harmful products such as toxic chemicals and nuclear weapons, using hazardous substances and radioactive materials, and consuming luxurious goods such as automobiles, refrigerators, and air conditioners, these countries have severely contributed to the emission of carbon (causing greenhouse effect), production of CFCs (depleting the ozone layer), destruction of forest (endangering plant and animal species), erosion of soil (degrading land), depletion of ground water (causing desertification), exhaustion of nonrenewable resources (diminishing the future resource supply), and so on.[105] For instance, since 1850, the industrial countries have been responsible for 75 percent of the global carbon emission.[106] The average per capita energy consumption (measured in terms of oil equivalent) is 4,840 kg in advanced industrial nations, but only 550 kg in Third World countries. While China has only 1 car per 1,000 people, the U.S. has 570 cars per 1,000 people.[107] With regard to this inequality in creating environmental problems and sharing environmental costs, it has been estimated by the UNDP that if the environment were correctly priced and tradable permits were issued to all countries according to their population sizes, the industrial countries would have to purchase most of the permits and transfer as much as \$500 billion to \$1 trillion a year to Third World countries.[108] Ironically, however, it is the poorest classes and nations which continue to suffer from environmental insecurity and catastrophes.[109]

UNEQUAL AND UNJUST WORLD ORDER

One most crucial factor that considerably affects and shapes the nature and mode of development in every society is the issue of world order, including its economic, political, military, cultural, and informational dimensions. In terms of the *world economic order*, after World War II, there emerged in the capitalist world predominantly an "American world order" based on various multilateral institutions such as the General Agreement on Tariffs and Trade (GATT), currently known as the World Trade Organization (WTO); the International Monetary Fund (IMF); the International Finance Corporation (IFC); and the World Bank.[110] Parallel to these capitalist arrangements of economic cooperation, most countries under the socialist bloc formed the Council of Mutual Economic Assistance (CMEA) to facilitate their version of economic collaboration. Many Third World countries, on the other hand, established the Non-Aligned Movement (NAM), formed the so-called "Group of 77," and adopted the New International Economic Order (NIEO) to obtain favorable terms of international trade and finance.[111] In addition, since the 1960s, Third World countries have established many regional and interregional organizations[112] to facilitate their politico-economic unity and development.

The outcomes of this postwar economic order have been unequal for different parts of the world. Although the advanced capitalist countries have gained significantly in terms of growth and stability from such a world economic system, it has hardly benefited the poorer Third World nations.[113] Despite the Third World's demand for a more equitable economic order, the "economic superpowers" have continuously increased their dominance over international trade and financial institutions.[114] In fact, international institutions such as the IMF and the World Bank, remain quite undemocratic in structure, because for these institutions, the composition of voting rights exercised by the member countries is largely based on a country's financial contribution and the size of its economy. The U.S. alone has about 21 percent vote in the World Bank, over 29 percent in the IFC, and 20 percent in the IMF; and since any major change in the IMF system requires 85 percent vote, the U.S. alone retains a veto.[115] The global economic dominance of these international bodies is also evident in their tendencies to impose policies and programs on Third World countries. Thus, the World Bank has come under attack for imposing the so-called structural adjustment programs that tend to subordinate Third World economies to transnational capital; for financing projects that have created environmental catastrophes and displaced the common people; for overpaying its own employees that amounts on average to $123,000 per year; and more recently, for receiving more money from Third World countries in repayments and interests ($20 billion) than the amount of loans ($16 billion) provided to these countries.[116]

In terms of exchange, in the 1980s, while the prices of primary commodities (exported by the Third World) had been falling at an average rate of 1.3 percent, the prices of manufactures (exported by developed countries) rose at the rate of 4.11 percent.[117] In fact, the whole international trade system based on the GATT (now WTO) rules ignores the realities of global economic power structure.[118] The existing trade system has served the economic interests of advanced industrial nations by remaining indifferent toward various forms of protectionism practiced by these nations, which cost Third World countries about $50 billion a year;[119] by authorizing Western nations (especially the U.S.) to use techniques such as the provision of Most Favored Nation (MFN) status to favor certain Third World countries that satisfy Western economic and military interests; by allowing the U.S. to practice the so-called provision 301 and Super 301 to punish its "unfavorable" trade partners; and so on. In addition, the recent trade agreement has produced specific international codes related to intellectual property, trade in services, and foreign investment, which are mostly in favor of advanced capitalist nations.[120] Increasingly, Third World countries are becoming the major export markets for goods produced by these capitalist nations. For example, about 47 percent of Japanese export, 42 percent of American export, and 47 percent of Western European export go to the Third World and the former Soviet-bloc countries; the U.S. exports more to the Third World than to Western Europe and Japan; and Western Europe exports twice as much to the Third World as it does to North America and Japan.[121]

It is often mentioned that the structure of world economic power has changed due to the declining economic leadership of the U.S. as reflected in its continuing budget and trade deficits and its decreasing shares in the world's capital goods industry and manufactured goods exports.[122] But the situation has become more complex in the context of the diminishing power of the socialist bloc over the world economic order due to the collapse of major socialist states and their growing dependence on Western economic powers.[123] Such complexity has increased further due to the emerging multiple linkages within the world market on the one hand, and the newly established regional economic blocs on the other.[124] The examples of economic regionalism include the creation of the European Community (EC), recently replaced by European Union (EU), and the formation of the North American Free Trade Agreement (NAFTA) comprised of the U.S., Canada, and Mexico. Moreover, the EU is planning to incorporate Northern, Central, and Eastern Europe and proposing to create a 40-country Euro-Mediterranean zone; and the Asia-Pacific Economic Cooperation (APEC) has a plan to expand into a free trade area that would incorporate the world's two top economic powers (U.S. and Japan), the fastest-growing region (East Asia), the fastest-growing major economy (China), and other advanced economies such as those of Australia and New Zealand.[125]

But the question remains the following: What implications do these changes in the world economic order, particularly in the regional economic structures, have for the majority of Third World countries that are poor? In fact, economic regionalism may be quite detrimental to most Third World countries, because it is likely to create few "islands of relative prosperity" in an unstable "sea of global poverty."[126] On the other hand, the recent decline in the developmental role of the UN and the potential diversion of foreign aid and trade to the emerging market economies in Eastern Europe and the former Soviet republics, may lead many of these poor countries to depend more upon the international dynamics of capital and production controlled by the transnationals.[127] This is likely to increase the external economic dependence of Third World countries further, which is already evident in the recent withering away of their North-South dialogue and the growing emphasis on their "adjustment" with the existing economic order.[128]

In terms of the *world politico-military order*, during the second half of the twentieth century, the rivalry between the North Atlantic Treaty Organization (NATO) and the Warsaw Pact[129] shaped the global power structure.[130] Most Third World countries were incorporated, directly or indirectly, into this world order dominated by the two superpowers and their allies.[131] The dominance of the two superpowers over the world military order was overwhelming: in 1985, the U.S. and the Soviet Union "accounted for 23% of the world's armed forces, 60% of the military expenditures, more than 80% of the weapons research, and 97% of all nuclear warheads and bombs."[132] More recently, after the demise and disintegration of the dominant socialist states and collapse of the Soviet-led military alliance (Warsaw Pact), this oligarchic power structure has been transformed into a near-monopolistic one under the command of the U.S. as the only remaining superpower of the world. Recently, in relation to the global power structure, the power of the U.S. and its Western allies has expanded further due to the weakening solidarity of Third World countries and the diminishing bargaining position of the socialist and post-socialist military powers (China and Russia) in the international security system, especially, due to their growing dependence on advanced capitalist nations for economic assistance, investments, and markets.

The legal structures of the world military order, especially the UN Security Council, have served the interests of the five world military powers, including the U.S., the Soviet Union (now the Russian Federation), Britain, France, and China.[133] The permanent membership and veto power of these five countries in the Security Council remain highly undemocratic because, in terms of the number of citizens and their international rights, many Third World countries deserve to have such privileges before most Western nations.[134] In fact, the whole UN has increasingly become an instrument of American global economic policies and military interests, because of its dependence on the U.S. for financing its peace-keeping expenditures (from $235 million in 1986 to $4 billion in 1994) and carrying out its operations in various parts of the world.[135] The growing hegemony of the U.S. over the UN Security Council is evident in some of its recent military operations in Third World countries (e.g., Panama, Iraq, Somalia, and Haiti) approved by the Security Council.[136] The U.S. is also using other international laws and institutions, such as the Nuclear Nonproliferation Treaty and International Atomic Energy Agency, to prevent Third World countries (e.g., North Korea, Iraq, and Iran) from having any nuclear weapons, while keeping its massive nuclear arsenal intact and overlooking the alleged possession of nuclear weapons by Israel and South Africa.[137]

However, the current politico-military hegemony of the U.S. is not without challenge. On the one hand, in this post–Cold War era, without the Great Other, the Soviet Union, it has become increasingly difficult for the U.S. to justify its hegemonic military position, and the role of NATO is now in question.[138] On the other hand, the U.S. is less capable of policing the global military activities because of its various economic difficulties caused, ironically, by its expansive defense expenditure itself.[139] In addition, after the Cold War, the U.S. military expansion is under challenge internally, because today American taxpayers are more interested in internal economic conditions than external security. Internationally also, the focus of international conflict is being shifted from the military to the economic realm.[140] Thus, the U.S. government needs to invent more "enemies," such as Cuba, Iraq, Libya, Iran, North Korea, and so on, to justify the big business in arms on behalf of the corporate defense industry.

From this point of view, it could be concluded that recent changes in the world economic and military orders in the post–Cold War era could have certain favorable implications for the economic and political emancipation of Third World countries. However, whatever opportunity has been created by such changes for an autonomous or self-reliant mode of development in these countries, is being lost due to the increasing Western dominance over another dimension of world order, i.e., the *world cultural-informational order*. In this age of revolutionary advancements in communication technologies, an unprecedented degree of globalization of Western media, and the universalization of Western information and cultural products, there has emerged a world order in this regard which is extremely unequal and hegemonic. Such world cultural-informational order based on Western hegemony is quite obvious from the near-monopolistic control and ownership by the Western (especially American) media tycoons in the domains of international news, television programs, radio broadcasting, film production, book publishing, advertisement, data processing, telecommunications, and so on.[141]

Although empirical evidence of this reality is presented elsewhere in the book, it can be briefly mentioned here that in the U.S. alone, there are 1,781 daily newspapers, 8,546 weekly newspapers, 10,794 radio stations, 11,000 magazines, 17,000 book publishers, major television networks (e.g. ABC, NBC, CBS, PBS, ESPN, CNN, MTV), huge film industry (producing about 500 feature films per year), and so on.[142] Internationally, the Associated Press (AP) gathers news from 300 bureaus in more than 70 countries and has subscribers in 112 countries. The CNN has millions of audiences in more than 110 countries.[143] More than 750 million TV sets, often broadcasting imported programs, are watched by 2.5 billion people everyday in more than 160 countries.[144] Recently, American media giants, including Viacom Inc., Time Warner Inc., Walt Disney Co., and Fox Inc., have been expanding their outlets all over the world.[145] In Asia, Western broadcasters (such as Murdoch's Star TV, Turner's CNN, Time Warner's HBO Asia, ESPN International, and so on) are building their media empires. Even in a relatively closed society like China, there are 500,000 satellite dishes, and millions of people watch Western television programs beamed by Murdoch's Star TV.[146]

This unequal world information structure has serious implications for the reinforcement and maintenance of inequality in the world's economic and politico-military orders. For instance, Western information and cultural products (both hardware and software, machines and messages) themselves have taken commodity forms, and they are sold worldwide like any other commodities for profit. Thus, the increasing inequality in the ownership, production, and dissemination of information and cultural commodities implies the generation of more revenues for the affluent capitalist nations, and thus, the expansion of inequality in the world economic order. However, a more crucial economic role of Western media is in its manipulative power to change the indigenous consumption patterns and lifestyles, and thereby, create demands for nonmedia products produced by various transnational firms, ranging from automobiles to electronic goods, fast foods to soft drinks, pharmaceuticals to cosmetics. For example, MTV (Music Television) and Murdoch's Star TV (broadcasting in English, Mandarin, and Hindi) are targeting millions of Asians, especially teenagers, for marketing fast-food, soft drinks, clothes, footwear, and so on.[147] In this regard, Angus and Jhally make a generalization that in the 1980s there has been a deeper integration between the media and transnational corporations, and the boundary between the economic and cultural spheres has become blurred.[148]

With regard to the world politico-military order, Western media may not only play an internal ideological role to promote and legitimize the interests and power of the elites[149] while disregarding social inequality, repression, and subjugation. Such media may also play a crucial international role in expanding and legitimizing the hegemony of Western nations over the world politico-military structures by convincing people of the superiority of Western social formations, demonizing the less pro-Western Third World countries, inventing external enemies, and thus creating a pretext for Western military intervention and hegemony.[150] Today, international television networks can construct and reconstruct instant world opinion through their selective news reporting based on the decontextualized, fragmented, and often fabricated audio-visual displays of various global events stripped of their historical, economic, political, and cultural contexts and meanings. According to Kellner, American television networks often provide distorted information to the world, sell the foreign policy agenda of the U.S. government, manufacture international conflicts, and demonize the "official" enemies of the U.S.[151] In fact, realizing the significance of such a role of transnational media in promoting Western interests, the U.S. government established Radio Free Europe and Radio Liberty to broadcast anticommunist and procapitalist programs in 22 languages, installed transmitters in more than 100 countries to broadcast in 35 languages for ideological propaganda, encouraged and financed ABC to create television empires in Latin America and the Middle East, and is now contemplating more extensive use of such media in pursuing foreign policies and international diplomacy.[152]

In short, although the recent changes in the world economic and military orders have created potential opportunities for Third World countries to break away from the unequal economic and politico-military structures dominated by the superpowers, the global expansion of Western media networks and their all-pervasive penetration into Third World societies have led to the reinforcement and legitimation of such unequal international structures serving the economic and military interests of advanced capitalist nations. As Parenti and Bandyopadhyaya suggest, the existing world information order has led to the perpetuation of unequal world economic order and the legitimation of capitalist politico-ideological interests—by creating biased images, molding international market and exchange, manipulating the outlook of Third World people, and reordering their consumption patterns and lifestyles.[153] Thus, the situation is such that in the current era, a fundamental restructuring of the world cultural-informational order has become a historical precondition to generate critical awareness among Third World nations regarding the adverse implications of hegemonic economic and military structures, to intensify Third World demand for a fundamental change in such economic and military orders characterized by inequality and subjugation,[154] and to pursue a more genuine form of Third World development based on self-reliance rather than dependence.

Conclusion

The above analysis of various forms of intranational and international crises indicate that the existing theories and policies of development have failed to accomplish many of their stipulated objectives. They have not made any considerable progress in resolving the problems of poverty, social inequality, ethnic and racial conflicts, and various forms of international hegemony. In many cases, the practical implications of such development theories and policies have rather been disastrous—in terms of the worsening conditions of external debt and dependence, budget and trade deficits, urban and industrial crises, crime and violence, and above all, the environmental and ecological catastrophes. Many of these development crises are prevalent even in advanced capitalist countries that are often considered exemplars of progress and models of success in the mainstream development literature.

In addition to these failures and adverse implications of the prevailing development theories and policies, some of the most recent policies, reforms, and events have created antidevelopmental outcomes despite some of their immediate favorable results. For instance, although most Third World countries have recently adopted policies of free trade, foreign investment, deregulation, and divestment in the name of efficiency and growth, such policies are likely to expand external dependence, compromise self-reliance, and endanger indigenous sociocultural traditions. Similar promarket reforms in the former socialist countries have brought about certain degree of openness and freedom, but they have exacerbated various forms of economic and political disorders such as poverty, inequality, dependence, instability, and conflict. The technological and industrial expansion in advanced capitalist nations has multiplied the production and consumption of goods and services, but it has worsened the environmental and ecological problems. The end of the Cold War has created a favorable demystifying atmosphere for Third World countries to overcome their subjugation to global ideological hegemony, but the worldwide expansion of transnational media has intensified both ideological and cultural hegemony further.

For Third World countries, these experiences of contradictory policy outcomes and paradoxical contemporary events pose serious developmental challenges: how to resolve economic poverty without perpetuating external debt and dependence; how to reduce state control over private market forces without worsening social inequality; how to adopt free international exchange without undermining national economic sovereignty; how to ensure technological and industrial advancements without endangering the environment; how to acquire authentic information and knowledge without being subjugated to the global media; and so on. The abovementioned failures, maladies, and dilemmas of development, in the ultimate analysis, suggest that there is a serious need to critically reexamine the existing theories and models of development and reconstruct them into an alternative development perspective.[155] For accomplishing this task, one of the most essential prerequisites is a proper analysis and understanding of these development theories and models, which begins with the next chapter.

CHAPTER 3

A Taxonomic Prelude to Development Theories

The quest for development, implying the contemplation and realization of good life and good society, was always a central concern in all great civilizations of the world, including the Aztec, the Chinese, the Egyptian, the European, and the Indian. However, the contemporary thoughts on development, including its concept, theory, model, and strategy, are predominantly European. The origin of this European tradition of development thinking can be traced back even to the idea of progress that evolved in the Greek period.[1] More direct roots of modern development knowledge, however, can be found in some major practical and intellectual events in European history, such as the rise of mercantilism and colonialism, the emergence of the Renaissance and the Enlightenment, the advent of scientific and industrial revolution, and the growth of industrial capitalism and its worldwide expansion.[2]

But several historical challenges, including the Great Depression, World War II, the decolonization of Third World countries, and the emergence of socialist nations and their worldwide influence, interrupted the process of consolidating the Eurocentric view of development. Thus, some theoretical adjustments were to be made in mainstream development thinking to accommodate such unprecedented national and international challenges.[3] On the other hand, since their independence, Third World countries have undertaken massive development programs to improve the living standards of people by transforming various socioeconomic sectors such as agriculture, industry, education, health, and communications. In the process, there has emerged varieties of development models, policies, and strategies encompassing almost every domain of society. In the academic sphere, on the other hand, numerous books, journals, and reports have been published to explain the concepts, theories, and models of development from diverse disciplinary perspectives, including economics, political science, sociology, and even psychology and geography.[4]

Owing to such diverse historical, international, and disciplinary origins, the scope of development theories is quite extensive. More complexity, however, has been created by introducing various overlapping classifications of these theories often based on inadequate taxonomic principles. Because of this enormity and complexity, it is not always easy to comprehend the varieties and substance of all development theories in a meaningful way, although such comprehension is a precondition for a critical study of these theories and their necessary reconstruction. It was realized even in the 1960s, when the development field was at an early stage, that a "deeper analysis of what development theory is supposed to cover may be an important step in the development of development theory."[5] Among the more recent scholars, it has been pointed out by Jaffee that a basic challenge to understand development literature "is to organize the theories [of development] in a way that illuminates the differences and similarities among the various theories."[6]

To resolve such theoretical confusion and controversies, the articulation of a sound typology or taxonomy of development theories is indispensable for the field.[7] In general, "a taxonomy is a naming and arranging in an order an aspect of reality. The taxonomist views reality and arranges it conceptually according to some order based on a set of principles, and names the categories he has created."[8] In any field of knowledge, a comprehensive taxonomy is essential not only to overcome the existing theoretical ambiguities, but also to facilitate future research and theory building.[9] For the development field, the construction of such a taxonomy of development theories is almost a precondition for accomplishing one of the main objectives of this study, which is to introduce a systematic analysis and facilitate a critical understanding of these theories. In this regard, it is necessary to apply certain basic criteria or principles to construct a comprehensive taxonomy.[10] The main objectives of this chapter are to explain some of the primary taxonomic principles needed for classifying development theories, to examine the shortcomings of the existing taxonomies in the development field, and to propose a revised taxonomy with a view to overcome the prevalent taxonomic flaws.

The Taxonomic Principles for Development Theories

DELINEATION OF TAXONOMIC SCOPE

Before classifying a certain issue, event, or object, it is necessary to delineate its scope or boundary, so that there is minimal ambiguity regarding what should and should not be included in the classification scheme. In this study, the focus of classification is on development theories, and it is essential to precisely determine the scope of such theoretical domain for constructing a meaningful taxonomy. However, there are varying connotations of the term "development theory," because almost all disciplines or fields of social science deal with issues related to development, and they have something to offer theoretically under diverse terminologies such as development theory, development model, development approach, development paradigm, development ideology, and so on.

However, in line with the arguments made by Hettne, one may conclude that all these conceptual categories can be considered "development theory" as long as they refer to the academic pursuit of knowledge regarding development, and that "development theory" should be distinguished from "development ideology" justifying development policies in terms of certain obsolete theoretical constructs.[11] The proposed taxonomy would cover all theories, models, approaches, and paradigms that have emerged in various disciplines or fields as a body of knowledge to explain different dimensions of society in relation to the question of progress, modernity, or development. This would become clearer in the analysis below and more specific in the next three chapters.

ADEQUACY OF TAXONOMIC CATEGORIES

There should be a sufficient number of taxonomic categories to cover all theoretical constructs included within the taxonomic scope, i.e., "development theory," mentioned above. Without an adequate number of categories, some theories of development could be left out from the overall taxonomy, because they might not fit in any of the selected taxonomic categories. At the same time, the number of selected categories should not be so many that the purpose of classification itself is lost, because it might lead to a situation in which each theory is placed under an individual category. In short, the number of taxonomic categories should not be so small that some important theories of development are abandoned and so large that the taxonomy becomes extremely detailed and meaningless.

LOGIC OF TAXONOMIC HIERARCHY

Another essential principle, which also mitigates the above problem of selecting an appropriate number of taxonomic categories, is to construct a hierarchy of classification, so that at different levels of this taxonomic hierarchy, development theories are divided into categories, categories into subcategories, subcategories into sub-subcategories, and so on. But some sequential logic should be followed in constructing such a taxonomic structure—it can move from the generic to the specific in a top-down direction or from the specific to the generic in a bottom-up direction. However, the higher level categories should be more generic and inclusive in nature, while the subsequent levels should increasingly be more specific. For instance, one may classify all development theories into conservative theories and radical theories; conservative theories into economic growth theories and modernization theories; economic growth theories into classical and neoclassical theories; and so on.

Such a taxonomic structure of development theories is likely to provide certain analytical autonomy to move along the generic-specific continuum depending on one's intellectual interests or practical needs to deal with development theories. Some scholars and practitioners might be interested in a more generic level of theoretical debate on development while others might require a more specific level of developmental analysis. In addition, a systematically arranged taxonomic hierarchy would facilitate a more meaningful understanding of each development theory, especially in terms of its differences from and relation to other theories, and its location within the overall taxonomic map encompassing all development theories.[12]

EXCLUSIVENESS BETWEEN TAXONOMIC CATEGORIES

The selected taxonomic categories should be arranged in such a manner that they are mutually exclusive, they should not overlap at the same level of taxonomic hierarchy. In other words, at the same level, each development theory should belong to only one category. It is easier to ensure this mutual exclusiveness between categories in classifying objects and issues that are relatively simple and tangible—such as classifying the world population in terms of variables like gender, race, age, and income. In this case, the exclusiveness between taxonomic categories— between male and female, between blacks and whites, between adult and old, and between rich and poor—is easily discernible. But it is quite difficult to maintain such a principle of exclusiveness in classifying issues such as development theories, which are quite broad, complex, and abstract in nature. For example, many development theories may contain both reformist and radical, both incremental and revolutionary, assumptions and arguments. However, it is possible to distinguish these theories by classifying them as "predominantly," if not "absolutely," reformist or radical, incremental or revolutionary.

In other words, despite certain difficulty in classifying development theories due to their complex nature and multidimensional scope, it is still feasible to create a meaningful taxonomy of these theories by using mutually exclusive categories at every level of the taxonomic hierarchy.

ABSTRACT-CONCRETE BALANCE IN SELECTING TAXONOMIC TERMS

To construct a taxonomy of development theories, the terminologies or designations used for various taxonomic categories should not be so abstract and ambiguous (e.g., "discontinuity" theories) that these terminologies themselves require much clarification before exploring the kinds of development theories they include. On the other hand, a taxonomic terminology should not be so concrete or localized (e.g., "Latin American" theories) that it is conceptually empty, and thus, unable to provide any clue regarding the nature of theories it encompasses. In other words, the term or designation used for each major taxonomic category should be precise, easily comprehensible, and conceptually reflective of development theories it represents. In addition, at the top of the taxonomic hierarchy, the broader taxonomic categories should be designated by terms that have more encompassing conceptual scope, so that each higher-level category accommodates many lower-level categories and subcategories of development theories, and conveys messages regarding various dimensions of these theories. For instance, under the term "economic" (theories of development), it is only possible to include development theories that predominantly deal with economic (rather than political and cultural) issues, and the term only expresses the content (which is economic) of such theories. But a terminology such as the "conservative" or "radical" (theories of development) not only encompasses theories dealing with varieties of issues (economic, political, and cultural) but also conveys the basic themes, ideological orientations, historical origins, and main proponents of these theories.

The Major Limitations of Existing Classifications

Before attempting a taxonomic reconstruction, it is necessary to critically examine the inadequacies of the existing classifications of development theories in order to justify the proposal for a new taxonomy. From the standpoint of the above taxonomic principles, it may be recognized that there are serious problems in the development field with regard to the classification of various development theories: such as the ambiguity in outlining the overall scope of these theories, the insufficiency of categories to include them in entirety, the lack of logical sequence in the taxonomic structure, the overlaps between different categories, and so on. These problems can be found in most disciplines and fields concerned with development theories. According to Leeson, development economics, a major field dealing with development theories, is a "hodgepodge of theoretical and empirical work."[13] The typologies of "social change" (development) theories offered by Moore, Smelser, and Etzioni, have been found inadequate by Appelbaum.[14] However, Appelbaum's own classification of social change theories into equilibrium, evolutionary, conflict, and rise-and-fall theories is not without flaws, especially with regard to the overlapping boundaries among these categories.[15]

In the following discussion, some recently constructed typologies of development theories are critically examined on the basis of taxonomic principles outlined above. First, there are typologies that are inadequate because they do not use enough varieties of taxonomic categories to encompass all development theories. For instance, the classification of development theories into modernization theory and world system theory by Kim, and into modernization theory and dependency theory by Valenzuela and Valenzuela, cannot cover many established theories of development such as classical and neoclassical growth theories, Marxian and neo-Marxian theories, and so on.[16] Similarly, the classification of development theories into neoclassical, Marxian, and structuralist by Srinivasan[17] does not involve classical growth theory, modernization theory, and neo-Marxian theory. The classification of development theories into capitalist and Marxist/neo-Marxist by Vengroff,[18] on the other hand, leaves out modernization theory and confuses Marxism with neo-Marxism.

Second, there are classification schemes that create ambiguity because the categories are mutually overlapping or repetitive; not mutually exclusive. For instance, the classification of development theories into orthodox, Marxist, development economics, and neo-Marxist by Hirschman[19] is quite overlapping, because the category "development economics" usually covers and overlaps with the other three categories. The categorization of theories into evolutionary, growing systemness, motivation, economic and political development, and modernization theories by Chodak and Bava[20] is also repetitive, because political development theories are parts of modernization theories, because modernization theories can be interpreted as evolutionary theories, and so on. Similarly, the division of theories into developmentalism, dependency, modes of production, and political economy by Laite[21] is overlapping, because the category "political economy" encompasses other theoretical categories.

Development theories have also been classified in terms of historical contexts, especially in reference to the specific periods of capitalist development, within which these theories emerged.[22] In line with this mode of classification based on historical origin, development theories have been classified by Larrain into three major historical categories, namely, the age of competitive capitalism (1700–1860), the age of imperialism (1860–1945), and the age of late capitalism (1945–present).[23] However, this typology remains overlapping, because it does not consider the fact that development theories that emerged in one period continued into other periods despite their reformulations. In addition, during the same historical period, different societies may follow different sets of theoretical frameworks or traditions. Realizing the existing taxonomic problems, Jaffee categorizes development theories in terms of their levels or units of analysis, including the individual level (focusing on attitudes and values), the organizational level (addressing industrial relations), the societal level (dealing with economic systems and state policies), and the international level (highlighting international economic forces).[24] But this classification is quite misleading, because there is rarely any development theory that applies only a single unit or level, most theories use multiple units of analysis.

Third, there are some schemes of classification that use extremely abstract and controversial terminologies for various taxonomic categories. For instance, after a review of various classification schemes presented by several authors, Nieuwenhuijze offers an ideal-type classification of development theories that seems to be quite problematic due to its use of a taxonomic criterion, "continuity-discontinuity,"[25] which is too abstract and ambiguous. In this case, before studying development theories categorized under such a classification scheme, one has to be clear about the vague taxonomic term "continuity-discontinuity" itself. Another example of this problem with the use of taxonomic terms is the classification of development theories by Steidlmeier into categories such as trickle-down, revolution, basic beeds, self-reliance, and rural development.[26] The controversy lies with the fact that these categories basically represent specific development "strategies" rather than "theories." In fact, these are practical strategies prescribed by certain development theories, and therefore could be inappropriate (and inadequate) for constructing a taxonomy for all theories in the development field.

Some scholars, on the other hand, have used Kuhn's idea of "paradigm" to classify development theories. For instance, Berger identifies the paradigms of modernization and imperialism; Wilber and Jameson make a distinction between orthodox paradigm and political economy paradigm; and Jolly presents three conflicting paradigms of development.[27] But objections have been raised by Foster-Carter and Elguea against the use of the term "paradigm" in the development field.[28] It is because in most of these cases, there seems to be a misunderstanding of or an indifference toward the basic principles or features of a paradigm suggested by Kuhn, including the incommensurability between the past and present paradigms and the impossibility of the coexistence of two competitive paradigms in the same historical period. Against these Kuhnian principles, development scholars often consider the past and present paradigms of development as mutually commensurable, and they often present two or more development paradigms as if they can coexist simultaneously.[29]

Finally, there are authors who have offered more exhaustive classifications, but these too are not without taxonomic flaws. For instance, the classification of development theories into neoclassical, structural, Marxist, and neo-Marxist theories by Clements[30] is relatively comprehensive in terms of its broad coverage and minimal overlap. But in this taxonomy, the author fails to include theories such as classical growth theory and modernization theory, and in his analysis, he tends to create confusion between dependency, Marxist, and neo-Marxist theories.[31] In addition, this kind of classification of development literature into three major schools has been found problematic by Toye due to its poor demarcation of specific theoretical boundaries.[32] Preston also presents a relatively comprehensive typology that divides development theories into three main categories:

growth and modernization theories, neo-institutional and structuralist theories, and neo-Marxian theory. However, he has placed the works of some leading development theorists in inappropriate theoretical categories.[33] In brief, the existing typologies of development theories offered by various development scholars suffer from varieties of limitations mentioned above, which implies that there is a need for constructing a more precise and comprehensive taxonomy of these theories.

Restructured Taxonomy of Development Theories

Based on the above set of taxonomic principles and critical review of the existing classification schemes, an alternative taxonomy of development theories is proposed below, which is tentative and subject to further revision and improvement. The central concern of the proposed taxonomy is to comprehend the existing theories of development in a more systematic and meaningful manner, and thereby facilitate the realization of the main objectives of this study—to reexamine the major shortcomings and adverse implications of the existing development theories, to restructure such inadequate theories into a more comprehensive theoretical perspective, and to operationalize this new theoretical perspective into a set of effective development policies. In line with the basic taxonomic principles articulated above, this proposed taxonomy attempts to ensure that the selected taxonomic categories are exhaustive enough to cover all major theories of development, that a balance is maintained in terms of the generality and specificity of taxonomic categories used at various levels of taxonomic hierarchy, that the categories at the same taxonomic level are mutually exclusive, and that the terms used for designating various taxonomic categories are conceptually unambiguous and easily comprehensible.

The scope of this taxonomy, which is basically concerned with development theories, covers various explanations or interpretations of development offered by diverse academic disciplines and fields, esepcially sociology, economics, and political science. The content and focus of such development theories range from the politico-economic to sociocultural dimensions of society, from internal condition to international system, from group composition to class structure, from past historical account to futuristic prediction. Beyond the domain of academic theoretical frameworks, there are also concrete models, approaches, and strategies of development (e.g., "basic needs"

approach) prescribed or practiced by development experts and practitioners. Since some of these development models and strategies
usually represent certain dominant theory or theories, they are also
covered within the scope of the proposed taxonomy.

However, it should be mentioned that in constructing such a
taxonomy of development theories, it is hardly possible to put a particular development thinker and his or her lifetime works in a single
category. This is because the same writer may have contributions to
more than one category of development theories. It is also difficult to
introduce the entire development-related works of a scholar in this
book due to the limitation of space. On the other hand, as mentioned
above, for a meaningful understanding of development theories, the
prevailing taxonomic duplications, overgeneralizations, and oversim-
plifications must be overcome by constructing a more comprehensive
taxonomy of these theories. Given such limitations and necessities,
in the proposed taxonomy, development theories are broadly classified into three major theoretical traditions, including the conservative tradition, the reformist tradition, and the radical tradition,
followed by their further division into more specific categories and
subcategories.

THE CONSERVATIVE TRADITION

The conservative tradition of development theories ideologically reflects the theories of capitalist development that emerged in Western
Europe and North America. There is a central common theme among
various development theories placed under this tradition: they consider all societal changes as gradual or incremental, and exclude the
possibility of any fundamental social contradiction and revolutionary
historical transformation. Under this conservative tradition, there
are established theoretical explanations that emphasize mainly the
economic dimension of development, which can be categorized as the
"theories of economic growth." Within this category, however, there
are some theories, such as the classical and neoclassical theories of
economic growth, that tend to oppose any significant state intervention, while other theories emphasize the interventionist role of the
state in ensuring economic progress in both developed nations and
Third World countries. The interventionist growth theories concerning
developed countries include both Keynesian and post-Keynesian
varieties, whereas the interventionist theories related to Third World
countries represent a set of theories that covers unbalanced-growth
theory, theory of dualism, stages of growth theory, and so on.

Beyond these extremely economistic theoretical categories, there are other theories within this tradition such as the theories of modernization, which focus on the social, political, cultural, and psychological realms affecting the process of development.[34] Thus, based on their specific focus on any of these societal realms, modernization theories are further classified into three main subcategories, including sociological modernization theory, political modernization theory, and psycho-cultural modernization theory. An overall taxonomic structure of the conservative tradition, composed of all these development theories, is presented in Figure 4.1 in chapter 4.

THE REFORMIST TRADITION

Unlike the above conservative tradition and the radical tradition discussed below, the reformist tradition tends to suggest that the nature of societal change is neither incremental nor revolutionary. Instead, the planned socioeconomic changes have to be brought about by introducing significant reforms at national and international levels. The theories and models under this tradition are reformist not only in terms of their choice for practical strategies of reform, they are also reformist in terms of their theoretical orientation since they mostly represent the revisions of various conservative and radical theories of development. Thus, the tradition is divided into three major categories: first, the conservative reformist theories, originating mostly from the conservative tradition and emphasizing some piecemeal reforms; second, the radical reformist theories, reflecting considerable influence of the radical tradition (explained below) but stressing basic socioeconomic reforms rather than revolutionary changes; and third, the critical reformist theories, representing mostly the contributions of critical theory (articulated by the Frankfurt School) that emphasizes the role of critique to uncover the reality of domination and enhance the process of emancipatory reforms.

Within the conservative reformist category, there are development models and strategies which focus on reforms at the national level, and there are those which highlight reforms at an international level. Among the national level models and strategies, some of them emphasize the strategy of "redistribution with growth" while others favor "redistribution with or without growth." The second broad category, i.e., the radical reformist theories, is divided into three subcategories depending on their theoretical contents and orientations—the theory of internal colonialism, the theory of underdevelopment, and the theory of dependent development. These theories of under-development and dependent development, broadly known as dependency theories, are radical reformist, because although they believe in fundamental societal change, they suggest accomplishing it through major reforms rather than revolution. However, there are other dependency theories that emphasize social transformation through revolution, and thus belong to the radical tradition discussed in the next section.

The third theoretical category under the reformist tradition, i.e., critical theory, does not directly represent development theory as such, because it hardly addresses the question of development as understood in the mainstream development literature, and according to some writers, it hardly possesses an adequate theory of social change.[35] However, the theory is included in the taxonomy because of its valuable contributions to the understanding of various short-comings in both the capitalist and Marxian frameworks of development thinking. As far as the overall nature of the reformist tradition is concerned, as discussed above, all theoretical categories under the tradition generally suggest reform rather than revolution as the dominant mode of social change. An overview of the whole reformist tradition can be found in Figure 5.1 in chapter 5.

THE RADICAL TRADITION

In the radical tradition, there are diverse theories of development that connote some common underlying themes: that there are various forms of contradictions within and between societies, that these contradictions lead to fundamental or radical changes in different dimensions of society, and that such basic societal changes occur through revolutionary historical events. The most prominent theories of development under this tradition are attached to two central figures, Marx and Engels, although the tradition has been extended in different directions during this century by its propo-nents, including both academics and revolutionary political leaders in different parts of the world. Thus, the original contributions of Marx and Engels and their direct proponents (who did not differ on their central theses) have been categorized as classical Marxist theories.

On the other hand, there are theoretical contributions made by more recent scholars who, in studying the contemporary socio-historical contexts of Third World countries, attempt to reexamine classical Marxism and restructure it without rejecting its basic arguments. These recent theoretical formulations have been placed under the category of neo-Marxist theories. Such neo-Marxist theories have been divided further into different subcategories depending on their varying emphases on some basic tenets of Marxism such as the modes of production, forms of exchange, compositions of the state, and class structures in different societies. In addition to these Marxian and neo-Marxian theories, there are other theoretical formulations that are not necessarily compatible with the basic Marxian arguments, but they belong to the radical tradition because of their emphasis on the radical transformation of society through revolutionary means. These relatively non-Marxian but radical development theories represent the works of radical dependency theorists, and they have been classified as such.[36] For all these theories, an overall taxonomic structure of the radical tradition is presented in Figure 6.1 in chapter 6.

In conclusion, for the last two centuries, scholars from different parts of the world, particularly Western Europe and North America, and from various disciplines of knowledge, especially the social sciences, have offered numerous theories and models of development that largely represent the conservative, radical, and reformist traditions of development thinking. These major theoretical traditions are discussed in the following three chapters: the conservative tradition in chapter 4, the reformist tradition in chapter 5, and the radical tradition in chapter 6. As mentioned above, it is hardly possible to introduce the life-time works of so many development thinkers who have contributed to the formation, expansion, and reconstruction of various development theories.[37] However, as much as possible, their basic theoretical arguments and critiques related to the question of development and underdevelopment will be examined in these three subsequent chapters.

CHAPTER 4

Conservative Tradition of Development Theories

Within the conservative tradition, various development theories, in general, deal with the economic, social, political, cultural, and psychological dimensions of society, although the economic realm has primacy over the other domains. Historically, the root of such overwhelming emphasis on the economic dimension can be traced back to the emergence of the capitalist mode of production, institutions of free market, and principles of exchange and profit, which increasingly became the primary forces not only to shape the nature of practical policies but also to influence the agenda of academic research. Almost simultaneously, changes in other domains—including the rise of liberalism in politics, individualism in social relations, secularism in culture, and hedonism in human attitudes—took place in line with the overall capitalist system and its dominant forces.

In this sociohistorical context, the intellectual perspective related to development or progress was largely influenced by the prevailing capitalist atmosphere: the classical theorists of economic growth, including Adam Smith, Thomas Malthus, David Ricardo, and J.S. Mill, were considerably affected by the emerging industrial capitalism characterized by the dominance of economic considerations. Within the conservative tradition, although the contributions of these classical theorists have been revised into neoclassical growth theory, and later, into Keynesian and neo-Keynesian frameworks and "new growth" theory, the dominance of economism still represents one of the most crucial features of this tradition of development thinking.

However, the principles of economic growth theories that emerged in advanced capitalist nations were found to be relatively inapplicable or ineffective in economically underdeveloped Third World countries, which led to the reformulation of these theories by emphasizing the economic role of the state and incorporating certain concerns for income distribution. On the other hand, within the scope of Third World development, the social, political, and psycho-cultural dimensions were also recognized, which gave rise to various "modernization theories" highlighting these specific domains of Third World societies. Even these theories of modernization, which attempted to address the relatively noneconomic (i.e., social, political, and psycho-cultural) realms of society, were expected to facilitate the achievement of "economic" progress as the eventual goal. However, modernization theories came to represent an established theoretical category within the conservative tradition of development thinking. Thus, there are two broad categories of development theories within the conservative tradition, including the theories of economic growth and the theories of modernization. Within each of these general categories, it is possible to identify more specific theoretical subcategories as shown in the taxonomic diagram presented in this chapter (see Figure 4.1).

Theories of Economic Growth

It is widely known that under the feudal mode of production in Europe, the expansion of agriculture, especially the surplus production of food and handicrafts, brought the demise of feudalism itself. Agricultural surplus expanded trade and commerce which, in turn, strengthened the power and capacity of the rising merchant class and facilitated the emergence of mercantilism. The merchant class continued to accumulate wealth, transformed handicrafts into export industry, converted agricultural labor into manufacturing labor, commoditized land and replaced feudal landlords, established foreign trade monopolies and colonies, and ushered in the emergence of rapid scientific and technological changes. Many of them from this merchant class increasingly invested their capital in industries and converted themselves into industrial capitalists, enhanced the process of industrial revolution, and finally augmented an overall shift in the mode of production from merchant capitalism to industrial capitalism. Compared to an active role of the state under mercantilism, under industrial capitalism, the emphasis was on the accumulation of wealth based on market competition and minimal state intervention.

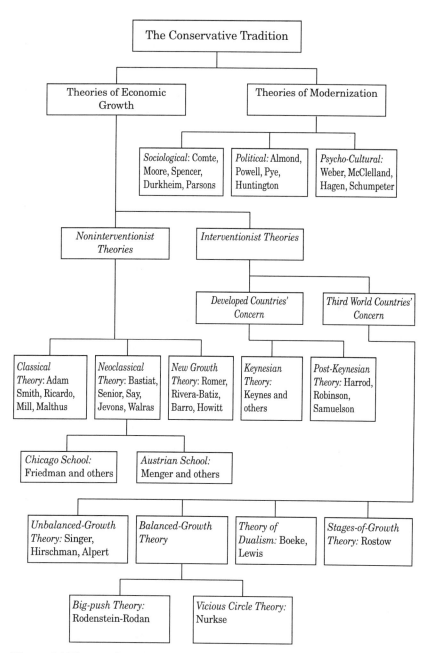

Figure 4.1 Diagram showing various taxonomic categories and subcategories of development theories and models within the conservative tradition. It displays the major intellectual sources of and theoretical differences among these theories and models.

Intellectually, the early phases of industrial capitalism, however, combined certain features of mercantilism with liberalism: it came to be a synthesis between the drive of mercantilism (1550–1776) for accumulating wealth and the concern of the physiocratic economic school (1756–1778) for economic and political liberalism. The principle of economic accumulation through the mechanism of market competition eventually became the core component of the noninterventionist theories of economic growth that flourished in the major capitalist nations.

NONINTERVENTIONIST THEORIES

In the course of its intellectual evolution, the noninterventionist perspective took two major theoretical forms, classical and neoclassical. The classical noninterventionist theory was concerned primarily with accumulation and growth, perhaps because during this formative period of capitalist industrial growth, there was an underlying fear of potential stagnation caused by factors such as population increase. However, by the end of the late nineteenth century, as the capitalist market economy demonstrated its continuous expansion, the fear of stagnation diminished, capital became relatively secured, and the market system became more institutionalized. In this context, there emerged an increasing emphasis on the maintenance, rather than rapid expansion, of the existing level of growth by ensuring the stability and efficiency of the market system.

Thus, another form of noninterventionist theory, the neoclassical theory, appeared along with various microeconomic laws and quantitative devices in order to ensure the maintenance of market competition as an institution of the capitalist system in general. But there has been a growing concern for the depletion and scarcity of material resources as a constraint to economic growth, which required economic thinkers to pay attention to alternative factors of production other than material resources. In this regard, there has emerged a more recent version of growth theory known as "new growth" theory, which emphasizes the continuing expansion of economic growth based on new knowledge, technological innovation, and human capital. Thus, under the category of noninterventionist theories, it is possible to include classical growth theory, neoclassical theory, and "new growth" theory.

Classical Growth Theory

One of the most important contributions, which laid the basic foundation of economic growth theory, was made by Adam Smith's *An
Inquiry into the Nature and Causes of the Wealth of Nations*. Further
articulation or consolidation of growth theory continued with other
classical economists such as David Ricardo, T.R. Malthus, and J.S.
Mill. The sociohistorical context that shaped the work of Adam Smith
(1723–1790) was the context of industrial revolution and the emerging
industrial capitalism. He was so impressed by the capitalist expansion of productivity based on an increasing division of labor that he
considered capitalism as the highest social formation in which the
acquisitive and selfish human desire for wealth accumulation could
be realized. In a simple term, his theoretical framework suggests that
the capitalist system ensures the existence of a free competitive market, a free market facilitates the free exchange of commodity based on
the division of labor, the division of labor increases the level of productivity, an increase in production brings more profit, and additional
profit leads to further accumulation. Thus, division of labor and free
market are the basic components: the former enhances the expansion
of commodity production and the latter provides the opportunity for
free exchange of such commodities.[1]

However, according to Adam Smith, when the market becomes
limited due to various reasons (such as the decline of exchange due to
local self-sufficiency), the process of growth reverses and the economy
becomes stagnant. Market can, however, be expanded through exchange between nations on the basis of the principle of specialization
and division of labor at an international level. But eventually, each
country, with all its resource endowments and relations with other
countries, attains a point of "full complement of riches." For Adam
Smith, this is a stationary stage of the economy when capital accumulation ceases and development stops.[2]

Thomas Malthus (1766–1834), another classical theorist, worked
as a spokesman for the wealthy, wrote against intellectuals supporting the working class (e.g., Condorcet and Godwin), and opposed
any attempt to provide relief to the poor. Malthus concluded that
poverty was natural and inevitable because of the uncontrolled
population growth. His relatively pessimistic theory of population,
which explains the causes, effects, and remedies of population growth,
is not of much relevance here. However, in relation to economic growth
theory, it is important to know his argument that an economy can fall

in a situation of overproduction—a situation when capital accumulation is increased by reducing consumption, when the effectual demand is less than supply.[3] The solution to this problem is to redistribute income to a group that would spend most of its income on consumption. For Malthus, it is mainly the landlords who constitute such a group: if they are allowed to increase their earning from rent, they would spend it not only on their own luxurious consumption but also for the maintenance of their servants (unproductive workers) who, in turn, would also spend all their incomes.[4] This, according to Malthus, would eventually expand the effectual demand.

David Ricardo (1772–1823), on the other hand, explains the nature of relationship between the relative sharing of income by three economic factors (i.e., profit for capital, rent for land, and wages for labor) and the dynamics of population growth.[5] At the initial stage, capital grows faster than the population, which causes an increase in actual wage beyond the subsistence level. However, this increase in wage leads to an increase in population, and such population increase leads to an economic stagnation. But how does this unfold itself? According to Ricardo, as the population increases, an increasing amount of land of lower quality is brought under cultivation. This leads to the diminishing returns from land and, thus, to a scarcity of food. This food scarcity increases both the prices of food and the rent on land, which, in turn, reduce the savings and (thus) investments of capitalists, because they have to spend more on food and land in such a situation. Finally, with this decrease in capitalist investment, the demand for labor falls, wage rates decline, starvation and deaths occur, family size shrinks, labor supply goes down, wages go up again, and the process repeats itself. However, in the short run, such an economic stagnation can be mitigated by opening new fertile lands abroad; by enhancing technological progress; and by introducing free trade among nations depending on their "comparative advantage," i.e., an advantage based on the international division of labor and the economic specialization of various nations. But eventually, in the long run, the rate of growth ceases and the economy becomes stationary.[6]

With regard to theoretical contribution to economic growth theory, John Stuart Mill (1806–1873), another classical thinker, focuses on capital accumulation. For him, the amount of capital accumulation depends on the magnitude of industrial production and "the strength of the disposition to save."[7] In a progressive economy, usually, an increase in capital and output expands the demand for labor, which in turn increases the level of wages. However, due to competition and the law of diminishing returns, the rate of profit declines and, thus, the increase in wealth stops. For Mill, this stationary economic state is desirable, because with a controlled and fixed population, this is a situation in which a higher level of economic development had already been achieved by technological progress and capital accumulation, in which there would be no struggle to get ahead, and in which there would be more opportunity for the moral, cultural, and social dimensions of progress.[8]

In summary, according to the leading classical theorists of economic growth, capitalism represents the highest stage or form of society, and the primary criterion of progress in such a society is the accumulation of wealth or capital. However, for these theorists, at the eventual stage of this process of accumulation, a stationary state would set in when further growth would end due to the market limitations and diminishing returns from capital and land. This stationary state could be overcome only for a temporary period by undertaking measures such as redistributing income to the land-lords, establishing international trade, and discovering new lands. However, among these classical theorists, Mill considers this stationary state desirable, and anticipates the neoclassical view that if population can be controlled, the importance of a growing or progressive economy declines.[9]

Neoclassical Theory

The intellectual shift from classical growth theory to neoclassical theory around the 1870s was primarily due to the successful realization of economic growth in advanced capitalist nations. This economic success—characterized by increases in real wages, profit rates, and technological progress—outstripped population growth and neutralized the classical theorists' fear of a "stationary state." As a result, the immediate short-run concern for the efficient allocation of resources and maximization of their utility became more important than the long-run process of economic growth. Despite this relatively static and short-run nature of neoclassical theory, it remains relevant to issues related to economic growth and development. Today, neoclassical theory represents a strong intellectual position in academic and government institutions in advanced capitalist countries, in the programs carried out by international development agencies, and in development plans and policies undertaken by Third World countries.[10] Therefore, it is relevant to discuss at least some major components of neoclassical theory, which was initiated indirectly by Bentham; founded by Say, Senior, and Bastiat; extended by Jevons, Menger, Walras, Marshall, Clark, and Bohm-Bawerk; and refined further by Friedman, Samuelson, and others.

Although Jeremy Bentham (1748–1832) did not write directly for neoclassical theory, his thoughts prevailed in the works of well-known neoclassical thinkers. On the basis of his hedonistic assumption of human nature,[11] Bentham developed his utilitarian social philosophy. According to this philosophy, an object has "utility" if it can produce pleasure or reduce pain, and this utility can be measured in terms of the quantity of such pleasure and pain.[12] Based on this utilitarian philosophy, he offered an economic interpretation that it was the utility (in consumption) of a commodity rather than its embodied labor (in production) that remained the primary source of value and wealth.

The founders of neoclassical theory, including Jean-Baptise Say (1767–1832), Nassau Senior (1790–1864), and Frederic Bastiat (1801–1850), accepted the principles of free market offered by classical theorists but rejected their labor theory of value that considered labor as the sole source of value. They rather followed Bentham's utilitarian principle, according to which the utility of a commodity determines its exchange value or price. For Say and Bastiat, the main source of capital is also not labor, as classical theory suggests, but the frugality and suffering of capitalists.[13] Thus, there is a tendency to justify profit for capital and exclude the possibility of capital-labor conflict. According to Say, the incomes of capitalists (based on the profit rate) and workers (based on the wage rate) are to be determined by the relative contribution of capital and labor.

Although Bentham, Say, Senior, and Bastiat laid the foundation of neoclassical theory, it was the works of Jevons, Menger, Walras, Marshall, Clark, and Bohm-Bawerk that helped build a more independent and comprehensive tradition of neoclassical theory.[14] These later scholars endorse the major neoclassical principles offered by the earlier thinkers discussed above—including the principle of utilitarian consumption behavior, prices determined by utility, profit based on the contribution of capital, existence of capital-labor complementarity, and so on. The main concerns of these later neoclassicists were how to determine the prices of consumption goods, assess the incomes of the factors of production, and maximize the consumer's utility and producer's profit. However, while Jevons, Menger and Walras focused more on the consumption side, Marshall, Clark, and Bohm-Bawerk dealt with the production side.

More specifically, in relation to the realm of *consumption*, Williams S. Jevons (1835–1882) extended neoclassical theory by presenting the idea of marginal utility, implying the utility or satisfaction gained from consuming an additional unit of a commodity. He also introduced the mathematical formulations of how utility determined prices and how total utility could be maximized. Based on this concept of marginal utility, Carl Menger (1840–1921) developed his law of demand: a decrease in marginal utility (diminishing marginal utility) causes a corresponding decrease in demand, which also leads to a decrease in price. On the other hand, realizing the dependence of commodity prices in one market on all other markets, Leon Walras (1834–1910) introduced the theory of general equilibrium. According to this theory, since in any disequilibrium, the total excess demand (resulting from those markets where demand is more than supply) is equal to the total excess supply (resulting from those markets where supply is more than demand), under perfect competition, all the disequilibrium would eventually be overcome through automatic price changes.[15]

With regard to the sphere of *production*, parallel to the principle of diminishing marginal utility and its effect,[16] Alfred Marshall (1842–1924) introduced the principle of "diminishing returns," which implied that as a firm employed more and more of a particular factor of production (labor or capital), the productivity of such a factor would diminish. Similar to how a household substitutes between various consumption goods, a firm also substitutes one factor of production (e.g., capital) for another (e.g., labor) by comparing their relative "marginal productivity/cost ratios" in order to maximize profit.[17] John Bates Clark (1847–1938) goes further to describe that every factor of production receives income (wage for labor and profit or interest rate for capital) that is equal to the value of its marginal product. In this sense, there is no surplus value and no exploitation. On top of this, Eugen von Bohm-Bawerk (1851–1914) adds the time dimension in order to calculate the total amount of capital that comprises not only the amount of original factors of production but also the duration of production period.

Accepting all the above assumptions and principles of the early neoclassical scholars, more recently, the neoclassical tradition has been divided on *methodological grounds* into the "rationalist" Austrian School (in the line of Carl Menger) and the "empiricist" Chicago School (represented by Milton Friedman). However, both schools endorse the mainstream neoclassical principles, especially the automaticity of market forces and noninterventionist role of the state. The list of neoclassical thinkers, ideas, and schools can be quite extensive. However, at this stage of analysis, without extending the list further, it is necessary to put all the aforementioned neoclassical thoughts together in order to have an overall view of this theoretical framework. In this regard, based on the above discussion, the essential components of neoclassical theory can be summarized as follows:

1. *On the consumption side*, each individual tries to maximize his or her utility through consumption. In the process of consumption, although individuals increase their overall satisfaction or *total utility* (up to a certain point) by consuming more units of a particular commodity, their incremental satisfaction or the *marginal utility* from each additional unit decreases. This condition is known as the condition of *diminishing marginal utility*. However, the same amount of utility can be obtained from consuming different commodities in various combinations depending on their mutual substitutability. As long as his total utility remains the same, an individual is indifferent toward the trade-off between commodities, which can be shown by the so-called *indifference curve* based on the principle of diminishing marginal utility. On the other hand, individuals have a limited budget. Under this budget constraint, which allows them to buy various amounts of specific commodities depending on their relative prices (usually depicted by the *budget line*), they maximize the total utility by continuously substituting various commodities they consume until the marginal utility ratio of these commodities equals their price ratio.

2. *On the production side*, a firm, given the prices of various factors of production such as capital and labor, tries to maximize its profit by reducing the cost of production. With the increasing use of a particular production factor, say labor, the amount of total product increases. However, beyond a certain point, the amount of product from each additional unit of that factor (known as the factor's *marginal productivity*) decreases. This is known as the law of *diminishing returns*. As long as the amount of product remain the same, the firm does not mind substituting one factor for another. But each of these factors has a price (e.g., wage for labor and interest for capital) determined by the value of its marginal product. Given such prices of different production factors, the firm, with its limited resources, can afford to obtain various combinations of different amounts of production factors, which is depicted by an *iso-cost* line. Thus, under the resource constraint, the firm maximizes its output by mutually substituting between various factors of production (labor

and capital) until their *marginal productivity ratio* equals their price (wage for labor and interest for capital) ratio.

3. *How do consumers and producers interact* to maximize welfare in terms of maximizing utility and profit? With the given amounts of labor and capital, it is possible to produce different combinations of commodities (e.g., food and clothing), which can be demonstrated by a *production-possibility curve*. By transferring inputs, the production of one commodity can be transformed into the production of another, and this is known as the *marginal rate of transformation*. Under equilibrium, the marginal rate of transformation between commodities reflects their price ratio. This equilibrium price ratio, on the other hand, equals the ratio of marginal utilities of consumers. Thus, under perfect competition, the marginal rate of transformation of two commodities produced by a firm, the ratio of their marginal utilities for a household, and the ratio of their prices in the market are equal.

4. Under perfect competition, this condition of equilibrium for both households and firms is known as the so-called *utility-possibility frontier*.[18] Under such an equilibrium, no change in production or exchange can be better for one individual without being worse for another. Under this equilibrium, it is difficult to make any individual better off without others being worse off. This condition of maximum welfare, in terms of optimum allocation, is known as a *Pareto optimum*, representing the theory contributed by Vilfred Pareto (1848–1923). J.R. Hicks and N. Kaldor have added a compensatory dimension to Pareto's theory: if anybody remains a net gainer even after compensating the losers, then it is efficient.[19] Academically, this logic of welfare maximization has become a legitimate ground to apply neoclassical principles to assess various policy issues. The neoclassical framework is often used to justify the instruments (e.g., cost-benefit analysis) of policy analysis, international trade, and development policies and projects. According to Clements, since the late 1960s, the theoretical framework used by decision-makers in the dominant nations and international agencies has been based on neoclassical assumptions.[20]

New Growth Theory

Based on certain differences from the above classical and neoclassical theories of economic growth, there is another version of economic growth theory, the so-called "new growth" or "endogenous growth" theory, articulated by scholars such as Paul Romer, Luis

Rivera-Batiz, Robert Barro, Philippe Aghion, and Petter Howitt. While classical and neoclassical growth theories emphasize physical resources and free trade as major factors contributing to economic growth, the main thrust of this new growth theory is on human capital and new technologies for growth. While classical and neoclassical theories stress resource scarcity as a major impediment to growth, the new growth theory remains optimistic about the continuity and expansion of wealth creation enhanced by new ideas, products, and markets.[21] According to Paul Romer (the main proponent of new growth theory), despite the challenge to economic growth posed by resource scarcity, there can still be continual expansion of such growth ensured by new ideas and technologies, which have enormous potential to rearrange or reorganize raw materials or physical resources to enhance productivity and growth.[22]

With regard to new ideas or knowledge, the proponents of new growth theory, especially Romer, attempt to distinguish knowledge (as a form of capital) from physical capital. In general, there are diminishing returns from investments made in physical capital. But in the case of knowledge, although the amount of new knowledge created from additional investment in research gradually declines, this investment eventually leads to much higher returns in terms of goods produced by applying such new knowledge—especially because the knowledge created by one firm has positive externalities for many other firms that can use the same knowledge to increase production.[23] With regard to these positive externalities, Romer explains that various forms of new knowledge (including new scientific law, mathematical result, software, design, etc.) are "nonrival" goods, because they can be used or copied by many firms at the same time.[24]

However, behind all forms of new ideas, knowledge, and technologies is the human capital. Thus, for Romer, among the major variables contributing to economic growth, the key factor remains the stock of human capital (creative and capable human resource, not the total population)—"an economy with a larger total stock of human capital will experience faster growth."[25] Since the low level of human capital largely accounts for minimal growth in underdeveloped countries,[26] these countries should invest heavily in education, encourage their citizens to acquire ideas from the world stock of knowledge (especially from advanced countries), and allow direct investments by foreign firms.[27]

Finally, the proponents of new growth theory emphasize international trade and global economic integration in order to enhance growth. As Rivera-Batiz and Romer mention, "economic integration can cause a permanent increase in the worldwide rate of growth. Starting from a position of isolation, closer integration [among countries with similar endowments] can be achieved by increasing trade in goods or by increasing flows of ideas."[28] With regard to poorer countries such as India, Romer mentions that India has remained poor due to its minimal openness to world markets and foreign ideas:

> India's commitment to closing itself off and striving for self-sufficiency has been as strong as Japan's commitment to acquiring foreign ideas and participating fully in world markets. The outcomes—grinding poverty in India and opulence in Japan—could hardly be more disparate.[29]

The above arguments offered by new growth theory make some theoretical contributions in terms of emphasizing the role of innovative ideas, new knowledge, human capital, and technological progress to overcome stagnation and create wealth. But these arguments are not only a matter of common public knowledge (except putting them in a more precise and quantitative manner by the new growth theorists), they also have certain shortcomings. For instance, this theoretical framework, similar to other growth theories, suffers from the fetish of economic growth without much concern for issues such as class inequality, unequal exchange, environmental problems (caused by industrial growth), and so on. In addition, this theory emphasizes global economic integration, recommends free flows of ideas, and encourages Third World countries to borrow new ideas and technologies from advanced capitalist nations and their corporations—these policy prescriptions, if adopted, may endanger Third World countries by subordinating them to the global capitalist system, displacing their indigenous knowledge and technology, and making them economically, intellectually, and technologically dependent on advanced industrial countries.

INTERVENTIONIST THEORIES

In advanced capitalist countries, the assumptions of invisible hand, perfect competition, and market automaticity underlying the classical and neoclassical theories of economic growth came under challenge due to their inadequacy to explain various unexpected events, including the market crises such as the Great Depression of the 1930s, the displacement of market competition by the oligopolistic corporate capitalism, and the continual expansion of the administrative state.

To overcome some of these critical problems, especially the Great Depression, the policy option for the capitalist economies was to expand the interventionist economic role of the state. As a result, it became imperative to offer alternative theoretical explanations to articulate and justify an increasing degree of state intervention in the capitalist system.

In Third World countries, on the other hand, the central concern was how to accelerate economic growth within an adverse context characterized by weak private capital, underdeveloped market, and excessive surplus labor. In this Third World context, instead of waiting for the uncertain, autonomous development of market capitalism, the preferred option was to adopt various interventionist theoretical frameworks endorsing some form of state planning. However, while the interventionist option in advanced capitalist nations was adopted largely to rectify serious market failures such as the Great Depression, the interventionist approach in Third World countries was in response to their post-independence economic poverty and lack of private capital and entrepreneurship. Thus, there emerged two sets of interventionist theories: one related to the market crises in advanced capitalist nations, another for resolving poverty and underdevelopment in Third World countries.

For Advanced Capitalist Nations

In the case of advanced capitalist countries, although the practical interventionist policies were already adopted by the state to overcome the market crisis, the theoretical framework for such an interventionist option was provided by John Maynard Keynes (1883–1946). Keynes provided a more systematic explanation of the economic crisis in capitalist countries and established the theoretical ground for interventionist economic policies in their market economies. This is commonly known as Keynesian theory that influenced government policies in the capitalist world.

Keynesian Theory

Although Keynes received training in Marshall's neoclassical school and accepted most of the basic principles of neoclassical theory, he did not agree with the neoclassical arguments that savings and investment are determined by the interest rate and vice versa. For Keynes, saving is a matter of the level of income and consumption: the rate of income-increase is inversely related with the "marginal propensity to consume" (MPC) and positively related with the "marginal propensity to save" (MPS).[30] On the other hand, the interest rate is determined by the demand and supply of money. While the supply of money is a matter of available cash, the demand for money depends on the individual's desire to keep savings in cash form, which is known as liquidity preference.[31] An ordinary form of depression can be overcome by the monetary policy of increasing the quantity of money or expanding the volume of money supply.[32]

However, a more critical depression starts when the continuous economic growth in a capitalist economy, together with its income inequality, causes a huge expansion of savings without further investment, because the factors of production are already fully employed and no investment opportunity is available. This was the situation during the Great Depression, which could not be corrected by undertaking simple monetary measures. Thus, in opposition to neoclassical theorists, Keynes recommended policies based on fiscal measures, which suggested that government should borrow the excess savings and spend it on projects that would benefit the low-income groups who have higher MPC and lower MPS (rather than the wealthy people who have lower MPC and higher MPS) in order to enhance the so-called multiplier effect.[33] However, the significance of Keynesian theory declined due to the fact that after the end of the Great Depression, the emergence of "big government" (supporting the corporate capital at the expense of small business) itself became a problem, which enhanced the revival of practical interest in neoclassical theory.[34] This has led to the formation of the so-called Keynesian-neoclassical synthesis, which represents a revised version of interventionist theory that incorporates certain tenets of neoclassical theory.

Keynesian-Neoclassical Synthesis

The proponents of this theoretical synthesis attempt to address crucial economic issues, including the problem of market instability, existence of oligopolistic corporations, need for public goods, and externalities of private enterprises, by mediating the relatively interventionist Keynesian fiscal policies with the noninterventionist principles of neoclassical theory. They suggest limited government intervention to mitigate the market crises, so that the functioning of the capitalist system could be maintained more effectively.

One of the most well-known liberal neoclassicists is Paul A. Samuelson, who tends to integrate Keynesian and neoclassical theories.[35]

Realizing some of the crucial negative implications of free market economy, Samuelson suggests some Keynesian form of government intervention to achieve economic objectives such as full employment, rational prices, and efficient resource allocation, which the orthodox neoclassicists themselves wanted to achieve. Instead of rejecting the basic principles of neoclassical theory, Samuelson recognizes that despite the need for government intervention to correct the situation of market imperfection, as an analytical tool, the principle of market competition remains important. According to Hunt, Samuelson's ideological belief in property ownership as the basis of income "is not essentially different from that of Say, Senior, Bastiat, Clark, and the conservative neoclassicists in general."[36]

For Third World Countries

After World War II, the advanced capitalist nations showed strong commitment to assist Third World countries in achieving rapid socioeconomic development, although the main reason for such a benevolent helping attitude has been explained in terms of the self-interest of capitalist nations to maintain certain relationship with these decolonized, newly independent countries in order to use them as the sources of raw materials, maintain them as markets for capitalist industrial goods, and prevent them from being affected by communist ideology. Whatever were the reasons for assisting Third World countries, it was realized that the neoclassical and Keynesian theories of economic growth were inadequate or insufficient to enhance economic development in these countries. The neoclassical framework was inadequate because of its static nature and its relevance mainly to the advanced market economies. Keynesian analysis was inadequate because the problem of Third World development was not excessive saving, which Keynes explained as the cause of economic depression. The trouble rather was insufficient saving and capital. Similarly, classical theory, despite its emphasis on economic growth, was not that relevant to Third World context, because while classical theorists emphasized free market and market competition for economic growth without much concern for the problem of surplus labor and scarcity of capital, most Third World countries suffered from these problems of excessive surplus labor and lack of capital.

Because of these unique contextual features of Third World economies, a revised version of classical growth theory, combined with a certain degree of Keynesian interventionist strategy, became the dominant theoretical framework for Third World development. This revised framework emphasized the accumulation of capital, expansion of industrial progress, and resolution of population problem in order to break away from the stationary state of economic situation in Third World countries. This was the beginning of what is known as "development economics" today. In response to the aforementioned features of Third World context—including a huge surplus labor, the scarcity of capital, and the absence of advanced market institutions—there emerged a new generation of development economists such as Nurkse, Rostow, and Lewis. In general, these theorists highlighted the importance of capital accumulation, investment, and some form of government intervention. Despite certain differences among these theorists in terms of their strategic preferences, most of them tried to explain the main cause(s) of economic backwardness and poverty in Third World countries, and they recommended certain interventionist strategies to overcome such adverse economic conditions. These relatively interventionist theories of economic growth related to Third World countries include the theory of balanced growth (with its three major versions), the theory of unbalanced growth, the theory of dualism, and the stages-of-growth theory, which are briefly discussed below.

Theory of Balanced Growth

According to this theory of balanced growth, capital shortage is the main cause of economic backwardness, and it is essential to undertake the strategy of balanced growth to overcome such a capital shortage. However, there are differences among three varieties of theoretical explanations—the big push, the vicious circle, and the critical minimum effort—regarding the causes and remedies of Third World backwardness. With regard to the causes of economic stagnation or backwardness in Third World countries, the big push theory of Paul Rosenstein-Rodan emphasizes the lack of three forms of indivisibility—indivisibility of capital, demand, and saving—in Third World countries, which constitute the main obstacle.[37] The indivisibility of capital is needed for undertaking big infrastructural activities (e.g., electricity) that precede other productive investments (e.g., textile); the indivisibility of demand among different industries is required to ensure markets for each other; and the indivisibility of savings is necessary to make any large investment.[38]

On the other hand, for the theory of vicious circle formulated by Ragnar Nurkse, the cause of poverty in low-income countries is poverty itself as it leads to the stagnant condition of both supply and demand.[39] Finally, according to the critical minimum effort of Harvey Leibenstein, the main problem in poor countries is that the forces which depress income, such as the high rate of population growth and the diseconomies of scale, are stronger than the forces which promote income.[40]

However, all these theorists offer similar solutions to the problem of such stagnation, low-level equilibrium, or backwardness in these countries. By implication, all of them feel the need for investing huge capital in industries, although such capital is in short supply from the private sector. Thus, these theorists suggest government intervention in order to ensure the planned and balanced investments of capital in mutually supportive industries.

Theory of Unbalanced Growth

In opposition to the principles of balanced growth, the proponents of unbalanced growth, including Albert Hirschman, Hans Singer, Paul Alpert, and others, argue that the process of development can rather be set in motion by creating a series of unbalanced-growth sequences, so that the decisions of private entrepreneurs and state planners are induced through various forms of tensions and incentives.[41] For this theory, investment has to be made in those leading sectors or industries which have extensive linkages with and positive external effects on other sectors or industries. The development of the leading sectors would advance the economy further by inducing the lagging dependent sectors. This theory puts more emphasis on investment in the agriculture sector that has multifarious positive implications for other sectors and industries.

The positive impacts of agriculture are described as follows: a small investment of capital in agriculture would bring larger output because of its high labor-capital ratio, and it would increase the purchasing power of rural population and help them establish small industries. In addition, surplus agricultural production would support the urbanized industrial population, the export of agricultural products would bring foreign exchange, and the higher income from agriculture would generate more tax revenue for future investment in infrastructure related to industrial development.

Theory of Dualism

W. Arthur Lewis identifies a form of dualism between the high productivity capitalist sector and the low productivity traditional sector.

The traditional sector is characterized by surplus labor, lower productivity, lower earnings, traditional technology, extended family, and family based production such as farms and handicrafts. On the other hand, the features of the capitalist sector include the existence of reproducible capital, hired labor, production for sale, and profit for capitalists.[42] For Lewis, it is essential to absorb the surplus labor of the traditional sector within the productive capitalist sector and to supplant gradually the traditional sector by the capitalist sector.[43]

J.H. Boeke introduced a different framework of dualism—i.e., social dualism—by distinguishing the Western mentality characterized by unlimited wants and materialistic interests from the Eastern mentality symbolized by limited wants and an ethical orientation. For him, the Eastern people or the orientals are also characterized by features such as the lack of competitive spirit, insensitivity to changes in prices and incentives, immobility of factors of production, inefficient resource allocation, and other precapitalist phenomena. Thus, according to Boeke, the usual efforts to transplant Western economic theories and models in the production systems of non-Western societies, particularly in the agriculture sector, may cause more harm and retrogression than development.[44]

Stages-of-Growth Theory

W. W. Rostow identifies the following five sequential stages of economic growth that every society has to pass through: the stage of traditional society, the preconditions for take-off, the take-off, the drive to maturity, and the stage of mass consumption.[45] For Rostow, the stage of "traditional society" is characterized by a hierarchical social structure, a food-producing agricultural economy, pre-Newtonian science and technology, concentration of power in religious groups, and strong family relations. The stage of "preconditions of take-off" has features such as a higher rate of capital accumulation, the commercial market, a risk-taking entrepreneurial class, an order-maintaining and modernizing national government, and higher investment in infrastructural activities. The "take-off" stage is featured by an industrial revolution, rapid growth in certain sectors, and the institutionalization of the sources of capital. The stage of "drive to maturity" is marked by an expansive use of modern technology, improvement in industrial skill, further expansion of urbanization, and the specialization of labor. And the stage of "mass consumption" is characterized by the abundance of durable consumer goods, market oligopoly, expansive military expenditure and concern for external power, the care for welfare, and the existence of social security and leisure.

However, the take-off stage is the most decisive for the transition from an agricultural to an industrial society. It requires three related conditions: (a) an increase in the rate of productive investment from 5 percent to 10 percent of national income; (2) the development of one or more sectors with a high growth rate; and (3) the existence or enhancement of a social, political, and institutional framework that would absorb the expansion of the modern sector and ensure continuous growth.[46]

Theories of Modernization

It has been pointed out that the theories of modernization emerged as a result of the decolonization of Third World countries and the Western Cold War policies to prevent these countries from being influenced by communist ideology.[47] Preston specifically mentions that "the USA offers 'modernization' to combat the [former] USSR's offers of 'socialism.' The US theory [of modernization] is thus the ideological child of 'containment'."[48] In addition to these vested ideological interests behind the formation of modernization theories, in general, these theories represent the Western ideas of progress and development, which have been used to explain and evaluate the social, political, cultural, and psychological realities in Third World countries. Although the intellectual credibility and practical application of modernization theories seem to have diminished, they still represent an established intellectual tradition in the current studies on Third World development. According to Goldthorpe, these theories still have many adherents, particularly in the United States.[49]

Modernization theories can be divided into three major categories in terms of their primary focus or emphasis on the specific realms (social, political, cultural, or psychological) of society: (a) the sociological theory of modernization explains various structural-functional dimensions of society, including social structures, social functions, and their changes; (b) the theory of political modernization deals with major political concerns such as the nature of political system, structure of political institutions, and causes of political change; and (c) the psycho-cultural theory of modernization focuses on the implications of various psychological and cultural factors for socio-economic development. A brief analysis of each of these theoretical categories is presented in this section.

The sociological theory of modernization dates back to the ideas of evolutionary progress offered by nineteenth-century scholars such as Auguste Comte, Henry Sumner Maine, and Lewis Henry Morgan. They attempted to explain social progress in terms of changes in society along various evolutionary stages—for instance, from savagery to barbarism to civilization.[50] In line with this intellectual trend, Herbert Spencer analyzed the evolutionary progress of society by using the metaphor of living organism.[51] The scope of his analysis encompassed the structures and functions of society and their increasing differentiation and integration. For Spencer, like living organisms, a society survives through its adaptation with the environment by increasing its level of complexity, implying its further differentiation, interdependence, and reintegration. Following such structural-functional analysis of social change by Spencer, Emile Durkheim focused his study largely on the situation in Western European societies. He extended the structural-functional perspective further by adding to it a methodological dimension—i.e., a causal and factual analysis of social change.[52] For Durkheim, the cause of social change is what he calls "social density," which increases with an increase in interaction among people.[53]

However, this genre of structural-functional analysis became relatively static and lost its dimension of historical evolution in the hands of anthropological functionalists such as Malinowski and Radcliffe-Brown.[54] Although Radcliffe-Brown took the historical origins and functions of social structure into consideration, Malinowski's functional analysis of culture ignored the historical dimension.[55] This ahistorical functionalism came under severe criticism for its inward-oriented analysis of single societies, its neglect of the dimension of change, its assumption of perfect functional harmony without conflict, and its overemphasis on stability and status quo.[56] In addition to these intellectual attacks, the unprecedented sociohistorical events of the 1950s and 1960s—including the decolonization of Third World countries, the worldwide expansion of communism, and the civil rights movement in the U.S.—became challenging to the ahistorical assumption of social stability and led to the reconsideration of the historical dimension in structural-functional analysis.

Such a reorientation in structural-functional analysis has been labeled the *neo-evolutionary revival*.[57] This neo-evolutionary structural-functionalism provided a theory of social change that not only focused on the processes of social differentiation, reintegration, and adaptation,[58] but also incorporated the notion of historical "inevitability and irreversibility" of the increasing level of such differentiation. However, this time, the concern was not so much for explaining the evolution of Western industrial societies from their early stage to the current modern stage, but for examining the features of newly independent Third World countries and prescribing how these traditional societies could be modernized largely in the image of modern Western nations. This tendency of the neo-evolutionary, structural-functional theory of social change continued with Talcott Parsons, Neil J. Smelser, Wilbert E. Moore, and others.

Talcott Parsons was influenced considerably by the biological explanation of society offered by Durkheim, the mechanical equilibrium postulated by Pareto and Marshall, and the action frame of reference articulated by Weber.[59] These intellectual sources are reflected in Parsons' interpretation of social change and modernization based on the perspective of system's equilibrium. His primary concern is for the survival of the system: for this survival the social system must deal with four "functional imperatives"—adaptation, goal attainment, integration, and pattern maintenance.[60] For Parsons, these hypothetical functions are givens, and what is necessary is to find out appropriate structures to perform these functions. This is almost a reversal of the position of Malinowski and Radcliffe-Brown, for whom social structures are rather pregiven, and the functions performed by such structures are to be identified.

However, in relation to the above four hypothetically "given" functions, Parsons attempts to delineate the necessary structural features of society. For him, this structure is constituted by social roles as manifested in behavior. He categorizes these social roles and behavior into five dichotomous patterns: (1) affective (emotional) versus affective-neutral, (2) collective oriented versus self-oriented, (3) particularistic versus universalistic, (4) ascriptive versus achievement-oriented, and (5) diffused versus specific.[61] It is in this analytical scheme in which the dichotomy between the traditional and the modern becomes obvious. While the traditional societies are characterized by affectiveness, collectivity, particularism, ascription, and diffusedness; the modern societies are featured by affective-neutrality, self-orientedness, universalism, achievement orientation, and specificity. Parsons had a very strong influence on the subsequent modernization theorists attached to various social science disciplines.

Similar to the Parsonian distinction between traditional and modern societies, Neil Smelser presents certain binary criteria of economic development in terms of various societal changes: from traditional to scientific knowledge in technology, from subsistence to commercial production in agriculture, from animal and human power to machine power in industry, and from the rural to urban form in ecology.[62] On the other hand, the scheme of modernization offered by Wilbert Moore focuses mainly on the conditions, processes, and consequences of industrialization. For him, the conditions of industrialization include the following: values such as economic growth and national identification; institutions for economic exchange, property, and political stability; existence of specialized and hierarchical organizations; and achievement-oriented motivation and personality.

POLITICAL REALM

The Parsonian version of structural-functionalism in sociology became one of the basic premises on which the theories and models of political modernization were built. By integrating this organismic structural-functional analysis of Parsons with the mechanistic systems (input-conversion-output) model of David Easton, Gabriel Almond offered a new theoretical framework for political analysis.[63] By applying this revised version of structural-functional framework, Almond and Powell explained political modernization in terms of a higher level of functional differentiation in political structure and the secularization of political styles.[64] For them, this differentiation and secularization would increase the capabilities of political systems in Third World countries. Despite some difficulties in applying this structural-functional measure, gradually it became the dominant analytical framework for not only Almond, Powell, and other theorists of political modernization, but also for the academics and experts in comparative administration.[65]

However, at a certain point, the all-pervasive application or excessive use of Almond's structural-functional framework by too many scholars eventually led to a considerable degree of diversity in the definitional criteria of political development. These conceptual variations were so significant that Pye became interested in reviewing the literature, and identified ten categories or typologies of the concepts of political development.[66] Pye himself suggested three essential features or criteria of political development such as differentiation, capacity, and participation.[67] The degree of conceptual diversity multiplied further due to the subsequent classification schemes related to different criteria and interpretations of political development. For instance, after examining Pye's classification, Chodak divides the existing interpretations of political development into three main categories.[68]

Helio Jaguaribe, on the other hand, divides these interpretations into six categories, and describes political development as an increase in the capability, representativeness, and serviceability of a political system.[69]

However, political development theory came under attack from two main sources. First, social anthropologists such as Joseph Gusfield, Lloyd Rudolph and Suzanne Rudolph, Paul Anber, and Reinhard Bendix, criticize this theory for its oversimplified concepts of tradition and modernity, and its unreal tradition-modernity dichotomy.[70] These critics, although labeled as modernization revisionists by Huntington, attempt to demonstrate from their various case studies that tradition is not a monolithic unity and that traditional and modern institutions can coexist and even complement each other. Secondly, political scientists themselves realized that disorder, violence, inequality, and military coups rather than democratization and participation, were the political realities in most Third World countries during the 1960s. This realization encouraged them to reevaluate and revise the earlier theory of political development. In this regard, Huntington recommended political institutionalization—implying adaptability, complexity, autonomy, and coherence of political institutions—for ensuring political stability and order.[71] Because of this new concern for political stability, many scholars (e.g., Johnson, Shils, Pye, and Huntington) even found a justification for military intervention due to the organizational skill, responsibility, unity, efficiency, and other qualities associated with the military, which they regarded as necessary for Third World modernization.

PSYCHO-CULTURAL REALM

There is another group of development theorists that tends to interpret development from a psychological or cultural perspective. These theorists attempt to demonstrate that it is the unique characteristics of various psycho-cultural factors in advanced capitalist societies which have contributed to their socioeconomic progress. It is also the unique psycho-cultural features in Third World countries that are held responsible for their backwardness. Some of the prominent theorists espousing this development perspective are Weber, Schumpeter, Hagen, and McClelland. The major theoretical contributions of these scholars are briefly discussed in this section.

In contrast to the Marxian materialistic interpretation that production forces are the prime determinants of capitalist development, Max Weber offers a relatively subjective, psycho-cultural explanation of capitalism and its institutions. In his *The Theory of Social and Economic Organization* (1947), Weber explains different typologies of social actions and orientations, and their bases of legitimacy and authority.[72] In Weber's framework, one kind of authority (e.g., rational legal) can be replaced by another (e.g., charismatic). However, among these various forms of authority, the main focus is on the bureaucratic, legal-rational authority which, for Weber, is a unique characteristic of capitalist society. Thus, he attempts to explicate the fundamental cause of the emergence of capitalism itself. In this regard, in his *The Protestant Ethic and the Spirit of Capitalism* (1958), Weber illustrates that the main cause of the emergence of Western capitalism is the so-called Protestant work ethic. For him, the essence of capitalism is the "pursuit of profit" through capitalist enterprise based on rational calculative behavior. Thus, the spirit of capitalism is rationality, which emerged within the context of *Protestant ethic* that repudiates all irrational ascetic and contemplative practices and emphasizes the practice of mundane asceticism.[73] In his explanations, although Weber implies the possibility of a nonlinear change in authority from its one form to another, he tends to hold a more linear view of cultural change in the direction toward increasing rationality.[74]

David C. McClelland accepts Weber's proposition that the Protestant ethic provides a conducive context for the process of capitalist development, but he tries to identify more specific and microlevel motives of individuals that enhance economic advancement. Among the three types of needs or motives, such as needs for affiliation, power, and achievement, McClelland tends to emphasize the "need for achievement" (n-Ach) or the achievement motive as the main supportive cause of economic progress.[75] He postulates that a higher level of achievement motive existing in a society creates more energetic entrepreneurs who can accelerate the pace of economic development. McClelland also suggests that since motives are learned mostly in early childhood, the achievement motive can be inculcated through child rearing, education, and training based on values such as self reliance, goal attainment, praise for work, and so on.[76]

Another prominent figure who contributed to the psychological dimension of development is Joseph A. Schumpeter who emphasizes the initiative and innovation of entrepreneurs as the prime force behind economic development, particularly capitalist development.[77] While the classical theorists of economic growth understand progress in terms of an increasing accumulation of wealth, for Schumpeter "development consists primarily in employing existing resources in different ways in doing new things with them, irrespective of whether these resources increase or not."[78] He interprets development in terms of adopting or creating anything new, such as new production methods, new organizations, new sources of supply, and new markets. Any organization that exhibits this creative venture is an enterprise and any person who carries it out is an entrepreneur. Thus, with regard to economic development, entrepreneurship and innovation are the key words for Schumpeter. Beyond such analysis, however, Schumpeter sees the possibility of what he calls the "creative destruction" of capitalism caused by its different countervailing forces such as overproduction, technical errors, oligopolistic corporations, and social welfare that discourages private investment.[79]

Lastly, according to the "theory of status withdrawal" presented by Everett E. Hagen, personality is a dominant factor in economic development.[80] He compares two types of personality. In traditional society, the nature of personality is "authoritarian," and it is featured by submissiveness, dependence, obedience, and lack of creativity. In contrast, in modern society, the nature of personality is "innovational" and characterized by openness to new experience, curiosity, and creativity. For Hagen, to achieve economic growth in a traditional society, it is necessary to break its self-perpetuating equilibrium by transforming its authoritarian personality into an innovational and reformist personality. This personality can be developed through a specific mode of child-rearing stimulated by a status-withdrawal.[81]

In summary, the proponents of various modernization theories basically assume that societies develop through certain distinct stages, particularly, from the stage of traditional societies (implying Third World countries) to the stage of modern societies (referring to Western nations). Such transition is caused or enhanced by factors such as structural-functional differentiation and integration (in the sociopolitical realm), achievement motives and entrepreneurship (in the psychological domain), and normative rationalization or secularization (in the cultural sphere). For these theories of modernization, the "modern" is characterized by a higher level of social differentiation, government stability, political participation, economic entrepreneurship, achievement motivation, and cultural secularism. In contrast, the "traditional" is marked by a fused social structure, political disorder, low achievement orientation, weak entrepreneurship, and strong cultural norms. Thus, these theories imply that to modernize traditional societies, it is necessary to enhance social division of labor, establish government order, expand political participation, rationalize culture, instill achievement motive, create entrepreneurship, and so on. Since these societal changes prescribed by modernization theories largely represent the past experiences and current features of Western nations, often the process modernization has been equated with that of Westernization.

CHAPTER 5

Reformist Tradition of Development Theories

The conservative and radical theories of development that emerged in the late nineteenth and early twentieth centuries in advanced capitalist nations were considered relatively inadequate to explain the development problems encountered by newly independent Third World countries. The unique politico-economic and sociocultural realities in these countries, which are considerably different from those in capitalist nations, required theoretical adjustments in the mainstream development thinking. Thus, the earlier theories of development had to be recast or reformulated, which led to the emergence of a different set of theories and models. In this chapter, these revised theories and models are integrated into a different tradition of development thinking, the reformist tradition.

One common tenet that brings these development theories and models under the reformist tradition is their emphasis on reforms as the primary means of societal development. Unlike theories within the radical tradition, these theories and models tend to disapprove revolution as a means of social transformation. Neither do they assume a spontaneous and conflict-free social change as postulated by theories within the conservative tradition. The reformist tradition recognizes different forms of conflict and instability at the national and international levels, and proposes considerable economic, political, and social reforms in this regard. Although some theorists within the reformist tradition believe in the eventual realization of a socialist society, they still prescribe substantive reforms rather than revolution as the means to accomplish such an objective.

However, there are variations among these development theories and models emphasizing reform as the dominant mode of social change, especially in terms of their intellectual sources and suggested reform programs. First, there are reformist scholars who stress the strategies of moderate economic reform to accommodate concerns such as income distribution, although their original intellectual sources are largely from economic growth theories within the conservative tradition. The contributions of these theorists can be classified into the category of "conservative reformist" theories. Second, there are development thinkers who are considerably influenced by various radical theories of development, and in line with these radical theories, they tend to emphasize a self-reliant mode of Third World development and suggest the eradication of internal and international economic domination and exploitation. However, these emancipatory development objectives are to be accomplished through major socioeconomic reforms rather than revolution. Based on this intellectual position, the theoretical formulations of these scholars can be placed under the category of "radical reformist" theories.

Lastly, there is another theoretical category within the reformist tradition that represents the contributions made by a group of critical theorists attached to the Frankfurt School. Despite its reformist nature, this theoretical category is significantly different from both conservative reformist and radical reformist theories, and has been labeled here as "critical reformist" theory. Although the critical analytical framework of the Frankfurt School is not usually included in development literature due to its minimal direct engagement in development discourse, it has made significant contributions to the critical assessment of both the conservative (capitalist) and radical (Marxist) traditions. The proponents of this critical theory moved away from their earlier revolutionary stance, and increasingly emphasized the realization of social change through critique and critical consciousness initiated by critical thinkers rather than through revolutionary means undertaken by the working class. This position of critical theory regarding social transformation is reformist rather than revolutionary in nature,[1] and thus, the theory can be located within the reformist tradition. However, it should be remembered that despite its significant theoretical contributions, critical theory has not yet established itself as a theory of development in the mainstream development literature. Based on the above description, this chapter presents a taxonomic structure of development theories under the reformist tradition (see Figure 5.1).

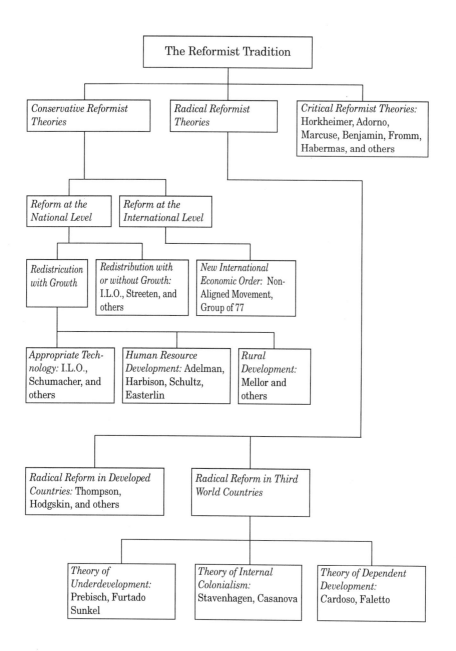

Figure 5.1 A taxonomic structure displaying various categories and subcategories of development theories and models within the reformist tradition. In this diagram, the major intellectual sources of and theoretical differences among these theories and models are outlined.

Conservative Reformist Theories

In the 1950s and 1960s, the mainstream conservative tradition of development theories was facing a theoretical crisis in terms of their incapacity to address many critical problems in Third World countries such as the deteriorating standard of living, an increasing level of income inequality, and the rise of military intervention and dictatorship. Under such circumstances, many Western development economists expressed their intellectual concern, especially for income inequality in these countries. Realizing the past failures of growth-oriented development strategies, in the late 1960s, a reexamination of such setbacks began with some international development experts, including Dudley Seers of the Sussex group, Mahbub ul Haq of the World Bank, James Grant of the Overseas Development Council, and others. During the 1970s, many of these development experts began to recast the prevailing development objectives by combining growth with income distribution.[2]

Thus, in the early 1970s, the ILO (International Labour Organization) model of development suggested the strategies of labor-intensive technology and small-scale industry to benefit low income population. In the mid-1970s, the "basic needs" approach went further to emphasize "redistribution with or without growth." In the same period, the school of "rural development" emerged also with an emphasis on income distribution. However, it is necessary to understand that all these strategies related to Third World development were not to redistribute the existing wealth but to redirect only a part of the additional or incremental economic growth in favor of the low-income groups. In other words, during the 1970s, these scholars attempted to reformulate the goals and objectives of development by emphasizing both growth and distribution, but without any fundamental shift in their intellectual identity with the conservative theories of economic growth. The impacts of such theoretical reforms were considerably reflected in various national development policies (emphasizing poverty eradication and income redistribution) adopted in Third World countries in the 1970s. However, at the international level, the ethos of reform mostly came from Third World leaders and scholars themselves, who wanted to change the existing international order and establish the so-called New International Economic Order (NIEO). Despite this international focus, in terms of basic objectives, the policy of the NIEO remains largely conservative-reformist in nature.[3] Thus, under the conservative-reformist perspective, there are development strategies that emphasize the internal changes in

Third World countries, and strategies that highlight reforms at the international level.

NATIONAL LEVEL STRATEGIES

The proponents of national-level reforms related to development can be broadly divided into two groups: the proponents who endorse the strategy of "redistribution-with-growth" and those who go further to stress "redistribution-with-or-without-growth." Although the theoretical distinction between the two might be insignificant, it is important to understand the nature of these development strategies widely used in formulating policies and programs in Third World countries.

Redistribution-with-Growth

There are various strategies of development introduced by international development experts, which emphasize the simultaneous achievement of both economic growth and income distribution. The list includes strategies such as employment through appropriate technology, human resources development, and rural development. As discussed below, these redistribution-with-growth strategies are relatively conservative in nature, and are less likely to have any radical impacts on the patterns of income distribution.

Employment Through Appropriate Technology. From the experience of its missions to Sri Lanka and other Third World countries, the ILO became interested in addressing the problem of urban unemployment resulting especially from rural-urban migration. Its possible solution to the problem was to encourage the growth of informal but entrepreneurial sectors and the use of an appropriate or alternative technology that was labor-intensive in nature. With regard to this issue of appropriate technology, Schumacher's contribution is also quite well known. He recommends the adoption of an intermediate technology that would utilize local resources to produce goods for local markets and increase the productivity of labor through small-scale enterprises.[4]

Human Resources Development. There are scholars, such as Frederick Harbison, Irma Adelman, Theodore Schultz, and Richard Easterlin, who pay special attention to the improvement of human resources (through education, training, motivation, and health programs) as a strategy for Third World development.[5] Both Harbison and Schultz consider human resource development as an active causal factor rather than a mere end-result of the overall national development. As Harbison mentions, "Human resources—not capital, nor income, nor material resources—constitute the ultimate basis for the wealth of nations."[6] Easterlin, on the other hand, explains that the dissemination of knowledge about the new techniques of production among the educationally motivated people has been a prime factor behind economic growth throughout the world. However, Adelman highlights the problems of slow growth at the initial stage of investment in human resources and its potential for political instability, and he suggests a strong government to deal with such problems.

Rural Development. The strategy of rural development was espoused by agricultural economists and other development experts. This development strategy, unlike the traditional development focus on industrial growth, recognizes the contribution of the agricultural sector not only to the employment generation and income distribution, but also to the process of industrialization itself. John Mellor, based on his experience in India, suggests that an increase in agricultural production through certain changes in techniques (such as the use of new seeds, fertilizer, and irrigation), is an important strategy for the generation of employment and distribution of income.[7] The process includes the following sequential steps: an increase in agricultural production would raise the level of farmers' income and spending, an increase in their income and expenditure would expand their demand for labor-intensive agricultural and industrial goods, an expansion of demand for (and thus, the production of) such goods would generate more employment, an improvement in employment conditions would create more demand for food, and this increase in demand for food would encourage further agricultural production.

However, A. Waterston observes that this "agriculture first" approach may increase the income gap by benefiting mainly the rich farmers because only they can afford these new agricultural techniques. To overcome this problem, he suggests an "integrated rural development" approach which contains six basic components: a labor-intensive but high-yielding agricultural technology which small farmers can afford; the adoption of smaller projects, such as building schools and dams, to absorb surplus labor and create employment; an emphasis on activities based on self-reliance; the creation of local level organizations to control functions previously performed by government; and regional planning to provide agricultural inputs and to process agricultural outputs.[8]

Redistribution with or without Growth (Basic Needs Approach)

The issue of income distribution became so central that increasingly development experts put more emphasis on the realization of redistribution even when economic growth could not be achieved. This led to the formation of the so-called basic needs approach. Although the basic needs approach to development originated from diverse sources—including the Indian experience with basic needs in the 1960s, the debate between the New International Economic Order and self-reliance, the United Nations Environmental Programme, and the World Bank's concern for the growing income gap[9]—its formal recommendation came from the ILO in its publication entitled *Employment, Growth, and Basic Needs.*[10] According to this ILO framework, an equitable distribution of income increases the demand for basic consumer goods that are produced by labor-intensive techniques: this would lead to more employment, more use of appropriate technologies and local resources, and less requirement for imports.[11] In general, there are four components constituting the basic needs: (a) certain minimum necessities related to household consumption such as food, shelter, and clothing; (b) some essential services provided by the community such as sanitation, safe drinking-water, transport, and basic health; (c) the provision of ensuring adequate employment; and (d) the opportunity for participation in decision-making.[12]

Realizing the inadequacy of economic growth policies to address the immediate needs of the poor, the proponents of this basic needs approach emphasize the redistribution of income to the lower-income groups in accordance with their basic needs regardless of the situation of economic growth.[13] For Streeten, the primary requirements for implementing the basic needs strategy include a labor-intensive system of production, an improvement in the labor force, the decline of fertility and population, and the mobilization of resources through people's participation.[14] Yet according to some scholars, the main limitation of the basic needs approach is that it "lacks a longer-term perspective of growth model, unlike its immediate predecessor of redistribution with growth."[15] But Streeten does not see any trade-off between economic growth and basic needs, because although this approach would increase economic growth at a slower pace during the distributional phase, growth would get highly accelerated after a certain point.

Moreover, it is pointed out that "growth will turn out to be the *result* of a basic needs policy, not its *objective*."[16] Streeten is hopeful

that more international assistance (particularly food) would be provided by Western nations because of the moral and political appeal
of the basic needs approach, and that transnational corporations
would play an important role in achieving the goals of this approach.[17]
At this point, it is necessary to realize that despite its concern for the
indigenous development of Third World societies, in many ways, the
basic needs approach is not very different from the previous development strategies. According to some authors, like other approaches to
development, this approach also originated in the West, was opera-
tionalized through international development networks and programs, and thus, became another smokescreen used by the First
World to avoid international distribution of power.[18] For Preston, the
basic needs approach is "an excuse for First World interference in
the affairs of Third World nation states."[19] In addition, according to
Weigel, there are serious *conceptual limitations* of this approach
which led to its premature dismissal by many economists.[20]

INTERNATIONAL LEVEL STRATEGIES

Within a few decades after their independence, many Third World
countries began to understand the adverse effects of their relationship with advanced capitalist nations, the strength of their own economic and political power, and the importance of their participation
in deciding international matters.[21] Such a realization became evident
in the growing consensus among Third World countries regarding
their economic needs and status in relation to the existing international structure dominated by international organizations (e.g., the
OECD, the GATT, the IMF, and the World Bank) that represented the
interests of advanced capitalist nations. As discussed in the second
chapter, Third World countries established the so-called "Group of
77," which demanded significant changes or reforms in international
economic structure, and thus initiated the proposal for the New
International Economic Order or NIEO. Recognizing the sources of
economic power exercised by advanced capitalist nations, particularly
their control over global market, finance, technology, labor, and nonrenewable resources, the proponents of NIEO made some concrete
proposals on behalf of Third World countries. The main proposals or
demands constituting the NIEO include the following: the liberalization of trade, regulation of transnational corporations, stability of
commodity prices, establishment of a common fund, assurance of
continual financial resources, debt relief, more stable exchange rates,
and so on.[22]

However, as mentioned earlier, these proposals associated with the NIEO are reformist rather than radical in nature, because its aim was to improve or liberalize the existing world order without any fundamental change in its structure. As Karl Sauvant mentions, despite its demand for a change in international economic order, "the underlying philosophy of the NIEO program is essentially reformist; it is aimed at improving the existing mechanisms, not at changing the existing structures."[23] Moreover, Third World countries established the "Group of 77" and endorsed the NIEO strategy mainly as a bargaining tool to reduce their trade and technological dependence. Their mutual commitment diminished as soon as the concerned issues took more concrete forms.[24] Finally, due to its overemphasis on international economic structure, the NIEO project is inadequate to address the structure of unequal resource distribution among people within each Third World country.[25]

Radical Reformist Theories

The radical reformist theories of development are influenced by diverse intellectual sources and practical events, including the critical reactions to various conservative theories, the basic theoretical underpinnings of the radical tradition, the emerging social problems in advanced capitalist nations, and the socioeconomic crises in Third World countries. In general, the development scholars associated with this theoretical category contributed to the development field by suggesting some radical socioeconomic reforms in the capitalist system, by radicalizing conventional or conservative theories, or by moderating the revolutionary strategies endorsed by the radical tradition of development thinking. Thus, although the proponents of radical reformist theories go far beyond the strategies of marginal changes preferred by the conservative reformists, they fall short of the revolutionary character of the mainstream radical tradition. It is true that similar to development thinkers in the radical tradition, some proponents of radical reformist theories consider dependency as the primary cause of economic underdevelopment, and feel the need for establishing a socialist society. But as mentioned at the beginning, the radical reformists suggest to bring about such a significant social change not through revolution, as in the case of the radical tradition, but through fundamental reforms.[26] In this section, these radical reformist theories of development are discussed under two broad categories—radical reforms proposed for advanced capitalist countries and radical reforms recommended for Third World countries.

REFORMS IN CAPITALIST COUNTRIES

The radical reformist perspective of social progress emerged in capitalist countries as early as the 1830s when Robert Owen endorsed the workers' movement against industrial exploitation, and recommended the establishment of voluntary cooperatives based on communal rather than private ownership, which would coexist, compete with, and eventually replace capitalist enterprises. This line of argument for replacing capitalist institutions through reform was reinforced by William Thompson and Thomas Hodgskin.[27] William Thompson was influenced by the labor theory of value offered by classical economists, Bentham's idea of utilitarianism, and Owen's philosophy of cooperatives. For Thompson, there is no wealth without labor, and capitalism is a system of exploitation, inequality, instability, and sufferings. However, accepting the utilitarian principle of Bentham, he suggests that all workers should own their capital and retain the fruits of their labor. In addition, according to Thompson, the best form of society would be a planned and cooperative socialist society created through peaceful change rather than revolution and characterized by communal wealth, common stores, free education for all, and the absence of any sexual division of labor.

Following the labor theory of value, Thomas Hodgskin also rejects the principles of private property and profit. He explains that a laborer is the natural owner of capital because he produces it and also uses it for further production. Hodgskin mentions that the ownership of capital by those who do not produce is unnatural and it causes most social ills.[28] He also distinguishes between the "natural price" (representing the amount of embodied labor in a commodity) and the "social price" (containing the unearned incomes of landlords and capitalists) of a commodity. He believes that through the self-education of workers and based on basic reforms, a society would emerge in which the natural price and the social price would be equal. Hunt describes the nature of such a society desired by Hodgskin as "competitive capitalism without capitalists."

In short, both Thompson and Hodgskin follow a labor theory of value and are critical of the capitalist notion of private property and profit. They also believe in the essence of utilitarianism in terms of their views that the voluntary exchange between various parties would increase the utility of each. Both of them suggest reforming the capitalist system to overcome the prevalent exploitation, injustice, and instability within the system. However, while Thompson recommends a planned and cooperative socialist society, Hodgskin endorses a competitive and free-exchange society without capitalists. Yet all these are to be achieved through reform, not revolution.

REFORMS IN THIRD WORLD COUNTRIES

With regard to Third World countries, the radical reformist theories of development, largely known as the reformist dependency theories,[29] introduced a considerable restructuring of the orthodox classical and neoclassical economic theories, and later, became the intellectual sources for radical dependency theories discussed under the radical tradition in the next chapter. Most of these reformist dependency theories are structuralist in nature, which was inherited mostly from Latin American scholars, although contributions from other sources were not insignificant. For instance, outside Latin America, during the 1930s and 1940s, the "doctrine of market failure" emerged in Britain, which challenged the fundamental principles of classical and neoclassical theories of market competition. A structural analysis of the ineffectiveness of price system was introduced by Rosenstein-Rodan,[30] which came to be known as the structuralist doctrine. This doctrine became a major intellectual source not only for some first-generation development economists, but also for the Latin American structuralist perspective of dependency espoused by the ECLA (United Nations Economic Commission for Latin America) group of economists led by Raul Prebisch.[31]

Despite this common structuralist nature of the reformist dependency theories, there are significant differences among the proponents of these theories, especially with regard to their views on the dominant causes of underdevelopment in Third World countries. The main causes of this underdevelopment are as follows: it is external dependency for the *theory of underdevelopment* (offered by Prebisch, Sunkel, and Furtado); it is internal structure for the *theory of internal colonialism* (presented by Stavenhagen and Casanova); and it is both external and internal factors for the *theory of dependent development* (espoused by Cardoso and Faletto). These three specific explanations of underdevelopment from three corresponding theoretical viewpoints are briefly discussed below.

Theory of Underdevelopment

In Latin America, due to the decline of export earnings caused by depression, many countries adopted inward-looking development strategies. Intellectually, such strategies were promoted by the ECLA established in 1948 under Prebisch as its first secretary general. Prebisch and other scholars attached to the ECLA, including Celso Furtado, Osvaldo Sunkel, Antonio Barros de Castro, Aldo Ferres, and Anibal Pinto, are relatively non-Marxist economists although they are quite critical of international economic imperialism. These ECLA scholars, in general, are reformist rather than revolutionary in their perspectives. As Arndt mentions, "ECLA thinking about dependency and structuralism, though clearly anti-market and near-socialist in its implications, was still a long way from revolutionary Marxism."[32] The basic conceptual and theoretical formulations of some of these radical albeit reformist scholars require further elaboration.

First, similar to some classical and neoclassical theorists of economic growth, these theorists of underdevelopment interpret development in terms of an accelerated and sustained process of economic growth and capital accumulation based on industrialization. They examine various structural constraints that inhibited such industrialization and perpetuated the condition of underdevelopment in Third World countries. *Second*, the prime cause of this underdevelopment is external—i.e., the external dependence of Third World countries (the periphery) on the advanced capitalist nations (the center). The nature and mechanism of such external dependence as a cause of underdevelopment is explained variously by the three main proponents of structural dependency. According to Prebisch, the cause of underdevelopment in Latin American countries is their trade dependence resulting from the specialization of the "periphery" in raw materials and the "center" in industrial goods.[33] International trade based on this specialization creates trade imbalance and the balance of payment problem for peripheral nations, which eventually leads to their dependence and underdevelopment.[34]

Like Prebisch, Osvaldo Sunkel (a Chilean economist) identifies a polarization between the developed metropolitan nations and the dependent peripheral countries.[35] He explains that the transnationals, by introducing capital-intensive technology and promoting consumption, destroy or subsume the national capital and entrepreneurship of peripheral countries, deprive them of their autonomous development, and thus lead them to a condition of dependency and marginalization.[36] For Sunkel, the international division of labor created by this transnational capitalism also incorporates Third World population into the transnational system, causes the fragmentation of various groups, and exacerbates the process of national disintegration.[37] Thus, according to Sunkel, the incorporation of Third World countries into the system of transnational capitalism is the main cause of their underdevelopment. On the other hand, Furtado describes underdevelopment as the existence of "hybrid structure" (composed of a subsistence structure, an export-oriented structure, and an industrial nucleus), which emerged due to "the penetration of modern capitalistic enterprises into archaic structures."[38] In addition, for Furtado, the condition of such underdevelopment and dependence has also been caused by an expensive pattern of consumption in Third World countries that is affordable only to higher income groups. It is because for producing those expensive consumption goods, the periphery has to depend on capital-intensive technologies manufactured mostly by multinational corporations from the center.[39]

Third, in order to overcome the condition of Third World dependence, these theorists of underdevelopment also make various recommendations. According to Booth, the ECLA even supported foreign investment and international economic cooperation on favorable terms to maintain a high rate of economic growth, to reduce the balance of payment gap, and to introduce new industrial techniques.[40] However, Prebisch preferred the expansion of industrialization based on import substitution, especially, to resolve the balance of payment problem. For him, the domestic production of industrial goods, previously imported from the center, would lead to an autonomous and indigenous capitalist development.[41] Sunkel, however, recognizes the limits of the import substitution strategy and recommends other domestic reforms such as agrarian reform and industrial reorganization, which would ensure the participation of marginal groups and enhance the capacity for autonomous economic growth. On the other hand, Furtado concludes that the import substitution strategy of merely transplanting rather than fundamentally changing the consumption patterns, would not generate any innovation.[42] He also feels the need for central planning to resolve the problem of underdevelopment. For Furtado, the restructuring needed for overcoming the condition of underdevelopment has to be based on "a more comprehensive ordering than that afforded by markets, and such an ordering is possible only through planning."[43]

It should be clear by now that the policy recommendations offered by the above theorists to overcome Third World underdevelopment are reformist rather than revolutionary in nature. The radical reformist position of the ECLA scholars is evident in the following comment made by Cardoso: the ECLA has been attacked by liberal economists because of its support for the prosocialist policy of state intervention, and by the ultra-left because of its failure to expose the mechanisms of socioeconomic exploitation that subordinate the working class to the bourgeoisie.[44] The radical reformist stance of Furtado is evident in his suggested option to adopt structural reforms in Latin America in order to reduce dependence and underdevelopment.[45] Sunkel, on the other hand, rejects any possibility of socialist revolution in Latin America.[46] Thus, O'Brien suggests that Furtado and Sunkel are "more squarely in the reformist ECLA tradition which wants national development without class struggle and independence without revolution."[47]

Theory of Internal Colonialism

Another group of structuralist scholars, including Rodolfo Stavenhagen and Pablo Gonzalez Casanova, interprets development and underdevelopment in terms of internal colonialism. An explanation of the meaning and nature of "internal colonialism" can be obtained from its analysis presented by Stavenhagen. He describes internal colonialism as the following social condition: "the subordination of modes of production and forms of precapitalist accumulation to the dominant mode of production, which leads to the subordination and exploitation of certain economic and social sectors, of certain segments of the population from certain geographical regions, by others."[48] According to Stavenhagen, internal colonialism also signifies the character of a hierarchical structural relation between different modes of production that evolved within the global framework of underdevelopment.

For Casanova, another proponent of this theoretical framework, some characteristics of the past colonial relations between different nations also exist today within each Third World country.[49] Casanova describes internal colonialism in terms of the following features: the dominance of the metropolis over isolated communities leading to the deformation of the native economy, the relations of production based on exploitation and the plunder of land, and the prevalence of a subsistence economy accentuating poverty and technological backwardness.[50] To overcome such a condition of internal colonialism, Casanova suggests an alliance between the workers and the progressive national bourgeoisie against imperialism to eliminate the precapitalist forms of production, to establish bourgeois democracy, and to ensure an eventual transition to socialism.[51] However, these theorists of internal colonialism are mostly in favor of social change through reform rather than revolution.

Theory of Dependent Development

In the above discussion, it has been pointed out that the theorists of "underdevelopment" emphasize external dependence, and the theorists of "internal colonialism" focus on internal structure. There is another category of radical reformist theory, the theory of "dependent development." The proponents of this theory, especially Fernando Henrique Cardoso and Enzo Faletto, recognize the role of both external and internal forces in the development of the periphery. For instance, instead of viewing dependency as an antithesis to development, Cardoso and Faletto emphasize the possibility of *dependent development* characterized by an alliance between indigenous state capital, national private capital, and international monopoly capital.[52]

Cardoso and Faletto interpret development mainly in terms of progress in productive forces, capital accumulation, and social division of labor, and they suggest that there is no contradiction between dependence of the periphery on monopolistic foreign capital and its own industrial capitalist development, although it remains dependent on external assistance for completing the full circle of the creation, expansion, and accumulation of capital.[53] In this regard, Cardoso suggests that "*dependency, monopoly capitalism* and *development* are not contrary terms: there occurs a kind of *dependent capitalist development* in the sectors of the Third World integrated into the new forms of monopolistic expansion [original italic]."[54]

Thus, while other dependency theorists put too much emphasis on the external world capitalist system and too little on the internal components within the periphery, Cardoso and Faletto try to explain how the external structure determines the dynamics of internal conditions and how both the external and the internal factors in combination determine the concrete economic, social, and political conditions in each dependent peripheral nation.[55] Although some Marxian ingredients can be found in Cardoso and Faletto's analysis of dependent development, they are not mainstream radical thinkers, they are radical reformists. This is because they want to overcome the status of dependence not through revolution but through major reforms. For Cardoso and Faletto, the proletarian route to socialism is not viable for Latin America.[56] However, they advocate the establishment of some form of socialism by enhancing national integration and creating organizations of unstructured masses, and they emphasize market and trade relations rather than production relations in their class analysis.[57]

At this point, it might be useful to make a comparison between these apparently very similar but different theories of development and underdevelopment: including the theory of underdevelopment of Prebisch, Sunkel, and Furtado; the theory of internal colonialism of Stavenhagen and Casanova; and the theory of dependent development of Cardoso and Faletto. *First*, in terms of the meaning of "development," the theory of underdevelopment interprets development as autonomous industrial growth and capital accumulation, the theory of internal colonialism explains it as the achievement of bourgeois democracy and ultimately socialism, and the theory of dependent development describes it as the realization of both autonomous industrial growth and certain socialist order. *Second*, the concept of "underdevelopment" is interpreted as a condition of external dependence by the theory of underdevelopment, and as the existence of precapitalist and predemocratic societal stage by the theory of internal colonialism. But for the theory of dependent development, there is a condition of dependent development rather than absolute underdevelopment.

Third, with regard to the causes of underdevelopment, the proponents of the theory of underdevelopment consider such causes as mostly external, which include colonial interference and disruption, intervention by multinationals, and unequal international trade. The theory of dependent development has almost similar explanations. But for the theory of internal colonialism, the main focus is on the internal precapitalist structure of domination as a cause of underdevelopment. *Fourth*, regarding the means to overcome underdevelopment, the theory of underdevelopment recommends certain reformist strategies such as import substitution, agrarian and industrial reforms, and central planning. Similarly, for the theories of dependent development and internal colonialism, the strategies are largely based on reforms, although they are more keen to support the realization of some form of socialism in peripheral nations. *Finally*, as to the agents of social change, both the theory of underdevelopment and the theory of dependent development suggest that it is primarily the state which should undertake the reformist strategies and introduce changes to overcome underdevelopment. But for the theory of internal colonialism, the condition of underdevelopment (indicating internal colonialism) is to be overcome mainly by forming an alliance between the national bourgeoisie and the masses.

Critical Reformist Theories

It is quite well known that the main proponent of *critical theory* is the Frankfurt School, which was founded in 1923 at the Institute of Social Research affiliated with Frankfurt University. Bronner and Kellner identify two generations of critical theorists who have been attached with the Institute: while Max Horkheimer, Theodor Adorno, Herbert Marcuse, Leo Lowenthal, Friedrich Pollock, Erich Fromm, and Walter Benjamin represent the first generation of critical theorists; the second generation include Jürgen Habermas, Oskar Negt, Alfred Schmidt, Claus Offe, Albrecht Wellmer, and others.[58]

However, the intellectual roots of critical theory can be traced back to the earlier contributions made by phenomenology, Freudian psychoanalysis, Hegelian dialectic, and Marxism.[59] In particular, the shift in the Institute's perspective from orthodox or scientific Marxism to critical Marxism[60] reflects the influence of two prominent critical Marxists, George Lukacs and Antonio Gramsci.[61] There were also practical events, including the rise of fascism in Europe, the Stalinist influence on the Soviet socialist system, the Soviet intervention in Czechoslovakia, and the American antiwar movement, which led the Frankfurt School to be critical of both late capitalism and state socialism.[62]

Although the first generation critical theorists, particularly Horkheimer, Adorno, and Marcuse, were initially supportive of critical Marxism that emphasized the revolutionary role of the working class, they changed this position and began to put more emphasis on the critical role of theoreticians or intelligentsia to reveal the process of ideological indoctrination, and thereby eliminate social repression and facilitate social transformation. Despite certain differences among critical theorists in this regard,[63] their common stance regarding social change remains reformist in nature: they tend to visualize the transformation of society by critical thinkers through intellectual reflection rather than by the proletariat through practical revolution. This emphasis on the critical role of the intelligentsia rather than on the revolutionary role of the proletariat in societal transformation makes critical theorists not only reformist but also critical reformist. Unlike the conservative reformists, they suggest fundamental changes in society, and unlike the radical reformists, they envision these changes to be introduced by critical intellectuals rather than the working class.

THE CRITIQUE OF CAPITALISM

In terms of the critique of capitalism, the analytical scope of critical theory covers some important domains of capitalist society, including an economic analysis of "postliberal" capitalism, a socio-psychological interpretation of family socialization and ego development, and a cultural-theoretical analysis of the mass media and mass culture.[64] First, with regard to the political economy of advanced capitalist countries, according to Horkheimer and Pollock, "state capitalism" has replaced the classical form of market capitalism, and the market system has been supplanted by both the state planning authorities (including the governmental power elites) and the management of capitalist conglomerates.[65] However, for Neumann and Kirchheimer, the authoritarian state represents only the husk of monopoly capitalism, and the primacy of the economic realm still remains.[66]

Second, regarding the politico-administrative sphere of the capitalist state, Habermas suggests that in the early stage of capitalism, individuals used to enjoy an autonomous public sphere that could protect them from excessive state control. However, this public sphere has significantly diminished, and it has become a matter of manufactured public opinion due to the increasing technical control over the political sphere and the depoliticization of the people. These changes in the role of the capitalist state represents its administrative efforts to overcome the crisis of economic growth by transforming the public sphere, which reflects the contemporary legitimation crisis of the capitalist state.[67]

Third, in examining the socio-psychological domain of capitalist societies, Fromm attempts to introduce a synthesis between sociology and psychology, and between historical materialism and Freudian psychoanalysis.[68] According to Fromm, in these societies, the change in family structure has not only caused the underdevelopment of the adolescent ego, it has also led to the rise of an authority-bound personality among individuals who easily surrender to the capitalist system of domination. For Marcuse, on the other hand, the Freudian psychoanalysis has become obsolete in advanced industrial societies, because the role of the family in socializing individuals has declined, the father's role in individuals' ego development has diminished, and these roles have been replaced by various sociocultural institutions such as the mass media, schools, and sports teams.[69] This new pattern of socialization has reduced the conflict between individual and society, and led to more social conformity in individual behavior.

Finally, with regard to culture and media, according to Horkheimer and Adorno, the mass culture in capitalist countries is not a popular culture. It is governed and imposed by the capitalist system through the contemporary culture industries that manipulate and indoctrinate individuals to accept the existing form of society based on domination.[70] It is observed by Lowenthal and Adorno that in advanced capitalist societies such as the U.S., there is an uncritical and conformist tendency in the commercialized culture.[71] However, deviating from this critical position of Adorno, Marcuse, and Lowenthal, a more optimistic view is held by Benjamin and Habermas regarding the emancipatory role of commercial mass culture and broadcasting networks.[72]

THE CRITIQUE OF MARXISM

A significant reformulation of Marxism by critical theorists is the reversal of Marxian interpretation regarding the relationship between the basic economic structure (including production force and production relation) and the superstructure (encompassing politics, culture, state, and religion). While the Marxian tradition emphasizes the primacy of the basic structure over superstructure, for critical theorists such as Adorno, Horkheimer, and Marcuse, due to various politico-economic changes in industrial democracies and socialist countries, the social formation has changed in favor of the primacy of the political over the economic realm.[73] It has been specifically pointed out by Pollock that under state capitalism (both democratic and totalitarian forms), the state exercises control over the command economy, the state planning provides guidelines for production, consumption, savings, and investment, and such a role of the state shows the primacy of the political sphere.[74] Similarly, in his reconstruction of historical materialism, Habermas tends to reverse the Marxian priority of labor over social interaction, of economic base over superstructure—for Habermas, due to the state intervention in capitalist economies, the state rather than market becomes the primary concern.[75]

In line with this reinterpretation of the Marxian analysis of base-to-superstructure relation, critical theorists also differ from Marx's position regarding the historical agent of social transformation.[76] For

Marcuse, the contemporary working class does not correspond to the Marxian concept of proletariat due to various factors—such as the incorporation of the working class into the capitalist system, the emergence of a workforce that includes white-collar employees and technicians, the diminishing gap between intellectual and material labor, and the existing process of "deproletarianization."[77] Similarly, for Habermas, there is a form of compromise between labor and capital, and the classic form of class struggle hardly exists in modern capitalism.[78] The above reformulation of basic Marxian constructs not only shows the reformist nature of critical theorists, it also indicates that these theorists are not neo-Marxists though some authors have described them as such.

CRITICAL THEORY AND DEVELOPMENT

For Horkheimer, the role of critical theory is to provide guidelines for transforming society, economy, and politics.[79] In this regard, although critical theorists have made valuable contribution to reveal the shortcomings of orthodox Marxism and corporate capitalism, they have largely failed to offer an alternative, fully developed social theory.[80] Some critical theorists tend to present a very sketchy view of the future society—a society that would be free from all the shortcomings and pathologies discovered by these theorists in the current social system. For instance, Marcuse emphasizes a "rational" form of society in which the potential, freedom, happiness, and rights of all individuals could be realized.[81] He outlines the nature of a more desirable society in the following words:

> The total reconstruction of our cities and of the countryside; the restoration of nature after the elimination of violence and destruction of capitalist industrialization; the creation of internal and external space of privacy, individual autonomy, tranquillity; the elimination of noise, of captive audiences, of enforced togetherness, of pollution, of ugliness.[82]

This interpretation of rational society and social change hardly offers anything new, it is quite similar to the narration of desirable social conditions presented by social scientists, particularly development theorists. Moreover, this view of society held by Marcuse is theoretically inadequate, because it does not explain how such a social change is to be introduced, what constraints are likely to be encountered in realizing it, and who the change agents are for accomplishing the task. In this regard, Habermas offers a more systematic theory of social evolution based on the "developmental logic" of the learning process. In his theory of social evolution, Habermas explains evolution in terms of an advancement in learning capacities in both the empirical-analytic and moral-practical domains.[83] The former represents the sphere of production force (located in technology and economy), the latter represents the sphere of various forms of social integration (embodied in worldviews and conflict resolution mechanism). In respect to the latter—i.e., the development of the forms of social integration—Habermas presents a scheme of hierarchical stages of social evolution such as neolithic societies, archaic civilizations, developed civilizations, and the early modern societies.[84] Such interpretation of the "developmental logic," however, is not very different from the traditional version of modernization theory. It is not only Eurocentric and parochial, it is also a relatively incomplete theory because it does not offer any explanation of developmental dynamics: How and why do such social changes occur and what implications do they have for various social groups and classes?

This brief discussion indicates that the main contributions of critical theory lies in its comprehensive critique of advanced capitalist societies, and its reexamination of some major philosophical and theoretical shortcomings of the capitalist and Marxist intellectual traditions. But it failed to construct a comprehensive theory of society and societal development of its own. With regard to the critique of capitalist society, critical theorists emphasize mainly the superstructural domains of politics, culture, and social psychology but fail to reach a consensus regarding the dialectical relationship between the basic economic structure and the superstructure. Moreover, they tend to exclude the significance of the historical origin of capitalist development in relation to the past colonial exploitation, the present unequal structure of international political economy, and the process of underdevelopment in postcolonial societies. This absence of a Third World dimension leads to the partial, if not misleading, explanations of the nature and dynamics of the capitalist system. In the context of today's global economic, military, cultural, and information networks, the intellectual focus of critical theory on merely the internal conditions of capitalist society is inadequate. Lastly, the overemphasis of critical theory on the role of intelligentsia and its suspicion about the progressive role of the working class in transforming society not only reflect the impractical nature of critical theory, it also implies an inherent tendency toward rationalizing the intellectual hegemony of theoreticians over the common masses.

In summary, it has been discussed in this chapter that the conservative reformists suggest incremental socioeconomic changes through minor reforms to accommodate some economic fairness (income redistribution) at the national and international levels, but without introducing any fundamental change in the system. On the other hand, the radical reformists recommend the introduction of major reforms to eliminate national and international economic domination and to establish an exploitation-free society, if necessary, by fundamentally transforming the system. But this societal transformation has to be brought about through significant reforms rather than revolution. Lastly, the proponents of critical theory propose the transformation of the existing capitalist system through the critical intellectual role of the intelligentsia rather than the revolutionary role of the working class. With respect to the mode of such social transformation, critical theorists are quite similar to radical reformists. But while the radical reformists tend to focus on the practical politico-economic strategies of change, critical theorists emphasize mainly the critical intellectual strategies of social transformation.

CHAPTER 6

Radical Tradition of
Development Theories

The radical tradition of development thinking is inseparable from the contributions of Marx and Engels: they synthesized and transcended the fragmented radical ideas of the past, constructed a philosophical foundation for radical thinking, and offered more systematic theoretical explanations of sociohistorical development from this radical perspective. In the course of time, however, this radical theoretical framework has not only been extended and developed further, it has been subjected to various forms of reformulations depending on the changing contexts and orientations of subsequent theorists and policy-makers.[1] There are other forms of radical development thinking that emerged not because of the direct influence of Marxism but mostly because of the reaction of Third World intelligentsia to the theoretical inadequacies and negative practical implications of conservative development theories.

In general, in opposition to the assumptions of social harmony and incrementalism in social change found in the conservative tradition, theories within the radical tradition recognize various forms of fundamental contradictions: such as the contradiction between production forces and production relations, between basic structure and superstructure, between the ruling class and other social classes, and between the world capitalist system and Third World economies. They also have a common belief that development or progress basically implies a radical transformation of society through the means of *revolution* that eventually leads to the establishment of a socialist society.

But due to the aforementioned reformulations of Marxism and the varying radical reactions to the conservative traditions of development thinking, today there exist significant differences between various radical theories and schools, including classical Marxism, dependency theory, and neo-Marxism. They differ not only in terms of their views on the nature, scope, and dynamics of capitalism, but also in terms of their interpretations of the causes, goals, and implications of capitalist intervention in Third World countries. In addition, under the radical tradition, there are disagreements between different categories of theories with regard to the necessity, possibility, and role of a bourgeois revolution in Third World countries and the character and capacity of indigenous social class(es) to carry out such a revolutionary social change.[2]

Because of the varieties and complexities of radical development theories and the lack of a clear consensus among theorists themselves, there exists a problem of taxonomic ambiguity in the radical tradition. More specifically, there is a tendency toward the sweeping generalization and overlapping classification of various development theories into different taxonomic categories without examining the basic differences and similarities among these theories. This often leads to analytical confusion and theoretical misunderstanding. However, before introducing or proposing any new classification of these radical theories of development, it is necessary to explore some of the existing taxonomic problems. First, there are writers (e.g., Foster-Carter) who consider almost all the post-Marxian radical thinkers, including Baran, Sweezy, Frank, Emmanuel, Amin, Alavi, Buchanan, Caldwell, Shanin, Mao, Castro, and Fanon, as neo-Marxists.[3] Second, there are scholars such as O'Brien, Gulalp, Lall, and Kay,[4] who regard many of the dependency theorists[5] as neo-Marxists due to their use of Marxist terms and their emphasis on the progressive role of capitalism in Third World countries. To avoid such a sweeping generalization, it is necessary to examine the basic similarities and differences between these theoretical categories.

Although there are certain similarities between dependency theory and neo-Marxism in terms of their use of radical terminologies, belief in the progressive role of capitalism, and support for establishing a socialist society, these two theoretical categories remain significantly different. For instance, while dependency theory emerged in reaction to the inadequacies of modernization theory, neo-Marxist theory evolved as a response to the dependency debate itself.[6] In fact, most dependency theorists exclude, contradict, or reject important neo-Marxist ideas and concerns such as the coexistence and articu-

lation of various modes of production, primacy of production relations rather than exchange relations, internal class structure and its
relationship with external capitalist intervention, nature of state-
class relation, and so on. Considering the relative absence of these
basic features of the neo-Marxist position, it is difficult to accept the
aforementioned claim made by some authors that dependency theorists
are neo-Marxists. The central concern is about the prefix "neo" that
connotes here a notion of revival, extension, or revision,[7] and about
the term "Marxism" that implies the theoretical contributions and
ideological position of Marx (and Engels). Randall and Theobald
explain that neo-Marxists are those who, after a close reading of Marx,
adjust Marxism based on its relevance to the new contexts of Third
World countries without rejecting the basic principles and arguments
of Marxism.[8]

In line with the above analysis, a critical examination of various
taxonomic schemes available in the existing literature would suggest
that radical theories of development could be classified into three
major categories: classical Marxism, radical dependency theory,[9] and
neo-Marxist theory. It is possible to identify considerable differences
among these three theoretical categories. For instance, one important
criterion that distinguishes these theories from each other is their
respective positions regarding the role of capitalism in Third World
development. For classical Marxist theories, the role of external capitalist intervention in the Third World is progressive; for radical
dependency theories, such a role is always regressive; and for neo-
Marxist theories, the role depends on the historically specific modes
of production in Third World countries, the composition of their state-
class relations, and the nature of their interaction with the external
capitalist system. There are other theoretical criteria or positions that
also differentiate these three categories of radical theories. In addition, there are variations within each of these major theoretical
categories (see Figure 6.1).

Classical Marxist Theories

There are variations in defining the scope of "classical" Marxism,
and there are controversies over the distinction between "critical
Marxism" and "scientific Marxism."[10] However, in line with the common understanding of classical Marxism in terms of its scientific or
orthodox version, the taxonomic category of "classical Marxist theories"
will cover the later works of Marx and Engels and the contributions

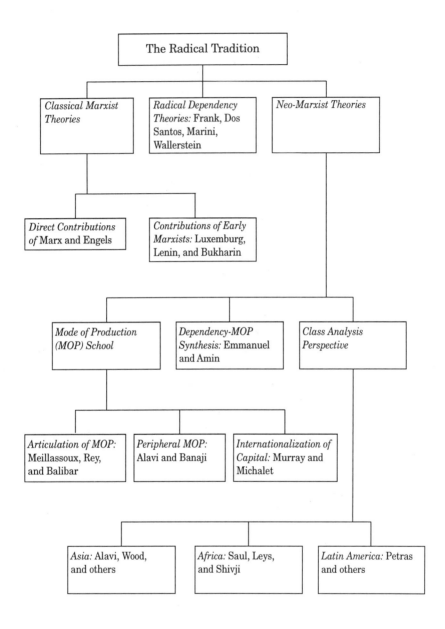

Figure 6.1 A taxonomic diagram exhibiting the major categories and subcategories of development theories and approaches within the radical tradition. The figure not only shows the major intellectual sources of these theories and approaches, it also outlines the main theoretical differences among them.

of those who have maintained and extended Marxian ideas without any fundamental revision.[11] Among these classical Marxists, however, a line can be drawn between the contributions of Marx and Engels and those of Hilferding, Lenin, Luxemburg, Bukharin, and other early Marxists, especially in terms of their intellectual stance regarding the role of external capitalist (colonial) intervention in the Third World. However, Marx's theoretical contribution, being the most original of these classical radical theories, is discussed in greater detail than others.

CONTRIBUTIONS OF MARX AND ENGELS

The major historical events and intellectual sources that influenced the radical thoughts of Karl Marx (1818–1883) and Friedrich Engels (1820–1895) included the rise of capitalism in Western Europe, the experience of the French Revolution, the German philosophy of Hegel and Feuerbach, and the British classical economics of Adam Smith and David Ricardo. Within this practical and intellectual context, Marx examined, challenged, and restructured the existing philosophy, history, and political economy of society and its development. However, the major contributions of Marx and Engels can be divided into four interrelated parts: (a) the critique of the existing philosophical traditions and the development of a philosophical perspective in line with the so-called dialectical materialism; (b) the application of this endorsed philosophical perspective to interpret the dynamics of social change based on a materialistic view of history; (c) the engagement of such a materialistic historical perspective to explain the origin, nature, and future of capitalism; and (d) the use of this analysis of capitalism to examine the cause and effect of capitalist intervention in the colonies. These basic contributions of Marx and Engels are briefly discussed below.

Hegel's dialectics and idealist interpretation of history and Feuerbach's philosophical materialism[12] were two major sources for Marx to develop his own philosophical orientation,[13] which has often been characterized as *dialectical materialism* by subsequent Marxist scholars. As a philosophical tenet, as far as dialectical materialism is concerned, there is a dialectical relationship between the objective material world and the subjective ideal world, and in the final analysis, matter determines and precedes idea. While according to Hegel's idealism, the state is the basis of "civil society" (private economic life), Marx holds an opposite view. In emphasizing the primacy of the (material) economic sphere, Marx was also influenced by Engels who was interested in economics.[14] Thus, Marx became engaged in the critical study of classical political economists, particularly Adam Smith, Ricardo, Malthus, and J.S. Mill, and the early neoclassicists such as Bentham, Senior, Say, and Bastiat.[15]

In philosophical terms, to a certain extent, Marx was influenced by his aforementioned philosophical position identified as dialectical materialism in interpreting the history of social change based on a materialistic view of history and the assumption of inherent contradiction in society. For Marx, in the course of time, society changes from one mode of production to another due to the perpetual contradiction between the forces of production (which are progressive) and the relations of production (which are regressive), leading to the eventual transformation of the latter through class struggle and revolution.[16] In general, every society, at different stages of its historical evolution, is supposed to change along a relatively fixed hierarchy of certain inevitable modes of production—i.e., primitive communism, slavery, feudalism, capitalism, and socialism.

Based on the above perspectives related to philosophy, history, and political economy, Marx dedicated the major part of his work to the study of the origin, composition, impact, and future of the capitalist mode of production. According to Marx, the basic feature of capitalism is not only commodity production[17] but also the transformation of labor itself into a commodity. Commodity production also exists in noncapitalist societies engaged in necessary production and exchange, but without the labor being transformed into a commodity and source of surplus value.[18] It is only in industrial capitalism where labor, like any other commodity, becomes a commodity and the source of surplus value. The capitalists invest money to acquire input commodities such as machinery and raw materials (the constant capital) and labor (the variable capital) to produce new commodities, such as automobiles, to sell them for profit. The source of such profit is surplus value and the only source of surplus value is labor (bought as a commodity).[19] This surplus value is added to the existing volume of capital for further profit, and thus capital accumulation continues.

The very composition of commodity production, however, leads to the crisis of capitalism.[20] The final demise of capitalism starts when capital becomes highly concentrated in few hands because of the elimination of small capitalists who cannot survive in a competitive situation where commodity production requires a huge amount of capital due to the rise of capital-labor ratio in the composition of commodity. On the other hand, despite the increase in workers' sufferings, the concentration of capital also assembles workers in larger industries, leading to their further socialization. The workers become conscious of how the surplus value they create is exploited by the capitalists and how they are alienated from their own products because of the capitalist system of production. Thus, the class struggle intensifies between the workers and the capitalists. Eventually, through a revolutionary process, workers replace the capitalist mode of production and establish a classless socialist society. And such is the interpretation of Marx about the inherent contradiction within the capitalist mode of production and the possibility of its transformation into a socialist society.

This labor theory of value, which explains the composition of commodity production and surplus value, also forms the basis for Marx to explain the cause and effect of capitalist intervention in the former Third World colonies. For Marx, the internal dynamics of capitalism in capitalist countries is the main *cause* of their colonial intervention in Third World countries. More specifically, he refers to the falling rate of the capitalists' profit due to the rising capital/labor ratio, the desire of capitalists to expand the scale of production while lowering its cost, and their desire for higher profit from selling manufactured goods in backward countries. Marx and Engels suggest that despite the primitive accumulation of capital through the plundering of wealth and introduction of slavery by capitalist nations, the *effect* of colonialism was largely progressive.[21] According to this Marxian model, "socialism can only be attained through capitalist development" and such capitalist development in the backward regions was possible only "by the impact upon them of the capitalism of Western Europe itself."[22]

Marx himself tends to believe that capitalism played a progressive role by colonizing non-European countries and thereby enhancing the emergence of capitalism in these countries, although such colonial intervention might have caused some human sufferings.[23] For instance, his articles on India clearly indicate his belief that one day the static, feudal, "barbarian" (he used the term many times), and rural colony of India, which was insensitive to foreign domination, would be transformed into a civilized, progressive, industrial, and capitalist nation-state by the colonial intervention of British capitalism. He wrote on the so-called Asiatic mode of production, which he considered static and without internal dynamism, and suggested that the penetration of European capitalism was necessary to mobilize such a static system.[24] It is mainly this interpretation of Marx and Engels regarding the progressive role of capitalist intervention in colonies which differentiates them from almost all other radical theorists. The departure starts with those Marxian thinkers who introduced a radical explanation of imperialism, particularly Hilferding, Luxemburg, Bukharin, and Lenin.

CONTRIBUTIONS OF THE EARLY MARXISTS

Different radical theorists of imperialism, including Lenin and some of his immediate predecessors, explained the *cause* of imperialism in various ways. According to Rosa Luxemburg, imperialist intervention is caused by the problem of "realization" or disposal of products due to insufficient demand (underconsumption) in the domestic markets in Western capitalist countries, and this creates the need for exchange with external economies.[25] For Rudolf Hilferding, the main cause of imperialist intervention is the emergence of "finance capital" (representing the fusion of "industrial capital" and "financial capital") in the form of monopolies and cartels: it encourages the export of finance capital and the acquisition of colonies for raw materials, markets, and cheap labor.[26] Nikolai Bukharin extends this argument further by explaining the process that involves the emergence of monopolistic finance capital, the alliance of finance capital with the state, the direct role of the state in exploitation on behalf of finance capital, and the intervention of such a state and capital in backward areas for higher profit.[27] In line with Hilferding, V.I. Lenin characterizes the imperialist stage of capitalism by the rise of monopolies, the merger of banking capital and industrial capital, the export of capital and formation of international cartel, and the division of the world among the great capitalist powers.[28]

Despite some differences among the above theorists with regard to their explanations of the *causes* of imperialism, they all agree that "the net *effect* [emphasis added] of imperialism is to develop the productive capacities of the colonial countries."[29] In opposition to the belief of the Narodniks,[30] Lenin, like Marx, recognized a progressive role of external capitalist intervention to enhance the emergence of capitalism, and thus socialism. In this regard, Lenin makes the following statement:

> The export of capital affects and greatly accelerates the development of capitalism in those countries to which it is exported. While, therefore, the export of capital may tend to a certain extent to arrest development in the capital exporting

countries, it can do so only by expanding and deepening the further development of capitalism throughout the world.[31]

However, Lenin's view about the role of capitalism in precapitalist nations changed for various reasons.[32] He started to believe that revolution was possible even in underdeveloped societies, that capitalism did not necessarily lead to socialist revolution, that capitalism assimilated the important segments of the working class, and that *imperialism might not be conducive to the development of underdeveloped societies*.[33] Despite Lenin's recognition of this retarding or paralyzing effect of imperialist intervention on capitalist development in the Third World, he still believed that after the withdrawal of this intervention, progressive change would occur. He did not go further to mention that imperialist intervention not only paralyzed Third World development, it also distorted the very potential for such development in the future. This issue has been the main focus of another category of theory, the radical dependency theory, which emphasizes the implications of the world capitalist system and its intervention for the distortion of capitalist development in Third World countries.

Radical Dependency Theories

In spite of its revolutionary view of social transformation, the radical dependency perspective of Andre Gunder Frank, Ruy Mauro Marini, Theotonio Dos Santos, and Immanuel Wallerstein did not emerge directly from the classical Marxist or Leninist interpretations of historical development and underdevelopment. Wallerstein, for instance, despite his use of Marxian concepts such as mode of production, class conflict, and the state, "reverses the causal direction" of traditional Marxism in linking these concepts.[34] It is necessary here to introduce a clear distinction between classical Marxism and radical dependency theory.

While classical Marxist theory emphasizes that the root of surplus is in the capital-labor relation within "production," radical dependency theory traces the root of surplus in the unequal "exchange" relations between capitalist countries and the Third World. While "class" is the basic unit of analysis in Marxist theory, the world "capitalist system" is the main unit in dependency theory. While Marxist theory identifies various modes of production in different parts of the world, dependency theory finds capitalism everywhere throughout the world; while Marxist theory focuses on the continuous changes in various modes of production, dependency theory finds a relatively stagnant structure of development and underdevelopment; and while Marxist theory emphasizes the progressive role of capitalist intervention in Third World countries, dependency theory finds it as the main cause of their underdevelopment.[35] Thus, based on the distinction made by different scholars between these two theoretical categories, Bernstein straightforwardly rejects the idea that dependency theory is Marxist.[36] After this brief overview, the remaining part of this section is devoted to an examination of the basic features and arguments of radical dependency theory as articulated by its proponents.

One of the main proponents of radical dependency theory is Andre Gunder Frank. Being influenced by the worsening economic condition in Latin American countries and the Castroist view that the oligarchic bourgeoisie was incapable of acting independently in these countries, Frank reacted not only against the conventional theories of modernization but also against the structuralism of the ECLA (Economic Commission for Latin America) scholars.[37] Although it is mentioned that Frank radicalized or Marxified the tradition of structuralism established by the ECLA, his theoretical framework is not directly based on Marxism.[38] It is rather influenced by the work of Paul Baran who finds a relationship between the development of Western nations and the underdevelopment of Third World countries.[39] However, in line with Frank's theoretical framework, Dos Santos, Wallerstein, and Marini made significant contributions to radical dependency theory.

The major conceptual and theoretical formulations of these theorists are related to various dimensions of development, dependency, and underdevelopment. *First*, it is necessary to understand what these theorists tend to connote by the terms "development" and "underdevelopment." Although they do not have a very clear interpretation of development, Frank's writings imply that development is "the attainment of economic sovereignty and the meeting of culturally determined needs for all people" rather than a mere increase in gross national product as stressed in the Newly Industrialized Countries (NICs).[40] However, these theorists are quite specific regarding the concept of underdevelopment, which refers to the condition of dependence of Third World countries (satellites/peripheries) on the advanced capitalist nations (metropoles/cores), what Dos Santos calls the "conditioning situation."[41] For Frank, the underdevelopment of a country basically means its incorporation into the world system but in a subordinated position.[42] In short, for the proponents of radical dependency theory, the indicator of development and underdevelopment is not economic growth but the condition of dependence.

Second, the radical dependency theorists also attempt to explain the nature and scope of this dependence. For Frank, dependence is characterized by a one-sided and unequal power relation, which implies that the course of development in the "satellites" (underdeveloped countries) is determined and controlled, consciously or unconsciously, by the "metropoles" (advanced capitalist nations).[43] The chain of this metropole-satellite relation is also extended to the regional and local centers within each satellite.[44] However, instead of two, Wallerstein identifies three hierarchical levels in the world system: the core, specialized in capitalist agriculture and industry; the periphery, specialized in export-oriented agriculture or mining; and the semi-periphery (such as the NICs), engaged in exporting raw materials to the core and manufactured goods to the periphery.[45] Similar to Wallerstein's idea of "semi-imperialism" exercised by the semi-periphery is Marini's view of "sub-imperialism," which implies a condition under which the dependent capitalist countries (such as Brazil) exercise an expansionist policy to dominate weaker nations. However, for these theorists, the sub-imperialist countries are incapable of having autonomous capitalist development, and they themselves are integrated into and dependent on the world capitalist system through international trade and financial relations.

Another dependency scholar, Dos Santos, interprets dependence as a situation in which the development and expansion of some countries (the dependent ones) are conditioned by the development and expansion of other countries (the dominant ones).[46] Moreover, he extends the dependency perspective by introducing three historical periods of dependence and three corresponding forms of dependency relations: (1) the colonial dependency, based on the monopoly of trade, land, mines, and labor in colonies; (2) the financial-industrial dependency, based on the monopoly of capital and its investment in colonies; and (3) the technological-industrial or "new" dependency, based on investment made by multinational corporations in the peripheral ex-colonies.[47]

Third, with regard to the causes of underdevelopment, for radical dependency theorists, the main cause of dependency and underdevelopment is largely the world capitalist system. According to Frank, dependence is not an original condition; it was created by the world capitalist system. It is the monopoly of metropolitan capitalism which results in unequal exchange: the monopsonic commodity market in the center (i.e., very few buyers of raw materials exported by many competing peripheral countries) and the relatively monopolistic status of the center's transnational corporations, force the peripheral nations to sell raw materials at a lower price and import industrial goods at a higher price.[48] As Frank himself mentions, "the non-realization and unavailability for investment of 'potential' economic surplus is due essentially to the monopoly structure of capitalism."[49] Dos Santos also attributes the structure of dependence to the international division of labor, especially the division between those producing primary agricultural products and those producing manufactured goods.[50]

Marini, in addition to his explanation that the dependent nature of "peripheral capitalism" results from unequal exchange between the periphery and the center,[51] goes further to incorporate the dimension of production in the dependency analysis. He suggests that to compensate the fall of profit rates caused by unequal exchange between the periphery and the center, dependent peripheral capitalists tend to introduce a form of *superexploitation* of labor within the periphery itself.[52] What makes this superexploitation of labor possible in the periphery is the fact that there is no strong link between the two basic elements of the capital cycle, i.e., the production and circulation of commodities.[53] While production and consumption in the center are interlinked and internally determined, production in the periphery largely depends on its exports to the center rather than on internal consumption in the periphery itself.

Fourth, in terms of the unit of analysis, it is quite clear from the above explanations of dependence and underdevelopment that for radical dependency theorists, the primary unit of analysis is the world capitalist system rather than class structure. For instance, according to Frank, the causal determinant of development and underdevelopment is the world capitalist system that not only encompasses the nation-states but also extends down to the structures existing in the remotest corners of the world.[54] It implies that for Frank, there is no dualism in the world economic system in terms of the modes of production. All the underdeveloped countries (though seemingly feudal) are capitalist,[55] because during the first phase of colonialism, they were thoroughly incorporated into the world capitalist system. Similarly, Wallerstein's "world systems analysis" explains that since the sixteenth century, there has been only one *world system* with a single unitary mode of production, i.e., capitalism.[56] Regarding other units of analysis, such as class, group, household, and the state, Wallerstein mentions that "all of these structures postdate, not antedate capitalism; all are consequence, not cause."[57]

Fifth, regarding the effects of dependency, according to these theorists, one of the most critical outcomes of dependency-based relationship between the metropoles/center (developed capitalist countries) and the satellites/periphery (underdeveloped countries) is the drainage of surplus from the latter to the former. While the peripheral countries experience varying forms and degrees of underdevelopment because of their loss of surplus, the center-nations get the benefits of economic development by accruing such surplus. *Sixth*, in terms of the evidence of dependency outcomes, Frank tries to confirm his thesis—that underdevelopment has been associated with the development of capitalism—by presenting the explanation that the satellites seem to experience more economic development when their linkages with the metropolis are weak.[58] He cites the examples of Latin American countries, which experienced more industrial development during the periods of their interrupted and weak relations with Western capitalist countries—e.g., during the periods of World War I, the Great Depression, and World War II. In addition, the regions that were the greatest colonial sources of surplus, and had the closest ties with the metropolis, are the most underdeveloped today.

Lastly, regarding the strategies or mechanisms to overcome the condition of dependency and underdevelopment, the proponents of radical dependency suggest revolutionary strategies. According to Frank, the satellites require the absence of capitalist interference, which indicates the need for a revolutionary break and delinking: for him, it is mainly a socialist revolution that can ensure such a necessary delinking with the capitalist metropolis.[59] Dos Santos and Marini also tend to suggest a socialist revolution to overcome the condition of dependency.[60]

Neo-Marxist Theories

In the past, radical dependency theory came under attack for various reasons: for its narrow interpretation of underdevelopment focusing on exchange rather than production relation, its relative indifference toward class structure and lack of class analysis; its deterministic pessimism regarding Third World development; its overemphasis on the world capitalist system at the expense of specific socioeconomic formations; its reduction of superstructural phenomena such as religion and ethnicity to pure economism; its circular or tautological argument of capitalist development, and its impractical desire for revolution.[61] Banaji concludes that the whole theory of dependency "is still today fundamentally a *petty-bourgeois* theory," and any revolutionary theory of world capitalism "must start by rejecting the entire framework of 'dependency theory'."[62]

More particularly, the dependency theory's lack of Marxian focus on production and class structure led to a "return to Marx" or a close reading and understanding of Marxism, and its application to the analysis of development and underdevelopment.[63] This extension or modification of Marxian principles to the analysis of development and underdevelopment can be brought under a single theoretical category—i.e., the "neo-Marxist theories"[64] that take three major forms, including the mode of production (MOP) school, the dependency-MOP synthesis, and the class analysis perspective.[65]

MODE OF PRODUCTION (MOP) SCHOOL

Although the origin of the mode of production (MOP)[66] approach can be found in the works of Marx, Engels, Lenin, and other earlier radical thinkers, the current interests in the MOP analysis largely emerged from certain recent sources. Some of these sources include the debate between Dobb and Sweezy on the "transition" from feudal to capitalist modes of production and their mutual coexistence, the conceptual analysis of noncapitalist modes of production by Hindess and Hirst, and the works of some French structuralists (e.g., Meillassoux, Godelier, Terray, Dupre, and Rey) in line with the methodological writings of Althusser and Balibar.[67] In general, the main thrust of this MOP analysis is on the extent, pattern, cause, and outcome of the coexistence of both capitalist and noncapitalist modes of production in societies. Within the MOP school, there are three main approaches, including the "articulation of MOP" approach, the "peripheral MOP" approach, and the "internationalization of capital" approach.[68]

"Articulation of Mode of Production" Approach

For Louis Althusser and Etienne Balibar, a certain mode of production can dominate the other modes and determine the dominant class; for Ernesto Laclau, a single economic system may contain more than one mode of production; and for Pierre-Philippe Rey, the transition from one mode of production to another mode takes such a long period that the transition itself becomes a normal condition.[69] Based on these diverse sources and interpretations, the "articulation of MOP" approach contains the following conceptual and theoretical positions. First, with regard to *the meaning of "articulation,"* the MOP approach indicates not only the coexistence of different modes of production and their mutual interdependence, but also the dominance of one mode of production over the others.[70]

Second, regarding *the stages of articulation* in capitalist development, Rey presents a general theory that identifies three stages of such articulation between the precapitalist modes and the capitalist mode of production: first, the interaction of the periphery's precapitalist modes with the capitalist mode, and the reinforcement of the former by the latter; second, the subordination and use of the precapitalist modes by the capitalist mode; and finally, the supplanting of the precapitalist modes (and their total disappearance) by the capitalist mode.[71] For this transformation to take place, capitalism needs to penetrate into the precapitalist modes and work from the inside.[72] Taylor also identifies three stages of capitalist penetration and its articulation, such as the period of merchant capital, the period of European capitalism, and the period of finance capital.[73]

Third, with regard to *the nature of transition between different stages*, the MOP approach differs from classical Marxism that suggests that at all stages, capitalism engulfs and inevitably and rapidly destroys the precapitalist modes of production. For the proponents of the MOP approach, at different stages, the transition involves various contradictions and problems depending on the changing needs of the capitalist mode in precapitalist societies. This means that "there is no single succession of stages of development in all countries."[74]

Fourth, as to *the causes of the transformation of precapitalist modes*, the MOP approach emphasizes the inevitable external effect of the capitalist mode from outside rather than the internal change within the precapitalist modes. This movement is guided by the functional needs of reproduction of the capitalist mode itself.

Finally, regarding *the notion of development and underdevelopment*, the MOP approach considers the expansion of the capitalist mode as development and the persistence of the precapitalist modes as underdevelopment. However, it suggests that capitalist development in the periphery is an "*uneven* process taking place over an extended period of time."[75]

"Peripheral / Colonial Modes of Production" Approach

While the proponents of the above MOP approach focus on the coexistence and articulation of the capitalist and precapitalist modes of production and the reproduction of the precapitalist modes under the dominance of capital, the advocates of the "peripheral or colonial mode of production" approach emphasize the transformation, not just the articulation and reproduction, of the precapitalist modes by the capitalist mode of production.[76] Although W. Ziemann and M. Lanzendorfer have examined the impact of colonial expansion on the economic structures of peripheral societies,[77] it is Hamza Alavi and Jairus Banaji who have conceptualized and theorized the "colonial mode of production" as a distinct social formation. For Alavi and Banaji, the colonial intervention changed the precapitalist mode of production to the effect that it served the capitalist mode: the precapitalist mode was transformed into an integral component in the hierarchical structure of a single capitalist mode, and it could be considered as the "colonial mode of production."[78]

Foster-Carter, however, finds it difficult to endorse the concept of "colonial mode of production," because there is no clear demarcation regarding its exact position between feudalism and capitalism, because of its transitional or impermanent nature, and so on.[79] D. McEachern attempts to overcome this problem of ambiguity related to this approach by introducing the idea of "the colonial forms of capitalist mode of production," and even by suggesting that India is not characterized by a "colonial mode of production" but by a "constricted form of capitalism" resulting from its international linkages.[80] This discussion related to the mode of production in India has been extended further by U. Patnaik, P. Chattopadhyay, and A. Rudra with special reference to the degree of capitalism in Indian agriculture.[81]

"Internationalization of Capital" Approach

This third variety of the MOP approach makes a shift in attention from the articulation of capitalist and precapitalist modes in the periphery to the structure and logic of development of the capitalist mode. For this approach, the multiple modes of production in the periphery have already been brought under the world capitalist system through the internationalization of capital. Its analytical focus is on the dynamics *within* the capitalist mode rather than the articulation *between* various modes in the periphery. In this approach, there is a tendency to synthesize Frank's concern for circulation and Laclau's concern for production by using Marx's analysis of the three circuits of capital, including commodity-capital, money-capital, and productive-capital. It examines how the expansive and global nature of these circuits of capital causes the subordination of different parts of the world to multinational corporations through the *internationalization* of such capital.[82]

Robin Murray highlights the Marxian interpretation that in the process of this internationalization of capital, some national economies remain more powerful than others, and the tendency of capitalist expansion is usually toward the precapitalist areas.[83] The contribution of C.A. Michalet is also relevant to this internationalization approach. He argues that multinational corporations themselves emerged from the process of concentration of capital into monopoly capital and its internationalization: this internationalization process involves not just the export of money capital, but also the export of the capitalist relations of production, which affects the structures of production or the capital-labor relations in peripheral societies.[84]

The basic difference between this "internationalization of capital" approach and the above two MOP approaches is summarized by Ruccio and Simon in the following words: "Underdevelopment and dependency are no longer associated with the persistence of noncapitalist modes of production, as they are with the articulation of MOP theorists, or with the dependent status of developing countries, as in the peripheral MOP approach; they are effects internal to the capitalist mode of production itself."[85] However, like dependency theory, this approach underestimates the inherent potential for change within the economic structure of peripheral nations and overemphasizes the international forces. The precapitalist or noncapitalist modes of production in the periphery and their determining power are hardly taken into consideration.

DEPENDENCY-MOP SYNTHESIS

In general, the proponents of radical dependency theory are attacked for overemphasizing the external factors and overlooking internal issues such as the modes of production and class structures, whereas the MOP approaches are often criticized for their relative indifference toward the adverse external impacts of the world capitalist system such as dependence and underdevelopment. In this regard, the contributions made by some scholars tend to address these shortcomings by synthesizing various components of these theories or approaches. Samir Amin, for instance, attempts to combine the basic theoretical concerns of dependency theory, the articulation of MOP approaches, and the theory of unequal exchange offered by Arghiri Emmanuel. As a theoretical framework, this dependency-MOP synthesis has been brought under the category of "neo-Marxist theories" because of the presence of some basic Marxian elements—including issues such as the mode of production and the production-based analysis of exchange—in the above intellectual sources constituting the synthesis. To comprehend the basic theoretical underpinnings of dependency-MOP synthesis, the relevant contributions of Amin are presented in this section. Before this, however, it is necessary to explain Emmanuel's theory of unequal exchange that represents an essential component of Amin's framework.

According to the ECLA structuralist perspective and radical dependency theories discussed above, the presence of monopoly capital and the differential elasticity of demand represent the main causes of unequal exchange between the core and the periphery, and the surplus extraction from the latter by the former. However, in this regard, Emmanuel revises Marx's labor theory of value and offers a different version of the "theory of unequal exchange." According to this theory, surplus is drained from peripheral nations even without monopoly capital and even under perfect competition in the world market.[86] How is this possible?

For Emmanuel, although the high international mobility of capital leads to a single international rate of profit, due to the relative immobility of labor, different levels of wages are formed in different countries—higher in the core and lower in the periphery—based on their specialization in different commodities reflecting the international division of labor.[87] Since the commodity prices incorporate wage costs and reflect the wage levels, an "unequal exchange" occurs when a high-wage capitalist country trades its relatively expensive commodities (reflecting higher wages) for the cheaper commodities (reflecting lower wages) produced by a low-wage underdeveloped country. As goods are exchanged unequally, "not in proportion to the value (hours of work) embodied in them," it leads to "a constant bleeding of value away from low-wage countries."[88] In fact, for Emmanuel, the poorer countries are "forced to exchange products in which a large number of labor-hours are embodied, with commodities produced with smaller number of labor-hours in richer countries."[89] Thus, this unequal exchange through trade leads to the "superexploitation" of peripheral countries by the core countries.

In his synthesis, Amin tends to integrate these basic tenets of Emmanuel's unequal-exchange theory with the basic features of dependency theory and various MOP approaches. First, Amin agrees with dependency theorists that the world capitalist system is divided into two interrelated poles, the core and the periphery. Through this interrelationship "the development of the center engenders and maintains the underdevelopment of the periphery."[90] Second, Amin borrows from Emmanuel to explain the implication of such core-periphery relations—that such relations lead to an "unequal exchange" between the core and the periphery (due to distorted prices based on wage differentials) and the "superexploitation" of peripheral workers.[91]

Third, for Amin, the underdevelopment engendered by such a core-periphery interaction is characterized by the reproduction of noncapitalist modes of production and the distortion of the capitalist mode in the periphery.[92] This coexistence of both precapitalist and capitalist modes, however, creates market distortion.[93] Here Amin uses the theoretical framework of the MOP school to overcome the static nature of dependency and unequal-exchange theories by recognizing the coexistence of both precapitalist and capitalist modes of production. Amin also explains how precapitalist modes are dissolved into the dominant mode of world capitalism, and how "peripheral capitalism"—as a distorted (export-oriented) form of capitalism—destroys the autonomy of precapitalist modes and yet perpetuates their existence. With regard to the nature of "social formations" in the periphery, Amin discovers the existence of an expansive bureaucracy, an increasing level of social inequality, and the dominance of agrarian capital that complements local merchant capital and foreign interests.[94]

Amin does not see any possibility of autonomous capitalist development in the periphery. The solution to the problem is an "autocentric" development in peripheral countries by "delinking" themselves from the world capitalist system and by establishing socialism through revolution by the peasants and working masses.[95] Despite such revolutionary views, however, Amin has been criticized for his inadequate analysis of class relations.[96]

CLASS ANALYSIS PERSPECTIVE

As already described in this chapter, the classical Marxists predicted that socialist revolution was inevitable in advanced capitalist societies, that colonial intervention played a progressive role in Third World countries for their capitalist development, and that the proletariat class would ultimately emerge in these countries and establish socialist societies. For the proponents of radical dependency theory, however, the peripheral nations are already capitalist because of their incorporation into the world capitalist system. To achieve an autonomous development in the periphery, they recommend its delinkage from the world capitalist system and the realization of socialist revolution by the masses. On the other hand, according to the MOP school, capitalism is the dominant mode of production but it coexists with other precapitalist modes in various combinations depending on the specific social formations in individual Third World countries.

However, there are sociohistorical phenomena which could not be adequately addressed by the deterministic version of classical Marxism, the overgeneralized dependency theory, and the economistic MOP school. Such phenomena include the nonrealization of socialist revolution in advanced Western capitalist nations, the "nonproletarian" socialist revolutions in noncapitalist countries like China and Cuba, the controversy over capitalist development and the coexistence of multiple modes of production in postcolonial societies, and the emergence of relatively autonomous but complex relations between class and state formations in these societies. Such inadequacies in the above radical theories led to the emergence of another category of neo-Marxist theory which examines and focuses on the role of class,[97] the nature of the state, and the patterns of state-class relations, particularly in postcolonial societies.[98] In this chapter, the contributions made by the proponents of this neo-Marxist framework are generalized into a broad theoretical category termed "class analysis perspective."

One major controversy among neo-Marxist theorists within this class analysis perspective is regarding the revolutionary character of specific social classes, particularly the peasants and the proletariats. Some neo-Marxists are skeptical about the role of Third World industrial proletariats in realizing social revolution as they constitute a certain form of "labor aristocracy," while they are quite optimistic about the peasants to play such a revolutionary role. There are others such as I. Roxborough and Lionel Cliffe who are in agreement with classical Marxists that the industrial proletariats rather than the peasants represent the main revolutionary class.[99] Still there are some neo-Marxists who emphasize the combined role of both classes. James Petras, for instance, explains that the socialist revolution begins in a more "advanced" (industrial) sector, but its success greatly depends on "joining efforts with the bulk of the social forces (peasants) located in the 'backward' areas of the economy."[100]

With regard to the issue of state-class relations, for various unique factors in Third World countries—such as the coexistence of multiple modes of production, the transitional nature of class structure, and the weak status of class articulation—different classes and their alliances often contend for political power, and they tend to use the state for this purpose. Thus, the class composition of the state has become one of the main concerns for neo-Marxist writers: they like to examine the nature and role of social classes or class alliances dominating the state and the relationship of such a state with other classes or class alliances. Departing from the classical Marxist view of the state as an instrument and superstructural manifestation of the dominant classes, these scholars find Third World states as relatively autonomous entities rather than the passive reflections of such dominant classes. However, the contributions of these neo-Marxist writers to the study of class, state, and development can be divided into three main sections depending on the study's focus on specific Third World regions, including Asia, Africa, and Latin America.

On Asia

There are neo-Marxist scholars, such as Hamza Alavi and Geof Wood, who deal with the question of state and class in Asia, especially the Indian subcontinent. However, it is mainly the contribution of Alavi that has created considerable debate. According to Alavi, in the process of imposing colonial rule, the metropolitan center not only carried out the bourgeois revolution but also created an "overdeveloped" state apparatus in the colonies to subordinate indigenous social classes: the state became an instrument of the metropolitan bourgeoisie, the dominant class.[101] Although after independence the direct control of the metropolitan bourgeoisie has ended, no single indigenous class has exclusive command over the colonially inherited overdeveloped state apparatus in postcolonial societies such as Pakistan and Bangladesh. It has led to the "relative autonomy" of this overdeveloped state apparatus represented by a bureaucratic military oligarchy. Such "relative autonomy" of the state is necessary for its role in mediating the interests and demands of the three propertied classes (i.e. the indigenous bourgeoisie, the metropolitan bourgeoisie, and the landed classes), and at the same time, acting on behalf of these classes to preserve the required social order, the institution of private property, and the capitalist mode as the dominant mode of production.[102]

The relative autonomy of the postcolonial state emanates not only from a "negative condition," i.e., the absence of a single dominant class, but also from certain "positive conditions"—especially the extensive economic intervention of the state as reflected in its direct appropriation and disposition of economic surplus, which constitutes the material base of such state autonomy.[103] Alavi also mentions that within the postcolonial state, there is a complementary relationship between the bureaucratic military oligarchy and the ruling political party and politicians, they may experience short-term conflicts but without any fundamental antagonism.[104] The political parties rather constitute an essential component of the oligarchy. Finally, for Alavi, since the bourgeois revolution was already introduced in the colonies by the metropolitan center, today the native bourgeoisie in postcolonial societies, unlike its counterpart in metropolitan countries, has cooperative rather than antagonistic relationship with the landowning classes: the landowning classes assist the native bourgeoisie in the "democratic" running of the postcolonial state by containing the local revolutionary forces and connecting the national-level state apparatus with the local-level power structures in rural areas.[105]

However, Geof Wood points out that Alavi's notion of "relative autonomy" is based on the role of the "overdeveloped" state apparatus in mediating the interests of different propertied classes rather than on the relation between the social formation and the nature of the state. He tends to oppose Alavi's argument that the inherited "overdeveloped" state apparatus remains dominant over the indigenous classes even after independence.[106] However, Moore finds Wood's understanding of Alavi's thesis problematical and makes a distinction between their basic arguments: while Alavi articulates the autonomy of the state apparatus in terms of its freedom "from" control by others (the dominant class), Wood refers to power "within" the state apparatus itself; while Alavi focuses on the relations of the state apparatus to the aspirant ruling classes, Wood emphasizes the relations of the state apparatus to society; while Alavi finds the autonomy of the state apparatus as a postcolonial phenomenon, Wood considers the dominance of the state apparatus over indigenous social classes as a colonial experience that has diminished after independence due to the politicization of the indigenous social classes and pressure from politicians.[107]

Some degree of reconciliation between Alavi's notion of the relative autonomy of the "overdeveloped" state apparatus and Wood's emphasis on the politico-ideological challenges to such a state apparatus can be found in the analysis of W. Ziemann and M. Lanzendorfer. Ziemann and Lanzendorfer examine the relative autonomy of the state, but for them, the primary source of such state autonomy is the peripheral economic structures rather than the overdeveloped state superstructure. For them, the dependent and heterogeneous nature of peripheral economic structures gives rise to fragmented, weak, and unstable class structures, which in turn require the mediation of the interests of various classes and groups by the state: this leads to the concentration of political power in the state apparatus and the emergence of its relative autonomy.[108] On the other hand, in line with Wood's skepticism regarding the "overdeveloped" status of the postcolonial state, Ziemann and Lanzendorfer suggest that the dependent and heterogeneous nature of peripheral economic structures, in fact, makes the peripheral states "weak," which is reflected in political instability, regional disintegration, and so on.[109]

On Africa

Among the neo-Marxist scholars dealing with African countries, Issa Shivji, John S. Saul, and Colin Leys are quite prominent. Saul extends Alavi's notion of the "overdeveloped state" and its "relative autonomy," and adds another dimension—i.e., the ideological function of the postcolonial state. Such a function is essential for creating the state's hegemonic position within the artificially drawn territorial boundaries and for establishing territorial unity and legitimacy: all these lead to, what Saul calls, the "centrality of the state" in the postcolonial social formations.[110] However, there are differences between Alavi and Saul with regard to the origins and implications of the overdeveloped state and its relative autonomy. While Alavi emphasizes the colonial creation of the overdeveloped state in the Indian subcontinent and its use for subordinating the native social classes, Saul stresses the role of such a state in East Africa in subordinating the precapitalist social formations; and while Alavi finds the basis of the relative autonomy of the state in its function of mediating between various class interests, Saul traces the root of such relative autonomy in the centrality of the state to ensure territorial unity and legitimacy.[111]

On the other hand, based on his study of Tanzania, Shivji focuses on the role of the postcolonial state in the class formation itself. He discovers the absence of a genuine bourgeoisie and the weakness of the petty bourgeoisie in a postcolonial society. Thus, the state becomes the means of transforming an embryonic or weak petty bourgeoisie into a proper ruling class comprised of the military, economic, and politico-administrative elites, what Shivji labels the "bureaucratic bourgeoisie."[112] However, for Leys, in postcolonial societies such as Kenya, there was a considerable degree of capital accumulation by the precapitalist accumulators before colonialism, which had led to the emergence of a class of indigenous bourgeoisie that dominated the nationalist movement and directed the state in the peripheral social formation.[113] Thus, while in some Asian cases,

Alavi finds the dependent nature of the native bourgeoisie, resulting in the relative autonomy of the overdeveloped state; in certain African cases, Shivji discovers the weak nature of the petty bourgeoisie that needed to be transformed into a proper ruling class by the state, and Leys detects the dominance of the national bourgeoisie over, rather than the relative autonomy of, the state.[114]

On Latin America

In the case of Latin America, one of the most well known neo-Marxists on the analysis of the state and class is James Petras.[115] He is critical of dependency theory for its overemphasis on the external world system, and of the MOP school due to its narrow concern for internal modes of production. With regard to Third World countries, Petras explains the nature of external and internal class interactions, describes how colonialism created a social stratum that was collaborative with metropolitan countries, and examines the role of the state in serving the interests of such external and internal classes or class alliances.[116] In addition, Petras identifies three phases of capitalist and imperialist development and the corresponding three forms of peripheral exploitation.[117] In relation to the recent development situation in the Third World, the most crucial is the last phase—the phase of "late monopoly capitalism" and its role in creating "dependent neo-colonialism." This last phase of capitalist development is characterized by the circular flow of capital into and out of the periphery through banking, industry, commerce, and services in the form of joint partnership, management contract, and royalty. During this phase, as colonies became independent nations, an intermediate social stratum emerged between imperial capitalism and the peripheral labor force, and such a social stratum included various propertyless intermediate groups that belonged to the army, the civil service, the university, and so on.

According to Petras, for the purpose of capital accumulation, the postindependence regimes usually have three strategies of class alliances: (a) the "neocolonial" (alliance with imperial forces to intensify surplus extraction from the indigenous labor force); (b) the "national developmental" (elimination of the share of imperial firms, but extraction of surplus from labor force under the auspices of the state); and (c) the "national popular" (alliance with working population, reinvestment of national surplus, and redistribution of income).[118] In addition, in the Third World, the most popular and nationalist regimes have been least durable and expansive, whereas the least popular and nationalist regimes have been most expansive and exploitive, and most effective in capital accumulation and growth. Petras also mentions that the role and nature of peripheral states could be best understood in relation to their relationship with the imperial states. This is because the imperial states, owing to their interest in surplus extraction, contribute to the establishment of neocolonial peripheral states while they tend to disaggregate the national-popular and developmental regimes.[119] However, with regard to the question of development, underdevelopment, and dependency, Petras suggests that the basic problem for the periphery is not simply its external dependency: the process of imperial exploitation is also inseparable from the class structure within the periphery itself. Thus, for Petras, "it is within this class structure and in the class struggles that ensue that this problem must be examined and eventually resolved."[120]

From the foregoing discussion, it can be concluded that with regard to development and underdevelopment in Third World countries, the main focus of the neo-Marxian class analysis perspective is not the world capitalist system. For the proponents of this perspective, the patterns of the world economy are not determined simply by impersonal market forces but by the interests and structures of various social classes within various nations. Their main emphasis is neither straightforwardly on the modes of production and their articulation, because intranationally and internationally, it is the actions of and interactions between various classes which maintain or transform such modes of production. Regarding the question of the state superstructure, they emphasize its nature and function in relation to various classes and class alliances within a social formation. In short, the neo-Marxian class analysis perspective considers "classes as the prime movers of history."[121]

CHAPTER 7

A Critique of Development Theories

In the last three chapters, the main traditions of development theories and approaches, including their intellectual origins, ideological inclinations, central arguments, and mutual interrelationships, have been analyzed. In addition, the basic similarities and differences among these theories and approaches have been discussed. Although in the process of examining these theories and approaches, some of their limitations have been pointed out in these chapters, a more rigorous critique is essential for understanding the major theoretical shortcomings in the development field, grasping the practical implications of these theoretical flaws, intensifying awareness among development scholars and experts of such theoretical and practical problems, and restructuring development theories and policies.

It should be pointed out that there is already an enormous amount of critical debates on development, which tend to evaluate various theoretical and practical problems of the development field from diverse perspectives.[1] However, in most instances, the existing critical studies tend to focus on specific dimensions and issues of development without analyzing them in relation to the overall intellectual atmosphere existing in the development field. These critical studies on development tend to be fragmented or piecemeal in nature, and often they fail to explain the multidimensionality of theoretical problems and decipher the implications of such theoretical shortcomings for the practical crises of development. This chapter is devoted to this task of presenting a more comprehensive critique of the development field in terms of its major theoretical inadequacies and their adverse practical consequences.[2]

Theoretical Shortcomings in the Development Field

For every discipline or field of knowledge, there are various criteria to assess its intellectual strengths and weaknesses. For instance, in the development field, the major criteria for evaluating development theories should include: the *epistemological flexibility* of development theories to accommodate various modes (e.g., empirical, interpretive, critical) of understanding development; the *analytical breadth and depth* of these theories to cover both specific and generic, internal and international, dimensions of development; and the *practical relevance* of these theories to the varying historical, economic, political, and cultural contexts in different societies, including the advanced capitalist nations, Third World countries, and the socialist states. In other words, any satisfactory theory of development should accommodate various modes of interpreting development issues and concerns, possess analytical rigor to encompass multiple dimensions of development, and address cross-national diversity in societal contexts. But the overall field of development suffers from serious shortcomings related to these concerns, although there are certain intellectual variations among the major mainstream theories and models of development.

More specifically, the development field suffers from intellectual problems such as: (a) a predominantly empiricist view of development that does not give enough credit to nonempirical interpretations; (b) a considerable degree of analytical reductionism based on a parochial focus on economic issues while ignoring the noneconomic dimensions of development; (c) a tendency toward normative indifference, which refers to the exclusion of cultural values and norms, especially those in Third World societies, from development studies; (d) a certain trend of ethnocentric prejudices, referring to Western cultural biases or prejudices underlying development thinking; and (e) an inclination toward unfounded universalism, connoting the prevalent tendency to claim universal validity of development knowledge despite its culture-boundedness. These major shortcomings of the existing development theories and models are explained below.

EPISTEMOLOGICAL EMPIRICISM

The theories of economic growth are epistemologically empiricist[3] in the sense that their primary focus is on the tangible and quantifiable economic criteria to know the extent of development. For instance, the main concern of classical growth theory is the amount of wealth accumulation. The neoclassical theory has been characterized as empiricist by authors such as Katouzian, McCloskey, and Caldwell, because it emphasizes the principle of observability and rejects subjective introspection as a source of true knowledge.[4] Similar empiricist tendency can be found in the case of "new growth" theory. The Keynesian theory also holds an epistemological stance which posits that the knowledge about the future "can only be gained via induction from past experiences."[5] In addition to the endorsement of this Keynesian epistemological position, the post-Keynesian scholars believe that "the ultimate test of a proposition lies in its empirical verification or falsification."[6]

In the case of modernization theories, although the focus appears to shift toward certain noneconomic (e.g., political and cultural) issues, they hardly overcome the empiricist epistemological position. For instance, the empiricist view of knowledge, introduced by Auguste Comte and extended by Emile Durkheim, was continued by the subsequent sociological theorists of modernization such as Talcott Parsons.[7] The proponents of political modernization also emphasize the empiricist criteria of political development, including the frequency of elections, forms of government, the voting patterns, and political stability. Similarly, the reformist theories and models, including human resource development approach, rural development strategy, basic needs approach, and new international economic order, are predominantly empiricist in terms of their main focus on the observable and measurable criteria (such as income, employment, food consumption, calorie intake, and trade and exchange) as the main indicators of development. With regard to the distribution of development outcomes, the reformist theories tend to highlight the empirical figures of income distribution, while excluding the relatively nonempirical determinants such as social class structure. The tendency toward empiricism is also evident in the case of dependency theories. The proponents of different versions of dependency tend to focus on the empirical (mostly economic) structures of unequal international exchange. For them, the main criteria for knowing the conditions of underdevelopment and dependence is the structures of economic hegemony created by international exchange within the world capitalist system. Brewer mentions that both Frank and Wallerstein emphasize descriptive generalization based on empirical facts.[8] This implies a relative neglect of internal class structures, which are often inseparable from international economic dependency and hegemony.

The classical Marxist and neo-Marxist views of development are not free from empiricism, although their epistemological positions are quite complex and not straightforwardly empiricist. For instance, while the "young" Marx emphasized both the subjective human action and morality and the objective social experience, the "mature" Marx presented a materialistic interpretation of history that highlighted empirical experience related to the material world as the main source of knowledge. However, unlike the traditional mode of empiricism, most Marxist scholars tend to integrate empiricist knowledge with historicism,[9] emphasize noumena (the essence) rather than phenomena (appearance) as the primary source of knowledge, and attempt to uncover "causal structures and mechanisms" underlying the "epistemic surface of empirical phenomena."[10] Marx himself analyzed capitalism in terms of the inherent nature and composition of commodity production, surplus value, and class structure rather than apparent phenomena such as exchange relations and market mechanisms. Among the neo-Marxist theories of development, the "articulation of mode of production" (MOP) approach stresses the abstraction of empirical observations.[11] The proponents of this school largely rely on the empirical features of various modes of production within and outside peripheral nations in order to configure the nature and effects of interaction between the precapitalist and capitalist modes of production.

However, one may find that among these various development theories and models, some are more empiricist than others. For instance, modernization theories are less empiricist than economic growth theories, especially because modernization theorists deal with relatively intangible domains such as politics, culture, and behavior, although they tend to interpret these domains in terms of observable indicators. Dependency theories are also less empiricist than growth theories, because while the latter emphasize quantifiable criteria of economic accumulation, the former highlight the national and international structures of such accumulation. However, dependency theories are more empiricist than classical Marxist theories, because while dependency scholars emphasize the apparent exchange relations within the world capitalist system, the classical Marxists stress the production relations underlying such capitalist structures of exchange[12] despite their tendency to deemphasize the importance of superstructural forces.[13] On the other hand, among the neo-Marxist schools, the MOP school tends to preclude the relatively nonempirical dimensions such as class structures and class interests, which are taken into account by other neo-Marxist schools, especially the class analysis perspective.

In general, however, the major theories of development mentioned above tend to overlook the nonempirical dimensions of development such as social relations, cultural beliefs, gender question, and ethnic identity,[14] which are important issues related to human development. For development scholars with empiricist predilection, it is necessary to understand that even their empirical knowledge of development is not free from their normative or ethical predisposition. Thus, Morgan emphasizes that in general, the pursuit of knowledge, "because of its essentially social nature, must be understood as being as much as ethical, moral, ideological, and political activity as it is an epistemological one."[15] In this regard, Gadamer holds a more radical intellectual stance and suggests that all observations are affected by historically inherited traditions or prejudices that constitute the precondition of the very possibility of understanding as such.[16] The point, in short, is that the fetish for the empirical sources of knowledge represent a major epistemological shortcoming, especially in the social sciences. Thus, the dominant empiricist tendency in mainstream development theories is an epistemological problem that requires serious rethinking.

NORMATIVE INDIFFERENCE

Related to the aforementioned epistemological shortcoming created by overdependence on empiricism, there is also a normative problem in the development field caused by its tendency to be indifferent toward the issues of human values, norms, ethics, and morality that are not empirically verifiable. For example, the theories of economic growth consider individuals as utility maximizing consumers, and tend to exclude other human motives based on values and ethics, or simply interpret them in terms of their relevance to economic utility.[17] In fact, the whole mainstream economics dealing with various growth theories tends to isolate itself from any moral or ethical discourse.[18] As McKenzie and Tullock claim, economic approaches are amoral and devoid of personal values.[19] Among the proponents of neoclassical theory, Bastiat, Senior, Menger, and Walras emphasize that in order to acquire its scientific status, political economy must be free from values and ethics.

The contemporary neoclassical theorists such as Milton Friedman suggest that economics has nothing much to do with values and it is independent of any ethical or normative judgments. The proponents of "new growth" theory even consider the indigenous values in Third

World countries, such as the value of self-reliance in India, as obstacles to growth, and they suggest that these countries should borrow ideas from advanced industrial nations. This disregard for indigenous norms and ethics is also evident in the case of Keynesian and post-Keynesian theories of economic growth, whose basic principles are not very different from the value-neutral neoclassical principles such as utilitarianism, individualism, and marginal productivity.[20]

Similarly, modernization theories hold the assumption of value-neutrality despite the inclination of some early modernization scholars (such as Max Weber) toward an interpretive intellectual position.[21] According to Macpherson, the theorists of political modernization believed in the value-neutralist utilitarian principle of political rationality that explained the behavior of voters largely in terms of their tendency to maximize political gains, a tendency that is common among consumers in the economic market.[22] In other words, the normative assumptions of modernization theories are not very different from those of economic growth theories emphasizing value-neutrality.[23] The psycho-cultural theorists of modernization, such as McClelland and Hagen, are interested mainly in identifying and prescribing strategies to enhance entrepreneurship and achievement orientation of people in order to facilitate economic growth in Third World countries, but these scholars seem to be quite indifferent or insensitive toward the indigenous cultural beliefs and norms found in these countries. Similarly, the reformist theories of development show a considerable degree of normative indifference. For instance, the basic needs approach highlights the basic economic necessities defined in empirical rather than normative and moral terms, and the NIEO strategy focuses mainly on the economic dimension of unequal international structure while overlooking its cultural and normative dimensions that have become increasingly significant for determining the future direction of world order in this age of hegemonic culture industry and global information network.

The classical Marxist perspective does not categorically exclude the normative and ethical issues, but it tends to render them secondary and a matter of superstructure. Marx himself declined to endorse ethics and morality as a basis for social action.[24] For the Marxists, even the project of socialist revolution is not based on any moral ground; it is considered as a consequence of the process of historical transformation.[25] The similar normative indifference is also inherent in neo-Marxist theories, especially the MOP school highlighting the articulation and transformation of the precapitalist modes into a capitalist mode of production but precluding the normative dimensions of this politico-economic transition. The class analysis perspective focuses on the role of class structure and the state, but pays inadequate attention to the formation of class consciousness and state ideology based on cultural norms, ethnic identity, and religious ethics in many Third World countries. On the other hand, dependency theories emphasize the condition of Third World underdevelopment characterized by international economic dependence, but their proponents are less concerned for the condition of dependence and underdevelopment in terms of cultural, normative, and attitudinal factors,[26] although these factors, especially the cultural influence, play a significant role in shaping the behavior and policy orientation of Third World elites, expanding their demands for foreign goods, and thus perpetuating economic dependence itself.

The above tendency of the major development theories to exclude normative factors from the development debate is in opposition to the fact that human development involves various social groups and classes holding diverse values and interests, which require development theories and models to address various sets of social and institutional values.[27] The significance of the issue is expressed in Boulding's observation that worldwide, there are about ten thousand societies, and "each with its own traditions, values, religious practices, special knowledge stocks, and languages/dialects."[28] Thus, in explaining the concerns of development in all these societies, it is imperative for development scholars and experts to address and accommodate such cultural, normative, and ethical diversities. In addition, development scholars must understand that even when they tend to exclude the normative and ethical questions from development discourse in the name of objectivity, they themselves often impose their own values, worldviews, and ideologies in the process of constructing development knowledge.[29]

ANALYTICAL REDUCTIONISM

Most development theories that are quite established and well-known, suffer from a considerable degree of reductionism[30] in terms of their one-dimensional focus on a single social domain (especially the economic realm) while excluding other spheres such as culture, ethnicity, gender, and environment. They are also reductionist in terms of their tendency to reduce every development issue or concern to its tangible, verifiable, and measurable criteria. For instance, economic growth theories disregard the political and social issues from the theoretical framework by rendering them as constant, and they tend to reduce the theoretical scope merely to the quantifiable criteria of economic accumulation. In the case of neoclassical theory, an extremely reductionist tendency is evident in its interpretation of society as a collection of fragmented and detached individuals. For Friedman, in a free exchange economy, "society consists of a number of independent households" or "a collection of Robinson Crusoes."[31] Neoclassical theorists also exclude issues such as class structure, class conflict, and historical change from economic analysis.[32]

It has been mentioned that to claim the scientific status of their theory, neoclassical economists borrowed considerably from physical science while excluding the moral, political, and sociological realms from such a "scientific" inquiry.[33] In the case of Keynesian and post-Keynesian theories, the reductionist theoretical nature is inherent in their policy recommendations based on narrow economic rationality that largely exclude the relatively noneconomic issues from consideration. In general, all these theories of economic growth (i.e., classical, neoclassical, Keynesian, and post-Keynesian) tend to ignore important development-related issues—such as class and power structure, cultural and normative patterns, international economic structure, and exploitive process of underdevelopment—although these factors have significant implications for the pace of economic growth and decay in different countries.[34]

Modernization theories are also reductionist, which is evident in their parochial analytical units such as government structure (for political modernization theory) and individual behavior (for psychocultural theory); in their exclusion of historical factors (e.g., colonial legacy) and international structure (e.g., unequal exchange); and in their indifference toward important societal issues such as economic relations, power structure, and ethnicity.[35] Some of the original proponents of modernization theories, e.g., Durkheim and Weber, do not adequately address issues such as class structure and class conflict in society that constitute an essential component of the Marxian perspective.[36] Within the reformist tradition, development approaches such as employment generation, human resource development, and rural development are also quite narrow in terms of their indifference toward the question of income redistribution. Although some of the reformist theories (e.g., theories "redistribution-with-growth" and "redistribution-with-or-without-growth") highlight the issue of distribution, they hardly take into account the social and political origins and causes of income inequality, and disregard the reality of extreme inequality in international economic structure causing underdevelopment.[37] The NIEO strategies shifted the attention from internal inequality within each Third World country to international inequality between the rich and poor countries,[38] but they remained relatively indifferent toward the issue of internal class structure, and toward the historical formation and politico-economic foundation of such unequal international structure.

Although classical Marxists take into account these internal class relations and international capitalist structure, their reductionist tendency lies in their interpretation of the political and cultural spheres as reflections of the forces and relations of production, and in their inadequate attention to issues such as gender, race, and ethnicity.[39] Although Marx stressed the reality of class domination and class struggle, he did not show equal concern for human subjugation based on these criteria of gender, race, and ethnicity.[40] In addition, for Marx, although the forces of production (material being) exist independent of human will (consciousness), it is the former which determines the latter.[41] Most Marxian analyses tend to ignore the roles played by conscious individuals in social transformation. Marx himself deemphasized the critical roles of individuals and considered them as the "personifications of economic categories, embodiments of particular class-relations and class-interests."[42] Similar reductionist tendency can be found among the proponents of neo-Marxist perspectives. For instance, the MOP school has been blamed for its propensity to overlook factors such as political structure, class relations, and the role of the state, although these issues are seriously taken into consideration by the class analysis approach. However, both the MOP school and class analysis approach tend to exclude the spheres of ideology, culture, and ethnicity, or they portray these dimensions as the reflections of the modes and relations of production.[43]

The reductionist inclinations also exist in dependency theories, because while they focus on the economic basis of dependence and underdevelopment such as the world capitalist system based on unequal exchange, they tend to ignore the role of other factors in the perpetuation of dependence, such as class structure, dominant ideology, and the state apparatus.[44] This relatively narrow focus of dependency theories on the economic dimension of the world capitalist system fails to examine the existing multiple modes of production and diverse social formations in Third World countries, and ignores crucial differences among these countries in terms of internal economic, political, and social structures.[45] In addition, like other theoretical frameworks discussed above, the proponents of dependency theories overlook the structures of domination based on gender, race, and ethnicity that exist in many of these countries.

This common reductionist tendency in most development theories is problematic, because the question of development and underdevelopment is not just a matter of impersonal market forces, production relations, government institutions, and structures of international exchange emphasized in various degrees by these theories. The process of development is also a matter of social, political, and ideological struggles,[46] a matter of ethnic identity, cultural sovereignty, and gender equality. However, it should be pointed out that the degree of reductionist inclination varies among different theories: while the conservative theories of economic growth and modernization are highly reductionist in terms of their tendency to have an extremely narrow focus on a single factor (social or economic or political), the Marxian and neo-Marxian theories of social progress are less reductionist due to their attempts to incorporate issues such as colonial history, precapitalist social formation, class structure, state apparatus, and international political economy.

EUROCENTRIC ETHNOCENTRISM

In addition to the aforementioned epistemological, normative, and analytical shortcomings, there is also the problem of ethnocentrism in the existing development theories[47] largely based on a Eurocentric worldview. Among the proponents of economic growth theories, the theoretical focus of Adam Smith, Ricardo, Malthus, and Mill was mainly on the emerging industrial capitalism in Western Europe, they had very little to say about the economic realities in non-Western societies such as China and India.[48] Adam Smith sequenced the stages of development from hunting (native tribes) to pasturage (Tartars and Arabs) to agriculture (medieval Western Europe) to commerce (contemporary Europe).[49] Such a ranking of different societies in terms of their positions in the hierarchy of social progress is culture-bound, and there is an inherent Eurocentric bias in this ranking.

In addition, the basic principles of both classical and neoclassical theories of economic growth, such as rational human nature, utility maximization, division of labor, and market competition, do not often represent the realities in Third World countries. The "new growth" theory not only believes in most of these Western classical and neoclassical principles, it also recommends Third World countries to imitate any new knowledge and technological innovation brought about by Western nations and corporations. Similarly, economic growth theories related to Third World development, such as Rostow's stages-of-growth theory, also suffer from Eurocentric predispositions.

For Rostow, Third World countries are at a lower stage of evolution than the West, and they have to pass through the stages of development that Western countries experienced in the past.[50]

The Eurocentric bias is quite evident in modernization theories in terms of their analytical frameworks that not only portray Third World countries as "traditional" and Western nations as "modern," but also suggest that Third World governments should modernize their societies by emulating the economic, political, cultural, and technological features of advanced Western nations.[51] The early scholars related to modernization theories held various forms of Eurocentric prejudices.[52] It has been pointed out that Durkheim described non-European peoples as "barbarous" in terms of their physiognomic features, Max Weber described Asian people as greedy, and Parsons allegedly considered the achievements of the Chinese empire as failures.[53] These early theorists explained societies in terms of various schemes of sociohistorical evolution, and in general they had a strong tendency to identify Third World societies at the lower ranks and Western societies at the higher or more advanced stages of development.[54] Thus, Hansen and So conclude that the concepts and theories of modernization represent European evolutionary theory.[55] The more recent proponents of political modernization have also been considered by many scholars as ethnocentric and prejudiced toward the Western worldview.[56] Thus, in his analysis of modernization theories, Preston mentions that "the 'modern' is the image of the West in general and the USA in particular writ large."[57]

Eurocentric tendency also exists in Marxian theories, which can be traced back to the Hegelian roots of these theories. For Hegel, human history involves a transition from the ancient Orient to modern Europe, and for Marx, Western Europe represented the future image of the world.[58] The Eurocentric bias led Marx to conclude that "Indian society has no history at all, at least no known history."[59] In fact, Marx's works seem to have endorsed the Europeanization of Third World countries through colonial intervention.[60] The followers of Marx, including Luxemburg, Bukharin, Kautsky, and Lenin, concluded that "there would appear in the post-colonial period new capitalist societies relatively similar to those in Western Europe."[61] Thus, there are scholars who attack the Marxist tradition for its Eurocentric predilections.[62] Similarly, under the neo-Marxist perspective, the MOP school considers changes toward the Western form of capitalism as progressive, while alluding the existence of the precapitalist modes as an indicator of underdevelopment in Third World countries. Although the class analysis perspective recognizes the historical role of the peasants and various coalitions among contradictory classes in Third World countries, they still follow Marxian ideas and categories, such as capitalism, class structure, and production relations, which were constructed largely in reference to Western societies.

Although the reformist development models attempt to address Third World concerns, they still remain biased toward the Eurocentric view of human development. For instance, Paul Streeten, a proponent of basic-needs approach, uses Rostow's stages of growth theory to explain how after meeting certain basic needs through land reform and investment in education, some countries (e.g., Taiwan and Korea) laid the runway for the future take-off and economic growth.[63] It implies that one of the central concerns of the basic-needs approach is to set a take-off stage as described by Rostow, whose Eurocentric theoretical framework (mentioned above) suggests that the final stage of Third World development has to be similar to the stage already reached by Western nations. Similarly, although the proponents of the NIEO attempts to focus on how to reduce Western hegemony by establishing more equal international trade and exchange, they are not free from Eurocentric bias, because they want to enhance development in Third World countries by reproducing the Western model in these countries.[64] In this regard, it has been observed that "the idea of a new international economic order is, itself, a profoundly western idea. It has been advanced and rationalized by western-trained leaders in developing countries."[65] Even the proponents of dependency theories tend to be Eurocentric in their theoretical formulations that consider the Western mode of capitalism as a sign of development and its absence in Third World countries as underdevelopment. It is true that they are against Third World dependence on the global capitalist system dominated by the West, but their suggested development model or framework is based on a Eurocentric view of development.[66] More specifically, their exemplars for autonomous economic progress in peripheral countries are still Western industrial societies. As Manzo points out, "The opposition of metropolis/satellite [in dependency theories] might have replaced that of modern/traditional [in modernization theories] but it was still the first of these terms, associated with the West, that was superior."[67]

The above Eurocentric outlook inherent in the major development theories is quite misleading because, in opposition to the evolutionist interpretation of Western superiority and Third World backwardness, historically the technological and intellectual achievements in many precolonial Third World countries were significant, and such achievements were comparable to those in Western nations.[68] In fact, the levels of scientific and technological progress in precolonial Third World societies such as China and India were more advanced, and they were often borrowed and adopted by Western countries during the centuries of colonial rule.[69] The historical process of Western progress cannot be reproduced in Third World countries, because it is not feasible for these countries to repeat the history of Western colonial exploitation and accumulation that considerably accounted for such Western progress.[70] In addition, it is almost impossible to transform all societies in the image of the Western world, because there are so much diversity among them in terms of their social, economic, political, cultural, intellectual, and attitudinal features.[71] Thus, some scholars conclude that the very assumption of a unilinear, inevitable, and irreversible Western pattern of social change in all societies has been proven hollow.[72]

UNFOUNDED UNIVERSALISM

Despite the aforementioned Eurocentric biases in the existing development theories and models, there is a tendency among development scholars to claim the universal validity and applicability of these theories and models.[73] For instance, it was assumed by most classical theorists of economic growth that the "colonial economies were simply an extension of metropolitan economies. . . . One set of principles, one theory should suffice for all."[74] The neoclassical theorists have similar tendency to claim universalism. Among the original proponents of neoclassical theory, Bentham asserted that "all human motivation, in all times and all places, can be reduced to a single principle: the desire to maximize utility."[75] In addition, the claim of theoretical universalism made by both the classical and neoclassical theorists of economic growth—including Adam Smith, Malthus, Ricardo, J.S. Mill, Bentham, Bastiat, Menger, Walras, and Friedman— is inherent in their endeavor to idolize, imitate, compare, and adopt the principles, methods, and status of physical science that are often considered universal.[76] Such universalist inclinations have also influenced the subsequent theories of economic growth, including the Keynesian and post-Keynesian theories, "new growth" models, and reformist theories discussed in the previous chapters.

On the other hand, underlying all modernization theories, there is a common assumption that the features of Western societies are universally adoptable, especially in Third World countries. For example, Emile Durkheim attempts to define the task of social science as investigating social facts like natural objects in order to produce universal scientific explanations. Talcott Parsons describes the idea of rationality as a universal category. Gabriel Almond considers the process of enlightenment and democratization as inevitable in Asia, Africa, and Latin America.[77] Similarly, the universal applicability of Western political systems is assumed by modernization theorists such as Martin Lipset, Karl Deutsch, David Apter, and Edward Shils.[78]

Within the radical tradition, the claim for universalism is quite significant among classical Marxists interested in discovering the universal laws of sociohistorical change and development.[79] For Marx, Engels, and their followers, the principles of dialectical and historical materialism, the stages of social change, and the basic modes of production and corresponding patterns of class structure and class conflict, are valid for all societies.[80] For Marx and Engels, despite the existence of certain politico-economic variations such as the Asiatic mode of production, all societies are subject to the universal and irreversible stages of historical development such as slavery, feudalism, capitalism, and socialism.[81] The universalist tendency is also evident in Engels' claim that after the discovery of the "materialistic conception of history" and "secret of capitalistic production" by Marx, "socialism became a science."[82] The belief in the universal applicability of Marxism became so strong that the subsequent classical Marxists became hesitant to tolerate any deviation from the original interpretations of Marx.[83] Such a Marxian assumption of universalism tends to discount the unique sociohistorical circumstances that exist, especially in Third World countries.

The neo-Marxist theories take into account the unique social formations in Third World countries such as the coexistence of multiple modes of production. But they also have universalist inclinations in terms of their application of common Marxian concepts and formulations, especially the rigid Marxian classification of various modes of production, to all Third World societies irrespective of their cross-national variations. In studying these postcolonial societies, the proponents of class analysis perspective recognize such cross-national differences with regard to the varying modes of production, the role and composition of the state, and the relationship between the state apparatus and social classes, but they still have the problem of relying on common conceptual categories (e.g., capitalism, class structure, proletariat, bourgeoisie) that largely emerged in the unique sociohistorical context of advanced capitalist nations rather than Third World countries. Thus, despite the use of these basic terms by neo-

Marxist scholars to analyze Third World phenomena, they are more relevant to Western capitalist nations and have less universal validity. Finally, among the proponents of dependency theory, the tendency to claim universalism is quite evident in their basic assumption that all societies and nations operate within, and thus reflect, the world capitalist system. Such an assumption tends to discount the cross-national variations in the modes of production, class structures, political systems, and cultural patterns.[84]

This tendency of development theories to claim universal validity and applicability represents a major intellectual flaw in the development field. First, in terms of knowledge construction, it is necessary to recognize that the process of constructing knowledge is conditioned by the specific social contexts of intellectuals, and the validity of knowledge is often relative to the belief systems in various communities.[85] It is also necessary to understand that the mode of thinking is influenced by the existing dominant ideology, the relevance and legitimacy of knowledge often depends on the nature of class and power structures, and the choice of methodology is affected by various cultural and biographical factors.[86] Thus, with regard to the nature of social science in the U.S., Gareau mentions that American social science is culture-bound, inward looking, and sectarian rather than neutral and universal.[87] In short, due to the varying contextual factors that affect intellectuals who construct knowledge, it is not possible to produce any universally valid knowledge. Therefore, the claim of universal validity made by any field of knowledge, including the development field, is not sustainable.

Second, in terms of knowledge application, the context-bound nature of human knowledge makes it almost impossible to apply the same knowledge to all societies and get similar outcomes. In other words, the knowledge produced in one societal context may be practically ineffective, even detrimental, in other societies with different sets of economic features, political institutions, and cultural beliefs. With regard to the development field, thus, the application of development knowledge produced by Western scholars may have adverse implications for Third World countries. At a more applied policy level, Korten's study of community organizations in India, Sri Lanka, Bangladesh, Thailand, and the Philippines shows that the universalistic "blueprint approach" to development was proven to be a hindrance rather than help to the process of rural development in these countries.[88] Thus, development scholars and experts, who formulate or apply development theories and models, should not claim that there are universal ideas, principles, processes, methods, and laws of development.[89]

Adverse Implications of Current Development Thinking

The above theoretical shortcomings in the development field have serious implications for practical development outcomes, because development theories and models provide the policy guidelines to political leaders and government officials who formulate and implement various development programs and projects. Directly or indirectly, the aforementioned theoretical limitations in the development field have led to the perpetuation of various adverse societal conditions related to development, which include critical issues such as the expansion of intellectual hegemony, legitimation of politico-economic domination, erosion of indigenous culture and identity, deterioration of environmental problems, and perpetuation of a distorted form of development. These adverse practical scenarios of development are often reinforced, if not created, by the theoretical problems of development discussed above. This section attempts to explain how such theoretical problems are related to various practical crises of development mentioned below.

PERPETUATION OF INTELLECTUAL HEGEMONY

In terms of impact on thinking, some of the theoretical shortcomings in the development field have considerable implications for the maintenance of intellectual hegemony between various academic disciplines, between experts and the people, and between different nations. In general, in the academic sphere, there is a common tendency to professionalize and standardize knowledge, specialize disciplinary boundaries, simplify social issues into measurable criteria, and reject alternative viewpoints.[90] This is a tendency of analytical reductionism discussed above. In the development field, there is such a reductionist tendency toward professionalization, specialization, and oversimplification, which leads to a form of intellectual hegemony among various disciplines dealing with issues related to development. For instance, the development field has a tendency to emphasize a narrow, economistic view of development, which has created a strong belief in the superiority of economics over other social science disciplines, especially due to the reductionist mathematical mode of knowledge in economics that often claims a higher level of precision and objectivity.[91] This superiority claim of an economistic view of development is also due to another theoretical shortcoming in the development field: a belief in the possibility of universal scientific knowledge that does not recognize the context-bound nature of knowledge (discussed above).

Since this belief in universalism is more compatible with the mainstream economics than other disciplines, such as sociology, political science, and cultural studies, it tends to reinforce and justify the intellectual dominance of economics. The dominance of this economistic view is not only due to these theoretical tendencies (analytical reductionism and universality claim) in the development field, it is also due to a more practical fact that the major national and international development institutions, which shape the mission and direction of development policies and programs, are largely managed by economists trained in the principles of classical, neoclassical, Keynesian, and post-Keynesian economics. This academic dominance of economics in development studies often leads to a parochial view of development and to the misunderstanding of development problems that are inseparable from various noneconomic issues.

The reductionist tendency and universalist claims of development theories also tend to rationalize and perpetuate the dominance of development experts over the nonexpert people.[92] In advanced capitalist nations, a strong belief in the universality of scientific knowledge often reinforced the dominance of elite technicians and scientists over the ordinary people, and the scientific and technological advancements facilitated the exploitation of the working class.[93] In Third World countries, the implication of reductionist development knowledge for the power of development experts is more serious because, due to a very low rate of literacy, the common people can hardly comprehend the expert knowledge and technical language of development. According to Goulet, these development experts are "one-eyed giants" who often claim the universal validity of development knowledge that legitimizes their knowledge-power and expands the intellectual subordination of the common masses.[94]

At the international level, the mainstream development knowledge has often played a considerable role in the legitimization of intellectual hegemony of advanced capitalist nations over Third World countries. In this regard, Moore explains how the centuries of colonial conquest and the neocolonial role of the media contributed to the very formation of the concepts of development and underdevelopment.[95] The dominance of Western knowledge in the development field represents an overall tendency to impose and disseminate Western social sciences all over the world, and yet consider such a process natural and desirable.[96] It has been pointed out that American sociology has come to dominate world sociology, and development economics has often advocated the Western patterns of social change in Third World countries.[97] In line with the overall structure of international intellectual hegemony, most development studies are characterized by the dominance of Western academics or the Westernized Third World intelligentsia, major development books and journals are published by Western publishers and universities, and intensive development debates have taken place mostly among Western or Westernized scholars.[98]

Although this hegemonic global structure of knowledge may have led to a "diploma disease" and intellectual "fossilization" in Third World countries,[99] it has often served the interests of people attached to the management of development studies and practices. It has been observed that the whole development enterprise has become a big business: it serves the interests of international development experts, financiers, and technocrats who are engaged in advising, financing, and influencing various Third World regimes to pursue certain development policies and programs.[100] But as Harrod suggests, these "development experts and advisors [themselves] were never personally responsible for, nor materially affected by, the policies they advocated."[101]

LEGITIMATION OF POLITICO-ECONOMIC DOMINANCE

In addition to the perpetuation of intellectual hegemony, the existing development thinking also has implications for the legitimation of practical domination and inequality between classes and between nations, which often results from certain theoretical shortcomings in the development field, such as its empiricist tendency, Eurocentric bias, and rhetoric of universalism. In fact, the mainstream social science as a whole has been accused of legitimizing such domination.[102] For instance, in the case of sociology, Witton mentions that in the past, the discipline "has typically served as a handmaiden to the domination of imperialist over colonised, rich over poor, urban over rural, male over female, and strong over weak."[103] Similarly, the founding fathers of economics are accused of codifying "their observations in a form that fitted well with the ambitions of the emerging interests: they offered a 'scientific' foundation to the political design of the new dominant class."[104] With regard to the studies in development, Nandy has a more extreme view that "development too has become a new reason of state in many societies. Today, hundreds of thousands of citizens can be legitimately killed or maimed or jailed in the name of development."[105]

Beyond internal class domination, the Eurocentric view of development plays a significant role in rationalizing various forms of international subjugation and dependence. It has been observed that historically, the colonially inherited social sciences, especially anthropology, introduced an evolutionist and Eurocentric view of social progress that held the assumption of Western superiority, and implied the colonial intervention in Third World countries as a justifiable act.[106] Even the radical thinker like Marx, who advocated the eradication of subjugation and exploitation, considered colonial intervention a progressive act to civilize the "barbarians" of the East by the "civilized" West.[107] As indicated by Ramirez-Faria, it is the Eurocentric view of progress that influenced Marx and Engels to endorse the British colonial intervention in India to play the historical role in social transformation.[108]

In the contemporary epoch, the idea of Third World development in the image of the West "provided the basic ideology for the formulation of aid and other policies in the United States and many of her partners in the Cold War."[109] According to Addo, the Eurocentric view of development, which tends to undermine the image of non-European societies and characterize them as underdeveloped, has significant implications for the perpetuation of Western dominance over the world system.[110] The critics of the existing development thinking often consider developmentalism as an ideology of neoimperialism and instrument of neocolonial subjugation.[111] For Murphy, the process of development, involving various national and international institutions, itself constitutes a superstructure of global capitalism, which preserves the international economic system, encourages Third World regimes to maintain the flow of resources to capitalist nations, strengthens the power of the privileged groups in Third World countries, and discourages these countries from pursuing their own autonomous or self-reliant development.[112]

One major economic implication of the Eurocentric view and universalist claims of development is for the expansion of external debt and dependence. It is because such a view of development impels Third World regimes to transform their societies in the image of Western nations, and this expensive development model often encourages these regimes to borrow the missing components (e.g., capital and technology) from advanced industrial nations.[113] As a result, in most Third World countries, the experience of this genre of development has been inseparable from the burden of foreign debt and dependence.[114]

Some development theories have come under criticism for their direct relations with the structure of international hegemony. For instance, modernization theory has been characterized as an ideological instrument of the U.S. against the socialist influence on Third World countries.[115] Gendzier suggests that the proponents of modernization theories, including Almond, Verba, Huntington, Pye, Shils, and Lerner, offered the interpretations of social change that were compatible with the expansion of Western capitalism.[116] However, it is the Eurocentric view of the world based on the assumption of Western superiority[117] that influenced these modernization theorists to interpret social change and development in line with such Western dominance. More recently, this bias led modernization theorists such as Huntington to offer a post–Cold War interpretation of world order, which predicts an alliance between the Islamic and Confucian civilizations, portrays such an alliance as a threat to Western civilization, and prescribes various measures to preserve and expand Western domination worldwide.[118]

EROSION OF INDIGENOUS CULTURE AND IDENTITY

The aforementioned theoretical limitations of development theories and models adopted by Third World countries have serious implications for the erosion of indigenous culture in these countries. It is because these mainstream development theories and models are predominantly empiricist (implying their indifference toward the subjective dimension of culture), reductionist (implying their overemphasis on economic factors while neglecting cultural concerns), and Eurocentric (implying their preference of Western cultural beliefs over Third World cultures). These theoretical flaws in the development field, especially its insensitivity to the cultural reality and diversity, often lead to the endorsement of the globalization of Western culture. This hegemonic process of cultural transformation is variously known as the Europeanization, Westernization, or Americanization of knowledge and life-forms.[119]

The global development endeavor tends to create "one world," and "calls for absorbing the differences in the world into an ahistorical and delocalized universalism of European origin. The unity of the world is realized through its Westernization."[120] For instance, the common formula of development prescribed by modernization theories is that "modernization = Westernization = progress."[121] Even for Marx, "The [Western] bourgeoisie, by the rapid improvement of all instruments of production, by the immensely facilitated means of communication, draws all, even the most barbarian, nations into civilisation."[122] Other theoretical traditions are similarly prejudiced by Western cultural predilections. Thus, it has been observed by some scholars that the contemporary development enterprise is counterproductive to the indigenous cultures of Third World countries, subversive of their cultural identity, and conducive to their cultural recolonization by the affluent nations.[123] According to Sachs, "From the very start, development's hidden agenda was nothing else than the Westernization of the world."[124] This challenge to cultural identity posed by the existing development thinking has been expressed by the author in the following words:

> The result [of development] has been a tremendous loss of diversity. . . . The mental space in which people dream and act is largely occupied today by Western imagery. The vast furrows of cultural monoculture left behind are, as in all monocultures, both barren and dangerous. They have eliminated the innumerable varieties of being human and have turned the world into a place deprived of adventure and surprise; the "Other" has vanished with development.[125]

Despite this concern that the wholesale Westernization of societies is likely to destroy cultural diversity, there is an increasing tendency toward "cultural indoctrination" through the dissemination of Western education and corporate values in the name of "universal" education.[126] As a result of such global homogenization, various languages and cultures are disappearing,[127] and increasingly the non-Western cultures are being transformed into Western cultural forms based on the "borrowed consciousness."[128] Due to such destructive cultural processes, the "entire conceptions of what it means to be human have evaporated during the development decades since 1950."[129] On the other hand, this loss of cultural identity has weakened the self-confidence of Third World people, weakened their intention to resist subjugation, and made them vulnerable to external exploitation.[130]

It has been suggested that Western cultural norms and values are not often compatible with non-Western (e.g., Islamic, Confucian, Japanese, Hindu, or Buddhist) cultures.[131] As a result, the endeavor to culturally modernize (Westernize) Third World societies has failed, and created a cultural dilemma: "The old ways have been smashed, the new ways are not viable. People are caught in the deadlock of development . . . they are forced to get by in the no-man's-land between tradition and modernity."[132] In the process of such cultural confusion, reinforced by the aforementioned loss of cultural identity, there has emerged in Third World countries a new breed of educated elite, who adore foreign (Western) lifestyle, consume imported goods, accumulate money in foreign banks, and eventually migrate to foreign countries. As a result, each year Third World countries lose a considerable amount of financial and human resources. However, the desire of Third World elites for Western goods, education, and lifestyle is not isolated from their attitudinal changes brought about by the above process of cultural subjugation based on the Eurocentric assumption of Western superiority,[133] which is a common assumption underlying most development theories and policies.

ECOLOGICAL AND ENVIRONMENTAL DISASTERS

The mainstream development thinking has considerable adverse implications for various forms of environmental and ecological predicaments, especially due to its reductionist focus on economic progress that encourages the mindless expansion of industrialization and production of goods based on excessive exploitation of nature. It is now being recognized that the industrial civilization has largely been responsible for environmental disorders such as global warming, ozone-layer depletion, deforestation, groundwater decline, soil erosion, sea-level rise, and so on. Between the 1850s and early 1980s, nearly 140 billion tons of carbon dioxide was released by burning fossil fuel.[134] Every year about 1,000 new ozone-destroying industrial chemicals are introduced, and their production increased from 7 million tons in 1950 to 250 million tons in 1985.[135]

This environmentally harmful industrial production is related to the fetish of consumerism in affluent societies, which is based on the assumption that it is a rational option for individuals to increase their satisfaction by maximizing the level of consumption. Despite the adverse environmental outcomes of consumerism, it represents an essential component of the contemporary development thinking: one of the basic indicators of development is often considered to be the level of consumption in a country. Today the so-called developed countries account for only 20 percent of the world population but they consume 70 percent of the world's energy and 75 percent of its metals; and the U.S. represents less than 6 percent of the world's population, but it consumes 40 percent of the world's natural resources.[136] With regard to the relationship between excessive consumption and environmental destruction, Shridath Ramphal mentions that "the question of consumption is central to the environmental crisis. It is the human impact that is endangering the planet's capacity to sustain life."[137]

At a more philosophical level, these tendencies toward overproduction and overconsumption are related to certain dominant assumptions of progress, including beliefs such as hedonistic utilitarianism, individualistic competition, and instrumental rationality. For instance, in capitalist market economies, the utilitarian desire for accumulation to maximize material satisfaction, and individualistic competition involved in this accumulation process, often lead to endless struggle among various capitalist forces to exploit natural resources (soils, minerals, forests, water resources), which eventually results in ecological and environmental degradation.[138] On the other hand, instrumental to this utilitarian desire for accumulation is the belief in scientific knowledge as a means to dominate and exploit nature: science is considered instrumental to the acceleration of production and accumulation, although it often leads to the production of environmentally detrimental commodities.[139] In fact, behind the history of modernity, there has been a strong human intention to transform reality into an object of technical control and to enhance mastery over nature.[140]

Thus, the dominant mode of development thinking—based on the assumptions such as industrialism, consumerism, utilitarianism, individualism, and scientism—has not been that conducive to natural environment and ecology. Despite the recent recognition of this problem, there is not much of a hope to rectify the situation. Because, in the name of economic progress, there has been an unprecedented intervention and expansion of transnational corporations in the recently reformed promarket economies in Asia, Africa, Latin America, and Eastern Europe, and these corporations are motivated not only due to cheaper labor but also due to lower environmental requirements in these regions.[141] This transnational corporate intervention, together with the recent global upsurge of commercial media, is likely to expand and strengthen the belief in utilitarian consumerism in different parts of the world, which is not very encouraging for the future of environmental and ecological conditions.

DEVELOPMENT FAILURES AND DISTORTED DEVELOPMENT

The decades of development endeavor seem to have produced many distorted rather than balanced socioeconomic outcomes in different parts of the world. In this regard, Korten mentions that during the 1980s, it was recognized that the world was replete with profound crises such as "dehumanizing poverty, collapsing ecological systems, and deeply stressed social structures."[142] In many Asian, African, and Latin American countries, there are worsening conditions of poverty, food crisis, unemployment, hunger, inequality, political repression, external debt, and dependence.[143] According to Hancock, "in the name of progress, lives have been destroyed in virtually every country of the Third World."[144]

In the case of the so-called success stories, including the advanced capitalist nations and the newly industrialized countries, the economic achievements have been overshadowed by various noneconomic catastrophes. Behind these stories of achievement and success often propagated by media, there have been serious catastrophic outcomes such as the marginalization of the poor, destruction of culture and family bonds, sacrifice of environments, and fragmentation of social solidarity.[145] Certain economic consequences have been quite disastrous even in affluent countries such as the U.S. where in the 1980s more than 35 million people lived below the poverty line, 20 million were hungry, 30 percent of employed workers earned wages below the poverty level, and 22.2 percent of children were living in poverty.[146] In terms of income distribution, it was found that in the U.S., the top 0.5 percent household owned over 45 percent of the privately held wealth, the top 10 percent owned more than 86 percent of all financial assets, and less than 1 percent of all corporations controlled nearly 67 percent of corporate assets.[147]

In these so-called developed countries, such a coexistence of economic affluence with various social, cultural, and environmental disorders represents a distorted form of development. In these countries, economic wealth coexists with inequality and class-based poverty, industrial expansion with environmental catastrophes, scientific achievements with nuclear threats, individual freedom with weakening community bonds, and so on. In addition, whatever achievements these countries have made are inseparable from the past colonial means of accumulation and the contemporary structure of hegemonic world economic order, which cost Third World countries in terms of perpetual underdevelopment. However, Third World countries continue to follow these advanced capitalist nations as the role models for their own development activities. This expensive but distorted model of development has encouraged Third World countries to embrace foreign assistance, which has expanded Third World debt and dependence.[148] As Gregory mentions, policies based on Western development model "are often the cause of underdevelopment rather than development, i.e., they cause poverty rather than eliminate it."[149]

In many Third World countries, the current reality of unbalanced development is predominantly due to the imitation of Western development model by Third World regimes. According to Goulet, "The mainstream development models exported by the West to Africa,

Asia and Latin America are flawed in their very roots—they are vitiated *in radice*."[150] Thus, there are critical development scholars who feel that Third World countries need to establish alternative development frameworks, because the dominant Western model of development has not been compatible with their own economic, political, and cultural contexts; because this dominant model itself is under challenge due to the current disorders in Western societies; and because the contemporary Third World development has been an inappropriate development serving the interests of Third World elites and transnational corporations.[151]

Newly Emerging Challenges to the Development Field

In addition to the existing theoretical and practical problems discussed above, there are various newly emerging challenges to the development field. In the past, the mainstream development theories and models—especially the classical, neoclassical, and Keynesian theories, and their revised versions such as the theory of unbalanced growth, stages-of-growth theory, and vicious circle theory—came under attack. In response, the parochial focus of these theories on economic growth and accumulation was broadened in the subsequent theories and approaches, ranging from basic needs approach and new international economic order to dependency theory and neo-Marxist perspective, which seriously took into consideration issues such as inequality, external debt, trade dependence, unequal exchange, and international hegemony.[152] These theoretical improvements made in the 1960s and 1970s, however, have almost been reversed since the early 1980s due to the contemporary rise of promarket forces and the replacement of state-centered approach by a market-centered approach to development.[153] Since the traditional models of development have been predominantly state-centered, the recent endorsement and expansion of "free market" principles reflect a "counter-revolution" in development thinking.[154]

This current theoretical transition has been identified as a shift toward the neoclassical model, which largely represents the theoretical basis of promarket policies adopted under the so-called structural adjustment programs. These market-oriented policies and programs based on neoclassical perspective assume the superiority of market forces over the public sector, accuse public enterprises of causing economic crises, advocate deregulation and privatization, prescribe the reorientation of the public sector based on market principles, and redefine the role of the state merely as a guarantor of private property and money supply.[155] With regard to the neoclassical origin of the current market-driven development in Third World nations, Smith makes the following observation:

> The dominant ideology of the decade, neo-classical economics, had a major impact on less developed countries in the 1980s. The state and national development planning were rejected as economically inefficient. In their place the free market was embraced through deregulation, privatization, and budget cuts.[156]

In the process of reviving and reinforcing the neoclassical model of development in Third World countries, the international development agencies or institutions have played considerable roles. For instance, the World Bank has not only shifted its own theoretical position from the earlier state-centered, neo-Keynesian model to this market-oriented neoclassical model, it has also imposed this model on Third World countries through structural adjustment programs as conditionalities for receiving loans.[157]

Such a theoretical reversal in the modes of development pursued by Third World countries has serious theoretical and practical impacts. In terms of *theoretical implications*, the development field has become extremely reductionist, especially due to the neoclassical theoretical principles underlying promarket reforms that overemphasize "the atomistic interaction of self-seeking individuals" while rejecting the crucial role of institutions such as the state.[158] In addition to this bias toward individualism, the neoclassical basis of market-oriented structural adjustment programs is reductionist also due to its narrow economistic focus that fails to consider the social, political, and cultural dimensions of development. Furthermore, the reductionist tendency of these neoclassicist, promarket reforms is inherent in their relative indifference toward environmental and ecological costs (e.g., air and water pollution, global warming, ozone-layer depletion, land desertification, soil erosion) of economic production and growth.[159] Even in pure economic terms, the structural adjustment policies consider mainly the criteria of efficiency, productivity, and growth but ignore other crucial economic issues such as income distribution, class structure, external dependence, and unequal exchange, which are central concerns of other theoretical traditions such as the NIEO, dependency theory, and neo-Marxian class analysis.[160]

Despite these theoretical limitations, the neoclassical arguments in favor of promarket reforms have reached almost an ideological status in the sense that these bourgeois reforms are being endorsed and adopted worldwide without much rational judgment and critical evaluation. Thus, regarding this dominant promarket model, Clements mentions that the model "fetishizes the role of market forces, reifies the 'invisible hand' and rests on a spurious assumption that the market will cure all evils."[161] Similarly, for Helleiner, the "ideology of individualism" and the "magic of marketplace" are being imposed on Third World countries by the conservative political forces through various international agencies such as the World Bank.[162] However, this conversion of neoclassical principles (underlying promarket policies) into a global ideology is not conducive to the contemporary developmental challenges faced by these countries. In this regard, Stein concludes that the neoclassical root of structural adjustment programs is ill-equipped to meet the future economic concerns in Third World nations, especially in Africa.[163]

In terms of *practical implications*, the recent theoretical shift toward the market model has adversely affected certain important dimensions of Third World development. In the past, the state-centered development models, despite many of their negative outcomes, did make some favorable contributions in many Third World countries.[164] For instance, in the 1960s and 1970s, the planned economic policies led to the reduction of poverty in Latin America, generation of employment in Asia and Africa, and expansion of literacy in most low-income countries.[165] But these achievements are overlooked by the proponents of contemporary promarket reforms which, in opposition to their claims of economic performance made by these reforms, have failed to show any significant improvement in the condition of Third World underdevelopment. For instance, during the prime period of promarket reforms between 1980 and 1992, the number of people in poverty increased from 136 million to 266 million in Latin America, and in terms of percentage, the number of poor increased from 41 to 62 percent of the total population in the region.[166] In the case of Africa, in the early 1990s, the average per capita income dropped to the level of income in the 1960s, and between 1980 and 1990, the average annual growth rate declined from 3.2 to 1.1 percent.[167]

The reversal of development framework toward the market forces has also adverse implications for inequality and dependence. It is because the parochial focus of this market model primarily on economic growth and efficiency is quite inadequate to address the problems of income inequality and unequal class relations. Under the market-centered development perspective, most governments appear to be so committed to market-based efficiency and growth that their responsibilities for people's basic needs have been forgotten, which is quite evident in the recent cutbacks in health, education, housing, and social security.[168] On the other hand, the interclass domination has expanded under the promarket policies of privatization, because while such policies favor big businesses and strengthen the power of organized capital, they tend to drain capital from small producers, weaken trade unions, and depress the wages and living standards of the working class.[169]

Similarly, at the international level, the overemphasis on the neoclassical development model and corresponding promarket policies is likely to expand inequality and dominance between advanced capitalist nations and Third World countries. One indicator of such inequality is the continuity of Third World debt. Despite the prevalent advocacy of the market miracle, during the period of promarket reforms, the external debt of most Third World countries has increased rather than diminished.[170] In fact, it was this burden of external debt that made Third World countries vulnerable to international pressure to accept the conditionalities of structural adjustment policies such as privatization, deregulation, and liberalization. The Western banks used the so-called debt-equity swaps to influence the highly indebted Third World countries, such as those in Latin America, to privatize their essential public assets and then buy them at low prices.[171] Thus, the promarket policies of structural adjustment have significantly expanded the opportunities for Western transnational corporations to own valuable assets in Third World countries.[172] In other words, structural adjustment programs have not only expanded income inequality in Third World nations, they have also led to the transfer of resources from Third World countries to advanced capitalist nations.[173] This new genre of foreign ownership has serious economic implications for Third World countries in terms of diminishing their self-reliance, expanding their external dependence, and increasing the dominance of foreign capital over their national economies.

Despite the aforementioned theoretical limitations and adverse practical implications of the current market-centered development model, apparently it has acquired worldwide endorsement. The overwhelming support for this promarket development framework is not only due to its fetishization into an ideology, but also due to the vested national and international interests benefiting from such a market-oriented policy stance. It has been observed that in general, policies such as privatization, deregulation, and liberalization have served the interests of institutional investors, merchant bankers, business executives, and professionals like accountants and lawyers.[174] More importantly, the Third World's promarket policies have benefited transnational corporations by facilitating their access to privatized assets, and by assuring them minimal environmental standards and lower labor costs.[175]

According to Martin (1993), these policies have also benefited foreign experts and advisers who provided consultancy for promarket reforms and received contracts (especially with international financial institutions) worth hundreds of millions of dollars.[176] The point here is that the recent worldwide transition in development thinking toward the principles and forces of market may have benefited the national and international promarket forces, but such a transition has often been adopted at the expense of certain adverse developmental outcomes discussed above. As Berthoud mentions, the current tendency to "impose market mechanisms and principles on a global scale" is conducive to those who "devote themselves to making economic profit," but it is pursued "at the expense of the whole gamut of social and moral obligations."[177]

Conclusion

The above critique of contemporary development theories and policies suggests that in most cases, the overall consequence of the development field has been a distorted form of development. Theoretically, the field has produced various development approaches and models that suffer from certain major intellectual shortcomings such as epistemological empiricism, analytical reductionism, normative indifference, Western ethnocentrism, and unsubstantiated universalism. On the other hand, in terms of practical outcomes, the development field has various adverse implications, including the perpetuation of academic hegemony, legitimation of socioeconomic domination, erosion of indigenous culture and identity, and destruction of environment and ecology. It has been explained that in recent years, these theoretical and practical problems of the development field have worsened further due to the reversal or redirection of development priorities toward the mission of economic growth based on market forces.

It has also been discussed that theoretically, the narrow focus of conservative economic-growth theories was overcome to a certain extent by another set of theoretical frameworks such as the basic needs approach, NIEO, dependency perspective, and neo-Marxian analysis, which addressed issues such as poverty, inequality, exchange, and dependence.[178] Although these relatively new categories of theories or approaches themselves suffer from different forms of parochial tendencies discussed above, they made certain theoretical improvements in terms of their inclusion of these essential but hitherto left-out issues such as income inequality, unequal exchange, and external dependence. However, these theoretical improvements have almost been reversed due to the recent revival of neoclassical economic principles underlying the current promarket reforms (including the so-called stabilization and structural adjustment programs), although this neoclassical position is extremely reductionist in terms of its narrow analytical focus on individualistic economic productivity and efficiency, and its relative indifference toward political, cultural, and environmental issues. Similarly, the practical implications of these promarket reforms have been quite adverse for many Third World countries in terms of their worsening conditions of poverty, inequality, external debt, and dependence.

However, what is more disturbing is the fact that under the influence of promarket thinking, most Third World countries have not only withdrawn or compromised their grievances against extreme inequality in world economic order, they have also given consent to such hegemonic economic structure, especially under the pressure of international institutions.[179] In fact, the critical development debate has been replaced by the conservative concerns for economic growth based on neoclassical economic tools that are often advocated by economic experts and managers attached to large multinational banks, international aid agencies, consultancy firms, and regional financial institutions.[180] Even the traditional development economics, which eventually recognized the importance of socioeconomic issues beyond economic growth, has almost been rendered obsolete by the advocates of promarket reforms.[181] Regarding the newly emerging development ethos based on the principles of market competition, Esteva suggests that such a promarket ethos is likely to destroy what was achieved during the last three decades, and it may lead to the restructuring of societies to adapt with transnational structures and cope with market demands.[182]

In short, based on the above analysis, it can be concluded that while the mainstream development theories and policies already have serious theoretical limitations (e.g., reductionism, empiricism, and ethnocentrism) and adverse practical implications (e.g., interclass inequality, global hegemony, and environmental disorder), the contemporary redirection of these theories and policies based on the fetish of market forces is likely to worsen such theoretical and practical problems further. Thus, in order to overcome the existing and newly emerging problems faced by the development field, there is a serious need for introducing a basic restructuring of development theories and policies. The remaining chapters in the book are devoted to the realization of this task.

CHAPTER 8

Restructuring Concepts and Theories of Development

The previous chapters were engaged in analyzing the major traditions of development theories, examining their intellectual shortcomings and practical problems, and exploring their contemporary challenges. After such a theoretical analysis and critique, this chapter is devoted to the restructuring of development theories into an alternative development perspective. However, it should be mentioned that some scholars have already made certain contributions to the rethinking of development. For instance, there have been shifts in development thinking from a binary scheme (developed-underdeveloped) to a multilinear framework, from a mechanical approach to an innovative and interdisciplinary approach, and from the usual economistic view to a more sociological outlook.[1] There is also growing interest in discovering the "African way," "Chinese way," or "Indian way" of understanding development.[2] There has also emerged a certain degree of optimism that Third World intelligentsia would be able to de-Westernize development thinking and introduce new concepts, ideas, and tools.[3]

Despite these signs of increasing intellectual awareness about the need for rethinking development, there have rarely been any serious intellectual attempts to redefine development and restructure development theory in a more fundamental and comprehensive manner.[4] As Nieuwenhuijze mentions, the legacies of previous approaches still exist in the current reorientations of development and continue to inhibit the formulation of an entirely new approach.[5] Moreover, whatever improvements were made in rethinking development by incorporating historical, social, and cultural dimensions, they have recently come under challenge. As discussed in the previous chapter, there has been a setback in development thinking since the late 1970s due to the worldwide proliferation of promarket policies (e.g., deregulation, privatization, liberalization, and foreign investment), the return of economistic interpretations, the demise of sociocultural considerations, and the delegitimation of development concerns for the less privileged masses. The earlier development issues—related to the eradication of poverty and hunger, reduction in interclass and international inequality, and liberation of Third World countries from the hegemonic world powers—are in eclipse in the current epoch.

In this intellectual and practical context, there is a need for a more rigorous, critical rethinking of development. In this regard, the main objective of this chapter is to introduce a theoretical reconstruction in order to overcome the limitations of the existing development theories discussed in the earlier chapters. To transcend any form of intellectual parochialism, this theoretical restructuring would encompass the following: the major dimensions (economic, political, cultural, ideological, and intellectual) of society and their interactive confluence; the diverse structures or analytical units (group, class, state, and international system) and their interrelationships; and various modes (natural-physiological, politico-economic, and cultural-intellectual) and levels (national and international) of human subjugation and human autonomy. The main thrust of this theoretical restructuring is on the fact that in the ultimate analysis, a genuine development involves the realization of human autonomy from these various modes or forms of subjugation that exist within and between nations (discussed below). This attempt to restructure development theory, however, requires a clear understanding of development as a concept. Thus, the first section is devoted to redefine development in line with the essence of human autonomy and to outline the major dimensions of such a liberating view of development.

Redefining Development as a Concept

For some development scholars, there cannot be a fixed and final definition of development, and the conceptual plurality of development itself is a strength rather than a weakness.[6] For managing such conceptual plurality, others have classified various definitions of development into different categories.[7] However, since the 1970s, there has been a growing concern for the ambiguous, vaguely defined, and controversial nature of development as a concept.[8] In recent years, with the additional definitions and redefinitions of development and other related terms, this conceptual controversy has multiplied further. Among these additional concepts, some are quite well known: such as the idea of "sustainable development," which implies the need-satisfaction of the present generation without compromising that of future generations; "authentic development," which refers to the full realization of human capabilities; and "maldevelopment," which means the achievement of economic growth at the expense of repression and authoritarianism.[9] With regard to this conceptual ambiguity and diversity, Sachs mentions that "development has become an amoeba-like concept, shapeless but ineradicable. Its contours are so blurred that it denotes nothing."[10]

In general, however, the meaning of development varies depending on whether it is articulated within the conservative, the reformist, or the radical theoretical tradition (see chapters 4, 5, and 6). Without delving into the detailed illustrations of the endless definitions of development accumulated for decades and centuries, one can derive the major categories of development concepts from the above theoretical traditions of development. In the conservative tradition, development is understood in terms of increased economic production, consumption, and accumulation; further social differentiation, adaptation, and integration; more political stability, participation, and institutionalization; or enhanced psychological orientation toward entrepreneurship and achievement. In the reformist tradition, on the other hand, development is perceived in terms of higher economic growth with some degree of redistribution, more equality in the structures of international trade and finance, or further improvement in international economic dependence. Finally, in the radical tradition, development is construed in terms of progressive changes in the forces and relations of production, freedom from all forms of class exploitation, the realization of a classless society, or the liberation of peripheral nations from the world capitalist system.

However, as discussed in the previous chapter, these prevailing views of development remain predominantly empiricist, reductionist, deterministic, and culturally biased. In addition, inherent in the existing development concepts is a common assumption that development always involves a change toward a more desirable stage of society. The final stage is variously construed as the capitalist stage, socialist stage, industrial stage, postindustrial stage, information stage, and so on. Such teleological views of development encourage and justify various forms of ideological hegemony because, in the name of actualizing the final stage of development, the dominant groups, classes, and nations often impose hegemonic economic, political, cultural policies. Once the idea of development is institutionalized as the attainment of certain ultimate social stage (e.g., capitalism and socialism), it becomes an ideological instrument of subjugation. To avoid such a tendency, in the proposed redefinition, development is not construed as the "confirmation" or approximation of universal laws to reach a predetermined social stage prescribed by external agents: development is understood rather as the "negation" of or autonomy from all undesirable human conditions[11] experienced by various groups, classes, and nations through their active engagement in the process of social transformation.

These undesirable human conditions are the conditions of subjugation that exist in different spheres of society at both intra-national and international levels.[12] Some scholars have already emphasized that there must be an inherent theme in the concept of development that focuses on human autonomy from the structures of subjugation.[13] Thus, as already pointed out, while the existing concepts of development tend to perpetuate various forms of subjugation by portraying development as the "confirmation" of developmental laws to attain the prescribed higher stages of society, the proposed redefinition of development would encourage human autonomy by presenting development as the "negation" of any form of subjugation that exists in various realms of society. This human autonomy should be total rather than partial, it should be an autonomy from all forms of subjugation.[14]

More concretely, according to the proposed redefinition, *development connotes human autonomy from all forms of subjugation, including the natural-physiological subjugation, the politico-economic subjugation, and the cultural-intellectual subjugation,[15] which exist at various levels such as between individuals, between groups, between classes, and between nations.* When this autonomy from all three forms of subjugation at all levels of human encounter is not adequately realized, or when different forms of subjugation still exist in various degrees and combinations at different levels, such adverse human conditions can be defined alternatively as undevelopment, underdevelopment, partial development, and maldevelopment or distorted development. *Undevelopment* is a condition in which none of these three forms of human autonomy has been realized; *underdevelopment* is a condition in which these three forms of autonomy have been suppressed or retarded further; *partial development* is a condition in which some but not all forms of autonomy have been achieved; and *maldevelopment*, is a condition in which certain forms of autonomy have been attained in such a distorted manner that other forms of autonomy have been compromised or endangered.[16]

From the proposed conceptual framework, it is hardly possible to find any society which is developed in terms of all forms of human autonomy at all levels, or undeveloped without any form of autonomy at any level.[17] The common conditions are rather those of underdevelopment, partial development, and maldevelopment. The advanced capitalist and socialist countries represent mostly a form of partial development: while in capitalist countries, a significant degree of natural-physiological and cultural-intellectual autonomy has been achieved but without adequate politico-economic autonomy; in socialist countries, a certain extent of natural-physiological and politico-economic autonomy has been realized but often without much cultural-intellectual autonomy. The Newly Industrialized Countries (NICs) represent mostly the condition of maldevelopment, because most of them have attained some degree of natural-physiological autonomy often by subjecting themselves to politico-economic and cultural-intellectual subjugation at the international level.[18] In the poorer Third World countries, the condition is that of underdevelopment, because they have the worsening conditions of all three forms of subjugation at both national and international levels. All these points will become clearer as these various forms of subjugation and the corresponding modes of autonomy are discussed below in further detail.

HUMAN AUTONOMY FROM NATURAL-PHYSIOLOGICAL SUBJUGATION

In almost all societies, people not only receive the conducive forces of nature such as land, air, water, minerals, and various plant and animal species; they also encounter the detrimental forces of nature such as flood, drought, earthquake, unfavorable weather, and other natural calamities. In addition, they encounter their own physiological forces such as hunger, disease, aging, and so on. People continuously try to liberate themselves from the unintended dominance of natural forces: they observe and experience these natural forces, discover their common properties and patterns of interaction and change, utilize and transform the positive factors (resources) into capital and consumption goods, and manage or adapt with the adverse forces: thus, they satisfy their physiological needs and ensure their continual survival. The domain of these human activities related to production and adaptation involves the establishment and reestablishment of science, technology, and industry. However, underlying this whole process of production and adaptation through scientific, technological, and industrial activities, what is most fundamental is human labor, both physical and mental.[19] It is this human labor which is behind the discovery of scientific laws, manufacturing of technology, establishment of industry, cultivation of land, production of goods and services, prevention and cure of diseases, and so on. Thus, human labor remains the core component in the process of human autonomy from the aforementioned natural and physiological forces to which the human species is always subjected.

However, since the patterns of the aforementioned supportive and detrimental material forces of nature (e.g., soil conditions, water resources, mineral deposits, vegetation status, natural calamities) vary from one geographic region to another (e.g., from Western Europe to South Asia), the modes of human adaptation with and transformation of these natural forces, or simply the means and techniques of production, also differ.[20] In addition, the orientation of a society toward natural forces (whether it believes in the adjustment and coexistence with them or in the subjugation and exploitation of them)[21] also shapes the nature of its means, techniques, and knowledge of transformation (production) and adaptation. In short, due to the variations in the (objective) context of nature and (subjective) social attitude toward it, the appropriateness and choice of the means of production and the modes of adaptation vary from one society to another.[22] Moreover, within the same society, in the course of history, the patterns of natural forces change, human knowledge about them expands, the means of their transformation improve, and thus the overall mode of production (including both the means and relations of production) shifts from one epoch to another.

However, the existing and potential diversity in the natural formation and transformation of the modes of production was affected by the colonial and neocolonial intervention, which led to the subordination of all the precolonial patterns of production in Third World countries to Western capitalist structure, suppression of their autonomous process of historical changes, and the conversion of their relatively self-reliant production systems into dependent components of the global capitalist system. The modes of production that evolved in the core capitalist countries are relatively inappropriate and impossible for Third World countries, not only because of their abovementioned differences in natural context and mental constructs, but also because of their incapacity and historical impossibility to repeat the same global process of colonization, extraction of material and human resources from colonies, and enhancement of capital accumulation—

a process that significantly contributed to the emergence of Western capitalism.

In fact, Third World countries cannot even maintain the resources they currently have due to the prevailing unequal international structures of production and exchange, and it is mainly these uneven structures of production relations, consumption patterns, and exchange within and between nations, that have maintained the capitalist system. Even if such transformation of the world into an autonomous and homogeneous form of capitalist system is hypothetically possible, it is humanly undesirable, because the deadly competition within and between nations for maximizing profit (the essence of capitalism) would lead to the exhaustion all the world's resources and irreversible damage to environment and ecology. In this sense, the Western form of development can be considered a distorted form of development because, in the process of natural autonomy, excessive exploitation and abuse of nature has been introduced. As Nasr mentions, "There is nearly total disequilibrium between modern man and nature as attested by nearly every expression of modern civilization which seeks to offer a challenge to nature rather than to cooperate with it."[23]

In short, the Western form of autonomous and advanced capitalist development in all Third World countries, prescribed by conservative development theories, anticipated by classical Marxism, and sought by dependency theories, is not only unrealistic, it is also less desirable from environmental and ecological perspectives. Such a capitalist framework of human autonomy from nature has increasingly proven detrimental to the whole human species as it may eventually lead to more vulnerability to natural catastrophes. The continuous craving for such development has brought some fragmented and dependent form of capitalist development, or simply maldevelopment, in various NICs. But a worldwide or large-scale capitalist transformation, perhaps, would remain unrealized.

HUMAN AUTONOMY FROM POLITICO-ECONOMIC SUBJUGATION

The second dimension of development is autonomy from all forms of politico-economic subjugation[24] that exist within and between nations. *Intranationally*, within each society, there are dominant social groups and classes which, by dint of their ownership and control over various means of production and sources of power (e.g., land, capital, technology, weapons, information, and expertise), exercise subjugation over other groups and classes. Such structure of the dominant and dominated classes prevails not only in Third World countries,[25] it also exists in advanced capitalist nations. This internal condition of politico-economic subjugation is often described as "internal colonialism."[26]

However, there is a diversity in the nature of interclass subjugation in different societies, because this subjugation is primarily based on the ownership of the means of production, and the patterns of such ownership vary from one society to another. As discussed above, the variations in the forces of nature and social attitudes toward them lead to differences in the means and processes of transforming or adjusting with such natural forces through varying modes of production—this diversity in the modes of production implies variations in class formation, state structure, and the patterns of economic and political subjugation. In addition to this internal subjugation based on unequal relationships between classes, between the class and the state, and between the state and society, there are other forms of internal subjugation based on gender, race, religion, and caste, which are usually discounted by the conservative and radical theories of development. In other words, politico-economic subjugation is not only exercised by the ruling class over other classes and by the authoritarian state over society at large, such subjugation is also practiced by the male over female, by the dominant race over other races, by the upper caste over lower castes, and by the dominant religious community over other religious groups.[27]

Moreover, in opposition to the reductionist interpretations of politico-economic subjugation, the situation is much more complex in most societies. The common denominator of male dominance focused by most feminist groups usually ignores the fact that in general, white women hold more power than black men in South Africa, upper-caste women have more power than lower-caste men in India, and the upper-class women have more power than the lower-class men in most societies. On the other hand, the class analysis approaches fail to recognize the reality of subjugation based on race, gender, caste, and religion within the same social class. For instance, women are usually subordinated to men within each class, each race, each caste, and each religious group. In reality, one may discover that these various forms of politico-economic subjugation may coincide and perpetuate each other. For example, in the U.S., it is usually the upper-class, white, and male persons who have more power, although class identity is more determining than race and gender in such capitalist societies. In India, it is the upper-caste, upper-class, and male individuals who dominate, although caste identity remains the most crucial factor. In South Africa, it is white, upper-class, and male persons who dominate, although racial identity is most important (this has not changed much even in the post-apartheid period due to continuity in the extremely unequal patterns of ownership). These are some examples of how politico-economic subjugation may vary across nations depending on their class, race, gender, caste, and religious compositions.

These differences in the politico-economic structures of subjugation are also reflected in the varying composition of the state in different countries. This dimension is largely absent in the Western conservative theories of development and liberal theories of the state that overemphasize the state as a homogeneous unit of analysis. In reality, it is usually the dominant class, dominant race, dominant gender, and dominant caste which hold the state power. There are also the cases of compromise, as reflected in the case of Malaysia where economic power is mostly held by the upper-class Chinese, and the state power is exercised predominantly by the upper-class Malays. In general, however, the nature of this interaction between political power and economic power depends on factors such as the dominant mode of production, the extent of capitalist development, ideological predisposition, colonial background, and so on. For instance, it is more likely that political power is determined by economic power in advanced capitalist nations, economic power is dependent upon political power in socialist countries, and both political power and economic power are subsumed within the state apparatus in Third World societies.

All these dimensions of internal politico-economic subjugation, although requiring more rigorous research and analysis, are presented here in general terms to make a point that there exist various forms of such subjugation, which vary according to the sociohistorical contexts, are irreducible to a simple class analysis, and thus require more adequate means or mechanisms to achieve autonomy from such subjugation. Be that as it may, this human autonomy from politico-economic subjugation is an essential component in the realization of development. From this perspective, many economically advanced Western societies, although they have achieved a significant degree of autonomy from the adverse forces of nature, are not genuinely developed, since there is a considerable extent of politico-economic subjugation exercised by the dominant class, race, and gender in these societies.

Similarly, at the *international level*, because of the ownership of and control over various means of power, including finance capital, military weapons, and international trade, Western nations dominated Third World countries economically and politically during the colonial and postcolonial periods.[28] According to Galtung, the U.S. has economic, political, military, social, and cultural dominance over the Caribbean, Latin America, and Southeast Asia; the European Community (now European Union) exercises economic, political, social, and cultural subjugation over most African countries, the Caribbean, and the Pacific; Japan has economic dominance over East and Southeast Asia; and the former Soviet Union used to exercise political, military, and social subjugation over Eastern European countries.[29]

The economic dimension of this international subjugation is easily discernible by the extent of control exercised by transnational corporations over Third World economies.[30] Although these corporations have branches or units located in Third World countries, the origin of their capital and the final destination of their surplus remain to the advanced industrial nations. For example, the main headquarters of the world's 161 largest food firms are located in the U.S., Japan, Canada, and Western European countries.[31] This uneven international economic structure leads to unequal exchange between the poor and rich countries.[32]

Politically, it is well known that Third World countries are under significant Western military subjugation, which has become more intensive and monopolistic after the demise of the Cold War that virtually eliminated any major challenge to Western military power. Within this global context, the achievement of some material prosperity in terms of higher economic growth by few NICs basically represents a form of "maldevelopment" mentioned above, because such economic growth has often been achieved at the expense of international politico-economic subordination and cultural-intellectual dependence (discussed below). In most Third World countries, however, the condition is that of "underdevelopment," because in addition to their experiences of worsening material conditions such as hunger, malnutrition, and natural disasters, they are also subject to similar politico-economic and cultural-intellectual subjugation exercised by advanced capitalist nations.

HUMAN AUTONOMY FROM CULTURAL-INTELLECTUAL SUBJUGATION

The third dimension of development is the autonomy of various social groups, classes, and nations from different forms of cultural-intellectual subjugation exercised by the dominant group, class, and nation. Beyond the aforementioned natural-physiological and politico-economic spheres, human subjugation also exists in various cultural, ideological, and intellectual activities. However, these superstructural activities have considerable impacts on the process of human cognition, and thereby, on the nature and composition of material production and social structure. As O'Manique and Pollock point out, the nonmaterial aspects of development coexist with the material ones, they "inform them, give them identity and life, and thereby form an essential part of the whole development process."[33]

The cultural-intellectual aspects of development are not universal, they vary in content and implications depending on their construction by and identity with particular groups, classes, and nations. However, a dominant group, class, or nation tends to impose its own culture, ideology, and knowledge on others, and thereby create intergroup, interclass, or international subjugation in these spheres.[34] For an adequate concept of development, it is necessary not only to emphasize human autonomy from natural-physiological and politico-economic subjugation, but also to stress autonomy from this cultural-intellectual subjugation. For Ghosh, such cultural-intellectual subjugation is maintained intranationally by the privileged social elites and globally through a hierarchical international structure.[35]

Internally, in most societies, cultural-intellectual subjugation is inherent in the process of ideological indoctrination and intellectual manipulation, particularly through educational institutions.[36] According to Garnham, being detached from the purpose of human liberation, the academics in the social science disciplines often exercise intellectual influence and use symbolic means to establish subjugation.[37] In economics, for instance, the depersonalization of real human needs and their conversion into abstract ideas of utility and market forces by economic experts[38] become the means of intellectual subjugation over those who rarely understand such jargons. However, as Ramos points out, the most effective weapons for "cognitive politics" today are the press, radio, and television that shape the people's understanding of reality.[39] In advanced Western nations, various forms of privately owned and profit-oriented mass media have become all-pervasive in society,[40] and they are extensively used by the rich and powerful to instill their dominant views among the common masses. As Dixon mentions, through mass-media indoctrination, U.S. citizens have been kept ignorant by the state about the true nature and role of the U.S. government and its policies.[41] In fact, the U.S. journalists (associated with various news media) themselves carry the established cultural and ideological biases inherited from their past socialization, education, and professional training, which they tend to inject into the news.[42]

However, cultural-intellectual subjugation is more effective at the *international level*. Historically, such subjugation was created during the centuries of Western colonialism by expanding missionary activities, instilling Western lifestyles among Third World elites, and replacing Third World educational institutions by Western educational systems.[43] About the past and present reality of such Western cultural-intellectual subjugation, a French author (G. Gusdorf) makes the following comment:

> In the colonial period, the Western nations projected their systems of values on all overseas territories where their flag flew, and on which they grafted their culture, language, economics and religion. . . . This absurd situation continues today; the European nations, having folded their flags, continue to export their ideologies artificially applied to local conditions.[44]

Today the most effective means of international subjugation in the cultural-intellectual sphere are different forms of mass media owned and controlled by the leading Western nations.[45] The extensive penetration of global media and culture industries (including radio broadcasts, television programs, books, periodicals, newspapers, magazines, films, commercial sports, and advertisements) into Third World societies has expanded the cultural hegemony of these Western nations.[46] Through their worldwide networks, these all-encompassing global media are transnationalizing Western culture, eroding the distinctiveness of other societies and cultures, and ushering the emergence of a "transnational ideology" based on Western economic and developmental beliefs.[47]

In the academic sphere, there also exists the dominance of Western knowledge in educational institutions, especially universities, in Third World countries. More recently, some Western scholars themselves have begun to point out this intellectual hegemony or "imperialism" of advanced capitalist nations over poor countries, particularly, in the area of development theory and research.[48] Historically, it is not only the Western philosophy of positivism that has dominated the institutional symbols and education systems in Third World countries,[49] according to some scholars, even Western mathematics, commonly considered as the most universal and culture-free knowledge, has caused cultural invasion in these countries.[50] With regard to such subjugation in the academic realm, Hettne suggests that Latin American universities symbolized the beginnings of colonial hegemony, Asian universities represented the consolidation and reproduction of such colonial influence, and African universities marked the eclipse of this overt colonial subjugation and its transformation into a neocolonial form.[51]

For Alatas, Third World academics have a "captive mind," which implies their uncritical imitation of Western thought, their alienation from indigenous social issues, their incapacity to separate the universal from the particular, and their unconsciousness of this captive condition as such.[52] For the realization of authentic development, human autonomy from this cultural-intellectual subjugation is essential. In fact, in the current epoch, such cultural-intellectual autonomy has also become an important prerequisite for natural-physiological and politico-economic autonomy (discussed later in this chapter).

In this section, it has been emphasized that for genuine human development, it is imperative to realize all three modes of autonomy from the three corresponding forms of subjugation, including the natural-physiological, the politico-economic, and the cultural-intellectual. Although these three forms of human subjugation and the corresponding modes of human autonomy—broadly representing the basic realms or dimensions of development—have been presented above separately, there is continuous interaction or confluence among these dimensions at both intranational and international levels, and the nature of such interaction changes in different epochs and varies from one sociohistorical context to another. A proper explanation of the nature of such relationships among these realms of development is a function of development theory. Thus, in the remaining chapter, the linkages among these major dimensions of development (i.e., various forms and levels of subjugation and autonomy) are presented in propositional forms, and these propositions together would represent the proposed theoretical restructuring of development thinking.

Restructuring Development Theories

It has already been pointed out that the aforementioned three forms of human subjugation and the corresponding three modes of human autonomy are mutually confluential. However, these forms of subjugation and modes of autonomy are interrelated not simply on the basis of unidimensional cause-effect relations as assumed by mainstream development theories. It may be recalled that the conservative theories of development emphasize the expansion of economic production, accumulation, and consumption based on continuous scientific and industrial advancements: this dimension implies mainly the need for human autonomy from natural and physiological forces. But these theories tend to overlook the significance of human autonomy from politico-economic and cultural-intellectual subjugation that exists within and between nations. On the other hand, although the radical theories of development (including the Marxian, neo-Marxian, and dependency theories) emphasize human autonomy from politico-economic subjugation, they tend to ignore the importance of cultural-intellectual autonomy and relegate this to a secondary status of the so-called superstructure.

Differing from such relatively reductionist nature of the existing theoretical frameworks, the main thrust of the proposed theoretical restructuring is that these three forms of subjugation and autonomy are interactive or interrelated, and the nature of these interrelationships is diverse rather than universal, particularly because of the variations in sociohistorical contexts. More specifically, in different societies and different epochs, various groups and classes of people experience various degrees of natural-physiological subjugation, politico-economic subjugation, and cultural-intellectual subjugation at both intranational and international levels, and they engage themselves in alternative modes of emancipatory activities, depending on which form and level of subjugation they consider most primary in relation to other forms and levels. However, it is possible that an inappropriate alternative might be adopted due to the misleading perception and identification of which form and level of subjugation are most crucial in a given sociohistorical context. In addition, in a certain context, human autonomy from one form and level of subjugation may enhance or weaken the potential for autonomy from other forms and levels of subjugation. In this regard, certain basic theoretical propositions—which constitute the proposed restructuring of development theories—are presented below to delineate the nature of interrelationships between the three major forms of human subjugation and human autonomy at both intranational and international levels.

Proposition 1: *The process of human autonomy from natural-physiological subjugation may lead to the emergence of politico-economic subjugation, and even cultural-intellectual subjugation. If pursued in a distorted manner, the process of natural-physiological autonomy itself may even create new form(s) of natural-physiological subjugation. Thus, the choice of the mode of natural-physiological autonomy is a crucial factor.*

As discussed above, in most ancient societies, people encountered various unfavorable forces and events of nature (such as flood,
earthquake, typhoon, drought, and adverse climate) that often
endangered their lives and constrained the fulfillment of their basic
physiological needs, and thus threatened their survival. Although
there were supportive natural conditions or endowments (such as
water resources, fertile cultivable lands, mineral deposits, and
various plant and animal species) as well, most of them had to be
utilized and converted into useful products or consumption goods.
Human incapacity to manage the adverse forces and utilize the
supportive factors of nature could be attributed mainly to the lack of
advanced technology, skill, and other means of production (except
rudimentary tools and techniques) at the beginning of civilization.
Paradoxically, this relative lack of the means of production in prehis-
toric societies, which caused the excessive dominance of natural
forces over human life, was also the reason why there was a relative
absence of politico-economic subjugation based on the unequal ownership of the means of production as found in contemporary societies.

However, throughout history, the constant endeavor or struggle
for realizing human autonomy from the dominance of natural forces
led to the planned and organized use of human labor, the discovery
and invention of various factors and means of production (e.g., land,
capital, and technology), and thereby the production of various agricultural and industrial goods for final consumption. In this process of
reducing human vulnerability to or increasing human autonomy
from the forces of nature, there emerged unequal ownership of the
factors and means of production by various classes and nations,
which constituted the structural basis of subjugation among these
classes and nations. However, in the course of time, the continuous
advancements in the quality and composition of such means of
production brought about fundamental changes in the historical
formation of these structures of subjugation—e.g., from slavery to
feudalism to capitalism. Thus, the emergence of the means of production, which enhanced human autonomy from natural-physiological
subjugation exerted by the forces of nature, paradoxically became the
means of politico-economic subjugation exercised by the dominant
class and nation. In addition to unequal ownership of the means of
production, the dominant class(es) and nation(s) also introduced
various means of coercion or threat, including all forms of lethal
weapons and technologies, to expand and reinforce the structure of
politico-economic subjugation further. In other words, the scientific
and technological means of production that enhanced autonomy of

human species from natural-physiological forces (e.g., from natural disaster, hunger, and disease), also became the means of politico-economic subjugation, and in different forms (e.g., nuclear weapons), even became the means of threatening human existence as such.[53]

Moreover, the very scientific and technological endeavor that led to continuous upgrading of the means of production to enhance human autonomy from the forces of nature, also inspired and facilitated advancements in the techniques and equipments used for cultural-intellectual subjugation, including modern technologies and electronic equipments for mass media owned and used by the dominant social groups, classes, and nations. The modernization of media-related technologies has significant implications for expanding inter-class and international subjugation in the cultural, ideological, and intellectual spheres. Even the technologies used for material production and consumption have cultural identities, and thus are not free from certain cultural implications, especially when they are transferred from one society to another. In this regard, it has been pointed out that "the Third World imports technologies and along with these technologies come new behaviour patterns, norms, values and systems of human relations."[54] In short, the very process of scientific and technological innovations, which enhanced human autonomy from natural and physiological forces, also led to the emergence and ownership of various means of production, coercion, communication, and information, which in turn accelerated politico-economic and cultural-intellectual subjugation, internally by the landlords and industrialists over peasants and workers, and internationally by advanced Western nations over Third World countries.[55]

On the other hand, although technological and industrial production contributed considerably to human mastery over natural forces in the past, in recent years, its all-pervasive expansion has created other forms of human vulnerability to nature. For instance, the overproduction and overconsumption of modern industrial goods, such as automobiles, refrigerators, air conditioners, chemicals, pesticides, cosmetics, and nuclear weapons, have caused environmental and ecological disasters, and thereby have increased human insecurity to more detrimental forces of nature or natural calamities. It is undeniable that the scientific, technological, and industrial activities helped increase human protection against unfavorable natural and physiological forces. But in their modern distorted forms based on the capitalist greed for endless production, accumulation, and consumption, such activities have led to the overuse of environmentally and ecologically detrimental substances causing disorders such as air and water pollution, greenhouse effect, sea-level rise and flood, land degradation, acid rain, and ozone-layer depletion.

These catastrophic changes in nature also have significant implications for the eventual human incapacity to resolve physiological problems such as hunger and diseases—because these disorders in nature lead to a decline in food production (caused by drought and flood), the contamination of human atmosphere (caused by air and water pollution), the weakening of human immune system (caused by ozone layer depletion), and so on. In addition, the excessive use and exploitation of nonrenewable natural resources implies that they will be in short supply for future generations. Thus, the eventual outcome of such a deviant mode of human autonomy from the dominance of natural forces through excessive production and consumption may well be the self-subjugation of the whole human species to these forces taking more catastrophic forms. From the above illustrations, it can be concluded that the mode of natural-physiological autonomy based on scientific, technological, and industrial production should be such that in the process, it does not worsen politico-economic subjugation by creating extremely unequal ownership of means of production, exacerbate cultural-intellectual subjugation by facilitating the invention of technologies used for cultural and intellectual hegemony, and reinforce natural-physiological subjugation itself by aggravating disorders in nature.

Proposition 2: *In the process of historical changes, politico-economic subjugation may lead to both natural-physiological subjugation and cultural-intellectual subjugation. In this case, human autonomy in the politico-economic realm becomes a precondition for such autonomy in the natural-physiological and cultural-intellectual spheres.*

First, politico-economic subjugation has significant implications for perpetuating human subjugation to natural and physiological forces discussed above. More specifically, various forms of intergroup, interclass, and international subjugation that exist in the politico-economic realm often thwart the scientific and technological progress of the subjugated groups, classes, or nations; inhibit advancements in their production systems; and thereby reinforce their dependence on or powerlessness to such natural and physiological forces. Due to the unequal ownership and management of the means of production and exchange by the dominant classes (e.g., the landlords, industrialists, corporate elites, higher civil servants, and top military officials) and affluent nations (e.g., America, Britain, France, Germany, and Japan), the subordinate and underprivileged classes (e.g., the landless peasants, industrial workers, and unemployed labor force) and nations (mostly Third World countries) have very little command over the processes of production, distribution, exchange, and surplus. As a result, the subjugated classes and nations are quite helpless in dealing with certain natural and physiological conditions such as flood, drought, hunger, and malnutrition, because they do not have much control over advanced technologies, factors of production, and exchange mechanisms that are essential for addressing such natural and physiological conditions.

The structure of politico-economic subjugation based on unequal ownership of the means and factors of production also has varying implications for different classes and nations in terms of their relative vulnerability to the aforementioned natural (environmental and ecological) disorders. While the affluent classes and nations are largely responsible for environmental and ecological predicaments resulting from their mindless production and excessive consumption of industrial goods, the poorer classes and nations suffer most from such natural catastrophes. Thus, toxic waste affects the health of urban underclass (often living in polluted neighborhoods) rather than high-income population in capitalist nations; and the greenhouse effect or global warming, which causes drought, leads to famine and hunger in Third World countries (especially those already with food scarcity) rather than in rich industrial nations. In other words, the poor and powerless classes and nations that encounter politico-economic subjugation are also more vulnerable to the dominance of the catastrophic forces of nature.

Even the potential opportunities of these underprivileged classes and nations for overcoming such dominance of natural and physiological forces through scientific and technological progress, have often been constrained by the structure of politico-economic subjugation. For instance, historically, through the politico-economic subjugation established under the colonial arrangements, the Western powers not only impoverished Third World countries economically, but also suppressed and retarded their progress in science and technology, and in many instances, dismantled their precolonial indigenous knowledge, skills, and technologies. Today, due to the uneven structure of international political economy characterized by unequal exchange, debt, and dependence, many Third World countries still continue to experience the process of scientific and technological underdevelopment, which constrains their autonomous and self-reliant progress in

science, technology, and industry, and thereby worsens their powerlessness to the vagaries of natural and physiological forces mentioned
above. From this brief analysis of how politico-economic subjugation
may perpetuate the subjugation of the subordinate classes and
nations to various natural and physiological forces, it can be concluded that the autonomy of these classes and nations from such
adverse natural and physiological conditions largely depends on their
politico-economic autonomy through the restructuring of the ownership of the means of production, distribution, and exchange.

Second, politico-economic subjugation also has serious implications for cultural-intellectual subjugation based on the ownership,
control, and use of various cultural, ideological, intellectual, and
informational means by the dominant classes and nations.[56] In this
regard, it has been mentioned by Miliband and Williams that in
advanced capitalist nations, the class which owns the means of
material production also controls the means of mental production,
including the press, cinema, radio, and television.[57] In the case of
Third World countries, it has been observed that the politically dominant classes have often used intellectual means such as development
theories and models to create "political mythologies."[58] How the
politico-economic dominance leads to such cultural-intellectual subjugation can be understood in more specific terms by examining the
monopolistic nature of control and ownership related to various
cultural-intellectual means.

While in most Third World countries, the state exercises control
over all major forms of mass media and education systems, at the
international level, it is usually the dominant Western corporations
or firms that own, control, produce, and distribute various means of
cultural, ideological, and intellectual products (e.g., book publishing,
news agencies, television networks, radio broadcasts, film industry,
and varieties of entertainment industries), and thereby exercise
cultural-intellectual subjugation at a global scale. In this regard,
Parenti points out that only ten American business and financial
corporations control the three major television networks (NBC, CBS,
and ABC), 201 cable TV systems, 34 subsidiary television stations,
62 radio stations, 20 record companies, 41 book publishers, 58 newspapers, 59 magazines, and various motion picture companies.[59]

Currently, international news is largely controlled by four Western
news agencies (AP, AFP, UPI, and Reuters) which, under the facade of
objectivity and impartiality, are often guided by their own political and
economic interests.[60] On the other hand, the major news-film agencies
dominating the world market include large companies such as CBS

News (U.S.), ABC News (U.S.), UPITN (U.K./U.S.), Visnews (U.K.), DPA-Etes (Germany), and so on.[61] Similarly, the massive industries of advertisement magazine and book publishing are dominated, both nationally and internationally, by American transnational corporations and firms.[62] In the U.S., about 95 percent of the markets for records and tapes is controlled by only five media conglomerates.[63] In recent years, this monopolistic tendency has been strengthened further by integrating different forms of mass media and cultural products and merging them with various corporations and companies.[64] In fact, many directors of television, newspaper, and radio are also partners or directors of banks, universities, insurance companies, and foundations.[65] For instance, in 1983, the Gannett Company (which owns 88 newspapers) shared directors with Standard Oil, Phillips Petroleum, McDonnell Douglas, Merrill Lynch, McGraw-Hill, Eastern Airlines, Kellog Company, and so on.[66]

The point here is that the extremely unequal ownership of and control over various means of cultural-intellectual subjugation are not isolated from the forms of unequal ownership and control that exist in the politico-economic realm of society. As Jhally rightly points out, although "culture cannot be reduced to mere economic factors, it cannot be understood either, without understanding the economic context that surrounds and shapes it."[67] In such a context, where the politico-economic power of the dominant classes and nations enables them to exercise subjugation in the cultural-intellectual sphere, it becomes essential for the subjugated classes and nations to achieve politico-economic autonomy in order to realize their cultural-intellectual autonomy.

Proposition 3: Human subjugation in the cultural-intellectual realm may perpetuate and expand subjugation in both the natural-physiological realm and politico-economic sphere. In this context, cultural-intellectual autonomy becomes a precondition for both natural-physiological and politico-economic autonomy.

First, the cultural-intellectual subjugation exercised by the certain group, class, and nation through the unequal ownership of and control over the abovementioned cultural and intellectual means may influence other groups, classes, and nations to imitate and import inappropriate technologies, abstain from indigenous scientific and technological innovations, and thereby perpetuate their vulnerability or subordination to various adverse forces of nature. More specifically, since many Third World leaders and policy-makers are influenced by Western culture, ideology, and knowledge through their upbringing, schooling, and media exposure, they tend to modernize their countries in the image of Western societies by borrowing Western capital, technology, and expertise. In most of these cases, however, such imitative processes of social change has led to the destruction of the indigenous technological foundation in many Third World countries, increased their external technological dependence, and weakened their initiative for technological innovation based on local needs and contexts. Eventually, it has perpetuated their technological backwardness, and thus diminished their capacity to encounter various cataclysmic forces of nature explained above.

Similarly, in the sphere of consumption, various means of global culture industry, such as television, films, advertisements, and tourism, have played a significant role in distorting the indigenous pattern of consumption and replacing it by the Western form of consumerism in many Third World countries.[68] For instance, by displaying the luxurious lifestyles of Western women in magazines and on television, transnational corporations often create demand among Third World women for Western products, ranging from contraceptives to cosmetics.[69] Similarly, while the global media have enabled McDonald's to establish 13,000 restaurants in 65 countries, and Coca Cola to sell 300 million Cokes per day in 155 countries,[70] the majority of Third World people do not have adequate food and drinking water. In short, Western cultural influence has changed the consumption patterns in Third World countries (especially among the elites) toward expensive foreign goods, and thus diverted their scarce resources from the provision of basic foods, education, housing, and health care for the common masses.[71] As a result, it has become increasingly difficult for the underprivileged Third World people to satisfy their basic physiological needs or to enhance their autonomy from physiological forces such as hunger. From the above analysis of various implications of cultural-intellectual subjugation—for reinforcing technological backwardness, and thus perpetuating human powerlessness to the forces of nature, and for displacing or distorting indigenous consumption patterns, and thus diminishing people's capacity to satisfy their physiological needs—it can be argued that for most Third World countries, an adequate degree of cultural-intellectual autonomy is a prerequisite for realizing their autonomy from these adverse natural and physiological forces.

Second, cultural-intellectual subjugation often leads to the expansion of politico-economic subjugation. For instance, the fetish for luxurious consumption patterns among Third World elites, often generated through various media, tends to perpetuate international politico-economic subjugation: because such consumption of imported Western products leads to the decline of domestic savings, underutilization of local resources, problem of balance-of-payment, and thereby further economic dependence of Third World countries.[72] In addition to the purchase of expensive consumption items propagated through global media, Third World elites import varieties of media hardwares (including audio-visual equipments such as television and VCR) and softwares (including news, films, music, and other entertainment programs), which also worsen their external economic dependence. In this process, while these global culture and information industries have increased employment in the U.S. by exporting cultural and informational products,[73] they have impoverished Third World economies to a certain extent. The U.S. sales of television programs to foreign broadcasters, and the revenues from the foreign sales of U.S. films, increased significantly in the 1980s.[74] In 1989, among the U.S. media companies, the overall sales of Time Warner amounted to $7.6 billion, Paramount $5.9 billion, ABC $5.1 billion, Walt Disney $4.7 billion, MCA $3.5 billion, and CBS $2.9 billion.[75] In the process of producing cultural goods, the profit from one particular cultural product does not end in itself, it is converted into or merged with other cultural products for more profits. For instance, films are often used to produce various imitation products such as toys, comics, and video games.[76] The point here is that the proliferation of Third World markets for Western cultural and informational products has led to the expansion of the Third World's economic dependence further.

The above means of information and culture not only facilitate the expansion of politico-economic subjugation over Third World countries, they also play a considerable role in legitimizing such subjugation.[77] For example, the U.S. media played a significant role to justify the invasion of Panama by creating a favorable public opinion to support such an invasion.[78] Similarly, although Western media created a liberating image of the U.S. army involved in the Gulf War, according to some scholars, the real concern was to protect Western economic interest in the supply of oil threatened by Iraq.[79] Such a role of Western media in legitimizing international subjugation has become more crucial in recent years, because the previous ideological pretext of such subjugation based on the anticommunist rhetoric, has become obsolete after the end of the Cold War.

Similarly, in the academic sphere, Western education has played important role in legitimizing both intranational and international politico-economic subjugation.[80] As a result, there has emerged the so-called movement of indigenization in various social science disciplines with a view to enhance liberation from the imperialist world system.[81] Briefly, what has been emphasized above is the role of different means and forms of cultural-intellectual hegemony in perpetuating human subjugation to adverse natural-physiological forces and unequal politico-economic structures. In this situation, cultural-intellectual autonomy is an essential prerequisite for encountering or addressing the adverse forces of nature, and for realizing the politico-economic autonomy of subjugated classes and nations.

Proposition 4: *Internal subjugation between classes or groups may lead to international subjugation between nations. Conversely, international subjugation may reinforce internal subjugation. Hence, human autonomy from internal subjugation is a precondition for autonomy from international subjugation, and vice versa.*

In the preceding section on the redefinition of development, it has already been elaborated that there are various dimensions (such as class, race, gender, caste, and religion) of internal and international subjugation. In the above propositions, this internal and international subjugation has also been discussed in examining the nature of relationship among the three major *forms* (natural-physiological, politico-economic, and cultural-intellectual) of such subjugation vis-à-vis the three corresponding modes of autonomy. However, the interaction between the internal and international *levels* of subjugation requires an independent analysis of its own, because the nature of this internal-international interaction is quite complex. This fourth proposition emphasizes this complicated nature of linkages between the internal and international levels of subjugation and between the corresponding levels of autonomy.

With regard to internal subjugation, the dominant ruling class, group, or power bloc exercises various modes of subjugation over the relatively weak or powerless classes or groups depending on the nature of social formation in a society. For instance, in advanced capitalist nations, the corporate elites exercise politico-economic subjugation based on their ownership of capital and direct or indirect control over the state, whereas in most Third World countries, it is primarily the military and bureaucratic elites who, based on their direct control over the state apparatus, impose similar forms of subjugation over the common masses. More importanlty, internal subjugation in advanced capitalist nations and that in Third World countries are interrelated, which is often reflected in various mechanisms and structures of international subjugation. The configuration of the structures of internal subjugation by these structures of international subjugation has been described as the "internalization of imperialism" by Evans, and as the "internalization of external interests" by Cardoso and Faletto.[82]

It is not always the total population of a powerful nation (e.g., the U.S.) that subjugates the total population of a weaker nation (e.g., the Philippines). It is often a few dominant groups or classes of certain dominant nations that, directly or indirectly, exercise different forms of hegemony over the common masses of the subjugated nations, and in between, the intermediary roles are played by the ruling classes or power blocs within the subjugated nations.[83] For instance, the corporate capitalist class of the U.S. had a certain degree of dominance over the common masses of South Korea and Taiwan facilitated by the South Korean and Taiwanese regimes.[84] The ruling political elites of the former USSR used to exercise power and dominance over the Vietnamese and Afghans through mediating roles played by the erstwhile ruling elites of Vietnam and Afghanistan. The central argument of this proposition is that various levels of subjugation—internal subjugation within the dominant (First World) nations, internal subjugation within the dominated (Third World) nations, and international subjugation between the dominant (First World) and the dominated (Third World) nations—are interlinked in a complex manner. These complex internal-external linkages of subjugation is implied in the following words of Bandyopadhyaya:

> The inequality and the relative poverty in the capitalist DCs [Developed Countries], the inequality and absolute mass poverty in most of the LDCs [Least Developed Countries], and inequality between the rich DCs of the North and the poor LDCs of the South, all seem to be not only structurally interlinked, but also causally connected.[85]

The reasons for the emergence of such internal-international structures of subjugation have been variously explained by different scholars. One common interpretation is that due to the falling rate of profit and the rise of organized labor in advanced capitalist countries, the industrial, business, and finance corporations of these countries (in alliance with their governments) have increasingly internationalized their capital[86] and expanded economic, military, and cultural interventions in Third World nations in order to acquire cheaper labor and raw materials, expand consumption markets for their products, and thereby accumulate more surplus. In addition to this global search for more surplus, there is increasing difficulty in legitimizing internal politico-economic subjugation within advanced capitalist countries due to the growing consciousness of their working class, which has also led to the externalization of such subjugation into Third World societies. Western transnational corporations are also attracted to Third World countries for their cheap natural resources, favorable tax situations, subsidized utilities, lax safety standards, and depoliticized and unorganized work force incapable of bargaining for higher wages.[87]

With regard to this international subjugation, however, the role played by the internal forces of subjugation within each Third World country cannot be discounted. Since many of the authoritarian Third World regimes, comprised of political, military, and bureaucratic elites, do not have much public support or legitimacy in their own countries, they tend to seek political, financial, and military support from the dominant global powers.[38] This creates a complementary relationship between the global economic and military powers that intend to exercise international subjugation over Third World societies and the Third World regimes that endorse such global powers in order to maintain their own internal subjugation in these societies. Thus, while in many newly independent nations, the ruling classes tend to practice "a brand of internal colonialism over their own people,"[89] such internal structure of subjugation can be meaningfully comprehended only in relation to the role played by external forces. These linkages between internal and external subjugation exists not only in the politico-economic sphere, but also in the cultural-intellectual realm.[90]

In short, the internal and international levels of subjugation are mutually interdependent, and therefore autonomy at one level of subjugation is difficult to achieve without simultaneous autonomy at another level. More specifically, since internal subjugation in many Third World countries is supportive to and maintained by various forms of international subjugation, it is necessary to address both internal and external dimensions of this hegemonic structure in order to ensure a more genuine autonomy of the common masses in these countries. The process of decolonization did not guarantee their complete autonomy from international subjugation. Internally, in many Third World societies, although the people's struggle for autonomy led to the emergence of certain popular governments based on elections, very soon these elected governments were replaced by more repressive regimes (usually through military interventions) that often served the interests of external powers. In fact, there are many instances which show that whenever African, Asian, and Latin American people protested against their repressive and corrupt regimes, the U.S. provided strong financial and military supports to such regimes, and whenever peoples were able to establish any popular governments, the U.S. dismantled them through economic blockade and military intervention.[91] Thus, a proper understanding of the role of international structures of subjugation in maintaining and reinforcing the internal structures of subjugation is essential in order to device strategies for interclass or intergroup autonomy within Third World societies.

Proposition 5: *The nature of interaction between the forms (natural-physiological, politico-economic, and cultural-intellectual) of subjugation and between the levels (internal and international) of subjugation are sociohistorically grounded: it differs from society to society and shifts from epoch to epoch. Therefore, the chosen modes of human autonomy, to be sociohistorically relevant and effective, must vary accordingly.*

In the existing theories of development, there is a reductionist tendency to exclude sociohistorical diversity in the forms of human subjugation and the modes of human autonomy. For instance, the conservative development theories emphasize mainly the physiological dimension of such autonomy (based on production and consumption) and the related scientific, technological, and industrial exploration and expansion. But they tend to exclude, or even legitimize, the politico-economic and cultural-intellectual subjugation that exists within and between societies. Similarly, the classical Marxist theories—although recognizing the changing nature of interaction between the forces and relations of production and between various social classes—stress the primacy of production forces over ideology and culture, while overlooking the possibility of a shift in this primacy from production forces to cultural and ideological superstructure. This theoretical perspective tends to overemphasize the internal composition of production and class structure, and even endorses external colonial intervention to accelerate changes in the internal modes of production in the colonies, although the contemporary neo-Marxist theories consider such intervention regressive rather than progressive for internal capitalist development.

On the other hand, dependency theories highlight the international structure of economic dependency and consider the global capitalist system as the main cause of Third World underdevelopment. But they tend to underestimate the structures of internal subjugation based on the coexistence and articulation of various modes of production and the corresponding class structures within Third World societies. They also have little concern for noneconomic (cultural, ideological, and intellectual) dimensions of international subjugation. Moreover, all the above theoretical traditions hardly take into account certain crucial internal dimensions of subjugation based on race, gender, caste, and religion. These relatively nonclass forms of subjugation, although received minimal attention in the existing theories, constitute a significant dimension of subjugation, and have become more prominent in different parts of the world after the decline of ideological conflicts attached to the Cold War that used to overshadow these microlevel subjugation.

Considering the above limits of the prevailing theoretical traditions, in this proposed theoretical restructuring, it is emphasized that there is diversity rather than uniformity in the sociohistorical contexts constructed and reconstructed by various social groups and classes, which leads to variations in the nature of interaction between various forms and between different levels of human subjugation and autonomy. In most societies, although different forms and levels of subjugation exist in various degrees, in the course of history, one particular form and specific level of subjugation comes to play the primary role in maintaining, expanding, or facilitating other forms and levels of subjugation. Due to such sociohistorical variations in the primacy of one form and level of subjugation over other forms and levels, the appropriateness of policies for enhancing human autonomy from such subjugation may change accordingly.

First, with regard to the *forms* of human subjugation, the politico-economic subjugation (based on the ownership of the means of production) could determine the structure of cultural-intellectual subjugation in capitalist countries at the classical stage of capitalism: the dominant social class, by dint of its politico-cconomic power, used to exercise control over the cultural, ideological, and intellectual means. In socialist countries, on the other hand, various ideological and intellectual means controlled by the top ruling-party elites could have maintained their politico-economic power in society. In other words, while politico-economic autonomy might be a prerequisite for ideological and intellectual autonomy in capitalist societies, the reverse might be the case in socialist countries. Moreover, within the same society, the nature of linkages between the forms of subjugation and between the modes of autonomy may change in different epochs. For instance, in the feudal Europe, the rigid feudal structure of politico-economic subjugation maintained the natural-physiological subjugation of people by constraining the advancements in production forces—especially scientific and technological innovations—that might enhance human capacity to meet physiological needs and face adverse natural forces but could challenge the feudal power structure. Whereas in the early capitalist Europe, although such advancements in production forces were encouraged, and led to a considerable degree of human autonomy from natural and physiological forces, there emerged the capitalist structure of politico-economic subjugation based on the ownership of such production forces, especially advanced technologies and large capital.

On the other hand, in the modern corporate-capitalist Europe, the all-pervasive network of cultural-intellectual subjugation began to perpetuate and legitimize the corporate structure of politico-economic subjugation. For these historical changes in the nature of interaction between the forms of human subjugation, it is essential to adopt corresponding changes in the modes of human autonomy. In other words, in a particular epoch, if politico-economic subjugation has the primacy over other forms of subjugation, then it is the corresponding politico-economic mode of autonomy that should have more historical relevance. If cultural-intellectual subjugation has the primacy, then it is the cultural-intellectual mode of autonomy that should have more priority.

Second, with regard to the *levels* of subjugation, different societies may experience different patterns of linkages between internal (intranational) and external (international) subjugation in different epochs. For instance, while the structure of internal, interclass subjugation in advanced capitalist societies is relatively autonomous from any external intervention, the nature of such internal subjugation in postcolonial Third World countries is greatly influenced by external forces, particularly the global capitalist powers. However, for Third World countries, the nature and intensity of such linkages between internal and external subjugation depends, especially, on the relevance of these countries to the world capitalist system: relevance in terms of their economic resources (e.g., Kuwait and Zaire), their geocommercial location for international trade and exchange (e.g., Hong Kong and the Philippines), their geostrategic position for military purposes (e.g., Turkey and Israel), their geopolitical setting to counteract the rival states (e.g., Taiwan against China and South Korea against North Korea), and, above all, their extent of incorporation into the world capitalist structure. Of course, the same Third World country could be relevant to Western capitalist interests in terms of more than one of these factors. Similar arguments could be made regarding the impact of the world socialist system on Third World countries, although the system itself has become relatively incapable due to the collapse of the major socialist powers.

In general, the more a Third World country is relevant to external capitalist interests in economic, geopolitical, and geocommercial terms, the more such a country is likely to experience external subjugation, which in turn might increase the intensity of internal subjugation. In countries that are less relevant to or less incorporated into the world capitalist system (and thus are less of its concern), the imposition of internal subjugation by the state often leads to more regime instability (e.g., Bangladesh) or the state may find it challenging to sustain such internal subjugation due to external pressure (e.g., Western pressure on Myanmar). However, the intensity of the linkages between internal and external subjugation not only depends on this relevance or usefulness of Third World countries to external interests, it also depends on internal factors within these countries themselves, including the duration and intensity of their colonial experiences, the degree of their economic self-reliance, and the overall composition and ideology of their state apparatus. For instance, in postcolonial India characterized by relatively democratic politics, vast territorial and population size, and economic self-reliance, it was possible to maintain a considerable degree of national autonomy from the forces of external subjugation, which coincided with a significant degree of internal politico-ideological freedom despite the prevalence of interclass subjugation.

Finally, there are other forms of internal subjugation based on race, gender, caste, and religion, which exist in most societies and, in many instances, are integrated with external subjugation. These relatively nonclass forms of subjugation are often used by Third World regimes to maintain their power and legitimacy by weakening public solidarity or reinforcing intergroup conflicts (e.g., between races, between castes, and between religious groups), and such conflicts may also be instigated by the dominant international actors to destabilize a relatively popular Third World government. This nonclass dimension of internal subjugation is often overlooked or deemphasized in the existing development theories, including Marxian and neo-Marxian theories.

The nature of linkages between internal and external subjugation is not only subject to cross-national variations, it also changes over time within each nation. For instance, in Third World societies, while the precolonial structure of internal subjugation was relatively autonomous from external influence, it became almost completely subordinated to the structure of external colonial subjugation during the colonial period. After decolonization, due to the increasing incorporation of many Third World countries into the world capitalist system, the internal structures of subjugation in these countries have often been shaped by the international structures of subjugation in a neocolonial form.[92] After the end of the Cold War, there has been a shift in the nature of linkages between internal and external subjugation. More specifically, there has been a change in global concerns from security or military issues to more economic and financial matters, which is evident not only in the recent formation of various trade blocs based on the geocommercial interests of the leading Western nations, but also in the declining geopolitical relevance of the previous Third World regimes (e.g., the Filipino and Pakistani regimes) to the world military powers (especially the U.S.). Such diminishing geopolitical relevance of these regimes has reduced their external military and economic assistance, weakened their capacity to exercise internal subjugation, pushed them to introduce some form of political democratization and economic reform, and so on.

From the above discussion, one has to come to the realization that due to the diverse and changing nature of the linkages among various forms and levels of human subjugation, there are variations in the relevance and appropriateness of the modes of pursuing human autonomy. The mode of autonomy that is relevant to South African blacks suffering from internal racial subjugation may not be appropriate for the people in Palestine who are primarily the victims of external subjugation based on Israeli occupation. In advanced Western nations such as the U.S., while it was largely the politico-economic autonomy that was crucial for blacks and other ethnic minorities to overcome the state-sponsored racial segregation in the past, today it is the cultural-intellectual autonomy that is more essential for them to understand and transcend a relatively concealed form of discrimination that exists under the facade of "open competition" and "equal opportunity" propagated through various means such as education and media. At the international level, the liberation strategies that were appropriate in the past for ending the overt and coercive colonial subjugation of Third World countries, are less effective today for overcoming the neocolonial form of subjugation based on more covert and manipulative means such as finance, information, ideology, and cultural products. These sociohistorical differences in the forms and levels of subjugation, and the corresponding variations in the modes of autonomy, are often overlooked even by the radical theories of development. But for adopting appropriate strategies of human autonomy, it is essential to correctly identify the most primary forms and levels of human subjugation experienced by various groups, classes, and nations in different epochs.

Proposition 6: Recently, in terms of the forms of human subjugation, cultural-intellectual subjugation has come to play the primary role in maintaining and legitimizing both natural-physiological subjugation and politico-economic subjugation. In terms of levels, increasingly, international or external subjugation has the primacy over intranational or internal subjugation.

In opposition to the deterministic and universalistic views held by mainstream development theories, it has been suggested above that the linkages between forms (natural-physiological, politico-economic, and cultural-intellectual) and between levels (internal and international) of human subjugation are sociohistorically grounded, and the nature of such linkages varies from society to society and epoch to epoch. In line with this statement, the main argument in this proposition is that in the current age of globalizing the cultural, intellectual, and informational products through advanced information technologies and all-pervasive communication networks, it is the cultural-intellectual form of human subjugation that has come to play the primary role in perpetuating both natural-physiological and politico-economic subjugation, and it is the international level of subjugation that has become a crucial factor in determining internal (interclass and intergroup) subjugation.

In terms of the forms of human subjugation, in advanced Western societies, the cultural-intellectual sphere of subjugation has become essential for maintaining internal politico-economic subjugation for various reasons.[93] For instance, in the economic realm, the decreasing rate of capitalist profit caused, among other things, by the diminishing local demand, had to be overcome by expanding such demand artificially through different forms of manipulation: the all-pervasive networks of mass media are engaged today in creating "opportunities to sell ideas, values, products, in short, a consumerist worldview."[94] The obsessive consumerism created through media and advertisement industry, has not only ensured continuity in accumulation, and thus, social inequality and subjugation. It has also increased the vulnerability of people in physiological and environmental terms, because many of the products, although sold by presenting their false but sensational images, are detrimental to public health and disastrous to environment and ecology.

Similarly, in the political sphere, the practice of human subjugation in Western societies was possible during the feudal and early capitalist periods by adopting ruthless coercive means without much need for their legitimation. But due to the increasing consciousness and organizational consolidation of the working class, the ruling class has replaced such coercive techniques by manipulative cultural and ideological means to maintain power and dominance. On the one hand, a significant part of the culture industry is engaged in commoditizing entertainment and recreational products, individualizing or atomizing collective social relation and interaction, and thereby depoliticizing the public at large. On the other hand, various intellectual and ideological means, including educational institutions, publications, and news media, are being used to commoditize politics, to sell political parties and their activities to the public, to propagate hegemonic capitalist ideology under the facade of democracy and freedom, and to portray serious public issues such as class inequality and racial discrimination as nonissues. These means and processes of cultural-intellectual subjugation have been quite effective in thwarting public consciousness, and thereby maintaining the politico-economic hegemony of the ruling class in Western societies.

In Third World countries on the other hand, human subjugation to the material condition of poverty and hunger, although it remains a historical outcome of external colonial rule and internal class structure based on inequality, has been perpetuated in the postcolonial period largely due to intellectual and ideological factors such as the inappropriate and exploitive views and models of development adopted by the ruling elites governing these countries. These views and models of development—which emphasize the adoption of high-cost technology, capital-intensive industry, urban-bias planning, and export-led production—often led to the borrowing of foreign capital and technology that caused external debt, the use of inappropriate technologies that exacerbated unemployment, the diversion of resources in favor of urban population that worsened rural impoverishment, and the replacement of basic food items by cash crops that perpetuated hunger and malnutrition.

In terms of politico-economic subjugation, the precolonial structures of intergroup and interclass subjugation within each Third World society became subordinated to or incorporated into the colonial structure of subjugation. Although this internal subjugation under external colonial rule used to be quite ruthless and coercive, with the growing anticolonial sentiments, Western rulers began to use certain cultural-intellectual means. In particular, they created a genre of native intellectual and bureaucratic elites through Western education, and used them to legitimize and perpetuate colonial subjugation based on the myth of Western superiority and its civilizing mission. After decolonization, these Westernized elites themselves came to constitute the ruling classes in many postcolonial nations. These ruling classes not only continued such a tradition of Western education and training as a means of their social power and domination, they also introduced more modern cultural-intellectual means such as newspapers, radio broadcasting, and television networks. In the face of the rising public awareness of and opposition to internal politico-economic subjugation, these modern means of cultural-intellectual subjugation are often used today by many Third World regimes to divert public attention, manipulate public opinion, and thus legitimize such internal subjugation.

With regard to the levels of human subjugation, currently the practice of external (international) subjugation by Western nations over Third World countries has become an important condition for maintaining internal (interclass and intergroup) subjugation within both of these societies. For instance, in Western societies themselves, it would be quite difficult for the industrial, business, and state elites to exercise internal economic and political dominance over the working class and underclass minorities without internationalizing capital, labor, production, and exchange. As mentioned above, it was mainly the declining rate of profit of Western corporations in their own countries that led them to internationalize their capital and invest in the Third World—often in collaboration with both the Western states and the pro-Western Third World regimes—for cheaper labor, less expensive raw materials, and higher surplus. The maintenance of international economic hegemony by these transnational corporations is also inseparable from the politico-military hegemony exercised by the Western states: the paramount military superiority is not only used as a coercive means for maintaining and expanding the global economic dominance of multinational corporations, the worldwide business in defense industry itself is a great source of economic surplus for many of these corporations.

However, the point here is that in the context of the declining rate of domestic profit, the extension of these Western corporations to Third World countries was essential for continuing and expanding their surplus or profit. Otherwise, these corporations would have to intensify internal economic repression in their own societies, which might enhance the consciousness and resistance of their working class against such subjugation and lead to more fundamental emancipatory changes in Western societies. In addition, a portion of the corporate surplus repatriated from the Third World is also used by the Western states to provide some form of social welfare to their underclass or underprivileged population. Beyond the rhetoric, various welfare measures have not only prevented the radicalization of working-class people, increased their dependence on the system, and influenced them to accept inequality and subjugation, such measures have also marginally increased their disposable incomes, expanded their demands for goods and services produced by private corporations, and thus ensured the continuity of corporate profit and accumulation.

Moreover, the externalization or globalization of corporate capital and sources of surplus has reduced the bargaining power of workers, weakened their solidarity, and perpetuated their subjugating condition in Western societies. This decline in the bargaining power of the working class is due to the fact that today almost all countries are in competition to supply cheap, disciplined, and skilled labor to large corporations controlling transnational capital and making worldwide investments—corporate capital now has more power over labor to determine wages, safety requirements, and working conditions at very minimal levels in order to maximize surplus. The point, in short, is that without the unequal international structure of economic subjugation, recently perpetuated further by economic globalization, it would be difficult to maintain the internal structure of economic subjugation within Western societies themselves.

In the case of Third World countries, the influence of international subjugation on the structure of internal subjugation is much more deep-rooted and intensive. As discussed above, the structure of internal subjugation that evolved under the colonial rule, became a legacy in many postcolonial countries currently ruled by pro-Western and procapitalist regimes. The recent expansion of the unequal international structures of economic and military subjugation has been so global in scope that it is almost impossible to find a single Third World country in which the internal structure of subjugation is not influenced or managed by the international structure. During the Cold War, very few Third World regimes could avoid the hegemonic influence of two superpowers, the U.S. and the U.S.S.R. The economic and political systems in most Third World countries were considerably affected by either of these superpowers.

However, after the fall of the major socialist states, the dominance of contemporary Russia over Third World countries has diminished. In the former socialist countries themselves, according to common knowledge, the demise of orthodox Marxist-Leninist ideology has enhanced people's autonomy from internal politico-bureaucratic subjugation imposed by the former communist or socialist parties. But this historical transformation has also incorporated these countries into the world capitalist structure, increased their economic subordination to transnational capital and investment, and exacerbated their external debt and dependence. In addition, in these emerging dependent market economies, there is increasing internal economic inequality and subjugation: the internal politico-ideological subjugation exercised by the former socialist states is being replaced by internal economic (class) subjugation imposed by new business conglomerates. Furthermore, the internal economic inequality and subjugation resulting from recent promarket reforms may lead to more political unrest, and thus to more political repression (as evident in the Russian situation under the Yeltsin administration), but this time, with active Western support.

As for the Third World, these historical events (including the end of the Cold War, the collapse of major socialist states, and the monopolization of world power by the U.S.) have intensified various forms of global hegemony exercised by Western nations, which is evident in their expansive transnational investments and economic control, their recurring military interventions in the name of democracy and human rights, their frequent use of selective trade preferences and economic sanctions, and their increasing control over international institutions such as the International Monetary Fund (IMF), the World Bank, the World Trade Organization (WTO), the UN Security Council, and so on. In the current era, these international structures of subjugation are increasingly shaping the structures of internal subjugation—of the rich over the poor, the military over the civilian, the urban over the rural, and the "modern" over the "traditional"—in Third World countries.

Whatever degree of autonomy Third World countries used to exercise during the Cold War by playing one superpower against another, has diminished due to the end of such ideological competition and the emergence of a more monopolistic ideological atmosphere dominated by the world capitalist system. Thus, today the international credibility and sustainability of many Third World regimes often depend on whether they endorse market ideology, privatize public assets, withdraw state subsidies, deregulate and liberalize markets for foreign goods, and encourage foreign investments made by transnational corporations. Without adopting this promarket ideological position and an antistate policy stance, many Third World regimes would face strong opposition not only from transnational corporations and their supporting capitalist states, but also from the aforementioned international organizations.[95] As Schiller mentions, in the current era of transnational corporations, the existence of national economy and sovereignty is under challenge, and increasingly governments and institutions are being compelled to accommodate the interests of such transnational forces.[96]

In terms of both the modes and levels of human subjugation, the structure of international politico-economic subjugation, which reinforces internal politico-economic subjugation in both advanced capitalist nations and Third World countries (explained above), would be difficult to sustain today without international subjugation in the cultural-intellectual realm. As discussed above, such worldwide cultural-intellectual subjugation is exercised by Western nations based on their nearly monopolistic ownership of and control over the global knowledge and culture industry, including international news agencies, television networks, radio broadcasting, film and music industries, advertisement companies, and book and journal publishing. It is explicated below how in the current epoch, this international level of cultural-intellectual subjugation has increasingly become an essential precondition for exercising international politico-economic subjugation, which in turn perpetuates internal politico-economic subjugation.

For Western people themselves, international politico-economic hegemony is made publicly acceptable through various cultural-intellectual means, especially the global media, which often present misleading information and images of other societies and peoples, and portray them as backward, inferior, unpredictable, undemocratic, and detrimental. Due to the constant propaganda and manipulation by the media, most Western people believe in such distorted information and images, compare them with their own images (which are also fabricated), consider themselves fortunate, and thus accept not only their own conditions of internal subjugation, but also the international politico-economic subjugation exercised by their political, military, and business elites. Without this process of manufacturing false consciousness through cultural-intellectual means, Western people could be more aware of the reality of such internal and international subjugation, and perhaps resist the policies and mechanisms used for maintaining such subjugating conditions.

In Third World countries, it is also these global means of cultural-intellectual subjugation through which Western patterns of production and consumption, politics and administration, knowledge and ideologies, values and norms, and luxurious lifestyles, have been introduced via the intermediary roles played by the Westernized Third World elites.[97] This process has considerable implications for the growing consent or diminishing opposition of Third World nations to international subjugation in the politico-economic sphere. Various means of cultural-intellectual subjugation play significant role in creating ideological support for the world capitalist system, portraying transnational capital and foreign investment as the panacea for Third World problems, and globalizing Western lifestyles and consumption patterns.[98] Through the worldwide networks of bourgeois culture and knowledge industry, in many Third World countries, the demands for indigenous products are being replaced by demands for foreign goods, a procapitalist model of social progress is being sold to policy-makers, local entrepreneurs are being motivated to be subordinate partners of foreign investors, and thereby domestic capital is being integrated with transnational capital and national economies are being brought under the control of dominant capitalist economies.

The global means of cultural-intellectual subjugation are used not only for perpetuating the economic subjugation of Third World countries, but also for reinforcing their political subjugation. Today the global networks of Western media are engaged in propagating the rhetoric of liberal democracy, demonizing self-reliant or nationalist political leaders, rationalizing military intervention in the name of human rights, and selling lethal weapons to procapitalist regimes in the name of preserving national security. In fact, recently these global media networks are playing a more effective role than direct military involvement to maintain Western political dominance. Depending on the ideological perspective of a Third World regime and its role in serving Western economic and political interests, such transnational media may glorify or demonize the regime by defining and redefining its character, manipulate domestic public opinion for or against the regime, present the favorable or unfavorable image of the regime to the world population, and thus cause the rise and fall of the regime in terms of its power, legitimacy, and survival. In other words, the Western media may present a popular Third World regime as authoritarian, unpredictable, and dangerous because of its anti-capitalist ideological outlook and policy stance; while a dictatorial or repressive regime may be portrayed as progressive and constructive because of its endorsement of and services to the international capitalist system.

However, the role of this cultural-intellectual means in maintaining international politico-economic subjugation has become more crucial after the end of the Cold War—because after the collapse of the Soviet Union and other socialist states, it has become difficult to justify Western economic and military hegemony over Third World countries in the name of neutralizing the Soviet threat or communist takeover. In the current global context of diminishing ideological rivalry, it has become more essential for Western powers to use various cultural, ideological, and intellectual measures not only to propagate the virtues of their market ideology, political institutions, and transnational corporations, but also to invent new international enemies[99] in order to justify their expansive defense industry, international business in arms, and military intervention in and dominance over Third World countries.

Within the above context of cultural-intellectual influence exercised by the leading Western nations through the unprecedented worldwide expansion of culture and knowledge industry, many Third World countries seem to have forgotten their experiences of colonial and neocolonial subjugation, given up their opposition to Western economic and military hegemony, and come to accept or endorse such hegemony in order to "modernize" or "Westernize" themselves economically and militarily.[100] In other words, today the external cultural-intellectual influence on Third World countries has reached such a stage that it not only facilitates and legitimizes their politico-economic subjugation to the global powers, it also diminishes their critical consciousness against such subjugating conditions.

Proposition 7: *In line with the above proposition (proposition 6), in the current epoch, cultural-intellectual autonomy has become a historical precondition for realizing both natural-physiological autonomy and politico-economic autonomy. In terms of level, international autonomy has become a prerequisite for internal autonomy in this epoch.*

This proposition basically represents an analytical extension of the preceding proposition: since the cultural-intellectual form and international level of human subjugation have the primacy over other forms and levels of subjugation, today it is the cultural-intellectual mode and international level of human autonomy that have become more central for the realization of other modes and levels of autonomy.[101] In terms of the *modes* of human autonomy, although most proponents (both conservative and radical) of historical determinism, who believe in the preordained laws of social change, emphasize economic autonomy as a precondition for cultural-intellectual autonomy in various epochs, in reality there has been a shift in this configuration toward a more determining role of the latter mode of autonomy. It is because the cultural-intellectual realm of society has become increasingly autonomous from and influential upon natural-physiological conditions and politico-economic structures. The proposition is explicated below in greater detail.

It has been pointed out that in Western societies, the culture of the emerging industrial capitalism in the seventeenth century was the industrial culture of the dominant class. The culture of corporate capitalism in the early twentieth century became the mass culture of consumerism created through media to expand the demand for surplus production. Today, under the extremely concentrated patterns of ownership, the economic and cultural spheres have merged, the difference between real life and images has become insignificant, and the cultural sphere has achieved relative autonomy.[102] This human autonomy in the cultural sphere is not only significant in its own right, it has also become central for changes in the socioeconomic realm itself.[103] More specifically, the cultural-intellectual influence on people through the bourgeois education system, culture industry, and news media has diminished their critical capacity to comprehend the structures and sources of politico-economic subjugation, and to understand the need for or importance of their autonomy from such subjugation.[104]

The aforementioned cultural and intellectual media usually display Western progress, power, and superiority, but they hardly provide adequate information about the pathological realities in Western societies, including the hardship of the underclass, discrimination against minorities, sufferings of the homeless, various forms of psychological disorders, and alarming crime rate and violence. In addition, these media networks often reinforce racial identities and ethnic differences that tend to camouflage the reality of interclass distinction and subjugation in society: "racist ideology and ethnic differences" are often used for concealing class hegemony.[105] Thus, in advanced Western societies themselves, the politico-economic autonomy of the common masses has become difficult without reestablishing and strengthening their critical consciousness about economic inequality and political subjugation, which in turn, requires their autonomy from various means of cultural-intellectual subjugation, including television programs, newspapers, magazines, film industry, radio broadcasting, and so on. Similarly, in Third World countries, cultural-intellectual autonomy has become essential for internal politico-economic autonomy, because in this age of information, the use of media for legitimizing and perpetuating politico-economic subjugation has become a common practice in many of these countries.

In terms of the *levels* of human autonomy, the internal politico-economic autonomy of Western people from their states and large corporations is related to the international politico-economic autonomy of Third World people from these states and corporations. Because, as discussed above, with this Third World autonomy, the Western states and corporations would lose their external sources of surplus from Third World labor and raw materials, cut back their welfare services provided to the underclass population, intensify their means of internal exploitation and repression, and thus risk their current legitimacy and face social demand for the end of politico-economic subjugation and realization of true human autonomy within Western societies.

Similarly, the internal politico-economic autonomy of common masses within each Third World country is inseparable today from its international economic and political autonomy. The postcolonial structure of international political economy is still dominated by advanced capitalist nations, and complementing such international structure, there are internal structures of subjugation within Third World countries exercised by their political, bureaucratic, and business elites. These Third World elites usually accept the existing inequality in world order, satisfy the requirements of foreign investors, ensure the availability of cheap labor and raw materials for foreign capital, and in exchange get enriched and empowered by external economic and military assistance from the affluent capitalist nations. Thus, the autonomy of Third World countries from the international structure of subjugation would require the end of this external support to many repressive Third World regimes and ruling classes, which would weaken their power and legitimacy, and thus lead to the eventual autonomy of Third World masses from internal subjugation exercised by such regimes and classes. In other words, without the demise of or autonomy from the current international structure of subjugation, it is difficult today to realize the internal autonomy of Third World people.

In terms of both *modes and levels* of human autonomy, the international politico-economic autonomy of Third World countries—which has become a necessary condition to enhance their internal politico-economic autonomy—is difficult to achieve today without the realization of their international cultural-intellectual autonomy.[106] As discussed above, based on the globalization of culture, knowledge, and information, today the Western education system, film industry, news agencies, television and radio broadcasting, and computer networks play a significant role in manipulating world opinion in favor of Western interests, and in inhibiting and deforming public consciousness about the unequal and hegemonic nature of international economic and military structures. In this process of manipulating public consciousness, the transnational media tend to glorify Western societies as civilized, democratic, and progressive, while demonizing Third World countries (except pro-Western ones) as uncivilized, authoritarian, and backward. But these Western media often fail to mention how in most Third World societies, the colonial exploitation caused economic backwardness, external military assistance helped dictatorial regimes, international aid agencies expanded foreign debt, multinational corporations replaced basic foods by cash crops and worsened hunger, and the global culture industry eroded indigenous culture and lifestyle. Moreover, it is never mentioned how the interests, ownership, and management of such transnational media themselves are integrated with those of the dominant Western states and corporations, and how the production and dissemination of their news, information, knowledge, and cultural products are guided by Western state policies and corporate interests.[107]

The above global means of cultural-intellectual subjugation—through the constant propagation of such ahistorical, prejudiced, and reductionist images of Third World societies, Western nations, transnational corporations, and international agencies—not only create and maintain a favorable procapitalist opinion among Western people regarding their own socioeconomic conditions vis-à-vis Third World people, but also mobilize their support for defense industry and military intervention, economic aid and technical assistance, and transnational investment and exchange. Thus, the people in advanced capitalist nations have become increasingly indifferent not only toward their own subjugating conditions but also toward the politico-economic subordination and impoverishment of Third World masses by Western states, corporations, and agencies. In this context, the cultural-intellectual autonomy of Western people is essential not only for their own internal politico-economic autonomy, but also for their proper understanding of the international structures of subjugation, and thus for creating pressure on their states and corporations to rectify such exploitive international structures.

Similarly, within Third World countries themselves, the infusion of such biased or prejudiced interpretations of societies, economies, polities, and cultures through Western or Westernized education systems, culture industries, and information networks, has led to the formation of distorted consciousness among the masses. Through these cultural-intellectual means, Third World masses are influenced to believe that their conditions of poverty and subjugation are the results of their own incompetence rather than of the colonial and neocolonial legacies and structures, that their modes of life and culture are "primitive" and must be transformed into modern Western patterns, and that their true happiness lies in individualistic consumerism rather than in collective endeavor and solidarity. They are also told that their economies are backward and cannot be improved without Western investment and assistance, that only transnational corporations and international aid agencies are capable of rescuing them from backwardness, that the Western politico-military intervention is necessary to ensure stability and democracy, and that only under Western leadership can they modernize themselves and become a part of human civilization. Although such images, symbols, and information are often based on the falsification of history and fabrication of reality, their constant and all-pervasive propagation and reification through the global means of cultural-intellectual influence has led Third World countries to accept such falsities and fabrications, believe in Western superiority, emulate Western economic models and cultural norms, solicit investments from transnational corporations, seek external economic aid and military assistance, and thus perpetuate their own subjugation to the hegemonic international structures.

Thus, while the colonial mode of politico-economic subjugation was coercively imposed by the leading Western nations but rejected by Third World people, the current postcolonial mode of international politico-economic subjugation is not purely based on coercion, but on the consent of Third World countries (particularly of their ruling elites) created through the aforementioned cultural-intellectual means. Today many of these elites endorse such international subjugation not only for personal material gains in terms of wealth, power, and status, but also due to the fact that they are often mystified by Western knowledge, culture, ideology, and information. These ruling elites not only have their own consent to Western politico-economic hegemony, they also help create such a pro-Western consent among Third World masses in general. Thus, in the current epoch when the global cultural-intellectual means are intensively engaged in eroding the consciousness of Third World people against international politico-economic subjugation, and influencing them even to accept such a subjugating condition, it is hardly possible to achieve their international autonomy in this politico-economic sphere without their autonomy from the world structures of intellectual, cultural, ideological, and informational hegemony.

In short, human autonomy in the cultural-intellectual sphere, at the international level, has become almost a historical precondition for other forms and levels of human autonomy. It is because there has been an unprecedented expansion of various global means of cultural-intellectual subjugation, including transnational news media, advertising agencies, computer networks, and culture and knowledge industry, which are increasingly engaged in manufacturing pejorative world opinion about Third World societies and peoples, subordinating their economic concerns to the interests of transnational corporations, replacing their self-reliant production and consumption patterns by imitative and dependent structures, and perpetuating their internal subjugation maintained by pro-Western authoritarian regimes. In this regard, there are scholars who have already pointed out that these Western means of cultural-intellectual subjugation are affecting all nations, and shaping the nature of the relationship between capitalist centers and Third World peripheries.[108] In addition, the need for cultural-intellectual autonomy has become more crucial after the Cold War when there is hardly any strong ideological, economic, and military opposition to the unilateral power and hegemony of the leading Western nations, especially the U.S. These dominant world powers are now intensely involved in incorporating Third World countries into the transnational capitalist structure, pressurizing them to adopt liberalization and privatization policies based on market ideology, dictating their state activities by imposing the standards of bourgeois democracy and human rights, rallying their ruling elites behind Western (especially American) leadership, and using various international organizations (e.g., the IMF, World Bank, WTO, and U.N. Security Council) to enhance Western economic and military hegemony: all these acts of imposing international politico-economic subjugation, however, are sold to the world as legitimate and desirable through the aforementioned global means of cultural-intellectual subjugation. Thus, although the realization of all forms and levels of human autonomy is essential for genuine development, in this epoch, it is the cultural-intellectual autonomy at the international level that has become most central, because today the worldwide structures of cultural-intellectual subjugation are playing the primary role in reinforcing both natural-physiological and politico-economic subjugation within and between nations. However, it does not mean the exclusion of other forms (natural-physiological and politico-economic) and levels (interclass and intergroup) of human autonomy: rather it means the articulation of such other forms and levels of autonomy under the overall primacy of international cultural-intellectual autonomy, which has become most crucial for the eventual realization of overall human autonomy (defined as development) in the current epoch.

In conclusion, it should be mentioned that the proposed redefinition of development as the realization of overall human autonomy, and the theoretical restructuring of development based on the basic principles of such autonomy from various forms and levels of human subjugation, are still tentative and subject to further articulation or consolidation. However, the aforementioned theoretical propositions— which explain the sociohistorical dynamics of these forms and levels of human subjugation and the corresponding modes of human autonomy—represent an emancipatory development perspective, and thus, can be considered *an emancipatory theory of development.* It is probable that the proposed conceptual and theoretical restructuring will encounter various intellectual critiques or disagreements. Such critiques or disagreements should be based on rational criteria rather than the vested interests of development experts—including the bureaucratic and intellectual elites affiliated with the hegemonic capitalist states, authoritarian regimes, international agencies, think tanks, and academic and research institutions—who gained significantly from the prevalent development enterprise that brought them wealth, power, and status through foreign assistance, research grants, fellowships, and lucrative careers. In addition, in assessing any theoretical restructuring like the proposed one, it is necessary to overcome the intellectual forestructures or biases inherent in the existing development field. It is essential for development scholars and experts to recognize that in the ultimate analysis, a genuine development would not only imply the autonomy of various groups, classes, and nations from all forms of human subjugation, it would also require their own intellectual autonomy from the hegemonic development discourse.[109]

CHAPTER 9

Reforming Development Policies

In this study, the preceding chapters covered the following issues: an analysis of the nature and extent of major development crises, a review and critique of the existing development theories, and a conceptual and theoretical restructuring of development thinking. The study would remain incomplete without converting the restructured theory of development into more concrete development policies. Thus, based on the theoretical reconstruction proposed in the previous chapter—which emphasizes that in the current epoch, human autonomy from cultural-intellectual subjugation has become a prerequisite for realizing human autonomy from natural-physiological forces and politico-economic hegemony—this concluding chapter is devoted to the reformulation of various development policies.

However, in articulating practical development policies, it is necessary to take into account all modes (natural-physiological, politico-economic, cultural-intellectual) of human autonomy. Thus, with regard to policy reforms, each of these dimensions of human autonomy is addressed in this chapter, although it is emphasized (in line with the proposed theoretical framework) that the adoption of appropriate policies for cultural-intellectual autonomy has increasingly become an essential prerequisite to achieve human autonomy in the other realms. It is also necessary to mention at the outset that in suggesting these policy reforms, the focus in this chapter is mainly on Third World countries, because it is largely the underprivileged common masses in these countries who remain the worst victims of the above forms of human subjugation that exist within and between nations. It should also be highlighted that the recommended policy reforms are basically *examples* of how the practical development policies should be prioritized or designed. The additional policy areas, and the specific details of each policy measure, have to be worked out by various Third World countries depending on their respective needs, opportunities, and contexts.

Reforming Policies to Achieve Natural-Physiological Autonomy

In advanced Western nations, it was not only the internal transformation of the forces and relations of production and the scientific and industrial revolutions, but also the external colonial exploitation and the neocolonial gains from unequal exchange, which led to their massive accumulation of capital, advancements in science and technology, and unprecedented industrial expansion. All these processes enabled them considerably to exploit the favorable forces of nature (e.g., land, water, and mineral resources), control the unfavorable natural forces (e.g., drought and flood), and mitigate undesirable physiological conditions (e.g., hunger and diseases), although ironically such achievements also led to disastrous environmental and ecological problems. Conversely, in Third World countries, the centuries of colonial and neocolonial subjugation and scientific and technological captivity perpetuated their incapacity to use available natural resources, their vulnerability to various natural calamities, and their adverse physiological conditions such as hunger, malnutrition, and diseases. In other words, the impoverished natural and physiological conditions in Third World countries cannot be separated from their adverse sociohistorical experiences.

After decolonization or independence, such a situation of human subjugation to natural and physiological forces has not improved much. The earlier state-centered policies of development were introduced by Third World regimes (often with the inspiration and assistance from Western nations and international organizations) in the name of higher income, better living standard, and more equality, although in reality, they produced almost opposite outcomes. On the other hand, in the current post–Cold War era characterized by the collapse of major socialist states and the worldwide rise of promarket ideology, various market-centered policies are being pursued by the emerging neoliberal regimes in Third World countries, often under the pressure of Western governments, transnational corporations, and international agencies.[1] The liberalization of trade, privatization of public assets, and expansion of foreign investments have been adopted by these regimes in the name of efficiency, productivity, and economic growth.[2] These policies may benefit the national business elites and transnational corporations at the expense of the deteriorating conditions of Third World poverty, inequality, and external dependence.[3] For some critics, these policies represent a form of "raw neocolonialism."[4] Given the disappointing records of the past and present policies of development[5] that often constrained rather than enhanced the autonomy of the common masses from the subjugating natural forces and physiological conditions, it is necessary to introduce fundamental policy reforms in this regard.

For actualizing this natural-physiological autonomy of people in Third World countries, it is essential to study, analyze, and synthesize two central issues or questions: What are their major crucial development problems in terms of adverse material conditions? What are the material and human resources available to overcome such development problems? With regard to *the most crucial problems*, the majority of Third World people suffer from hunger, malnutrition, diseases, and illiteracy.[6] There are, of course, other material problems, such as backward technology, scarce capital, lack of skill, poor infrastructure, and so on, which can be considered as second-order problems, because they have relevance mainly in terms of their instrumentality to the first-order problems—i.e., hunger, malnutrition, disease, and illiteracy encountered everyday by the common masses in poor countries.[7] In order to overcome these most critical problems (i.e., hunger, malnutrition, disease, and illiteracy), it is necessary to achieve self-sufficiency in food production, ensure adequate health care, and expand educational facilities.

To attain these objectives of overcoming the above crucial problems by ensuring adequate food, health care, education, and so on, it is also essential to examine the second central question regarding what *necessary material and human resources* Third World countries have to achieve these objectives. In general, many of these countries possess adequate human resources, cultivable lands, minerals, water resources, and other primary resources.[8] As far as possible, development policies should be based on these indigenous resources rather than foreign assistance, and should be directed toward the basic necessities (food, health, and education) of the majority common masses rather than the luxurious consumption patterns of the few affluent elites. In short, development policies that serve few vested interests and create dependence must be rejected, and these policies should focus more on the needs of the majority, the principle of self-reliance, and the eventual well-being of all. The guiding principle of development policies should not be the quantitative and instrumental criteria of economic growth, efficiency, and productivity that often conceal poverty, dependence, and repression beneath the bourgeois economic indicators. Rathor the most essential principle is to enhance the overall quality of life for the common masses suffering from starvation, malnutrition, diseases, and illiteracy. With this brief note on the context within which natural-physiological autonomy (an essential material dimension of development) has to take place, some required changes in development policies are outlined below.

FROM THE URBAN-INDUSTRIAL TO THE RURAL-AGRICULTURAL PERSPECTIVE

First, the whole perspective of development has to shift from urban-industrial to rural-agrarian questions, because except few oil-rich countries and small NICs (Newly Industrialized Countries), most Third World societies are still predominantly agrarian, and the majority of Third World people live in rural areas and earn their livelihood from agriculture. The number of rural people as a percentage of total population is 70 percent in Sub-Saharan Africa, 74 percent in South Asia, 69 percent in East Asia, 70 percent in Southeast Asia, 79 percent in least-developed countries, and 65 percent in all Third World countries.[9] The percentage of labor force in agriculture is 58 percent in all Third World countries, and 72 percent in low-income Third World countries.[10] For these countries, agriculture remains the source of most essential commodity—i.e., food—because about 18.25 million people die every year from hunger.[11] In poorer Third World countries, about 60 to 80 percent of the labor force is dependent on agriculture.[12]

In fact, agricultural productivity (traditionally a rural phenomenon) has been a historical precondition for industrial growth (predominantly an urban issue) in modern affluent societies.[13] But in most Third World countries, despite the rhetoric of agricultural progress, rural development, and poverty eradication, the top policy-makers have often overlooked the agricultural sector, ignored the rural poor, and adopted prourban and proindustrial policies by allocating resources to cities, setting low prices for agricultural products, guaranteeing high prices for industrial goods, and so on.[14] Since such policies are quite discouraging for agricultural productivity, they have eventually worsened the conditions of food scarcity and hunger. It is necessary for agrarian Third World countries to transcend this obsession for industrialism and urbanism, and introduce more comprehensive policies for enhancing rural and agricultural advancements.[15]

This does not mean the rejection of the industrial sector altogether; it means the creation of a complementary relationship between the urban and rural sectors, between industry and agriculture, and between labor and capital.[16]

FROM EXPORT-LED GROWTH TO NEED-BASED PRODUCTION

The above restructuring in the intersectoral composition of development policies—i.e., urban vs. rural and agricultural vs. industrial alternatives—would be less effective unless changes are also made in the orientation of production, particularly, from the current export-led production for foreign markets to more need-based production for indigenous consumers. In agriculture, for instance, the production of cash crops for export should be replaced by the production of basic food items to satisfy the needs of the common masses, because in the food-deficit Third World countries, the production of adequate basic foods should be the first priority from any consideration.[17] Unfortunately, the colonial policies of plantation agriculture and cash crops based on the conquered land and slave labor still continue in different forms in many decolonized Asian, African, and Latin American countries in the name of economic growth.[18] In these countries, the policy shift from the production of basic foods to the production of cash crops has worsened their international food-dependence and subordinated them to the hierarchy of foreign agribusiness firms that produce, distribute, process, and market food products all over the world.[19] For instance, only three conglomerates control 70-75 percent of the world's banana market, and six corporations have command over 70 percent of its cocoa trade.[20]

The production of cash crops has served the affluent Western consumers, but it has transformed many Third World countries into dependent monocultural economies. It was found from a study of 58 Third World countries that the degree of dependence on a single commodity was over 90 percent in 15 countries, 80 percent in 10 countries, 70 percent in 11 countries, 60 percent in another 11 countries, and 50 percent in the remaining 11 countries.[21] On the one hand, there has been declining terms of trade for these export-oriented cash crops,[22] but on the other hand, there is increasing food import dependency of Third World countries. Between the periods 1969 to 1971 and 1988 to 1989, the overall food import dependency ratio of Third World countries increased from 6.7 percent to 10.5 percent.[23] Beyond the question of food dependency, a basic policy reorientation is essential for meeting the nutritional needs and maintaining the overall public health in Third World countries. According to an earlier report published by the World Health Organization, the export-led commercialization of agriculture reduced the capacity of the rural poor to satisfy their nutritional needs, leading to the deterioration of health condition in these countries.[24]

This policy of moving away from export-led production is necessary not only in agriculture but also in the industrial sector that has come under increasing control of transnational corporations.[25] Although some scholars, such as Rice and O'Cleireacain,[26] have discredited import-substitution policy for its limited success in the past, they have failed to recognize that import-substitution alone cannot resolve the problem unless the consumption patterns are changed. It is not affordable or feasible for poor countries to produce expensive items (e.g., luxurious cars, refrigerators, washing machines, air conditioners, television sets) by themselves, which are often less expensive to import from industrial nations. What may be essential in this regard is to introduce a fundamental shift in the consumption pattern—from the imported foreign goods consumed by Third World elites to the indigenously produced goods that satisfy the basic needs of common people. As Mittelman rightly suggests, it is necessary "to harmonize the sectors of an economy so that indigenous peoples produce what they consume and consume what they produce."[27]

Although export-led policies are often justified by Third World governments in the name of earning foreign exchange to repay foreign debt and import capital and consumption goods, in reality it constitutes a vicious cycle. While export-led production policies bring foreign exchange, they also create more need for such foreign exchange.[28] It is because governments have to import the very basic consumption items that they once used to produce locally, but are now replaced by the export-led production system itself. The need for foreign exchange and external assistance can be reduced by cutting down the import of foreign goods. But it requires the aforementioned changes in development policies: from the elitist consumption of expensive foreign goods to the mass consumption of indigenous products, from showcase urbanization and capital-intensive industrialization (both require foreign capital) to labor-intensive rural advancement and agricultural progress,[29] from production for export (e.g., cash crops) to production for indigenous needs (e.g., basic food items and need-based industrial products). Such policy reforms would help reduce the necessity for foreign exchange and foreign aid, and thus diminish the need for export-led production.

FROM ELITIST HEALTH SERVICES TO PEOPLE-CENTERED HEALTH CARE

Another critical factor in Third World countries is the issue of health, because most of these countries have serious problems related to the quantity and quality of physicians, hospitals, and medicines. In many instances, although the elitist health policies have created few city-based hospitals, produced some modern physicians, and ensured certain costly imported medicines,[30] most of such facilities remain unaffordable to the common masses. It is necessary to introduce the following basic changes in such health policies: (a) the replacement of the existing centralized, urban-centered, and expensive hospitals by more decentralized, rural-based, and affordable hospitals; (b) a shift from the production of few high-cost, elitist, and urbanized physicians (who are indifferent toward rural life and often leave the country) to the creation of many low-cost and people-oriented physicians (who are willing and skilled enough to address the common health problems faced by the majority of poor people); and (c) the gradual replacement of expensive, scarce, and often unreliable imported drugs by less expensive, easily available, and locally produced medicines.

In addition, it is essential for Third World physicians to acquire adequate knowledge of nutrition, particularly about the compositions (vitamins, minerals, proteins, and amino acids) of various food items and their implications for human health, because the causes and cures of most diseases are inseparable from foods. In Western nations themselves, the significant improvements in health have occurred over the past 150 years "not as a result of the 'miracle' drugs of the pharmaceutical industry, but because of improvements in nutrition, sanitation, and hygiene."[31] But the increasing dominance of agribusiness corporations guided by the principles of mass production and maximum profit, has created disasters to public health in many of these countries. Their extensive use of fertilizers, pesticides, and various chemicals has led to the deterioration of soil condition, and therefrom to the depletion of vitamin and mineral contents in grains, vegetables, fruits, meat, and milk products.[32] Moreover, in the process of refining, preserving, and packaging foods, the food industries destroy most of the remaining nutrients[33] and add hundreds of physically detrimental chemicals. The final damage is done by all varieties of fast food restaurants which, although selling unhealthy foods and drinks, have multiplied all over the world. The above scenario is well reflected in the following comment of an American nutritionist, Adelle Davis:

Our national health began to decline at the onset of the Industrial Revolution, as families moved from self-sustaining firms into crowded cities. It declined still further with the invention of machinery for milling grains, and with each new method of refining and processing foods, each new trick for forcing hybrid crops to yield higher tonnage per acre on worn-out soil.[34]

Thus, the modern transnational food industries make billions of dollars, and at the same time, cause varieties of human diseases such as diabetes, cancer, ulcers, high blood pressure, heart and kidney problems, various mental disorders, and so on, which were relatively unknown in traditional societies untouched by Western "civilization."[35] However, the eradication of nutrients from foods has significantly benefited transnational drug industries, pharmaceutical companies, private hospitals, and the affiliated scientists and physicians: the rise of the food industry, the deterioration of public health, and the expansion of the drug industry are highly correlated.[36]

In recent years, even the Third World countries have come under such cataclysms because, in the name of modernity, they are replacing basic foods by cash crops, importing Western foods and drugs, multiplying fast food restaurants and confectioneries, and being flooded by transnational corporations with junk foods, soft drinks, sweet bakery products, packaged cereals, baby foods, and so on.[37] Third World governments must realize the disastrous implications of such a situation for public health. In recent years, there has been a growing awareness among Western people themselves about the empty promises and potential dangers of all packaged foods and drugs, and many of them are shifting toward naturally grown foods and medicines (including herbs) that constitute now a profitable industry. Such natural foods and medicines that are available now in the worldwide network of expensive health-food stores, have been inexpensive, common consumption items in Third World societies for centuries. Third World physicians, instead of specializing only in modern medical knowledge and techniques, and using expensive imported medicines, must consider the above reality and learn the root causes and inexpensive cures of diseases. They must understand that the patterns of Third World diseases are quite different from those in advanced industrial countries. While the main killer-diseases in industrial countries are linked with unhealthy diet and lifestyle, the major causes of deaths in Third World countries are infectious and parasitic diseases usually caused by poor nutrition and polluted water.[38] In this regard, one commentator mentions the following:

> For the poor countries of the world, the Western approach to health has been a total disaster. It has focused on lavish buildings, imported equipment and drugs, and expensively trained personnel. Its cost has put health care of any kind way beyond the reach of the majority in almost every Third World country.[39]

Third World physicians must also have a critical understanding of the political economy of transnational food and drug industry that not only influences the world health system, but also guides their own medical knowledge and practices. More specifically, they should be aware of the fact that the transnational pharmaceutical industry is more interested in profit-based marketing than in research, it maintains close liaison with the medical profession for such marketing, and it has significant influence on physicians and health workers around the world through its control over information about medicines.[40] They should also know the fact that most of the tens of thousands of drugs on the world market produced by such transnational industry are unnecessary, ineffective, and unsafe: according to Health Action International, at least 70 percent of the drugs on the market are unessential, over 75 percent of vitamin preparations and 80 percent of cold remedies and antidiarrheals are ineffective, and 75 percent of analgesics and 73 percent of nonsteroidal anti-inflammatory drugs on the market are unsafe or dangerous, although these products are openly sold in Third World countries.[41]

FROM CONTEXTLESS EDUCATION TO NEED-BASED EDUCATION

Another important policy that requires fundamental reform is education policy because, after food and health, education represents a basic requirement for improving the quality of life in Third World countries. This reformulation of education policy is essential, especially for creating appropriate and adequate human resources needed to formulate and implement various development programs. In this regard, one basic shortcoming in education system in most Third World countries is that its basic components, including the institutional structure, course content, and reading materials, are either colonially inherited or adopted recently from the West. In addition, the most influential teachers or instructors at the university level are trained abroad and have degrees from advanced Western nations. What kind of human resource can this imitative, pro-Western education system create?

According to Barnett, the adoption of the Western education model in Third World countries has led to the emergence of an elitist educated class (including economists, lawyers, sociologists, physicists, etc.) without local relevance, the establishment of the superiority of mental as opposed to physical work, the creation of "diploma disease," and the perpetuation of wealth and power of the elite.[42] On top of this, Third World governments incur huge expenditures to send their fresh graduates and working professionals to Western nations for higher study, which isolate them further from their own societies and peoples. These are the foreign-trained modern professionals whose expertise and skills are more appropriate for advanced industrial nations, whose imitative or borrowed values and attitudes are less suitable to the indigenous context, and who are always interested to leave their own countries and settle down in some affluent nations. This brain-drain costs Third World countries not only in terms of their loss of skilled human resource, but also in terms of their loss of scarce financial resource invested for creating such human resource.

Thus, the current education policies must change toward more need-based knowledge and expertise by emphasizing indigenous social contexts and people's necessities. In most Third World countries, since the education system is highly subsidized and the common people bear the expenses, it is only fair to redirect all educational institutions and course curricula to produce human resources that satisfy people's needs and expectations. Therefore, it is necessary to establish more rural schools for the common masses[43] rather than city-based universities for social elites; to generate locally needed rather than internationally attractive knowledge and skills; and to exchange knowledge and expertise among Third World nations perplexed by similar development problems rather than spending scarce resources for expensive foreign training from industrial nations with a different set of problems.

FROM CITYWIDE TO NATIONWIDE TRANSPORTATION AND COMMUNICATION

In addition to the above policy reforms, there is a need for similar reforms in other sectors such as transportation and communication. In most Third World countries, the transportation and communication system remains city-centered and serves a limited number of urban population while the majority rural people do not have access to such a system. More specifically, while the urban elites enjoy luxurious private cars and have access to public transportation such as buses and trains, the rural poor cannot travel even to the nearest towns due to the unaffordability and unavailability of such transportation and the undeveloped road systems in remote areas. While the urban population enjoy advanced means of communication such as telephone and fax machine, the rural population have hardly any access to such communication networks. This lack of access to adequate transportation and communication facilities not only implies the backwardness of this sector, it also constrains the implementation of policy reforms in other areas discussed above.

For instance, due to poor transportation and communication in the peripheral rural areas, various rural communities are isolated from each other, delinked from cities, constrained in getting necessary goods and services, faced with difficulties in selling or marketing their products, and restricted in terms of receiving necessary information. Thus, even if there are changes in policies from urban-biased to rural-centered perspective, from export-led to need-based production, such changes would remain less effective without the required reforms in the transportation and communication sector. In this regard, it is essential to change transportation and communication policies—from the expansion and upgrading of roads and highways in few large cities to the construction of basic transportation infrastructures nationwide (including rural areas), from the multiplication of expensive private cars to the increase of more affordable public buses and trains. As Illich comments on the Brazilian transportation system, "Each car which Brazil puts on the road denies fifty people good transportationation by bus."[44] Without considerable improvements in the nationwide extension of adequate and affordable public transportation in Third World countries—especially its extension to rural areas where the majority of the population live—it would be difficult to enhance mobility of human resources, exchange of commodities, mobilization of capital, and distribution of goods and services. In other words, a basic shift in transportation and communication policy (from its urban-biased to nationwide outlook) is essential to effectuate policy reforms related to other sectors (e.g., education, health, agriculture, and industry), especially in terms of activating both material and human resources in these sectors.

In the above discussion, an effort has been made to present the general outlines of how various development policies have to be reformulated to enhance human autonomy from adverse material conditions, such as hunger, malnutrition, disease, and illiteracy, especially in poorer Third World countries. These policy reforms are also conducive to the mitigation of environmental and ecological catastrophes. For instance, the redirection of policies from urban, industrial, and capital-intensive to rural, agricultural, and labor-intensive orientation is likely to reduce the pollution of air and water, decrease the emission of greenhouse gases and ozone-depleting substances, and thereby alleviate the intensity of related predicaments. Although such global problems cannot be resolved without the policy changes in advanced industrial nations that are considerably responsible for various environmental disorders, the aforementioned policy reforms suggested for Third World countries would generate immediate and direct environmental benefits for Third World people themselves. For instance, a shift from the export-led cash-crop production to need-based agriculture is likely to reduce the extensive use of irrigation, pesticides, and fertilizers, and thus lessen the depletion of ground water, salinization of water and soil, desertification of land, and so on.[45] Conversely, this improvement in environmental and ecological conditions would have positive implications for better public health and higher food production.[46] In other words, the above policy reforms recommended for addressing basic necessities such as food, health, and transportation, are also conducive to a favorable environmental and ecological atmosphere, which in turn is essential to meet such basic necessities.

In short, for most Third World countries, the realization of human autonomy from adverse human conditions and natural forces requires certain basic reforms in development policies discussed above. However, since existing state policies are linked with the interests and power of the dominant groups and classes in Third World societies,[47] they may pose a formidable challenge to the proposed policy reforms. For instance, the urbanized civil and military bureaucracies are more interested in transferring resources from the rural areas to urban centers, they would oppose any redirection in the process.[48] Similarly, the industrial and business elites, based on their alliance with government representatives, often influence the state not to adopt policies that replace their profitable capital-intensive industries. Thus, in most Third World countries, policies may remain biased toward the urban centers, large industries, and affluent elites.[49] It is unlikely that the poor majority in these countries would be able to influence national policies since they lack resources, organization, leadership, and power.[50] It has been suggested that there are social causes of hunger based upon human-made political and economic structures.[51] Thus, for effectuating the above policy reforms—suggested for enhancing human autonomy from the unfavorable physiological-natural conditions or forces—it is imperative for Third World countries to adopt fundamental policy reforms in the politico-economic sphere as illustrated in the next section.

Reforming Policies to
Realize Politico-Economic Autonomy

In Third World countries, human powerlessness to adverse physiological conditions and natural forces is not only perpetuated by the aforementioned inappropriate policies (related to agriculture, industry, health, education, and transportation) undertaken and maintained by the national and international vested interests, it is also caused by politico-economic factors such as extreme income inequality, excessive military expenditures, international unequal exchange, and external debt and dependence. Because, these factors representing the structure of human subjugation in the politico-economic sphere, lead to the diversion of scarce resources in favor of the affluent classes and nations, and thus to the further impoverishment of the poorer classes and nations that already lack resources needed for managing adverse natural-physiological conditions. With regard to the significance of power structures and vested interests in understanding development, Johnston and Clark mention that "the fight for *whose* interests will be served imparts to the development process an inherent political dimension . . . one of the truest but least useful observations that can be made about development programs is that their failures to help the poor are 'essentially' political failures."[52]

It is necessary, therefore, to introduce major policy reforms with a view to overcome the existing inequalities and subjugation in the politico-economic realm by ensuring equitable property ownership, redistributing income, reducing defense expenditure, restructuring international trade, and so on. In fact, the realization of a more equal politico-economic structure is significant on its own right, because equality is an essential feature of human existence, and autonomy from politico-economic subjugation represents a basic component of development.[53] However, in adopting policy reforms for ensuring human autonomy from such politico-economic subjugation, it is necessary to identify the major dimensions, agents, and means of this subjugation at both the internal and international levels.

POLICIES FOR INTERNAL AUTONOMY

In Third World countries, there are dominant groups and classes, commonly known as Third World elite, who tend to impose or exercise internal human subjugation. For Nafziger, Third World elite includes big landowners, political leaders, top military officers, senior civil servants, leading professionals, business magnates, and corporate executives.[54] The landlords impose subjugation over marginal and landless farmers based on extreme inequality in land ownership; the industrial and business tycoons exercise subjugation over workers due to their control over industrial and financial assets; military personnel pursue subjugation over the civilian population by possessing coercive military weapons and centralized organizational structures; and bureaucrats and professional experts exercise subjugation over ordinary people based on their control over official positions, government resources, information networks, and expertise. These dominant groups and classes often reinforce each other's power, and some of them may form alliances to expand politico-economic subjugation over the common masses. For instance, there may be alliances formed between big landowners and local-level bureaucrats, between the business class and the military, between the intellectual and political elites, and so on, depending on the specific sociohistorical circumstances. Thus, for the autonomy of powerless groups and classes from internal politico-economic subjugation, it is essential to adopt appropriate policies in accordance with the degree, forms, and mechanisms of such subjugation. In this regard, although some scholars have offered some generic suggestions,[55] it is necessary to delineate more specific policy options.

Undertaking Fundamental Reforms in Landownership

First, for the autonomy of small or landless farmers from the subjugation of landlords or big landowners, it is necessary to introduce fundamental land reforms. In most Third World countries, the rural structure of interclass subjugation is usually based on extreme inequality in the patterns of land ownership. In Latin America, for instance, small farmers representing 50 percent of rural population, own less than 20 percent of all cultivable lands, while the remaining 80 percent is owned by landlords.[56] In the case of South Asia, the number of near-landless rural household is about 40 percent.[57] This inequality in land distribution enables the landowning class to exercise political and economic dominance over the dependent landless and small farmers. It is essential, therefore, to undertake radical land reforms in order to redistribute land. The redistribution of land from the absentee landlords to poor farmers would not only ensure more equality in rural power structure, and thereby mitigate politico-economic subjugation, it would also create more incentives for land-less farmers to produce more, because they would be able to claim and enjoy whatever crops they could produce in their own lands gained from land reform. In addition, according to Johnston and Clark, redistributive land reform often creates a favorable atmos-phere for the improvement or modernization of numerous small-scale farm units in Third World countries.[58]

Emphasizing Labor-Intensive Production and Technology

Another policy reform needed for overcoming politico-economic subjug-ation is a shift from capital-intensive technologies to labor-intensive ones. In the agricultural sector, it has been found that the so-called Green Revolution that introduced capital-intensive technologies and inputs, benefited rich farmers, increased landlessness and income inequality, and made the poor poorer.[59] Labor-intensive technologies are appropriate for Third World countries to expand employment for the unemployed rural population, to expand the capacity of small farmers (who cannot afford capital-intensive agricultural production) to survive in competition with big landowners, and to enhance the power of landless farmers to demand higher wages and more favorable terms and conditions from the affluent landowning class.

In the industrial sector, for reducing the hegemony of corporate elite over the working class, it is necessary to adopt similar policy of emphasizing labor-intensive technology and production in order to increase the bargaining capacity of workers vis-à-vis the power of industrialists. It is also necessary to encounter the dominance of monopolistic large corporations by encouraging and assisting smaller business enterprises—so that there is less corporate power over the labor market, there is higher demand and competition among enter-prises for the labor force, and thus the workers have more influence and bargaining power related to their compensation and service conditions. More importantly, it may be necessary to increase the involvement of workers in industrial and business management and ensure some form of workers' ownership of industrial assets. The above policy changes are essential for enhancing the autonomy of poor farmers and low-income workers from the dominance of rich farmers and corporate elites respectively.

Streamlining Military Establishment and Expenditure

With regard to the overwhelming power and influence of the military in Third World countries, it is necessary to cut military expenditures, reduce the scope of the defense sector to its most essential activities, and transfer resources from the military to more productive and people-oriented programs. Such reduction and redirection in military expenditure are essential, because it accounts for the increase of foreign debt, drainage of resources from essential development programs, and misuse of scientific and technological innovations.[60] In general, while the excessive military expenditure has economically impoverished, politically disintegrated, and internationally subordinated Third World nations, it has enriched affluent Western defense industries and strengthened many repressive Third World regimes. Thus, basic policy reforms are essential for changing the size, role, and power of the military in these countries.

In addition, policy changes are needed in relation to the structures and attitudes of the military. On the one hand, it is necessary to introduce a more decentralized structure in the defense sector in order to reduce the power of the military and its ability to intervene; on the other hand, it is essential to create a people-oriented, responsive, and accountable national defense through intensive attitudinal training and reorientation, so that the basic rights and freedom of people are ensured while maintaining national security. In short, the expensive, expansive, and repressive military establishment should be replaced by relatively inexpensive, need-based, decentralized, and people-oriented national defense, so that the process of subjugating the powerless common citizens by the powerful military through its direct or indirect intervention could be overcome in Third World countries.

Transforming Bureaucratic Structure, Culture, and Attitude

It is necessary to introduce fundamental reforms in the colonially inherited elitist bureaucratic and professional organizations to overcome their excessive power over the common masses. The state bureaucracies in Third World countries have been known for their centralized structure, secretive nature, inaccessibility, social isolation, hegemonic tendency, and so on.[61] In this regard, first, the rigidly hierarchical and centralized bureaucracies should be replaced by more democratic and participative institutions, so that they are equally accessible to various groups and classes of people and responsive to their needs and expectations. One effective means is to place the local branches or field offices of various state agencies under the control and supervision of the locally elected public representatives, provided these local representatives themselves do not have opportunity to abuse unequal power structure based on the aforementioned inequality in landownership.[62] The transfer of bureaucratic programs to local institutions and representatives would enhance people's accessibility to goods and services based on their local needs, and reduce people's dependence on the hegemonic state bureaucracy controlling scarce economic resources. The direct knowledge of local needs acquired by these local representatives is quite important, because the programs undertaken for the rural poor "must be based upon intimate knowledge of local conditions obtained by firsthand, village-level assessment."[63]

There is also a need for replacing the closed and secretive bureaucratic culture in government organizations by a more open and trustworthy organizational culture, so that the people have access to public-sector information, opportunity for scrutinizing government agencies, and thus the guarantee of bureaucratic responsiveness and accountability. One of the basic requirements for realizing such public accessibility and scrutiny is the replacement of complex bureaucratic jargons, which reflect the colonial legacy and the language of subjugation, by more indigenous interpretations and terms that are intelligible to the common masses. Such reforms in organizational structure and culture must be complemented by basic attitudinal changes among top government officials through appropriate training and education, especially in terms of changing their elitist mentality, and reorienting them toward the basic needs and expectations of people whom they are supposed to serve. This transformation of the structural, cultural, and attitudinal features of public organizations is likely to encounter strong bureaucratic resistance, and thus requires strong and committed political leadership to realize such organizational transformation.

Developing People-Centered Political Institutions

All the above changes in agrarian and industrial structures, rural and urban economies, military expenditures and powers, and bureaucratic cultures and attitudes cannot be realized without dedicated, people-centered political leadership emphasizing the needs and expectations of common people.[64] But in many Third World countries, political leaders themselves are highly corrupt and repressive, they often form alliances with the above dominant social forces (i.e., the landlords, industrial and business tycoons, top military officials, higher civil servants, and professional elites), and they are neither interested in, nor unilaterally capable of, introducing the aforementioned changes. Instead, these political leaders tend to adopt policies that strengthen and perpetuate the economic and political hegemony of these dominant forces over the common masses. In some Third World countries, the recent replacement of military regimes by elected ones without introducing any of the above changes, has hardly altered the hegemonic system. In this regard, one should not be mystified by the current fetish of Western democracy that ensures voting rights while the people are depoliticized and powerless, that perpetuates ideological biases and commoditizes politics through the profit-seeking media, and that tends to overlook the structures of inequality and subjugation.

One of the most essential prerequisites for realizing human autonomy from such internal inequality and subjugation is the unity of politically conscious and organized people who can form critical public opinion, challenge state policies serving the dominant social forces, and create pressure on the state for adopting reforms toward greater politico-economic equality. For this purpose, it is necessary to develop collective and integrative institutions: the formation of such liberating collective organizations or associations should not be confused with the existing local-level organizations that are dominated by the rural landowning class, urban elites, or foreign interests. In many Third World countries, the local government institutions have perpetuated the power of the rural elite,[65] the village cooperatives have benefited the rich farmers, and the professional and industrial associations have strengthened the influence of educated urban elite.

The earlier version of community organizations established under the so-called community development programs in many Asian, African, and Latin American countries did not take into account the question of local power structure, and allegedly these programs benefited the traditional village elites.[66] More recently, there has been unprecedented growth of the so-called nongovernment organizations (NGOs) in Asia, Africa, and Latin America often under the auspices of Western financial supports that may require serious critical examination due to the involvement of foreign interest and agenda. In this regard, Tandon brings the following charges against the foreign NGOs that are engaged in diverse agricultural and educational programs, health services, community development projects, and women activities: these NGOs, created and funded by Western governments and private corporations, are secretive about their decisions and activities, have hidden ideological and religious agenda, demonize African normative standards and impose Euro-American culture, judge African societies based on decontextualized and ahistorical Western standards, and are engaged in anticommunist crusade while supporting certain repressive and racist African organizations.[67]

Since many of these existing organizations themselves are means of internal subjugation, it is essential to establish indigenous local organizations based on economic and political equality. The subjugated groups and classes, including the landless farmers, industrial workers, underprivileged women, and ethnic minorities, should create their own organizations or associations. Structurally and financially, these organizations should be free from dependence on landlords, business magnates, bureaucratic officials, and political elites. Although a certain degree of complexity is likely to arise due to the overlaps between class, gender, and ethnicity within these organizations— due to the fact that there are gender and ethnic inequalities within the same class in many Third World countries—it is still essential to establish a strong solidarity among the subjugated groups and classes based on their common experience of being the victims of repression and exploitation in order to realize their autonomy from such subjugation.

POLICIES FOR INTERNATIONAL AUTONOMY

As explained in the previous chapter, in addition to the internal structures of interclass and intergroup subjugation, there are international structures of politico-economic subjugation that need to be overcome. Often these internal and international structures are mutually complementary and reinforcing. Although the direct form of colonialism has ended, for scholars such as Itty, such a demise of colonial rule has not diminished the need for Third World autonomy from the international structures of subjugation in the economic, military, and cultural realms.[68] In this section, some basic policy reforms are suggested in relation to the realization of this autonomy of Third World countries from the contemporary global structures of politico-economic hegemony.

Restructuring International Political Economy Based on Equality

For realizing autonomy from international politico-economic subjugation, it is necessary to examine the structures of such international subjugation, analyze their critical implications, and outline alternative policy measures. It has been discussed in the preceding chapters that in the economic sphere, advanced Western nations exercise considerable global dominance by dint of their favorable positions in the colonially inherited international division of labor, their influence on the patterns of Third World production and consumption through transnational corporations, their control over international trade and exchange through various world bodies such as the World Trade Organization (WTO), and their use of protectionist economic and trade blocs.[69] In the international financial system, it is also the leading Western nations that control the world financial institutions (including banks and stock markets), shape the world monetary system through institutions such as the International Monetary Fund (IMF), and perpetuate the financial dependence of Third World countries through the mechanism of foreign aid and external debt.[70] Western governments have often used foreign aid as an "instrument of intervention" in Asian, African, and Latin American countries, and currently these countries have a total debt of $1,500 billion to Western governments, private banks, and international financial institutions.[71]

However, a more intensive form of international economic subjugation that has expanded significantly in recent years is the worldwide intervention of transnational corporations, which have established a significant amount of control over the terms of trade, investment, production, and finance in Third World countries.[72] Today, each of the large corporations, such as Ford, General Motors, IBM, Exxon, Shell, Mobil, Texaco, and British Petroleum, has an annual output larger than that of many Third World countries.[73] In the year 1989–90, the annual sales of General Motors ($126.9 billion) and Ford Motor ($96.9 billion) were larger than the annual GNP of Iran ($100.1 billion) and Saudi Arabia ($92.6 billion) respectively.[74] The poorer Third World economies are much more insignificant compared to these global corporations. The operational scope of transnational firms is extremely expansive. For instance, the top 380 transnational corporations have 25,000 foreign affiliates, and they control 33 percent of world production and 40 percent of the world trade.[75] In terms of control over the regional economic markets, the U.S. has monopoly on Latin America, Western Europe has control over Africa, the U.S. and Western Europe share the Caribbean and the Pacific, and the U.S. and Japan have command over East and Southeast Asia.[76] Even the dominant international institutions, such as the IMF, the World Bank, and the WTO, have served Western economic and political interests instead of contributing to the politico-economic autonomy of the Third World.[77] As Dogra mentions, the IMF and the World Bank have played significant role in promoting Western foreign investment, facilitating the expansion of transnational corporations, ensuring interest payments by Third World countries to Western commercial banks, and protecting Western economic and political interests in general.[78] According to Nafziger, there are detrimental implications of such foreign investment by transnational corporations for Third World countries, such as the displacement of local industries, inappropriate production and consumption, technological dependence, income inequality, balance-of-payment deficits, foreign intervention in national politics, and so on.[79]

Similarly, in the politico-military realm, most Third World countries are under the hegemony of advanced Western nations (especially in terms of direct and indirect military interventions and threats) based on their possession of massive and lethal military weapons, their control over military research and information, their strong military alliance such as the North Atlantic Treaty Organization (NATO), and their control over international bodies such as the UN Security Council.[80] After the collapse of the socialist superpowers, Third World countries have been brought under more monopolistic Western military subjugation not only by informal coercive means (e.g., military threats and covert operations), but also through "legalized" interventions approved by the United Nations under the influence of Western powers, especially the U.S.

In order to enhance autonomy from the above global structures of politico-economic hegemony, it is essential for Third World countries to reexamine the critical implications of foreign assistance and foreign investment for perpetuating their external dependence. They must introduce fundamental changes in the patterns of production and consumption in accordance with available local resources and commodities, so that the need for external assistance, advice, and investment could be minimized. In the case when the borrowing of capital and technology and the import of goods and services are unavoidable, the process of such exchange should take place among the economically complementary Third World countries themselves. The conditional foreign assistance and investment from advanced capitalist nations should be avoided, and when unavoidable, must be received only on favorable terms and conditions in order to reduce external economic subordination. Similarly, in the case of national defense and security, each Third World country needs to rethink its waste of resources to amass arms based on the assumption to protect itself from other Third World neighbors. These countries must work out their cross-national differences and disagreements, view each other as partners and friends, reduce the need for defense built-ups, and stop purchasing weapons from Western military powers. This policy reorientation in defense will not only reduce the external military dependence and subordination of Third World countries, it will also diminish the capacity of global military powers that gained considerable financial strength based on profits from selling arms to these countries. This policy reform will also unleash resources needed for Third World development (mentioned above), and expand the scope of collective security among the neighboring Third World countries (discussed below) against any military threats launched by the global powers. In addition to this need for rejecting the unequal international structures maintained by the world economic and military powers, it is also imperative to challenge hegemonic international institutions such as the IMF, the World Bank, the WTO, the UN Security Council, and other UN organizations, which tend to facilitate and perpetuate such structures of international subjugation.

Resolving Conflict and Competition among Third World Countries

In order to overcome the subjection of Third World countries to international politico-economic subjugation, it is necessary to identify the major weaknesses of Third World countries themselves. One such weakness is the aforementioned concern that among these countries, there are serious ideological disagreements, territorial disputes, ethnic conflicts, and religious differences—inherited as colonial legacies or created by the postcolonial regimes—which have weakened their mutual unity and reinforced their subjugation to Western nations.[81] The potential for Third World unity has also been diminished due to the increasing division within the Third World caused by the emergence of the NICs, regional economic rivalries, cross-national competition for foreign aid and investment, national economic crises, and so on.[82] Recently, many Third World countries have been engaged in severe mutual competition for expanding their trade with advanced industrial nations.[83]

Although a considerable number of initiatives have been undertaken by Third World countries to enhance their unity at various levels, such endeavors have mostly failed due to insufficient resources and expertise, weak institutions and commitment, the gap between collective decisions and individual national policies, and poor communication and information exchange among them.[84] In addition, in adopting the existing conventions or treaties related to such unity and cooperation, Third World regimes put more emphasis on how to facilitate international negotiations, and demanded the transfer of capital and technology from advanced industrial nations to Third World countries; but they often overlooked the unequal structures of the international political economy, and compromised the need for fundamental changes in such international structures.[85] In this regard, Amin observes that as long as Third World countries continue to pursue their capitalist development within the structure of global capitalism, they will be bound to compete among themselves, and therefore conflict rather than cooperation among them will be the rule.[86]

In other words, although the realization of autonomy of Third World countries from the hegemonic global capitalism require the resolution of conflicts among these countries themselves, the process of resolving such conflicts has often been constrained by many factors, including the lack of resources, institutions, commitment, and communication, and the choice of inappropriate international policies and development models. In order to overcome these barriers to conflict resolution among Third World countries, it is essential that the governments of these countries allocate resources, build relevant institutions, show strong commitment, and facilitate cross-national communication or information exchange with regard to mitigating such conflict. In addition, they must adopt development policies based on the principle of self-reliance and mutual cooperation rather than on the principle of capitalist growth that often intensifies economic competition among Third World countries, especially for foreign investment and foreign markets. Instead of asking for the transfer of capital and technology from the affluent capitalist nations—which often proliferates competition among Third World countries for such foreign capital and technology, and perpetuates their dependence on the world capitalist system—these poorer countries should demand more autonomy from and maintain certain dissociation with global capitalism (discussed below).

Delinking Third World Societies from International Structures

For Third World countries, it is not enough just to comprehend the nature and forms of international subjugation, challenge international policies and institutions associated with the structures of such subjugation, and understand the shortcomings of various liberating attempts. For realizing genuine autonomy from the condition of such international subjugation, it is essential to adopt alternative policies. In this regard, some scholars suggest the dissociation or delinking of Third World countries from advanced capitalist nations, at least temporarily, so that they can achieve a certain degree of self-reliance and sustainable development with regard to their economies and societies.[87]

However, in the economic realm, today it is difficult for Third World countries to maintain any form of separation from the global capitalist structure due to their dependence on and subordination to the world capitalist system. On the other hand, they cannot overcome their international economic subjugation without establishing some form of delinkage in their modes of production, patterns of consumption, and processes of exchange. In fact, such delinkage could have more positive implications for Third World countries, because their very association with the global capitalist system, which they want to maintain for economic development, has led to their dependence and underdevelopment. For instance, to enhance the rate of economic growth, many Third World countries have replaced the self-reliant production of basic foods for local consumers by the export-led production of cash crops for foreign customers, and thus integrated themselves into the world capitalist structures. But such export-led policies have not only exacerbated the external dependence of these countries on the fluctuating state policies and market demands in affluent nations such as the U.S., in future, the newcomers in the game will face more difficulty in exporting their goods as the foreign markets become increasingly overloaded by such Third World exports.[88] As some scholars suggest, simply there is no room for "new Japans" or a new "Gang of Four" in the world market.[89] During 1997–98, the severe currency and market crises in East and Southeast Asia (especially in Korea, Indonesia, Malaysia, and Thailand) showed the vulnerability of export-led economic growth based on close linkages with the global capitalist system.

Thus, the problem is not that the dissociation of Third World countries from the world capitalist system will lead to their economic collapse. The problem is rather with the global dominance of Western capitalist nations, which would not allow such delinkage, and if necessary, would not hesitate to use coercive military force to maintain and expand their unequal and exploitive international economic relations with the Third World. However, as far as Third World countries are concerned, while pursuing closer economic unity among themselves, they need to detach from the hegemonic structure of global capitalism in order to pursue their economic self-reliance and autonomous (as opposed to dependent) development. In fact, similar disassociation of Third World countries needs to be introduced with regard to their defense pacts with, and military dependence on, the world military powers. In most Third World countries, the military establishments not only represent the colonial legacy, but also reflect their neocolonial subordination to Western military powers in terms of mission, training, weapons, technologies, and organizational structures. Of course, there are serious internal and external barriers to the realization of this delinkage, but it needs to be adopted in order to enhance the autonomy of Third World countries from the existing structures of international security dominated by the global military powers. However, to maintain this challenging but necessary dissociation from the hegemonic world order, Third World countries need to establish a genuine economic and strategic solidarity among themselves.

Establishing Effective Institutions for Third World Solidarity

In addition to the delinkage or dissociation of Third World countries from unequal world order, it is also imperative to reconstruct the existing fragmented and dependent organizations related to Third World cooperation into more effective institutions of solidarity, autonomous from the unequal global structures of subjugation. Alternative institutions are needed, because the existing organizational arrangements for Third World cooperation—including the Non-Aligned Movement, the North-South dialogue, the New International Economic Order, and the South-South Cooperation—have largely been articulated within the existing world order based on inequality and hegemony. In fact, the realization of solidarity among Third World countries and the process of their delinkage from the global powers are mutually interdependent and complementary: some degree of such delinkage is necessary to articulate a more self-reliant Third World solidarity, and this solidarity is essential for effectively maintaining this delinkage from the hegemonic world powers.

As far as economic solidarity is concerned, Third World countries have quite favorable conditions in terms of resources. For instance, they have over 80 percent of the world's oil reserves (the Middle East alone has 56.4 percent); they represent four (Saudi Arabia, China, Mexico, and Venezuela) of the world's top ten energy producers; many of them (especially African countries) are rich in valuable minerals such as gold, chromium, platinum, manganese, iron, lead, zinc, and nickel; and most of them have abundant lands for agricultural production.[90] Thus, against the established belief in their resource scarcity, Third World countries possess abundant resources, and it is highly feasible to establish a genuine Third World solidarity based on self-reliance without being subordinated to the structures of economic subjugation maintained by the economically dominant nations, transnational corporations, and various international agencies.[91]

In this regard, Senghaas, Abdalla, and Patel emphasize Third World integration and cooperation at the continental, regional, and subregional levels based on their similarity and complementarity in production and exchange, export and import, transportation and communication, technologies and skills, research and development, bilateral and multilateral negotiation, and so on.[92] For the creation of regional blocs based on each region's self-sufficiency in resources, capital, and know-how, Mamadou Aw proposes to restructure the world into the following five regions: (a) Western Europe, North America, Japan, and Australia; (b) Eastern Europe and China; (c) South America, Central America, and the Caribbean; (d) Africa and the Middle East; and (e) Asia and Far East (without China, Japan, and the former Soviet republics).[93] He emphasizes the primacy of such regional blocs over the dominant global economic system comprised of organizations such as the IMF, the World Bank, the WTO, and the UN institutions. Although this international reordering might require further rethinking due to some unprecedented changes such as the collapse and disintegration of the Soviet Union and the Eastern European states, the basic point here is that the formation of more liberating Third World associations or institutions at the regional and interregional levels is crucial. In brief, it is essential to establish self-reliant economic solidarity among Third World countries, which would include different forms and levels of economic unity based on their common and complementary historical contexts, resource compositions, production structures, consumption patterns, geographic proximity, technical feasibility, and so on.

Similar strategic change is needed in the politico-military realm to replace the fragmented, mutually conflicting, and internationally subordinated military structures of Third World countries by more cohesive, mutually beneficial, and internationally autonomous defense mechanisms based on genuine cooperation and unity among these countries. It is essential to overcome their dependence on the unequal world defense structures (including weapons, technologies, rules, and organizations) dominated by the leading Western nations. For establishing such collective defense mechanisms, it is imperative for Third World countries to resolve their historically inherited territorial, ethnic, and religious conflicts that weaken and impoverish them; to engage themselves in serious dialogue and mutual understanding for comprehensive regional and interregional security arrangements (independent of Western security systems) based on mutual power-sharing; and to subordinate their parochial (national) military out-looks and ventures to these collective arrangements of external security.

Unfortunately, many Third World regimes seem to endorse the current structures of global security dominated by Western military powers instead of pursuing their autonomy from such hegemonic structures. It is quite evident, for example, in the recent acceptance by Third World states (with few exceptions) of an unconditional and indefinite renewal of the Nuclear Non-Proliferation Treaty,[94] which might perpetuate the powerlessness of these nonnuclear states and their politico-military subordination to Western nuclear powers, espe-cially the U.S. and its allies. Instead of consenting to these hegemonic Western powers, Third World countries must enhance their own col-laboration and solidarity with regard to external security in order to protect themselves from the threats and challenges posed by the world military powers, because, compared with these global powers, they are relatively powerless as individual countries. In addition to this advantage of stronger external protection, collective security may also reduce military expenditures in individual Third World countries, ensure a more combined and larger pool of resources for advanced military research and technology, and thus expand Third World power in relation to the existing military superpowers. Furthermore, the system of mutually binding, collective Third World security would also ensure a more accountable military institution in each Third World nation, discourage military intervention or the formation of authoritarian military regime, and thus reduce the process of inter-nal subjugation.

It is also mainly by achieving this internationally autonomous collective military power that Third World countries can bargain for more equality and nondiscrimination in international forum (such as the UN Security Council and the Nuclear Non-Proliferation Treaty), create pressure on Western powers to introduce more genuine and comprehensive programs of denuclearization and demilitarization, and thus overcome the legacy of unilateral military subjugation that began with Western colonialism. However, the structures of interna-tional subjugation are much more complex: many Third World coun-tries are so economically dependent on Western nations that it is difficult for them to reject Western military hegemony; and conversely, they are so militarily dependent and powerless that their attempts for economic self-reliance are often undermined by Western military threats and interventions.[95] As a result, Third World countries should pursue the suggested policy reforms in both economic and military realms simultaneously, because their economic autonomy and military autonomy are interdependent and complementary.

Identifying and Uniting Emancipatory Change-Agents

Despite the need for the above politico-economic solidarity among Third World countries for their autonomy from the structures of international subjugation, it may not be easy to achieve this objective due to the fact that there are many Third World regimes that practice internal repression and collaborate with the international forces of subjugation. It has already been explained in the previous chapter that Western nations (especially the U.S.) have provided billions of dollars in arms to violent and repressive Third World regimes, while these regimes, in return, have served Western interests, especially by welcoming Western transnational corporations and investments.[96] Third World people have frequently experienced such dictatorial military regimes supported by the Western states and defense industries.[97] For instance, since 1950, the U.S. has trained more than 500,000 military personnel from 85 countries, which include the world's most brutal police forces (e.g., Iran's Savak and Uganda's "public safety unit") and the heads of the state (e.g., Chile's General Pinochet and Nicaragua's Somoza).[98] Thus, Sparks and Roach suggest that there is no hope for a just world order as long as Third World state structures "are themselves the product not of the needs of workers and peasants but of their ruling classes."[99] In addition, there are Third World countries—such as the NICs that have made some economic gains and acquired certain dependent development from the current unequal structures of international exchange—which tend to associate more closely with the hegemonic global politico-economic structures. As a result of such variations among these countries with regard to their support of and opposition to the hegemonic world order, it is not easy to achieve a clear Third World solidarity.

However, in spite of these adverse internal and international forces or vested interests undermining the autonomy of Third World masses from the international structures of subjugation, in each country, still there are many social activists or change agents, including political figures, grassroots leaders, public employees, and the academics, who recognize the need for international politico-economic autonomy of their societies and peoples. These liberating change-agents should identify their cross-national counterparts, establish information and communication links among them, overcome their cross-cultural differences, strengthen their cooperation and unity, establish regional and international organizations as alternatives to hegemonic global structures, and undertake the role of leadership in adopting and implementing policies for politico-economic autonomy of all subjugated Third World countries and peoples.

These emancipatory change agents, however, need to be aware of the fact that despite good intentions and commitment, their policy choices could be influenced by false assumptions and outlooks propagated by the global information networks, intellectual products, and culture industry dominated by the leading Western nations. The networks of transnational media may persuade them to believe in the ideology of economic growth, the miracle of market forces, pleasures in consumerism, benefits from transnational corporations, assistance from international agencies, the liberating role of Western governments, and so on. The media also tend to portray a self-reliant economy as inefficient, indigenous production and consumption as primitive, people-oriented but less Westernized leaders as dictators, and the common Third World masses as backward.

In effect, the global means of information, knowledge, and culture are engaged in perpetuating politico-economic hegemony exercised by advanced capitalist states and corporations; in manipulating Third World societies and peoples to accept the conditions of subjugation; and in manufacturing favorable world opinion to justify or legitimize the prevailing structures of international hegemony. In these circumstances, it is imperative for the liberating change agents, including certain Third World leaders and intelligentsia, not only to be aware of these media-created biases that might affect their own policy choices, but also to undertake initiatives to liberate their societies and peoples from such international networks of cultural-intellectual subjugation. The next section is devoted to an analysis of this cultural-intellectual dimension of human autonomy in Third World countries.

Reforming Policies to Enhance
Cultural-Intellectual Autonomy

Despite the relative indifference toward the cultural-intellectual realm in the current development literature, as far as the human species is concerned, the realization of cultural-intellectual autonomy represents a basic dimension of development.[100] In the present era, as discussed in the preceding chapters, such cultural-intellectual autonomy has become a determining factor also for the realization of natural-physiological and politico-economic autonomy at both the internal and international levels. The previous chapter already presented an extensive analysis of the nature of cultural-intellectual subjugation imposed by the leading Western nations on Third World countries through education systems, culture industry, intellectual products, and news media. The main thrust of this section is to delineate some basic policy reforms that are imperative for transcending such subjugation. In this regard, scholars such as Cees Hamelink, Samir Amin, and Gerald Sussman prescribe a delinkage of Third World countries from the global cultural-intellectual networks in order to overcome cultural subjugation, reduce communication dependency, and achieve autonomy and self-reliance.[101]

Although it has become extremely difficult to practice such a delinkage due to the globalization of education systems, cultural products, news media, and other information networks (largely controlled and owned by Western governments and corporations), there are hardly any other alternatives for Third World countries but to protect themselves from such cultural and intellectual hegemony by adopting this measure of delinkage or disassociation. However, in pursuing this delinkage for cultural-intellectual autonomy, Third World countries not only need to critically scrutinize the existing global structures of subjugation,[102] they should also reexamine and restructure their own policies related to education, culture, news, and information. In this regard, brief analyses are presented below on various forms of cultural-intellectual subjugation, followed by the corresponding sets of policy recommendations for augmenting the cultural-intellectual autonomy of Third World countries.

INDIGENIZATION OF EDUCATION AND KNOWLEDGE

As discussed in the preceding chapter, most Third World countries have inherited an education system that reflects their colonial past and the neocolonial influence. More specifically, "the structure and curricula of colleges and universities in the Third World are generally based on European and North American models. They represent Euro-American enclaves within these countries."[103] These colleges and universities produce civil servants, military officials, political leaders, development experts, and other professionals who are relatively isolated from their local conditions and indifferent toward societal problems, but they exercise power over the common masses, and play a significant role in subordinating indigenous culture and knowledge to the global structure of cultural and intellectual hegemony.[104] With regard to education, the process of Western intellectual hegemony is perpetuated through means such as books and journals, conferences and seminars, fellowships and assistantships, and lucrative projects and assignments.[105] In many Third World countries, there are also extensive networks of Western schools, colleges, and universities that are detached from the indigenous social contexts, and that produce graduates whose knowledge, skills, and attitudes are more appropriate for advanced industrial nations and transnational corporations than for the Third World's local needs. Moreover, since the whole global structure of intellectual production (including books, journals, reports, and papers) is predominantly controlled by Western nations, it is quite difficult for Third World universities and colleges to be free from such academic hegemony.[106]

In this regard, it is not only necessary to reduce Third World dependence on foreign education provided by Western educational institutions, it is also crucial to critically examine the assumptions of these institutions' intellectual supremacy in philosophical traditions, concepts, theories, and models that have very little relevance to Third World contexts. It implies the need for reevaluating the texts, journals, and reports owned and produced by Western institutions and scholars, especially in terms of their ideological predispositions, cultural underpinnings, and intellectual prejudices. This critical outlook toward the global dominance of Western educational institutions would generate more self-confidence among Third World scholars, enhance their urge for generating indigenous knowledge, diminish their dependence on foreign training, and reduce the incidence of brain-drain.

Within Third World countries themselves, there is a need for the critical scrutiny of their Eurocentric education systems, of their institutional linkages with the global education networks, of their course curricula based on Western education models. More specifically, in each Third World country, the existing education system has to be reassessed in terms of whether it is relevant or irrelevant to the local context, whether it creates positive or negative impact on indigenous knowledge, and whether it increases or diminishes intellectual self-reliance. Education policies should be restructured in such a manner that they not only produce human resources appropriate for local economies and domestic needs, not only enhance indigenous human capacities for addressing people's needs, but also reduce external educational dependence and expand intellectual self-reliance by gradually replacing the imitative institutional structures, borrowed concepts and theories, and imported texts and reading materials.

PROTECTION AND ADVANCEMENT OF INDIGENOUS CULTURAL HERITAGE

The intensity of the current cross-national cultural exchange is unprecedented in human history. The increasingly powerful culture industry, including television programs, radio broadcasts, films, musical recordings, cartoons, comics, videotapes, magazines, and so on, is shaping the cultural patterns worldwide by introducing artificially packaged norms and values.[107] Such cultural exchange is highly unequal and unidirectional since the global cultural industry is owned and controlled by few Western, especially American, transnational corporations.[108] For instance, the American films alone account for 95 percent of the total film imports in South Korea, 88 percent in Jamaica, 74 percent in Angola, and 70 percent in Sierra Leone.[109] Today, the imported videocassettes and videodisks are undermining film industries in Third World countries and perpetuating their subjection to Western cultural hegemony.[110] The worldwide expansion of Western cultural subjugation has considerably taken place through international television networks that were already expansive in the 1970s,[111] but have proliferated more massively in recent years. Currently, the imported Western television programs occupy more than 55 percent of the annual broadcast hours in Africa, 46 percent in Latin America, 42 percent in the Arab states, and about 87 percent in some Caribbean countries.[112] Similarly, the Western transnational agencies account for 92 percent of the advertising market in the Caribbean, 83 percent in Africa, and 58.2 percent in Latin America.[113]

Through this process of unequal cultural exchange, the utilitarian Western values of individualism, consumerism, and industrialism (compatible with the business norms of transnational corporations) are being introduced in Third World countries, although such cultural diffusion has allegedly led to more violence, crimes, perverted sexuality, suicide, and other pathologies in these non-Western societies.[114] Even tourism, which represents an emerging component of the global culture industry, has affected many Third World countries in terms of eroding their cultural traditions, commoditizing their indigenous arts and artifacts, increasing the number of drug addicts and prostitutes, and undermining the people's pride and dignity.[115] Although a certain degree of distortion took place in indigenous values, symbols, and

artifacts under the colonial rule, it is in the current age of transnational culture industry when the very survival of such indigenous
cultural forms has come under critical challenge.

To protect their cultural heritage from being subordinated, distorted, or supplanted, Third World countries rarely have any choice
but to put restrictions on the wholesale importation of the aforementioned Western cultural products. There are advocates of free cultural
exchange who might attack this policy stance as isolationist without
considering the gross inequality and subjugation that currently exists
in such a cultural exchange. They need to be reminded that the U.S.
itself practices restrictions on the foreign ownership of its broadcast
facilities while expanding its global hegemony over various forms of
media; and more recently, even the leading Western European countries have become increasingly protectionist against such hegemonic
American media to maintain their cultural identity.[116] At any rate,
the extreme vulnerability of Third World countries to Western cultural hegemony requires considerable safeguards based on a critical
scrutiny of the imported cultural products.

More specifically, in importing or borrowing foreign cultural
goods, each Third World country must critically examine whether
these cultural goods satisfy some basic terms and conditions—whether
they are neutral of implicit Eurocentric cultural biases and ideological
predilections, whether they express valid messages related to events
and information, whether they are contextually relevant to the local
conditions, and whether they create favorable politico-economic and
sociocultural outcomes for various social groups and classes. As discussed above and in the previous chapter, most of the borrowed or
imposed Western cultural goods do not satisfy these criteria—they
contain Eurocentric biases and bourgeois predilections, convey false or
distorted messages, contradict and erode local cultural conditions, and
often provide symbolic support to socioeconomic inequality and subjugation. Thus, based on a serious critical assessment, Third World
countries should import or allow openness to only those foreign cultural products that meet the above criteria of fair and beneficial cultural exchange. However, in order to satisfy the internal public
demands for cultural programs and recreational activities, the suggested protectionist or defensive cultural policy in Third World
countries must be supplemented by varieties of indigenous cultural
and recreational products, including television programs, radio broadcasts, films, theaters, musical recordings, magazines, and so on. The
forms and substance of these indigenous cultural products should not
be imitative of the Western culture industry (which has become a

common practice in many Third World countries), they should be based on indigenous contexts, and should represent the norms and expectations of the common masses rather than Westernized elites.

ESTABLISHMENT OF INDEPENDENT NEWS AND INFORMATION NETWORKS

In addition to education and culture, there is also overwhelming Western dominance over the sources of news and information through similar media networks such as newspapers, television programs, radio broadcasts, computer systems, and so on. The international flow of news is dominated by four major Western news agencies, including Reuters (Britain), AFP (France), AP (U.S.), and UPI (U.S.). There is 56 to 76 percent dependence of Asian, African, and Latin American dailies on these news agencies for international news.[117] The Western dominance over international news is also exercised through the networks of radio broadcasting, including Voice of America, British Broadcasting Corporation, Deutsche Welle, Radio France International, Radio Liberty, and Radio Free Europe, especially in Asian, African, and Eastern European countries.[118] Thus, Third World countries receive almost 80 percent of their news from New York, London, and Paris.[119] Moreover, through various electronic means, the U.S. transnational corporations have established control over nearly 75 percent of the international flows of data.[120]

In this regard, it is imperative for Third World countries to be selective in importing the commoditized forms of news that are advertised and sold globally like any other commercial goods. Since Western nations exercise almost monopolistic control over advanced information technologies that can reach the remotest parts of the world, Third World countries must invent or look for alternative technologies and mechanisms to screen (even block) transnational media in order to protect themselves from being bombarded by the relatively manufactured news and biased interpretations of national and global events broadcast by Western television and radio networks. They also need to overcome their information dependence on the hegemonic global news media by upgrading information technologies, developing broadcast skills, selecting appropriate news items, and above all, establishing independent news and information networks of their own. However, the content of news and information must be carefully delineated in order to overcome the structures of informational subordination of Third World countries.

First, a considerable amount of television and radio programs broadcast by these countries should be engaged to overcome the hegemony of transnational Western media by exposing the ideological roles, cultural biases, political motives, and economic interests of such transnational media. In other words, one basic task of the restructured Third World media is to generate critical public consciousness regarding the actual roles, motives, biases, and interests of the hegemonic global media, so that the people are not easily mystified by the foreign sources of news and information. Such an effort to raise critical public consciousness must go beyond Third World countries, and should reach advanced capitalist nations where the underclass and powerless people are often misled by their transnational media regarding internal and international events, have no access to these media to express their basic concerns, and need to free themselves from the deep-rooted false consciousness created by such media.[121]

Second, beyond this task of exposing the actual motives and interests of the global media, and forming public consciousness in this regard, Third World media have to play an essential role to produce more objective and critical news about political activities, economic conditions, social structures, and cultural issues in different parts of the world. The coverage of news and information should not only include these political, social, economic, and cultural realities within each Third World country, advanced capitalist nation, and former (or remaining) socialist state, it should also address crucial events related to various cross-national conflicts, exchanges, and treaties. Finally, in order to play the above essential roles by Third World media—in exposing the vested interests of global media, generating critical public consciousness, and producing more objective and reflective news—it is imperative to ensure that these Third World media themselves are not monopolized and used by certain dictatorial regimes and political elites for their personal gains, images, and legitimacy.

EXPANSION OF THIRD WORLD COOPERATION IN KNOWLEDGE AND INFORMATION

Given the existing inequality in the international structure of cultural, intellectual, and informational exchange, it is extremely difficult for Third World countries to reduce external dependence and achieve self-reliance in the realm of culture, knowledge, and information. In addition, since most of these countries suffer from external economic, political, and technological dependence on Western nations, they have almost no choice but to accept the hegemonic role played by the globalized Western media. In this regard, what remains to be most crucial is the establishment of much stronger cooperation and unity among Third World countries in the cultural-intellectual sphere based on appropriate regional and interregional institutions that are autonomous from the global media networks.

In the past, many Third World countries tried to make such attempts. For instance, with the support of the United Nations Educational, Scientific and Cultural Organization (Unesco), many Third World countries, especially those constituting the Non-Aligned Movement, tried to establish the so-called New World Information and Communication Order. In various conferences and meetings of Unesco, these Third World countries questioned the existing flows of international news, television programs, advertisements, and communication technologies, and demanded a restructuring of the world information order.[122] But since the U.S. and Britain rejected these Third World demands, and even withdrew from Unesco, this new information order failed to materialize.[123] It became evident that the rectification of inequality in the global information and cultural order could be difficult without transforming the existing institutional structures maintained by the dominant Western powers.

Thus, as suggested above, it is imperative for Third World countries to consolidate and deepen their mutual cooperation and unity independent of the existing international structures in order to pursue their cultural, intellectual, and informational autonomy. Without such cooperation and unity, the realization of the above policy recommendations regarding education system, culture industry, and news media is also difficult. More specifically, based on their cultural similarity, intellectual interdependence, and informational complementarity, Third World countries need to establish regional and interregional blocs for designing their educational curricula and institutions, exchanging their cultural programs and intellectual activities, and sharing their information and research outcomes. They must have strong commitment for such mutual cooperation, so that they have the collective capacity to create indigenous knowledge, develop able intellectuals, upgrade journalism skills, establish common information networks, improve communication technologies, and above all, ensure protection against the influence of the hegemonic global media. Such cooperation and unity among Third World countries is also essential to develop their own news agencies, radio and television networks, film industry, and other cultural and entertainment infrastructure; to overcome their external dependence on various forms of global media; and thus to enhance their autonomy from the structures of international cultural-intellectual hegemony.

PRIORITIZATION OF POLICIES RELATED TO CULTURAL-INTELLECTUAL AUTONOMY

Although the proposed policy reforms for enhancing human autonomy in the natural-physiological, politico-economic, and cultural-intellectual realms have been presented above separately, it is necessary to emphasize that policies for such autonomy in the cultural-intellectual sphere deserve utmost priority in the current age. Because, in line with the restructured theory of development presented in the previous chapter, it is genuine policy reforms in this cultural-intellectual realm (encompassing the education system, news and information networks, cultural products, entertainment industry, advertising enterprise, tourism industry, and so on) that have increasingly become essential for effectuating the suggested policy reforms in the natural-physiological and politico-economic spheres. For example, various networks of transnational media have serious implications for the perpetuation of the impoverished material conditions in Third World countries—the transnational advertisement industry plays a crucial role in reinforcing consumerism, replacing indigenous consumption patterns, expanding Third World dependence on foreign consumption goods, and introducing packaged solutions that are unaffordable and detrimental to most Third World people.[124] The predominantly media-created craze of Third World elites for luxurious imported goods often motivates them to accumulate more wealth and foreign exchange through different unfair means—including official corruption, foreign borrowing, capital flight, export-led production, and maldistribution—in order to purchase such expensive foreign goods. These unfair activities, largely reinforced by the commercial media, have diminished the Third World's self-reliance in basic consumption goods, and worsened the condition of poverty among the common masses. As a result, the policy reforms in various cultural-intellectual means, especially the media, are essential to reduce the volume of manipulative commercial messages, neutralize elitist consumerism, indigenize consumption patterns, cut down foreign goods, decrease external borrowing, and so on. Thus, the outcomes of these policy reforms could eventually enhance the alleviation of Third World poverty, and promote public awareness of the above causes of such adverse material condition.[125]

Similarly, the adoption of appropriate policies for the cultural-intellectual autonomy of Third World countries has become crucial for the realization of their politico-economic autonomy. Because, on the one hand, the globalized Western media are often engaged to maximize the profits of transnational corporations; to facilitate their worldwide expansion; and to perpetuate their control over Third World economies by advertising their products, advocating their contributions to economic progress, and legitimizing their worldwide economic hegemony (see chapters 2 and 8). On the other hand, the political and bureaucratic elites of Third World countries, due to their exposure to foreign education and transnational media, often adopt imitative and exploitive models of development, which require foreign capital, technology, and expertise, and thus, lead to further expansion and perpetuation of these countries' external debt and dependence.

Today the national sovereignty of Third World countries has increasingly come under challenge, especially due to the unprecedented capacity of Western information network to collect critical information regarding their internal socioeconomic issues and politico-military matters.[126] On the other hand, political solidarity among Third World countries is being weakened or diminished due to the influence of the global media.[127] As Dorfman and Mattelart mention, Western television networks, radio broadcasts, magazine, newspapers, and textbooks have weakened the "international solidarity" of the oppressed people, distorted their self-image, and separated them from each other.[128] More recently, various Western news media have intensified their influence to shape world opinion regarding Third World regimes and their political positions. Since these global news media work largely under the auspices of transnational corporations (discussed in chapter 8), they tend to glorify and legitimize regimes that serve such transnational corporate interests, while demonizing or delegitimizing regimes that are in favor of national interest and political sovereignty. The global media also tend to set the ideological agenda for the world population to evaluate, interpret, accept, and reject various political systems by propagating the self-serving conceptual categories such as dictatorship vs. democracy, central control vs. open market, state repression vs. individual freedom, and so on.[129] The images of Third World regimes manufactured and disseminated by the global media have become quite effective in rationalizing Western military interventions in different parts of the world.

Thus, since various global means of disseminating culture, knowledge, and information, especially by the transnational Western media, have become extremely effective to influence people's understanding and opinion worldwide, such cultural-intellectual means have serious implications for the perpetuation of Western politico-economic hegemony over Third World countries. Therefore, the adoption of the above policy reforms proposed for the cultural-intellectual autonomy of these countries has become almost a precondition for realizing the policies suggested for their politico-economic autonomy based on economic self-reliance and political self-determination. What has been emphasized above, in short, is that although the relevant sets of policy reforms are needed to enhance human autonomy from natural-physiological forces, from politico-economic subjugation, and from cultural-intellectual hegemony, in the current epoch, it has become essential to give more priority to the last set of policy reforms related to the cultural-intellectual domain. Thus, in articulating, selecting, and implementing various policy alternatives, this emerging priority should be seriously taken into consideration by the leading policy-makers in Third World countries.

Summary and Conclusion

In this book, the primary intellectual agenda was to explore the nature and extent of contemporary development crises, examine the major shortcomings of development theories, restructure these theories into an alternative development perspective, and articulate various policy reforms in line with this new perspective. In this regard, the first two chapters of the book not only presented an overview of both the practical and theoretical crises in the development field, but also analyzed more specific problems of development faced by Third World countries, the 'advanced capitalist nations, and the former and remaining socialist states. The list of these specific development crises included poverty and inequality, unemployment and homelessness, external debt and dependence, ethnic and racial conflicts, authoritarianism and repression, severe crimes and violence, erosion of community and family bonds, loneliness and mental disorder, drug abuse and alcoholism, environmental and ecological catastrophes, and unjust world order based on hegemony.

Following this discussion on the practical crises of development, the next four chapters (chapters 3, 4, 5, and 6) were devoted to an analysis of the existing development theories and models offered by both early and contemporary development thinkers with diverse theoretical perspectives, including the conservative, the reformist, and the radical. The discussion on the conservative tradition encompassed the major theories and models of economic growth—including classical and neoclassical theories, "new growth" models, Keynesian and post-Keynesian theories, theories of unbalanced growth and dualism, and so on. It also covered various modernization theories, including the sociological, political, and psycho-cultural versions of these theories. Under the reformist tradition, on the other hand, the focus was not only on development theories and models founded upon the relatively conservative reform principles such as "redistribution-with-growth" or "redistribution-with-or-without-growth," but also on theories emphasizing more substantive or fundamental reform such as the theory of underdevelopment; the theory of "dependent development," and the "critical theory" of the Frankfurt School. Within the radical tradition, the discussion began with the original contributions of classical Marxists, including Marx, Engels, and their direct proponents. This was followed by an analysis of neo-Marxist theories, which encompassed the mode-of-production schools, the radical version of dependency theory, and the class analysis perspectives related to Third World societies. The main purpose of examining all these development theories and models was to trace their intellectual origins, decipher their mutual similarities and differences, clarify their central arguments, and identify their basic theoretical shortcomings.

The last three chapters (chapters 7, 8, and 9) of the book not only offered a critique of development thinking, but also attempted to restructure development theories and policies. In addition to an analysis of the major intellectual flaws existing in the development field—such as epistemological empiricism, normative indifference, analytical reductionism, Eurocentric ethnocentrism, and unfounded universalism—it has been pointed out that there are adverse practical outcomes of the current development theories and policies such as the perpetuation of intellectual hegemony, legitimation of politico-economic dominance, erosion of indigenous culture, deterioration of environmental situation, and so on. It was explained that some of these development problems have worsened further in recent years due to the worldwide revival of the bourgeois development model emphasizing economic growth based on market forces. In the restructuring of development theories, on the other hand, the central focus has been on the realization of human autonomy from various modes (natural-physiological, politico-economic, and cultural-intellectual) and levels (intergroup, interclass, and international) of subjugation. It is argued that in terms of mutual articulation among these major modes and levels of human subjugation in the current epoch, it is the cultural-intellectual mode that has primacy over other modes of subjugation, and it is the international level that has preeminence over other levels of subjugation. Thus, in the current context, the realization of human autonomy from these subjugating conditions requires that among various modes and levels of such autonomy, priority should be given to the cultural-intellectual mode and the international level of autonomy.

Following such a theoretical restructuring of development thinking, this final chapter has been devoted to the reformulation of practical development policies, especially with a view to enhance the autonomy of Third World societies and peoples from various modes and levels of subjugation. More specifically, in order to overcome the vulnerability and powerlessness of the common masses in these countries to the vagaries of natural and physiological forces (e.g., natural calamities, hunger, malnutrition, and diseases), some macro-level policy reforms have been suggested in relation to agricultural production, industrial growth, health services, education system, and transportation and communication. Second, some policy reforms have also been proposed for enhancing the autonomy of Third World people, particularly the poorer classes, from the politico-economic hegemony exercised internally by their own rural and urban elites, and exter-nally by the leading Western nations, transnational corporations, and international agencies. Lastly, for the autonomy of Third World masses from the current global structures of cultural-intellectual hegemony, some recommendations have been made to rethink and reform the existing policies and institutions related to the distribu-tion and exchange of culture, knowledge, and information.

However, in line with the restructured theory of development, it has been emphasized in this chapter that among these three sets of policy reforms related to the three modes (natural-physiological, politico-economic, cultural-intellectual) of human autonomy, in the current age, it is essential to emphasize the policy priority of the cultural-intellectual mode of such autonomy. It is because the policy changes needed for the liberation of Third World masses from adverse natural-physiological conditions such as poverty and hunger, are less likely to be adopted not only due to the vested interests of the ruling elites in the existing policies, but also due to the inap-propriate policy outlook of these elites reinforced by various cultural-intellectual means—especially the global media—that tend to propa-gate and serve the interests of the world capitalist system at the expense of Third World needs. Similarly, policy reforms required for the politico-economic autonomy of Third World societies from the hegemony of capitalist nations, corporations, and agencies are less likely to be adopted by these ruling elites not only because of their self-serving alliance with these capitalist forces, but also because of the cultural-intellectual impact of the bourgeois global media that influences them to be indifferent toward unequal politico-economic structures and disinterested in undertaking any radical policy reforms in this regard. Thus, the central concern in the current age is how to enhance the critical public consciousness regarding this condition of worldwide cultural-intellectual hegemony, how to make Third World people and policy-makers understand the significance of their cultural-intellectual autonomy for the realization of their politico-economic autonomy, and how to achieve this autonomy in the cultural-intellectual sphere.

Despite this historical necessity to overcome the global structures of cultural, intellectual, and informational hegemony, it is possible that any policy reforms in this regard might be rejected by Third World elites who benefit from such hegemonic structures.[130] For instance, the elitist education system based on the colonial experience and neocolonial framework often enables these elites to occupy top government positions, control public resources, monopolize information sources, and thereby enhance their own power, status, and wealth. Most of these elites are so accustomed to Western living standards, consumption items, and cultural products[131] that they are unlikely to sacrifice such a luxurious lifestyle. In addition, since these foreign cultural and informational products are quite effective in influencing public opinion based on sensationalism and fabrication, they are often imported and used by many Third World regimes to diminish people's critical consciousness, weaken their social solidarity, marginalize their voice against hegemony, and create their consent to subjugation.[132]

It is also possible that any policy reforms suggested for defending cultural-intellectual autonomy would be similarly opposed by the advanced capitalist nations, transnational corporations, and international agencies, because such policy reforms might challenge their media-created claims to ideological superiority, reduce their profit from business in cultural and informational products, diminish Third World demand for their goods and services sold through advertisement, weaken the media-based rationale of their worldwide military intervention, and so on. In short, the policy proposal for any fundamental reforms in the global structures of cultural-intellectual hegemony is likely to be resisted by the dominant national and international forces that benefit from such hegemonic structures.

It is also likely that the suggested policy changes related to culture, knowledge, and information would be perceived by many Western academics and Third World intelligentsia as too protectionist or inward-looking, and too constraining for free international cultural exchange, intellectual competition, and information flow. But in the current context of extreme inequality in cultural, intellectual, and informational orders, this free competition and exchange may only expand and perpetuate the existing hegemony of advanced Western nations over Third World countries in the cultural-intellectual sphere. When the structures of exchange are already based on inequality and hegemony, it is unfair and unjust to propose such free exchange in the name of fairness and justice.[133] Third World countries may contemplate such idea of free exchange only after overcoming external dependence and achieving a certain degree of self-reliance in culture, knowledge, and information based on their external protection, internal innovation, and collective solidarity.

In fact, without the realization of such cultural-intellectual autonomy of Third World societies, the required transformation of development thinking itself is hardly possible. It is mainly after attaining a certain degree of self-reliance in culture, knowledge, and information, the intelligentsia and policy-makers in these societies will have a deeper understanding of the fact that the mainstream development theories and policies have been subjugating rather than liberating, that there is no universal framework of development for all societies,[134] and that they should adopt their own development alternatives in order to rescue the common masses from poverty and hunger, economic and political subordination, and cultural and intellectual subjugation. It is this freedom of societies and peoples to determine their own theoretical and practical alternatives that signifies a major hallmark of authentic development.[135]

As emphasized in this study, today the global culture and entertainment industry, knowledge and information networks, and news and advertisement agencies are extremely effective in infiltrating procapitalist beliefs, ideas, and values into Third World societies; shaping their patterns of production, consumption, and interaction; impoverishing their social solidarity, cultural identity, and human dignity; and marginalizing their indigenous voices and oppositional forces. Due to such unprecedented globalization of bourgeois culture, knowledge, and information, the subjugated groups, classes, and societies are losing their critical consciousness against hegemony: they are increasingly unable to distinguish true sociohistorical reality from fabrication and misinterpretation, uncertain about the roots and nature of their subjugating conditions, prone to believe in the media-created images of their inferiority and powerlessness, and inclined to blame themselves while giving consent to the very agents and structures that subjugate them. Therefore, although a genuine development should encompass human autonomy from all modes and levels of subjugation, today the autonomy of the subjugated subjects has to begin with autonomy from their own false consciousness produced and reinforced by the prevailing transnational structures of cultural, intellectual, and informational hegemony. This study has been devoted to articulating the historical significance of this particular dimension of human autonomy that has become the essence of development in the current epoch.

Notes

Preface

1. Similar to this observation made by Sachs (1992a, p. 1), there are other scholars who hold critical views on the existing development field. See, for instance, Amin (1990), p. 1; Edwards (1989), p. 121; Goulet (1983), p. 610; Korten (1990), p. 70; Nandy (1989), p. 35; Preston (1985), p. 4; Wiarda (1981), pp. 191–92.

2. See Amin (1990), p. 1; Preston (1987), p. 1.

3. Chaudhry (1994); Haque (1995).

4. Bello, Cunningham, and Rau (1994); Clarke (1994).

5. Chaudhry (1994), p. 1; Halachmi and Holzer (1993); Henig, Hamnett, and Feigenbaum (1988).

6. Bello, Cunningham, and Rau (1994); Dixon (1995); Sharma (1994); UNDP (1994); Veltmeyer (1993).

7. See Bello, Cunningham, and Rau (1994); Jain (1994a).

8. For further analysis and empirical evidence, see Haque (1995); World Bank (1994), pp. 200–201.

9. Cook and Kirkpatrick (1995), ILO (1995), Martin (1993), Sarkar (1991).

10. Clements (1994), p. 88; Pai (1994), p. 159; Stein (1994), p. 1845.

11. Pieterse (1991a), p. 26.

Chapter 1. An Introductory Overview

1. These critical observations have been made in various recent studies on development. For further illustration, see Amin (1990), p. 1; Braun (1990), p. 55; Edwards (1989), p. 121; Goulet (1983), p. 610; Mathur (1989), pp. 470–71; Nandy (1989), p. 35; Palmer (1978), pp. 95–96; Pieterse (1991a); Preston (1985), p. 4; Trainer (1989), p. 3; Wiarda (1981), pp. 191–92.

2. For further analysis, see Esteva (1992), p. 16; Goulet (1983), p. 612; Hancock (1989), pp. 113–14; Hexing (1991), p. 43; Holm (1990), p. 1; Jolly (1987), p. 61; Korten (1990), p. 70; Srisang (1984), p. 47; Szeftel (1987), pp. 87–88; World Bank (1991), p. 2.

3. For Murphy (1990, pp. 33–35), the national and international institutions of development (both public and private, bilateral and multilateral) constitute a "necessary superstructure" of global capitalism to serve its economic and political interests. On the other hand, Manzo (1991, pp. 3–4) and Preston (1987, p. 1) suggest that confidence in development studies has declined significantly and there is an intellectual impasse in the field.

4. Edwards (1989), p. 116.

5. Caporaso (1980), p. 606; Jolly (1977), p. 20; and Sinaceur (1983), p. 5.

6. These practical and theoretical levels of crises in the development field represent the current crises in overall social thinking. In this regard, Holton (1990, p. 39) suggests that the idea of "crisis" has become so all-pervasive in social thinking that there is no need for convincing anyone about its existence: What is necessary is to delineate the nature, forms, and extent of this crisis.

7. For instance, in terms of poverty, nearly 1.3 billion people are in absolute poverty in Third World countries, more than 38 million people are below the poverty line in an advanced capitalist nation like the U.S., and the situation of poverty has become severe in the former socialist states. See Cohen (1994), UNDP (1994), World Bank (1994).

8. There are taxonomic controversies among various schemes (e.g., the Nehruvian, the Soviet, and the Chinese) of the tripartite division of the world (Ahmad, 1992). In general, however, the *First World* refers to the market-oriented, advanced capitalist countries represented by the Organization for Economic Cooperation and Development (plus Israel and South Africa); the *Second World* includes the former centrally–planned, socialist countries of the East that once constituted the Council for Mutual Economic Assistance; and the *Third World* encompasses all other Asian, African, and Latin American countries, most of which were colonies. See Merriam (1988), Mittelman (1988), Steidlmeier (1987). Although the ideological collapse of

the Soviet Union and Eastern European countries raises question regarding the existence of the "Second World," and therefore, the "Third World," the fact remains that the Russian Federation continues to be a world military power, most Eastern European countries (e.g., Poland, Hungary, Slovakia, and Bulgaria) have reestablished socialist governments in new forms, and all of them identify themselves more with Western Europe, and even North America, than with Asia, Africa, and Latin America. More importantly, this phenomenon has not changed the sociohistorical identity of "Third World" countries in terms of their colonial and neocolonial experiences and their dependent status in relation to the world capitalist system. Despite the rejection of the "Third World" as a conceptual category by Ahmad (1992) for its varying interpretations, its inherent heterogeneity, and so on, he himself uses ambiguous categories, such as "backward formations" and "metropolitan countries," without adequate clarification. One needs to realize that there is hardly any unit of analysis which is perfectly homogeneous: Within a nation there are various classes, within a class there are various ethnic and religious groups, within an ethnic group there are different classes, and so on. What is most crucial is that the primacy of a conceptual category over others (not its exclusiveness from others) should depend on the formation of sociohistorical context and the priority of certain emancipatory policies within that context: All these may change from one epoch to another. In the current epoch, when the national economic, political, and cultural sovereignty of many countries is under challenge due to the increasing hegemony of Western corporations, military networks, and culture industry, the practical need for "Third World" solidarity, and hence the intellectual use of the category "Third World," is essential since it is hardly possible for a single nation to protect itself from these transnational powers. In fact, for many scholars, the term "Third World" has more advantages than other available terms. For instance, it is easily translated in other languages, it is manageable and functional, it represents the hopes and aspirations of three-fourths of humanity, and so on. See Merriam (1988), Mittelman (1988), Holm (1990). Considering all these factors, the term "Third World" is used throughout this book.

9. Nguyen (1989), p. 19; Nicholson and Connerley (1989), p. 385; Urquidi (1988), p. 86.

10. These critical problems of Third World development are elaborately discussed with adequate information in chapter 2.

11. According to Merriam (1988, p. 16), the very definition of development carries Western bias, especially in terms of its inherent dominant values such as materialism, change, progress, and science.

12. Damman (1979), Worsley (1984).

13. Braun (1990), p. 55.

14. Pieterse (1991a), p. 24.

15. In this chapter, the forms of crises in advanced capitalist countries are briefly mentioned. A more extensive analysis of these crises is offered in chapter 2.

16. Agazzi (1988), Baran and Sweezy (1968), Diwan and Lutz (1985), Kassiola (1990), Norwine (1988).

17. Diwan and Lutz (1985), p. 4.

18. See Bell (1981), Gurley (1979), Segal (1993).

19. Although the commonly perceived Cold War emerged as an ideological war between the capitalist and socialist blocs under the leadership of the U.S. and the U.S.S.R. respectively, according to some authors, the Cold War was a unilateral creation of Western powers to justify their intervention in Third World markets. See Minhas (1979), p. 76; Peck (1984), p. 51; Trainer (1989), pp. 165–67. On the other hand, for Landau (1990, p. 32), although socialism has declined in its first epoch, it will reemerge in Third World countries because of their increasing economic poverty, which capitalism cannot resolve.

20. See Pomfret (1994), pp. 1, 8.

21. These global-level problems of development are extensively discussed in the next chapter. Only a brief illustration of some of these problems is presented here.

22. During the Cold War, the U.S. and its allies pursued foreign aid and other policies to introduce a Westernized form of development in the Third World (Minhas, 1979, p. 76). After the end of the Cold War and the disintegration of the Soviet bloc, the procapitalist and anticommunist rationales for such policies of Third World development are questionable.

23. It has been pointed out that major international laws and institutions are based on the capitalist principles of Western Europe and North America (such as order, property, and accumulation), which justify Western economic and political interests and domination through institutions such as the IMF and the U.N. Security Council. See Rourke (1986), p. 343; also Huntington (1993), p. 39.

24. Jhally (1989), Kellner (1990).

25. Kellner (1990), pp. 13, 87–88; Welsh and Butorin (1990), p. 718.

26. Eder (1990), p. 81.

27. The theories of development range between the two dominant ideologies of the world, capitalism and socialism. However, in terms of their perspectives, they can be conservative (e.g., economic growth theory and

modernization theory); reformist (e.g., basic needs approach and theory of dependent development); and radical (e.g., classical Marxist theory and radical dependency theory). The origin, scope, and content of each of these theoretical perspectives are discussed in chapters 4, 5, and 6.

28. The incapacity of the existing development theories to address various forms of practical crises indicates a profound impasse or a confidence crisis in the development field. Pieterse (1991a). This crisis of confidence reflects a crisis in the explanatory and emancipatory power of development theories. Alexander and Sztompka, (1990, p. 3). For Eder (1990, p. 81), the recent crisis of environment and ecology has posed serious challenges to the last bastion of confidence in development.

29. Dopfer (1979).

30. Goulet (1983), p. 613.

31. See Addo et al. (1985), p. 4; Hancock (1989), p. 115; Harrod (1982), pp. 2–4; Sheth (1987), p. 156.

32. Aseniero (1985), p. 53.

33. Mathur (1989), pp. 468–71.

34. For Mathur (1989, p. 468), it covers not only the conventional theories of development but also alternative theoretical frameworks that should be brought under critical scrutiny.

35. Helleiner (1990), p. 41; Rist (1990), p. 10.

36. Apter (1987), Dopfer (1979).

37. Dopfer (1979), Pieterse (1991a).

38. See Devine (1988), Edwards (1989), Khoi (1986), Lauer (1973), Mathur (1989), Nuscheler (1988), Pieterse (1991a, 1991b), Redclift (1987), Vogeler and Souza (1980), Wallerstein (1989), Weigel (1989).

39. Reuveny (1979), p. 54.

40. Even the theoretical perspectives based on Third World concerns, are not devoid of problems. Dependency theory, for instance, has been accused of its inadequate attention to the political realms such as the state and the role of other relatively nonempirical issues such as religion, ethnicity, and gender. See Kay (1991), pp. 51–54.

41. Alcalde (1987), Nieuwenhuijze (1982), Weaver (1973).

42. This tendency of indifference toward indigenous values and norms is quite common among the major development theories—including the conservative theories (classical, neoclassical, Keynesian, post-Keynesian) of economic growth; Marxian and neo-Marxian theories; and various dependency perspectives. See Miller (1984), Nuscheler (1988), Steidlmeier (1987).

43. Agh (1984), Dopfer (1979), Laite (1988), Nieuwenhuijze (1982), Nisbet (1969).

44. In recent years, the unprecedented expansion and globalization of various forms of media have played a crucial role to vindicate the hegemony of capitalist nations over Third World countries by demonizing insubordinate Third World regimes as public enemies, manufacturing world opinion to punish these "invented" enemies in the name of democracy, delegitimating various emancipatory Third World movements, and portraying the acts of global hegemony as the desires of the world community. See Angus and Jhally (1989), Huntington (1993), Kellner (1990).

45. Halachmi and Holzer (1993); Henig, Hamnett, and Feigenbaum (1988).

46. Babai (1988), McGowan (1994), Petrazzini (1995).

47. See Berthoud (1992), Esteva (1992).

48. For details, see Global Economy (1994), Guocang (1994), Huntington (1993), Kapoor and Kohli (1994), Kappen (1994), Martin (1993), Nash (1994), UNDP (1994), Weiss (1994), Welsh and Butorin (1990), World Economy (1992), Zagorin (1994).

49. In most Eastern European and Third World countries, promarket policies have led to the expansion of wealth of the former *nomenklatura* and black marketeers, to the acceleration of corrupt income for the ruling cliques and their cronies, and to the legitimation of all these antipublic activities under the facade of people's capitalism. See Carchedi (1994), p. 91; Dwivedi (1994), p. 362; Heald (1990), p. 11; Martin (1993), p. 9.

50. Briones (1985), p. 389; Martin (1993), pp. 1, 11, 95; Sarkar (1991), p. 2308.

51. It has been suggested in various studies that in the Third World, the main beneficiaries of promarket policies include the top political leaders, bureaucratic elites, business firms, transnational banks, and international agencies. See Dwivedi (1994), p. 358; Malloy (1989), p. 328; Martin (1993), pp. 100–101.

Chapter 2. Practical Crises of Development

1. See Braun (1990), p. 56; Burki and Beckmann (1986), p. 95; Durning (1990), p. 139; Estes (1988), p. 127; Galtung (1990), p. 17; Jennings and Weiss (1982), p. 115; Sivard (1986), p. 1991; UNDP (1994), p. 26; Urquidi (1988), p. 86; World Bank (1994), p. 1.

2. Frank (1988), p. 189; Sivard (1989), p. 19.

3. Amin (1990), p. 7; Wesson (1990), p. 419; World Bank (1988), p. 2.

4. With regard to the scope of the NICs, different authors have used different sets of criteria. For instance, Shaw (1988) and Ingalls and Martin (1988) use per capita income, the pace of industrialization, the share of manufacturing sector in world market, and the speed and sustainability of economic growth as the criteria for determining which countries belong to the NICs. In addition to these criteria, Wolf (1988) emphasizes the size of a country. For the demographic figures, see Global Economy (1994), Rourke (1986), UNDP (1994).

5. See UNDP (1994), pp. 134–35.

6. Dixon (1995), p. 202.

7. It has been found that the current living standards in Latin America and Sub-Saharan Africa are lower than they were in the early 1970s. Smith (1991), p. 33.

8. Trainer (1989), pp. 9–17.

9. Brown (1987), p. 31; Durning (1990), p. 141; George (1977), p. 14.

10. In African and Latin American countries, according to Jain (1994a, p. 47), structural adjustment policies have mostly served the economic interests of the affluent social sections.

11. See Avery (1990), pp. 504–5; Dogra (1994), p. 25; Durning (1990, 1991); Lal (1985), p. 124; O'Cleireacain (1990), p. 3; World Bank (1987, 1990).

12. Chidzero (1987), p. 133; Taylor (1989), p. 10; Wiarda (1990), p. 411.

13. Laite (1988), p. 183.

14. UNDP (1994), World Bank (1994).

15. UNDP (1994).

16. In Third World countries, the overall cumulative military expenditure during the period 1977–82 was more than their total outstanding debt in 1982. See Renner, 1989, p. 137. It was found that since 1960, the total military expenditure of Third World countries increased by 5.3 times, although their per capita GNP increased only by 2.0 times; and as they imported arms worth $250 billion, their external debt increased by $580 billion. See Sivard (1986), p. 12; Straubhaar (1986), p. 137.

17. For further details, see Avery (1990), pp. 511–16; Frank (1988), pp. 188–89; George (1990), p. 332; Henry (1986); Korten (1990), p. 22; O'Cleireacain (1990), pp. 30–31; Redclift (1987), p. 57.

18. Steidlmeier (1987), p. 149.

19. Fagen (1994), p. 4.

20. Dogra (1994), p. 25.

21. Fagen (1994), p. 4.

22. George (1990), p. 329.

23. See Brown (1991), p. 16; Brown, Flavin, and Postel (1990), p. 175; E-Shagi (1990), p. 88; Estes (1988), p. 122; Korten (1990), p. 14; Rensberger (1994), p. 1; Singh (1994), p. 25.

24. See Arnold (1989), p. 175; Brown, Flavin, and Postel (1990), p. 175; Jacobson (1988), p. 152; UNDP (1994), p. 175. It should be mentioned here that this demographic trend is largely caused by the decreasing fertility rate in industrialized countries and the increasing fertility rate in the Third World. Because of this trend, by the year 2025, while the proportion of population aged 60 and over will be 26.4 percent in North America and 27.0 percent in Europe, there will be an increased proportion of population aged 0–14 years in Asia, particularly South Asia. See Jacobson (1988), Kono (1989).

25. Bradley (1986), pp. 93–94.

26. For this view see Skinner (1988), p. 60. However, to be balanced, it should be mentioned that there is a problem of overpopulation in many Third World countries, although this problem is often exaggerated while the issue of unequal distribution is hardly expressed in official statements.

27. Bradley (1986).

28. Bunge (1986), Patterson and Shrestha (1988).

29. See Anderson (1988), p. 180; Kamal and Fisher (1988), p. 198; Lieske (1988), p. 255.

30. Thrift (1986), p. 56.

31. See Sachs (1994), p. 24; UNDP (1994), pp. 35, 65.

32. Buchanan (1985), p. 93; Langley (1990), p. 56.

33. Welsh and Butorin (1990), p. 681.

34. For instance, in research and development, 87 percent of the world's scientists and engineers work in advanced industrial countries. See Khoi (1986), p. 24.

35. Arnold (1989), p. 176.

36. See Arnold (1989), p. 176; Brown and Jacobson (1987), p. 40.

37. Jaguaribe (1990), p. 163; Chakravarty (1987), p. 91.

38. Sachs (1987), p. 102; Ward, (988), p. 347.

39. Mittelman (1988), p. 169; Trainer (1989), p. 49; Wasi (1984), p. 57.

40. See Durning (1990), p. 140; Estes (1988), p. 127; Freeman (1980), p. 5; Housing (1992), p. 33; Lamar (1988), p. 34; Marsh (1990), p. 44; Poverty Figures (1988), p. A22; Sivard (1986), p. 51; Sivard (1989), p. 45; UNDP (1994), pp. 25–28.

41. Freeman (1980), p. 97; Inequality (1994), pp. 19–20; and Sivard (1986), p. 51.

42. Darden (1989), p. 4; Skolnick and Currie (1985), p. 91.

43. Durning (1990), p. 140.

44. See Kuttner (1988), p. 10; Lamar (1988), p. 38; Sivard (1986), pp. 48–51; Wilson (1988), p. 87.

45. See Kassiola (1990), pp. 5–6.

46. For further details, see Besharov (1986), Lieske (1988), Parenti (1988), Segal (1993), UNDP (1994).

47. See Federal Bureau of Investigation (1986), p. 6. According to Parenti (1988, p. 33), in the U.S., there are nearly 24,000 killings, 27,000 suicide cases, and 25 million cases of violence or theft per year.

48. See Koven (1989), p. 580; Sage (1988), p. 150; Kemp's Commission (1986), p. 3).

49. Kassiola (1990), pp. 5–6.

50. For details, see Durning (1990), Keller (1988), Korb (1990), Pear (1988), Sivard (1986).

51. For instance, the elected Russian president Boris Yeltsin has ruthlessly overthrown the Russian Parliament, abolished constitutional order, sent tanks to destroy parliament building, ruled the nation by decree, and used brutal military force to stop the separatist movement in Chechnya. See Cohen, (1994).

52. Cohen (1994); Reuters (1995), p. 15; "Yeltsin's Economic" (1992), p. 19.

53. UNDP (1994), p. 185.

54. World Bank (1994), pp. 200–201.

55. For example, Western nations are after the Caspian oil reserves located in Azerbaijan, Turkmenistan, and Kazakhstan: Azerbaijan has already signed contracts worth $8 billion with Western firms, such as Amoco, Pennzoil, Unocal, and British Petroleum. See Hoagland (1994), p. 6.

56. See Landau (1990), p. 30. It may remind observers about the historical status of Eastern European countries as appendages of the West during the period between 1400 and 1770. See Worsley (1984), pp. 11–12.

57. Korten (1990), Landau (1990), Phillips (1990).

58. For instance, Poland has increasingly fallen into the trap of inflation at home on the one hand, and the external pressure from Western governments, banks, and the IMF to introduce privatization and austerity programs on the other. See Petras (1990), pp. 170–71.

59. Perlez (1994), p. 2.

60. Guocang (1994), p. 30; Petras (1990), pp. 170–72.

61. *International Herald Tribune*, August 17, 1994, p. 13.

62. Some of these new states themselves are at war with each other (e.g., between Azerbaijan and Armenia, between Russia and Chechnya, between Georgia and its breakaway state Abkhazia), and there is potential for ethnic violence in each of these new states, including Estonia, Latvia, Lithuania, Moldavia, Ukraine, Kazakhstan, Turkmenistan, and Tajikistan, because of their multiethnic compositions. See Segal (1993), p. 147.

63. Petras (1990), p. 170

64. For details, see Durning (1989), p. 135, (1991), p. 153; George (1977), pp. 4–33; George and Paige (1982), p. 76; World Bank (1991), p. 1.

65. See Archibugi, Nijkamp, and Soeteman (1989); Holm (1990), p. 3; Jennings and Weiss (1982), p. 116; Mittelman (1988), p. 11; Roy and Sen (1989), p. 255; Skinner (1988), p. 61; UNDP (1994); "World Economy" (1992).

66. UNDP (1994), pp. 21, 35.

67. Sivard (1991), p. 5.

68. See Rourke (1986), pp. 255–56.

69. Brewer (1980), p. 2.

70. Miszlivetz and Kaldor (1985), p. 56.

71. In the Caribbean countries, for instance, European conquests led to the destruction of native people, and to the acquisition of slaves from Africa and contract workers from South Asia to satisfy the labor needs of plantations. See Anderson (1988), pp. 172–73.

72. Segal (1993), p. 63.

73. For instance, the postcolonial creation of artificial boundaries in Africa hindered national unity and spawned political instability and civil strife. Fisher (1988), p. 232.

74. For details, see Gonzalez (1988), p. 185; Hulme and Turner (1990), pp. 78–79; Hutchful (1985), p. 63; Kamal and Fisher (1988), pp. 201–5; Peters (1988), pp. 249–50.

75. This can be found, for instance, in the failure of the administrative state to accommodate religious and cultural diversity in South Asia. See Sukhwal (1988), p. 217.

76. Amin (1989), Boulding (1990), Morrow (1991a), Segal (1993).

77. Segal (1993).

78. Taylor (1995), p. 2.

79. Kurspahic (1994).

80. See Lewis (1994), Marlowe (1994), Winik and Mehic (1994).

81. Fairhead et al. (1994), Rademaekers (1994).

82. Segal (1993), pp. 147–51, 208.

83. Brown (1986), p. 196; Sivard (1989).

84. Sivard (1988), Renner (1989), Saunders (1990).

85. See Rourke (1986). According to the World Bank (1994), while more than 20 percent of federal expenditure was for the defense sector, less than 2 percent was for education.

86. Sivard (1989), p. 21.

87. World Bank (1994), pp. 180–81.

88. UNDP (1994), p. 51.

89. See Brown (1990), InterAction Council (1990), Korten (1990).

90. The greenhouse effect is caused by the increased density of carbon dioxide surrounding the earth which, being transparent to visible light, allows the sun rays to warm the earth surface, but absorbs the infrared rays carrying excess heat given off by the same earth surface. Thus, some of this excess heat remains in the atmosphere warming the earth.

91. Brown and Wolf (1987), Flavin (1990).

92. Brown, Flavin and Postel (1989); Postel (1987).

93. Brown (1990, 1991), Wolf (1988).

94. Flavin (1990), p. 17.

95. See Brown and Young (1990), p. 59. For some specific examples of the implications of global warming, see Cowley (1988), p. 99; Sanction (1989), p. 27.

96. Ozone is a three-atom form of oxygen which prevents harmful ultraviolet radiation of the sun from reaching the earth surface by absorbing this radiation. Shea, (1989), p. 77. This radiation is dangerous to life on earth because it damages DNA and thus disrupts the working cells. However, the depletion of this essential ozone is caused by chlorine and bromine that come from the production and use of goods such as aerosols, refrigerants, air conditioning, foam, and fire extinguishers. See Jacobson (1989), Shea (1989).

97. Shea (1989), p. 77.

98. French (1990), Jacobson (1989), Shea (1989).

99. Shea (1989), p. 82.

100. French (1990), p. 107.

101. See Brown and Young (1990), pp. 60–61. Also see Jacobson (1989), Postel (1989).

102. Postel (1990), p. 44.

103. Brown (1990, 1991), Brown and Young (1990).

104. UNDP (1994), p. 29.

105. For the empirical evidence of these arguments, see Commoner (1985); Durning (1991), p. 155; Flavin (1990), p. 37; Lowe (1990), pp. 120–23; Ramphal (1992), p. 4; Renner (1991), pp. 133–50; Shea (1989), pp. 86–87; South Commission (1990), p. 6.

106. Human Environment (1982), p. 10.

107. See UNDP (1994), p. 177; Global Economy (1994), p. 35. With regard to the current environmental problems caused by affluent nations, Mathieu and Gottschalk (1992, p. 113) specifically mention that the higher standard of living "enjoyed by the majority of the Northern population is based on just this: global environmental destruction."

108. UNDP (1994), p. 68.

109. Gare (1994), UNDP (1994).

110. See Bhagwati (1986), Friberg (1985), Gilpin (1987), Hettne (1990), Sheth (1987).

111. Hoogvelt (1982), Sklair (1991), South Commission (1990).

112. Some of these organizations include the Organization of American States, the Rio Group of Eight, the Central American Common Market, the Organization of Eastern Caribbean States, the Organization of African Unity, the East African Economic Community, the Economic Community of West African States, the Economic Community of Central African States,

the Association of Southeast Asian Nations, the Pacific Economic Coopera-
tion Council, the Asia and Pacific Economic Cooperation, the South Pacific
Forum, the South Asian Association for Regional Co–operation, and so on.
For details, see South Commission (1990).

113. Aziz. (1978), p. 6.

114. Hancock (1989), p. 51; South Commission (1990), pp. 2–19.

115. Rourke (1986), Segal (1993).

116. Kapoor and Kohli (1994), p. 57; Zagorin (1994), p. 31.

117. Hexing (1991), p. 44.

118. Welsh and Butorin (1990), p. 994.

119. UNDP (1994), p. 66.

120. Kapoor and Kohli (1994), Sachs (1994).

121. For further information, see Global Economy (1994), p. 10. According to the U.S. government projection, by 2010, while American exports to
Japan will amount to $88 billion, its exports to the rest of Asia will reach
$248 billion, and to Latin America $232 billion. Sanger, (1994), p. 1.

122. Friberg (1985), Gilpin (1987).

123. Petras (1990).

124. See Gilpin (1987), pp. 191–93. Today the major regional markets,
particularly in Southeast Asia, are dominated by Japan; the surpluses are
generated by Germany, Japan, and the OPEC (Organization of Petroleum
Exporting Countries) nations; and the financial centers have mushroomed
in Germany, Hong Kong, and Singapore. See Streeten (1989b), p. 1350;
Petras (1990), p. 163.

125. Dale (1994), p. 11.

126. Gilpin (1987), p. 400; Petras (1990), p. 175.

127. For further explanations, see Coate and Puchala (1990), pp. 132–33;
George (1990), p. 335; Linnemann and Sarma (1991); Mittelman (1988), p.
59.

128. See Emmerij (1986), p. 5.

129. The NATO was formed after World War II as a U.S.-dominated military alliance of North America and Western Europe against the *perceived*
threat posed by the former Soviet Union, and in response, the Warsaw Pact
was established as a Soviet-dominated military alliance of Eastern European
communist countries in 1955.

130. Sklair (1991).

131. For instance, there is significant dependence of Third world countries on Western nations, especially the U.S., for their arms supply and arms production. See Arnold (1989), Rosh (1990). Similarly, many Third World nations with socialist governments were militarily dependent on the former Soviet Union.

132. Sivard (1986), p. 9.

133. Arnold (1989), pp. 10–29.

134. For example, India has a population (880.1 million) larger than the combined population of Britain (57.7 million), France (57.1 million), the U.S. (255.2 million), and Russia (149 million); Brazil has a population (154 million) larger than the combined population of Britain and France; and this is true for Indonesia (191.2 million), Pakistan (124.9 million), and Bangladesh (119.5 million). See UNDP (1994).

135. See Rourke (1986), p. 321; Global Economy (1994), p. 20.

136. Arblaster (1991), Drake (1994), New World Order (1991), Segal (1993).

137. Segal (1993).

138. For further analysis of this issue, see Irvin (1991), p. 93; Petras (1990), p. 175; Talbott (1991), p. 30.

139. See Galtung (1976), Gilpin (1987), Petras (1990).

140. As Petras (1990, p. 175) mentions, "the major conflicts in the last decades of the twentieth century will be played out in Tokyo, Bonn and Washington. And the weapons of this conflict are economic, not military."

141. For more detailed information, see Babbili (1990), p. 312; Childers (1990), p. 13; Harrison (1979), pp. 56–57; Mattelart (1983), p. 40–60; Meyer (1989), p. 247; Roach (1990), pp. 290–92; Sklair (1991), pp. 78, 148.

142. Bethell (1993); Frederick, Post, and Davis (1992).

143. Bethell (1993), Olson (1993).

144. Kellner (1990), p. 1.

145. Covington (1994).

146. *Time*, December 6, 1993, p. 10.

147. See Agnew, 1994, p. 269; Fuller, 1994, p. ix. On a further note, largely due to the all-pervasive influence of the global media, Pizza Hut has been able to open 10,800 outlets in 88 countries; the consumers in many countries (e.g., the middle-class in India) are replacing their indigenous food items with imported food products; and the demand for imported cigarettes is expanding among women and youngsters in Asia, Africa, Latin America, and Eastern Europe. See Chao (1994), Moore (1994), and Tagliabue (1994).

148. Angus and Jhally (1989), p. 2.

149. Kellner (1990), p. 67.

150. As Kellner (1990, p. 9) mentions, the media have played a significant ideological role in legitimating the capitalist system and delegitimating its opponents, particularly the anticapitalist liberation movements in Third World countries.

151. Kellner (1990), pp. 9, 114–15.

152. See "Cross–Frontier" (1992), Kellner (1990), Whitney (1994).

153. Parenti (1986), Bandyopadhyaya (1988).

154. This restructuring of the world economic and military order should not be confused with the so-called North-South division which, according to Murphy (1990, pp. 28–30), remains predominantly a division within the single international system composed of the dominant social classes of the world.

155. In this regard, Sachs (1992a, p. 5) mentions that "at a time when development has evidently failed as a socio-economic endeavour, it has become of paramount importance to liberate ourselves from its dominion over our minds."

Chapter 3. A Taxonomic Prelude to Development Theories

1. For a further analysis of the European origin of development thinking, see Nisbet (1980), pp. 10–46.

2. These practical sociohistorical events had significant influence on the formation of development thinking. The major changes in the concepts and theories of development are inseparable from these contextual changes. Intellectually, the idea of "progress" based on human reason was one of the most basic components of the Enlightenment and post-Enlightenment traditions. Practically, the rise of industrial capitalism had considerable impact on mainstream development theories, especially the classical theories of economic growth. On the other hand, the history of Western colonial hegemony, culturally based on its supremacy claim, is inseparable from the existing Eurocentric predilection in development thinking.

3. One of the main theoretical outcomes from the process of decolonizing Third World countries and transforming some of them into socialist states was the emergence of various modernization theories, which were allegedly used as the ideological means for maintaining control over these newly independent countries and preventing them from being influenced by socialist ideology. See Preston (1985); Randall and Theobald (1985).

4. Larrain (1989), p. viii.

5. De Vries (1968), p. 46.

6. Jaffee (1990), p. xi.

7. For further details, see Nieuwenhuijze (1982), p. 24.

8. Ottaway (1983), p. 373.

9. Chafetz (1978).

10. With regard to the need for certain principles in constructing a taxonomy, B.S. Bloom, D.R. Krathwohl, and B.B. Masia mention that "a true taxonomy is a set of classifications which are ordered and arranged on the basis of a single principle or on the basis of a consistent set of principles." Quoted in Ottaway (1983), p. 374.

11. Hettne (1982), pp. 7–8.

12. For instance, one may study the inherent intricacies of the "basic needs" approach to development, but may not know its theoretical identity in terms of its relation to other theories and its belongingness to a broader theoretical category. At a micro level of the taxonomy, this "basic needs" approach might be different from other approaches, but at a macro level, all these approaches (including the "basic needs" approach) could belong to the same generic theoretical category.

13. Leeson (1988), p. 8.

14. Appelbaum (1970), pp. 117–37.

15. For instance, one can argue that there are evolutionary theories, such as Marxian theory, which hold the assumption of inherent conflict; and there are other evolutionary theories, such as Comte's theory of three evolutionary stages, which hold the assumption of stability and equilibrium.

16. Kim (1984), p. 9; Valenzuela and Valenzuela (1978), p. 536.

17. Srinivasan (1988), p. 5.

18. Vengroff (1977), p. 613.

19. See Streeten (983), pp. 1–2.

20. Chodak (1973), Bava (1981).

21. Laite (1988).

22. This approach is highlighted by Larrain (1989, p. 3), who suggests that "one must study theories of development not only as conceptions of such and such an author of such and such an academic tendency, but also as products of a particular period of development of capitalism and its specific characteristics."

23. Larrain (1989), p. 3.

24. Jaffee (1990), p. 9.

25. See Nieuwenhuijze (1982), pp. 98–99.

26. Steidlmeier (1987), pp. 207–24.

27. See Berger (1976), Wilber and Jameson (1979), Jolly (1977).

28. For further details, see Foster–Carter (1976), Elguea (1985).

29. In addition, Chambers (1987, pp. 230–31) argues that the application of Kuhn's paradigm is more appropriate for the physical sciences that are significantly different from the social sciences: (a) while basic reality is assumed to be relatively fixed in the physical sciences, it is assumed to be constantly changing in the social sciences; (b) while the deriving forces of change in the physical sciences are matters of observation and measurement, they are matters of action and experience in the social sciences; and (c) when the competing paradigms can hardly coexist in the physical sciences and a paradigm shift may take a generation, the competing paradigms often coexist for a long time in the social sciences.

30. Clements (1980).

31. Ibid.

32. Toye (1987), p. 23.

33. For details, see Preston (1985).

34. However, it will become clear from the analysis and critique of modernization theories in the subsequent chapters that despite their focus on social, political, cultural, and psychological factors, the proponents of these theories are eventually interested in economic growth. Most of them consider these relatively noneconomic dimensions of modernization as instrumental to economic achievements.

35. In this regard, it has been pointed out by Bronner and Kellner (1989, p. 7) that the proponents of critical theory have largely failed to provide an adequate social theory.

36. It has already been pointed out that in terms of the mode of social change, radical dependency theory is quite different from reformist dependency theory: While the former emphasizes radical social change through revolution, the latter believes in such a change through substantive reforms.

37. Recognizing this taxonomic problem, Jaffee (1990, p. 11) mentions that "many theories of development cannot be pigeonholed into a single level of analysis."

Chapter 4. Conservative Tradition of Development Theories

1. This exchange of commodities takes place according to the law of demand and supply, which is guided by the forces of an "invisible hand" or the desire for economic gain. If the "market price" (the price that actually exists in the market) is higher than the "natural price" (the price determined by exchange value composed of wage, rent, and profit), the profit goes up to the extent that it attracts many producers guided by the desire for further gain. Thus, the supply increases, and the market price goes down again to the level of natural price.

2. See Smith (1930).

3. According to Malthus, this decrease in effectual demand occurs either when capitalists receive too much income but cannot spend it for additional capital (because of technological difficulty and the shortage of labor) or when there is a replacement of workers by capital which reduces workers' demand. See Gianaris (1978), p. 42.

4. Malthus (1989); also see Hunt (1979).

5. Ricardo (1957).

6. Under this Ricardian condition of stagnation, the population is at the maximum level, the real wage rate is at the subsistence level, the rents are high, the profit rate is near zero, the total output remains stationary, and further capital accumulation does not take place. See Meier (1984), p. 118.

7. However, the amount of savings depends on their expected returns and people's willingness to sacrifice present goods for future ones. See Mill (1909); also see Meier (1984).

8. Gianaris (1978), Meier (1984), Mill (1909).

9. Meier (1984), p. 118.

10. See Albelda, Gunn and Waller (1987); Villamil (1977).

11. Bentham's assumption is that all actions, motives, and thoughts of individuals are governed by two basic factors, pleasure and pain, which are quantifiable.

12. Bentham (1969).

13. See Hunt (1979).

14. Ibid.

15. Hunt (1979), Walras (1954).

16. According to the principle of diminishing marginal utility, a household substitutes its consumption of one commodity (e.g., tea) for another

(e.g., coffee) by comparing their relative marginal "utility/price ratios" to maximize the total utility.

17. But in the short run, capital is fixed. Only the amount of labor can be increased up to a point at which the average productivity of labor is maximized. In the long run, however, nothing is fixed; both labor and capital can be substituted for each other in order to maximize output.

18. Hunt (1979), p. 357.

19. See Hicks (1981), pp. 104–6; Targetti and Thirlwall (1989), pp. 3–4.

20. Clements (1980), p. 6.

21. See Romer (1990).

22. Ibid., pp. S71–S72.

23. Romer (1986), p. 1003.

24. In this regard, Romer mentions that "a purely nonrival good has the property that its use by one firm or person in no way limits its use by another." Romer (1990), p. S74.

25. Ibid., p. S99.

26. (Ibid.)

27. Romer (1993), p. 186.

28. See Rivera-Batiz and Romer (1991), p. 531.

29. Romer (1993), p. 186.

30. For further discussion, see Keynes (1936).

31. This liquidity preference, on the other hand, depends on the individual's motives of transaction (for immediate exchange), precaution (for security), and speculation (to see what happens in the future).

32. In a simple depressive condition, saving is more than investment and, thus, aggregate demand is less than supply. This decrease in demand leads successively to less production, more unemployment, less workers' income, further decrease in demand, further reduction in production, and so on. This simple depression can be corrected by monetary policy—i.e., by increasing the quantity of money which would decrease interest rate, discourage savings, and encourage investment.

33. Because of their higher MPC, this group of people would spend most of their income on consumption. Thus, the original money spent by government would pass from one hand to another, and in the process, it would create a chain of increasing demand. This increase in demand would lead to more investment, to more employment, to more workers' income,

and again, to more demand. Thus, it would finally lead to the restoration of the economy.

34. Clements (1980), p. 11; Hunt (1979), pp. 420–30.

35. Samuelson (1976).

36. Hunt (1979), p. 429.

37. Rosenstein-Rodan (1957).

38. Ibid.; also see Gianaris (1978), p. 99.

39. See Nurkse (1964), pp. 4–11. Briefly, on the supply side, in economically poor countries, the limited capacity to save results from their low level of real income (or poverty), the low level of income emanates from their low level productivity, the low level of productivity reflects their lack of capital, and the lack of capital emerges again from their limited capacity to save. On the demand side, in poor countries, the low inducement to invest is caused by their lack of buying power, the lack of buying power reflects their limited amount of real income, the limited real income is due to their low level of productivity, the low level of productivity is caused by their limited use of capital for production, and such limited use of capital for production indicates again their low inducement to invest.

40. Leibenstein (1957).

41. See Hirschman (1958), Singer (1975). Also see Gianaris (1978).

42. Meier (1984), pp. 152–53.

43. For Lewis, the key to the process of transforming the traditional sector into the capitalist sector is the reinvestment of surplus and its transformation into new capital. With this expansion of capital, an increasing amount of surplus labor from the traditional sector would be attracted by the higher wages in the capitalist sector, and thus would be absorbed into the latter. In the process, the traditional sector would gradually diminish and be replaced by a more productive capitalist sector. See Lewis (1955).

44. See Gianaris (1978), p. 92.

45. Rostow (1962).

46. Rostow (1973), p. 291.

47. See Preston (1985, 1987), Randall and Theobald (1985), So (1990).

48. Preston (1986), p. xv.

49. Goldthorpe (1984).

50. Comte (1973), pp. 14–19; also see Appelbaum (1970), pp. 23–27.

51. Spencer (1973), pp. 9–13.

52. Durkheim (1982).

53. However, with the increasing level of density, a society comes to be founded upon "technical solidarity" characterized by common values, norms, and beliefs; and this solidarity enhances social integration and stability. But a further increase in such density leads a society to be founded upon an "organic solidarity" (featured by individualism), which creates anomie, and thereby, increases the rate of suicide. See Pope (1976).

54. Smith (1973), pp. 2–3.

55. See Burrell and Morgan (1979), p. 51.

56. Smith (1973), pp. 3–6.

57. Ibid., pp. 12–16.

58. Society needs adaptation with the external environment (by expanding its control over the environment), this adaptation requires social differentiation (because the specialized units are more capable of controlling the environment), and such differentiation implies a need for reintegration (for coordinating the differentiated or specialized units).

59. Burrell and Morgan (1979), pp. 109–10; Taylor (1979), p. 9.

60. "Adaptation" is necessary for enhancing control over the environment; "goal attainment" for using resources to achieve objectives; "integration" for effective coordination among various units; and "pattern maintenance" for maintaining the value system and motivation. See Parsons and Smelser (1965).

61. Parsons and Shils (1951).

62. See Smelser (1973), pp. 268–80.

63. Randall and Theobald (1985).

64. Almond and Powell (1966).

65. For instance, following the structural–functional framework, Fred W. Riggs uses the metaphor of "prism" to explain the relationship between the level of differentiation in developing (prismatic) societies and the performance of their social, political, and administrative organizations. Riggs (1964). In spite of his recent efforts to incorporate the issue of integration and other categories into his prismatic model to improve its theoretical status, the model remains structural-functionalist in nature. Ibid (1987).

66. Pye (1966).

67. However, at a later stage, Pye recognized the limitations of applying such a narrow and Eurocentric framework to understand politics in Third World countries. See Pye (1978), pp. 79–93.

68. The three categories of such interpretations are: (a) political development as the generation, solidification, and maturation of political entities, sometimes known as political integration or nation–building; (b) political development as the growing systemness or institutionalization of political interaction through various forms of political participation; and (c) political development as the formation, maintenance, and self-differentiation of political culture. See Chodak (1973), pp. 231–44.

69. Kim (1984), pp. 82–83.

70. See Randall and Theobald (1985), pp. 34–66.

71. Huntington (1965, 1968).

72. Weber classified social actions in terms of four modes of orientation, including the "traditional" based on habit, the "affectual" based on emotion, the "rational" based on absolute value, and also the "rational" but based on individual choice. These four modes of action and orientation are correspondingly related to four "criteria of legitimacy" in society, including the tradition, the affectual attitude, the belief in absolute value, and the legal basis. The last criterion of legitimacy—i.e. the legal basis—is derived either from a mutual contract or from an imposed legitimate authority. This "legal authority" itself is of three types in terms of its three grounds of validity claim: traditional authority (based on traditions or customs), charismatic authority (based on individual charisma), and rational–legal authority (based on legal rationality). The last variety of legal authority—i.e. the "rational legal" authority—is characterized by features such as impersonal rules, competence, hierarchy, and so on, which represent, in fact, the features of Weber's "ideal-type" bureaucracy.

73. Weber (1958).

74. See Etzioni-Halevy and Etzioni (1973), Nelson (1972).

75. McClelland (1961).

76. Chodak (1973).

77. See Schumpeter (1951).

78. Quoted in Gianaris (1978), p. 52.

79. Gianaris (1978), Schumpeter (1951).

80. Hagen (1962).

81. In traditional societies, for various reasons, some groups within the male population would lose their status or disregard their social roles and beliefs. This would lead such groups to a retreat or "status withdrawal." However, the women (wives) would resent such retreatism and weakness of their husbands, and in reaction, would try their best to instill a strong desire

for achievement and self-reliance in the minds of their sons. When grown up, these sons would acquire innovational personality, challenge existing elites, break the prevailing self-perpetuating equilibrium, enhance economic growth, and thus modernize society. Thus, Hagen places great importance on *child rearing* to create this innovational personality needed for economic growth. See Chodak (1973), pp. 161–62.

Chapter 5. Reformist Tradition of Development Theories

1. As Bronner and Kellner (1989, p. 18) mention regarding the Frankfurt School, "its members never based their critique of advanced industrial society on any positive theory of revolution."

2. For instance, the issue of Third World income inequality was seriously taken into consideration by Hollis Chenery (former vice president of the World Bank) and others in their book *Redistribution with Growth*. Chenery et al. (1974).

3. Browett (1982, p. 149) discusses both the "worst-first" approaches (including basic needs, employment generation, self-reliance, redistribution with growth, and rural development) and the NIEO strategies under the same reformist tradition.

4. See Schumacher (1973).

5. Frederick Harbison (1973), Irma Adelman (1975), Theodore Schultz (1971, 1980), Richard Easterlin (1981).

6. Quoted in Meier (1984), p. 180.

7. See Mellor (1966), Weaver and Jameson (1978).

8. Weaver and Jameson (1978), pp. 90–92.

9. Green (1978).

10. ILO (1976).

11. See Ewing and Koch (1977), p. 459.

12. Jolly (1977), pp. 22–23.

13. More specifically, the main focus of basic needs approach is on the mobilization of "*particular* resources for *particular* groups which are identified as deficient in certain resources (e.g., caloric adequacy by age, sex, and activity)." Streeten, (1979), p. 73.

14. Streeten (1979), p. 78.

15. Livingstone (1981), p. 3.

16. Streeten (1979), p. 98.

17. Ibid, pp. 78, 114–19.

18. Goulet (1983), p. 615.

19. Preston (1986), p. xvi.

20. Weigel (1989), p. 9.

21. Bhagwati (1985), pp. 13–14.

22. See Helleiner (1990), Streeten (1979), Weaver and Jameson (1978), Weiss (1982).

23. Quoted in Mattelart (1983), p. 20. Similar view is also held by Wionczek (1979 p. 651) who feels that the NIEO was interested to improve rather than fundamentally change the existing structures of international relations.

24. Seers (1979a, 1979b).

25. Goulet (1983), p. 615.

26. Chilcote (1984), p. 112.

27. For details, see Hunt (1979), pp. 135–53.

28. Ibid., p. 152.

29. These reformist dependency theorists include scholars such as Fernando Henrique Cardoso, Osvaldo Sunkel, Celso Furtado, Helio Jaguaribe, Aldo Ferrer, and Anibal Pinto. See Kay (1991), pp. 46–47.

30. Rosenstein-Rodan analyzed that the ineffectiveness of the price system to correct the maladjusted international balance of payment was due to a rigid cost and price structure in capitalist economies and the immobility of various production factors. Arndt (1987), pp. 122–24.

31. Ibid., pp. 122–24.

32. Ibid., p. 126.

33. Prebisch (1963); also see Attewell (1984).

34. Attewell (1984) and Kay (1991) present Prebisch's analysis in the following manner. The periphery exports raw materials and imports industrial goods, while the center exports industrial goods and imports raw materials. On the demand side, the center's demand for raw materials is inelastic, for which an income increase in the center does not increase its demand for raw materials exported by the periphery. However, the periphery's demand for industrial goods is elastic, for which an income increase in the periphery also increases its demand for industrial goods exported by the center. This creates the problem of balance of payment for the periphery.

On the supply side, when the periphery's productivity and supply of raw materials increases, their prices decline because of the following: the center's limited (inelastic) demand for these raw materials, intensive competition among peripheral nations to export them, and available cheap labor in the periphery to produce them. But an increase in the center's productivity and supply of industrial goods does not reduce their prices, because of their higher (elastic) demand in the periphery, the monopolistic nature of industrial enterprises, and the political pressure of unionized industrial labor. Thus, in the case of an increased level of productivity, while the center benefits in terms of more profit for its enterprises and more wages for its workers, the periphery loses in both instances.

35. See O'Brien (1975), p. 14.

36. Chilcote (1984), pp. 27–30.

37. Kay (1991), p. 47.

38. Furtado (1976), p. 41; see also Furtado (1970).

39. See Furtado (1970, 1973).

40. Booth (1975), pp. 58–59.

41. Chilcote (1984), p. 35.

42. The strategy of import-substitution without any change in the consumption pattern would reduce the external markets for raw materials, and after a certain period, the substitution process of modern goods consumed by the rich minorities would also be exhausted. The process may at best create a form of peripheral capitalism, which is dependent on external decisions, and thus may lead to the self-sustaining process of underdevelopment. Ibid., pp. 32–35.

43. Furtado (1987), p. 225.

44. Cardoso (1979), pp. 56–62.

45. Furtado (1970).

46. See Sunkel (1969).

47. O'Brien (1975), pp. 24–25.

48. Quoted in Kay (1991), p. 40.

49. Ibid., p. 41.

50. See Chilcote (1980), p. 303.

51. Chilcote (1984), pp. 35–40.

52. See Cardoso (1972), Cardoso and Faletto (1979), Kay (1991), Manzo (1991).

53. Cardoso and Faletto (1979); also see Caporaso (1980).

54. Cardoso (1972), p. 89.

55. Based on the experiences of Argentina, Bolivia, Brazil, Mexico, and Venezuela, Cardoso and Faletto (1979, pp. xvii–xviii) mention that "the analysis of structural dependency aims to explain the interrelationships of classes and nation–states at the level of international scene as well as at the level internal to each country."

56. Kay (1991), p. 49.

57. See Chilcote (1984), p. 47; O'Brien (1975), p. 20.

58. Bronner and Kellner (1989), pp. 2–3.

59. Kellner (1989), p. 10.

60. Gouldner (1980) differentiates between "critical Marxism" and "scientific Marxism": the former reflects the works of the young Marx on alienation, dialectic, and commodity fetishism, which emphasized a voluntarist, historicist, and cultural perspective; whereas the latter refers to the works of the mature Marx (e.g., his analysis of the modes of production) characterized by materialism, evolutionism, and economism.

61. Lukacs challenged orthodox Marxism and emphasized the role of proletarian class consciousness in transforming capitalist society: it is necessary to overcome the false consciousness of this class created by the capitalist system through the process of reification and alienation. Lukacs (1971). Similarly, Gramsci challenged orthodox Marxism for its determinism and indifference toward the need for the class consciousness of workers, and suggested that the capitalist system of domination was based not only on the material means of domination but also on "ideological hegemony." See Gramsci (1971).

62. Antonio (1983), pp. 325–29.

63. For instance, while Horkheimer shifted his position away from Marxism significantly, Adorno and Marcuse retained some components of Marxism, particularly their endorsement of the Marxian concepts of "class." See Adorno (989c), Marcuse (1989c).

64. Habermas (1989b), p. 292; Honneth (1987), p. 353.

65. See Honneth (1987), pp. 353–54.

66. Habermas (1989b), pp. 292–94.

67. For further details related to this Habermas' critique of the changing politico-administrative sphere in advanced capitalist societies, see Habermas (1970, 1973, 1975, 1989a).

68. Fromm (1989a), pp. 37–39; (1989b), pp. 213–18.

69. Marcuse (1989b), pp. 234–35.

70. See Adorno (1973, 1989a), Horkheimer and Adorno (1972), Antonio (1983).

71. Lowenthal (1989a, 1989b), Adorno (1989b).

72. Benjamin (1989), Habermas (1989b).

73. Benhabib (1986), p. 161.

74. Pollock (1989), pp. 95–118.

75. Habermas (1971, 1975, 1979).

76. See Bernstein (1978), p. 206.

77. Marcuse (1989d) pp. 288–89.

78. Habermas (1975).

79. Horkheimer (1972, 1989).

80. Benhabib (1986), p. 11; Bronner and Kellner (1989), p. 7.

81. Marcuse (1989a), p. 65.

82. Marcuse (1989c), p. 283.

83. For further details, see Habermas (1979). Also see McCarthy (1978), pp. 236–37.

84. First, the stage of neolithic societies is characterized by a conventional structure of interaction, a mythical worldview interlaced with the action system, and a conventional mechanism of conflict resolution; second, the stage of archaic civilizations is marked by a conventional structure of interaction, a mythical worldview but set off from the action system, and a mechanism of conflict resolution based on conventional morality that represents a dominant figure; third, the stage of developed civilizations is demonstrated by a conventional structure of interaction, a break from mythical thought and the formation of a rationalized worldview, and a conflict resolution mechanism based on impersonal conventional morality; and fourth, the stage of early modern societies is characterized by a postconventional democratic structure of interaction, a universalistic worldview, and a conflict resolution mechanism based on the principle of legal-moral separation and legal-rational law. See McCarthy (1978), pp. 252–53.

Chapter 6. Radical Tradition of Development Theories

1. For instance, within the radical Marxian perspective, there is a distinction between the Marxists (such as Plekhanov, Kautsky, and Lenin)

who emphasize the pregiven structural conditions of human action and the Marxists (such as Lukacs, Bauer, and Gramsci) who stress the importance of the transformational capacity of various political agencies. See Bertramsen, Thomsen, and Torfing (1991), pp. 2–3. With regard to such diversity in Marxian thinking, Immanuel Wallerstein mentions that the "Marxist era of Marx himself (1840s to 1883), the era of orthodox Marxism (from 1880s to 1950) and then the era of 'thousand Marxisms' (since the 1950s) are the three phases in which styles of utopia, rhetoric, and analytical rigours have undergone changes substantially." Quoted in Dhanagare (1990), p. 9.

2. Randall and Theobald (1985), p. 138.

3. See, for example, Foster-Carter (1973).

4. O'Brien (1975), Gulalp (1983), Lall (1975), Kay (1991).

5. These dependency theorists include Ruy Mauro Marini, Theotonio Dos Santos, Andre Gunder Frank, Oscar Braun, Vania Bambirra, Anibal Quijano, Edelberto Torres-Rivas, Tomas Amadeo Vasconi, Antonio Garcia, and so on. Kay (1991), pp. 46-47.

6. Randall and Theobald (1985), pp. 137–38; also see Werker (1985), pp. 84–86.

7. In general, any original or classical idea, concept, theory, and ideology, at a certain point in history, may become inadequate to explain the newly emerging practical realities or may face a crisis because of its critique by various intellectual sources. Under such circumstances, some of its proponents may revive the original framework by introducing some reformulation or modification. This revival of the original conceptual, theoretical, or ideological position through certain revision or reformulation is often presented with the prefix "neo" to qualify its revised version.

8. Randall and Theobald (1985).

9. Various dependency theories dealing with the question of development and underdevelopment can be broadly divided into two major categories: the theories that are predominantly reformist (believing in change through reforms) and the theories which are radical (believing in change through revolution) in nature. The reformist theories of dependency have been already discussed in the previous chapter. For radical dependency theory, the proponents (Marini, Dos Santos, Frank, Braun, Vasconi, and Garcia) tend to interpret "underdevelopment" as an outcome of capitalist intervention in Third World countries, explain the relationship between development in advanced capitalist nations and underdevelopment in Third World countries, and recommend a radical or revolutionary change in the existing world capitalist system.

10. For instance, Cammack (1988, pp. 93–99) places the contributions of Marx, Engels, Lenin, Trotsky, and Gramsci under the category of classical

Marxism based on their common focus on the nature of class formation in specific national circumstances, including Third World countries. But there are others who consider Gramsci a critical rather than classical (orthodox) Marxist. Burrell and Morgan (1979), pp. 288–90. For the distinction between critical Marxism and scientific Marxism, see Gouldner (1980).

11. According to Kautsky (1989), "classical" or "orthodox" Marxists include those intellectuals who analyzed social conditions similar to Marx's analysis, such as Georgi Plekhanov (1856–1918), Rudolf Hilferding (1877–1941), Karl Kautsky (1854–1938), and others.

12. According to Hegel's dialectic, there are continuous changes in all phenomena which occur through the endless stages of contradiction between the thesis and antithesis mediated by a synthesis. According to his interpretation, history unfolds through the self-objectification of nature and culture into spirit, and the process ends at the stage of "absolute knowledge," although there might be an alienation of mind to recognize something subjective as objective. Tucker (1978), p. xxi. The philosophical interpretation of Hegel that man is a self-alienated spirit, is placed under a "transformational criticism" by Ludwig Feuerbach. Feuerbach reverses Hegel's philosophy by describing the spirit or God as self-alienated man himself in the sense that he worships an imaginary God which is his own idealized image. Thus, "Man was not the personification of spirit; rather, spirit was the thought-process taking place in man" (ibid., p. xxiii). This was a more materialistic interpretation by Feuerbach.

13. As Onyewuenyi (1977, p. 62) writes: "Influenced by Feuerbach's interpretation of Hegelian ethicality and his material inversion of the Hegelian idealistic system, Marx took philosophical stand which improved greatly on Feuerbach's materialism while at the same time retaining the dialectic method of Hegel."

14. For this dimension of Marx's view, see Marx (1978b), pp. 16–25. Also see Tucker (1978), p. xxviii.

15. See Hunt (1979), pp. 180–81.

16. Every society contains certain kinds of "production forces" which include the following: the "means of production," such as tools and equipment, which are both creations and means of labor; the "objects of labor," such as raw materials and minerals, on which labor is applied to transform them into useful goods; and the "subject of labor," i.e., workers and peasants, who provide the labor. Depending on the nature of production forces, there exists a corresponding form of "production relations" between different classes based on their ownership of various means of production. These two, the production force and the production relation, constitute the "basic structure" of society. On this basic structure, there develops the institutional "superstructure" including politics, religion, culture, and so on. All

the components included in the basic structure and superstructure together constitute the "mode of production," although production forces remain the most basic factors for shaping the nature of other dimensions of society, including production relations and the superstructure. Marx (1978a), pp. 3–6. The forces of production, especially the labor force, advance continuously, but production relations fall behind and are retained as such by the "dominant class" that owns the means of production and benefits from the existing relations. Thus, a contradiction starts between the advanced production forces and the obsolete production relations. The working class, being the most progressive force because of its close relation to the ever-changing material forces of production, becomes conscious of both the changes in objective material forces and the existence of dominating but obsolete production relations. They organize themselves and transform such production relations through a revolution, which leads to corresponding changes in the superstructure. In short, the continuous dialectic between the production forces and production relations, and thus between classes, is the prime source of fundamental changes in the modes of production from one epoch to another.

17. For Marx, capitalism represents a particular form of commodity production. Brewer (1980), p. 28. Any object becomes a commodity when it contains both the "use value" (value in use) and the "exchange value" (expressed in price). Although the social division of labor or specialization in production leads to exchange between commodities facilitated by market and money circulation, the determination of exchange value presupposes something common in all commodities to become the basis of such exchange. Labor is that common component, which is embodied in each commodity during its production and quantifiable in terms of labor time. However, each particular commodity—e.g., textile—requires a unique kind of specialized labor known as "useful labor." Thus, it is difficult to compare different commodities in terms of their respective useful labor. That is why various kinds of useful labor are abstracted away and translated into general, "socially necessary" labor time: it largely refers to labor that is required to produce a commodity in normal condition. This Marxian assumption of the homogeneity of labor, however, has been considered flawed by Elster (1985).

18. In noncapitalist societies, exchange takes place either directly between producers themselves for their own immediate consumption or indirectly, through merchants. These merchants do not produce commodities, they only buy them to sell again. Therefore, one's profit is the other's loss, and thus, there is no net surplus value.

19. A worker gets his labor capacity from his subsistence consumption of food bought from the wage he earned previously. With this renewed labor capacity he is supposed to provide an equivalent amount of labor, known as "necessary labor," during a certain number of his working hours. But he is compelled to work extra hours during which he creates extra value, known as "surplus value."

20. For various reasons, including an increase in competition and wages, the capitalists tend to replace the variable capital (labor) by constant capital (machinery). But since labor is the only source of surplus value, due to this replacement of the labor component in the capital-labor composition of the commodity, the rate of profit declines, accumulation declines, profit declines further, and so on. On the other hand, the workers lose their jobs and become unemployed, which leads to less income, less demand for commodity, less production, and further unemployment of workers. Thus, the process finally leads to an economic depression.

21. See Brewer (1980), pp. 52–59.

22. Palma (1978), pp. 886–89; Attewell (1984), pp. 209–10.

23. Marx (1978c), pp. 653–58; Marx (1978d), pp. 659–64; Marx and Engels (1978), pp. 469–500.

24. See Binder (1988)

25. Luxemburg (1951).

26. Hilferding (1981).

27. See Luxemburg and Bukharin (1972).

28. Appelbaum (1970), p. 91; Jessop (1982), pp. 33–35.

29. Attewell (1984), p. 213.

30. The Narodniks represent a group of Russian intelligentsia who wanted liberation from the csar to establish socialism based on the peasant communes. They believed that capitalist development was neither possible nor desirable; it could be bypassed to expedite the realization of socialism.

31. Quoted in Brewer (1980), pp. 113–14.

32. The reasons include the success of strikes and revolts in underdeveloped Russia in 1905, the opportunism of the European working class to abandon international solidarity in favor of nationalism, and the rise of nationalist movements against capitalist intervention in precapitalist colonies.

33. Randall and Theobald (1985), pp. 100–102.

34. See Attewell (1984), p. 244.

35. Berberoglu (1984), pp. 401–2; Booth (1975), p. 69; Brewer (1980), pp. 158–59; Laclau (1971), p. 25.

36. Bernstein (1979), p. 94.

37. Randall and Theobald (1985), Attewell (1984), Booth (1975).

38. Leys (1977, pp. 97–101) mentions this Marxified tradition of structuralism. To clear the controversy about whether Frank is a neo-Marxist or

non-Marxist, Richard Leaver wrote an independent essay, in which he mentioned that Frank should be correctly located outside Marxist theory. See Leaver (1977), pp. 108–15. According to Brenner (1977, p. 90), Frank's original theoretical formulations, in fact, aimed to destroy the orthodox Marxian theory of evolutionary stages. From these viewpoints, it is difficult to categorize Frank as a Marxist.

39. For Baran, the effects of colonial rule on the colonized nations include the destruction of self-reliant agriculture and indigenous manufacturing in the colonies, the extraction of surplus through taxation and exploitation of cheap labor, and thus, the simultaneous development of the colonizing nations and the underdevelopment of the colonized countries. Baran (1957); Attewell (1984). Baran also suggests that although international trade provides cheap primary products to advanced capitalist countries, it is discouraging for industrial development in underdeveloped areas due to the challenge of competition posed by imported manufactured goods: such trade leads to the flow of surplus from underdeveloped areas to advanced capitalist countries, depriving the former of resources needed for investment while creating excessive surplus in the latter. See Baran (1957); also Brewer (1980).

40. Browett (1985), p. 791.

41. Dos Santos (1976), p. 76.

42. Brewer (1980), p. 18.

43. See Simon and Ruccio (1986), Ruccio and Simon (1988).

44. Frank (1967).

45. Wallerstein (1984a, 1984b).

46. Dos Santos (1970).

47. Ibid., pp. 231–36.

48. See Attewell (1984).

49. Frank (1967), pp. 6–7.

50. According to Dos Santos, in the situation of "new dependency," for industrial development, the peripheral nations have to import capital goods for which they need foreign currency. This foreign currency has to be acquired by exporting goods produced in the traditional sectors. But these traditional sectors are usually under the control of oligarchies tied to foreign capital.

51. See Blomstrom and Hettne (1984), p. 66.

52. Ibid.

53. Kay (1991), p. 50.

54. Frank (1984), Simon and Ruccio (1986), Brewer (1980).

55. Unlike classical Marxists, both Frank and Wallerstein explain that capitalism is not characterized by specific class relations, but by the world system of exchange, the production structure oriented toward such exchange, and the exploitation of some areas by others through such exchange. See Brewer (1980), Laclau (1977), Simon and Ruccio (1986).

56. Wallerstein (1974, 1984a, 1984b).

57. Wallerstein (1980), p. 745.

58. Frank (1969).

59. However, Frank's optimism for such revolution is said to have diminished recently due to Wallerstein's influence on him: Wallerstein tends to believe that there is no need for revolution or delinking from the world system since capitalism itself may bring its demise as it progresses. See Browett (1985), p. 791; Gulalp (1987), pp. 134–35; Soldatenko (1982), p. 36.

60. See Chilcote (1984), pp. 63–66.

61. For a detailed analysis of these points, see Binder (1988), p. 45; Booth (1985), pp. 762–763; Fitzgerald (1983), pp. 17–22; Forbes (1984), pp. 70–88; Kay (1991), pp. 51–54; Leys (1977), pp. 94–96; Smith (1983), pp. 77–84; Smith (1981), p. 761; Taylor (1974), pp. 7–12.

62. Banaji (1979), p. 488.

63. Fitzgerald (1983), p. 22; Randall and Theobald (1985), p. 136.

64. Neo-Marxist theories, according to Foster-Carter (1973, pp. 21–33), are characterized by an antibourgeois ideology and their concerns for totality, history, revolution, class, imperialism, moral issue, nationalism, ecology, and so on. Based on these criteria developed by Foster-Carter, Blomstrom and Hettne (1984, pp. 36–38) make a comparison between Marxism and neo-Marxism. But the oversimplification of the term "neo-Marxism" by Foster-Carter is evident in his characterization of dependency theorists (such as Frank) as neo-Marxists despite the fact that dependency theory excludes many of his own neo-Marxist criteria mentioned above. Similar oversimplification is found in Smith's identification of the Frankfurt School as neo-Marxist (Smith, 1984), although the School is highly skeptical about some basic tenets of Marxism (see chapter 5). For taxonomic consistency, the category "neo-Marxism" should include mainly those theories that accept and use at least the basic formulations of Marxian analysis, including the modes of production, labor theory of value, theory of surplus value, and class analysis, although such formulations might be extended or revised when applying to the newly emerging sociohistorical conditions.

65. These theoretical frameworks are neo-Marxist because they accept, extend, and use the basic constructs of Marxian analysis. The MOP school, for instance, is a contemporary attempt to develop a "Marxian theory of

development," and it has moved beyond the conceptual limitations of "non-Marxian dependency theory." Ruccio and Simon (1986), p. 211. Within the MOP school, the theory of "articulation" rejects the focus of dependency theory on a single mode of production and exchange relation, and along the Marxian line, it emphasizes the multiple modes of production and production relations. Gregory (1988), p. 9. This is why the MOP school has been brought under the neo-Marxian category, and dependency theory under a separate category.

66. Ruccio and Simon (1988, p. 143) summarize the connotation of "mode of production" offered by E. Laclau, which represents a combination of the following four factors: "the pattern of ownership of the means of production, the form of appropriation of what he [Laclau] called an economic surplus, the degree of the division of labor, and the level of development of the forces of production."

67. Foster-Carter (1978), p. 52; Chilcote (1984), pp. 125–26.

68. Ruccio and Simon (1988).

69. See Althusser and Balibar (1970), Brewer (1980), Laclau (1977).

70. Ruccio and Simon (1988), pp. 145–46.

71. Foster-Carter (1978), p. 56.

72. Moreover, according to Rey, capitalism could expand rapidly where it was protected very early by feudalism. But the expansion of capitalism is resisted by all other precapitalist modes, in which case, violence is necessary to implant capitalism through the creation of an extra stage of "transitional modes of production" or to "articulate the articulations." Foster-Carter (1978), pp. 60–62.

73. See Forbes (1984), p. 95.

74. Ruccio and Simon (1988), pp. 150.

75. Ibid.

76. See Westergaard (1985).

77. According to Ziemann and Lanzendorfer, the expansion of colonialism and the incorporation of peripheral societies into the international economic system have led to the disruption of these societies' economic structures, distortion of their self-contained economic development, and heterogeneity in their production relations—there is, however, "preservation" of the traditional modes of production (rather than their transformation into a different mode) as a necessary component of peripheral reproduction. See Westergaard (1985), pp. 8–9.

78. Alavi (1975), Banaji (1972).

79. Foster-Carter (1978), p. 72.

80. See Foster-Carter (1978).

81. Brewer (1980), Westergaard (1985).

82. Ruccio and Simon (1988).

83. See Murray (1971). For the author, the process of internationaliza-tion leads to "the decreasing independence of national economies, and their vulnerability to changes in external economic conditions." Ibid., p. 106.

84. Brewer (1980), pp. 277–78.

85. Ruccio and Simon (1988), p. 156.

86. See Attewell (1984), pp. 235–38; Chilcote (1984), pp. 106–7; Fitz-gerald (1983), pp. 18–19.

87. Brewer (1980).

88. Attewell (1984), p. 237.

89. David (1986), p. 187.

90. Amin (1976), p. 104.

91. Amin (1977).

92. See Ruccio and Simon (1988), p. 160.

93. The coexistence of the capitalist mode (which increases productivity) and non-capitalist modes (which accommodate surplus labor) creates an imbalance between productivity and wages. See Ruccio and Simon (1988), p. 159. This imbalance results in a distorted market characterized by the production of export goods and consumption of luxury goods.

94. Leaver (1979), p. 332.

95. Amin (1984), p. 5–6; Smith (1983), pp. 76–77.

96. See Mkandawire (1983).

97. According to Mittelman (1988, p. 85), although no fixed definition of class was assigned by Marx, there are three prevailing usages of the concept: (1) class as a statistical category in terms of income levels, such as upper class and middle class; (2) class as an economic entity, such as workers and bourgeois; and (3) class in terms of the birth origin rather than social origin, such as different castes. However, the author concludes: "Properly under-stood, class is a grouping of agents who occupy a definite place in the social division of labour. In other words, classes must be seen in reference to the means of production. And it makes no sense to speak of a single class. The concept denotes opposition. Classes must be discerned in regard to their ever-changing relations with each other." Ibid., p. 86.

98. See Randall and Theobald (1985), p. 6.

99. Ibid., pp. 143–45.

100. Petras (1983), pp. 217–18.

101. Alavi (1972).

102. Ibid.; also see Randall and Theobald (1985), White (1977).

103. Alavi (1972), p. 72.

104. Alavi (1972), Westergaard (1985).

105. Ibid.

106. Geof Wood (1977, 1980).

107. Moore (1980), pp. 140–41.

108. See Westergaard (1985), p. 9.

109. Ibid. p. 10.

110. See Saul (1974, 1979), Westergaard (1985).

111. Westergaard (1985).

112. Shivji (1976); also see Leftwich (1993).

113. Leys (1977), Randall and Theobald (1985).

114. In fact, Colin Leys rejects Alavi's notion of the "overdeveloped" state on the ground that postcolonial societies did not inherit an expansive military and administrative apparatus from the colonial past; the rapid expansion of the civil service and armed forces took place mostly after their independence. See Westergaard (1985), pp. 7–8.

115. Petras (1970).

116. See Petras (1978).

117. For Petras, the three phases of capitalist and imperialist development include primitive accumulation during 1500–1880, early monopoly capitalism during 1880–1945, and late monopoly capitalism during 1946–1975. The corresponding three forms of peripheral exploitation are pirate colonialism, extractive colonialism, and dependent neocolonialism. Petras (1983), pp. 201–4.

118. Ibid., p. 210.

119. An imperial state can enhance the building of neocolonial peripheral states by establishing ties with their political and military leaders, influencing their plans and budgets, training their bureaucracies, and creating new state power; and it may also disaggregate the national-popular

and developmental regimes by utilizing financial and military networks and imposing financial and credit constraints. Ibid., pp. 210–15.

120. Ibid., p. 217.

121. See Fitzgerald (1983), p. 24.

Chapter 7. A Critique of Development Theories

1. For these critical perspectives on the development field, including development theories and policies, see Caporaso (1980), Goulet (1983), Preston (1985), Sinaceur (1983).

2. It should be mentioned, however, that this critique will address theories and models that are directly related to the idea of progress, development, or modernization. Since the critical theory of the Frankfurt School is not directly related to development issues, it will not be analyzed in this chapter. In their major works, the proponents of critical theory tend to omit issues related to Third World countries (Pieterse, 1988). Even in their analyses of advanced capitalist societies, they ignore the relevance of Third World experiences (both colonial and postcolonial) to the understanding of Western capitalist development. Thus, despite its credibility as a rich theoretical tradition, critical theory will not be examined in this chapter since it is not straightforwardly a development theory. As mentioned elsewhere, the proponents of critical theory have been accused for being isolated from practical social realities and for being unable to offer a fully developed social theory. Benhabib (1986), Bubner (1988).

3. Epistemology is that domain of philosophy which deals with the nature, scope, sources, and validity of knowledge (Ayer and O'Grady, 1992, p. 486). For the empiricist epistemology in general, the main source of knowledge is experience. See Ayer and O'Grady (1992), p. 485; Machan (1977), p. 229; Urmson and Ree (1989), p. 183.

4. Katouzian (1984), p. 44; McCloskey (1984), p. 323; Caldwell (1984), p. 137.

5. See Brown (1984), p. 443.

6. Amariglio, Resnick, and Wolff (1990), p. 118.

7. For further analysis, see Taylor (1979), p. 7.

8. Brewer (1980), p. 169.

9. Dhanagare (1990), p. 3.

10. See Mills (1990), p. 5.

11. Forbes (1984), p. 98.

12. As Brewer (1980, p. 169) mentions, "Both Frank and Wallerstein are looking for *descriptive generalisation*, based directly on the observed facts. Marx, by contrast, insisted on the necessity of *abstraction*."

13. See Amin (1990), p. 69.

14. Marxian and neo-Marxian theories recognize the cultural and normative dimensions, but they tend to render them as matters of superstructure. However, the Marxist theoretical tradition is less empiricist than the conservative theories of economic growth and modernization, because the former seek to explore the noumenal structures of economic production and class relations beneath the manifest economic phenomena.

15. Morgan (1983), p. 373.

16. See Lamm (1993), p. 168.

17. Macpherson (1972), Sinaceur (1983).

18. Bell (1981), Weigel (1989).

19. McKenzie and Tullock (1978).

20. For more details regarding such normative indifference of neoclassical theory, "new growth" theory, and Keynesian and post-Keynesian theories, see Hunt (1979), McCloskey (1984), Friedman (1984), Romer (1993), Solo (1975), Brown (1984).

21. See Preston (1985), Dhanagare (1990).

22. Macpherson (1972).

23. Valenzuela and Valenzuela (1978).

24. See Miller (1984).

25. Mills (1990), pp. 17–18.

26. Nuscheler (1988), pp. 107.

27. Baster (1972), Chaturvedi (1978), Montgomery (1976), Vyasulu (1977), Galt and Smith (1976).

28. Boulding (1990), p. 37.

29. Bernstein (1988), Carson (1983).

30. Methodological reductionism means an emphasis on parts over the totality: the interpretation of a phenomenon or concept is reduced to its narrower and simpler form so that it is amenable to empirical confirmation. See Ayer and O'Grady (1992), p. 496; Rosenau (1988), p. 428.

31. Friedman (1962), p. 13.

32. See Bagchi (1982), Lall (1976), Nafziger (1979).

33. Abdalla (1980), p. 13; David (1986), p. 25; Seers (1979a), p. 4.

34. In this regard, Furtado (1979, p. 139) concludes that the more sophisticated the growth model, the more remote it is from the multidimensional reality of society.

35. Apter (1987), p. 26; Kim (1984), p. 14; Nohlen (1980), p. 85.

36. See Giddens (1971), p. 195; McCaughan (1993), p. 86.

37. Nafziger (1979), pp. 33–34.

38. Hershlag (1984), p. 57.

39. See Jones (1973), p. 29; McCaughan (1993), p. 85; Mills (1990), p. 19.

40. McCaughan (1993), p. 85.

41. Marx (1978a), p. 4.

42. Marx (1978e), p. 297.

43. For further analysis of such reductionist tendencies of these neo-Marxist frameworks, see Foster-Carter (1978), pp. 55, 77; Leys (1977), p. 105; Forbes (1984), p. 105.

44. See Banaji (1979), Blomstrom and Hettne (1984), Foster-Carter (1976), Kay (1991), Leys (1977).

45. Laclau (1977), O'Brien (1975), Smith (1981), Taylor (1974).

46. Bernstein (1988), p. 79.

47. There are many authors who consider the existing concepts and theories of development Eurocentric, because their origins, assumptions, paradigms, motives, criteria, and orientations are predominantly Western. See Addo (1985), p. 24; Alcalde (1987), p. xv; Dwivedi and Nef (1982), p. 62; Edmonds (1977), p. 13; Furtado (1979), pp. 130–31; Lauer (1973), p. 10; Macpherson (1972), p. 206; Nafziger (1979), p. 35; Nieuwenhuijze (1982), p. 8; Southall (1972), p. 143; Steidlmeier (1987), pp. 166–73. There are also development scholars who began with sympathetic attitudes toward non-Western societies, but subsequently changed their positions and became prejudiced by Western biases. For instance, Peter Berger was critical of both capitalism and socialism, and sympathetic to the desires of non-Western nations in his *Pyramid of Sacrifice* (1976). But recently, he attacked the economic, political, and cultural features of Third World countries; demonized their political leaders and peoples; and declared himself a spokesman for "democratic capitalism." See Berger (1985), pp. 6–16.

48. Meier (1984), p. 112; Said (1978), p. 14.

49. Hunt (1979), pp. 38–40.

50. Berberoglu (1978), p. 57.

51. See Berger (1988), Hansen (1989), Preston (1986), Valenzuela and Valenzuela (1978).

52. In this regard, the observation made by Gilderhus (1992, p. 71) regarding Comte's three historical stages (theological, metaphysical, and positive) is noteworthy: "Straightforwardly Eurocentric, he [Comte] intended to focus his attention on the 'vanguard of the human race,' by which he meant the inhabitants of Italy, France, England, Germany, and Spain." It has been pointed out that the evolutionary scheme common to all modernization theories has been based on the Eurocentric assumption of Western superiority. See Welsh and Butorin (1990), p. 322. The proponents of such Eurocentric evolutionary schemes include modernization theorists such as Maine, Spencer, Durkheim, Tonnies, Becker, Linton, Riesman, Lerner, Parsons, List, Philippovitch, Schmoller, and Sombart. See Nieuwenhuijze (1982), pp. 103–12.

53. See Barnett (1988), pp. 21–22; Harrod (1982), p. 8; Smith (1973), p. 36.

54. Among the mainstream sociological theorists, the assumption of evolutionism can be found in Comte's three stages of social change; in Maine's view of social progress as a transition in the basis of society from status to contract; in Morgan's explanation of progress from savagery to barbarism to civilization; in Spencer's belief in social change from its religious militaristic to its modern industrial form; in Durkheim's assumption of social change from a simple mechanical solidarity to a more complex organic solidarity; and in Parsons' choice of some evolving societal variables and his identification of three stages of civilization such as primitive, intermediate, and modern. See Harrison (1988), p. 3; McCaughan (1993), pp. 85–86; Nieuwenhuijze (1982), pp. 103–12; Smith (1973), pp. 32–33.

55. Hansen (1989), p. 176; So (1990), p. 18.

56. See Chodak (1973), Crow et al. (1988), Kim (1984), O'Brien (1979), Wiarda (1981, 1989–90).

57. Preston (1986), p. xv.

58. See Mills (1990), p. 22; Tucker (1978), p. xxi.

59. Quoted in Tokei (1982), p. 298.

60. Berberoglu (1984), p. 399.

61. Palma (1978), p. 896.

62. See Addo (1985), pp. 28–29; Jose (1987), p. 497; Laite (1988), p. 166; Wiarda (1981), p. 174.

63. Streeten (1979), p. 95.

64. See Cooper (1979), p. 247; Rist (1978), p. 50.

65. Cooper (1979), p. 247.

66. Forbes (1984, p. 71) identifies the Eurocentrism of dependency theorists in their failures to recognize the importance of "autonomous histories," "class formation," and "anti-colonial resistance" in Third World countries.

67. Manzo (1991), p. 18.

68. Shamuyarira (1976), Wallerstein (1984a, 1984b).

69. See Goonatilake (1988), Khoi (1986).

70. Berberoglu (1978), p. 51.

71. Adams (1986), Griffin (1987), Wiarda (1989–90).

72. See Dos Santos (1976), p. 59; Mitsuo (1982), p. 605; Van Leeuwen (1970), p. 3.

73. Universalism implies that the general laws of science have universal applicability irrespective of time and place. See Benton (1977), p. 33.

74. Brookfield (1975), p. 7.

75. Hunt (1979), p. 114.

76. See Bastiat (1964), p. 487; Friedman (1984), p. 139; Hunt (1979), pp. 114–15; Hutchison (1981), p. 188; Nafziger (1990), p. 77; Walras (1954), p. 48.

77. See Benhabib (1986), p. 2; Taylor (1979), p. 9; and Almond (1970), p. 232.

78. See Lipset (1963), Deutsch (1969), Apter (1965), and Shils (1965).

79. Esteva (1992), and Feng (1986).

80. According to G.V. Plekhanov, often considered the father of "Russian Marxism," the ideas of Marx are universally relevant, irrespective of historical differences between societies. See Baron (1989), pp. 20–21.

81. See Sawer (1978–79).

82. Engels (1978), p. 700.

83. For instance, Reglar (1987, p. 229) blames Mao Zedong for his analysis of class and class struggle because it is different from Marx's interpretation.

84. According to Tony Smith (1979, pp. 247–88), dependency theory subordinates the analysis of the parts to the analysis of the whole, and thus, interprets the local actors as "pawns of outside forces."

85. See Morrow (1991b), Rosenau (1992).

86. Binder (1988); Mafeje (1978); Tice and Slavens (1983).

87. Gareau (1990), p. 62.

88. See Korten (1980).

89. Schlegel (1977).

90. See Chambers (1987), pp. 233–34.

91. Leeson (1988).

92. According to (Said, 1983, p. 2), "For the intellectual class, expertise has usually been a service rendered, and sold, to the central authority of society. . . . Expertise in foreign affairs, for example, has usually meant legitimization of the conduct of foreign policy."

93. See Klompe (1977), Stanley (1972).

94. Goulet (1980).

95. Moore (1983).

96. Easton (1991), Harrod (1982), Said (1983).

97. Munch (1991), p. 318; Nafziger (1979), p. 40.

98. Chambers (1987), p. 233; Edwards (1989), p. 123.

99. Chambers (1987), pp. 232–33.

100. Edwards (1989), p. 116; Korten (1990), p. ix.

101. Harrod (1982), p. 5.

102. With regard to the linkage between knowledge and class, Karl Mannheim discovered a relationship between the class position of an individual and his or her points of view. See Mannheim (1991); Noble (1982). Benson (1983, p. 334) also mentions that "interests and power bases, institutional settings, and class affiliations affect the concerns of social scientists and their practices."

103. Witton (1988), p. 22.

104. Esteva (1992), p. 18.

105. Nandy (1989), p. 35.

106. For further discussion, see Raghaviah (1987). For an analysis of the Eurocentric foundation of social science based on the assumption of Western superiority, see Khoi (1986), Said (1983).

107. Marx and Engels (1978), see also Blomstrom and Hettne (1984).

108. Ramirez-Faria (1991).

109. Minhas (1979), p. 76.

110. See Addo (1985), pp. 17–19.

111. Kappen (1994), p. 5; Pieterse (1991a), p. 19.

112. Murphy (1990), pp. 33–35.

113. Healey and Clift (1980), Lipset (1978), Rondinelli (1987), Streeten (1983).

114. In this regard, it has been pointed out that Third World countries with the inherited Eurocentric economic structures are more likely to experience an extreme burden of external debt. See Magdoff (1986).

115. Preston (1986), p. xv; So (1990), p. 17.

116. Gendzier (1985) p. 12.

117. Zack-Williams (1982), p. 125.

118. Huntington suggests that it is in the interests of the West to enhance unity within its own civilization in Europe and North America, to incorporate Eastern Europe and the Westernized Latin America into Western civilization, to exploit conflicts among the Confucian and Islamic states, to prohibit the military capability of such Confucian and Islamic states, to maintain military superiority in East and Southwest Asia, to support other civilizations that are sympathetic to Western interests and values, and to strengthen those international institutions that serve and legitimate Western interests. Huntington (1993), p. 49.

119. See Easton (1991), Dallmayr (1991), Munch (1991), Ritzer (1991).

120. Sachs (1992b), p. 104.

121. Forbes (1984), p. 57.

122. Marx and Engels (1978), p. 477.

123. Kappen (1994), p. 6; Sheth (1987), p. 156; Tri (1986), p. 4.

124. Sachs (1992a), pp. 3–4.

125. Ibid., p. 4.

126. Bruton (1985), p. 1102; Schiller (1989), p. 320.

127. It has been mentioned that although there are currently 5,100 languages spoken worldwide (99 percent of them are in Asia, Africa, the Pacific, and the American continents while merely one percent are in Europe), it is most likely that within a generation or two, only 100 of them will survive. See Sachs (1992b), p. 102.

128. Easton (1991), p. 27.

129. Sachs (1992b), p. 102.

130. Addo (1985), O'Brien (1979).

131. Huntington (1993), p. 40.

132. Sachs (1992a), p. 3.

133. "Eurocentrism is a circular and self-justifying affirmation of absolute cultural superiority." Ramirez-Faria (1991), pp. 4–5. Historically, the rationale of Western cultural hegemony has been based, to a great extent, on this assumption of Eurocentrism that emerged in Western Europe and was extended to other parts of the world. See Arndt (1987), Grassi (1990), Nieuwenhuijze (1982), Sachs (1992b).

134. New Internationalist (1982), p. 10.

135. Ibid.

136. Sachs (1992a), Ullrich (1992), UNDP (1994).

137. Ramphal (1992).

138. Routh (1975).

139. See Cutter (1994), Khoi (1986), Rapaczynski (1987), Shils (1989), Shiva (1987).

140. Dallmayr (1991), p. 75.

141. Simons (1994).

142. Korten (1990), p. 1.

143. See Amin (1987), p. 1144; also see chapter 2 of this book.

144. Hancock (1989), p. 131.

145. These adverse outcomes of the contemporary development models and policies have been discussed extensively in chapter 2. However, for further information and analysis, see Pieterse (1991a), p. 17; Goulet (1983), p. 612; Hancock (1989), p. 114.

146. See Farazmand (1989), p. 191; Parenti (1988), pp. 27–31.

147. Parenti (1988), pp. 10–11.

148. However, instead of enhancing socioeconomic progress, foreign aid has expanded economic dependence, increased economic inequality, perpetuated class domination, strengthened corrupt and authoritarian regimes, undermined democratic institutions, worsened people's sufferings, and deepened underdevelopment in many Third World countries. See Gregory (1988); Hellinger, Hellinger, and O'Regan (1988); Lappe, Schurman, and Danaher (1987); Mittelman (1988); Trainer (1989).

149. Gregory (1988), pp. 8–9.

150. Goulet (1983), p. 613.

151. Black (1983), Blacking (1987), Pieterse (1991a), Trainer (1989).

152. Attewell (1984), Randall and Theobald (1985), Ruccio and Simon (1986).

153. In this newly emerging global context, the state–centered paradigm of Third World development came under attack, and was overwhelmed by the advocacy of market–oriented policies in the 1980s. See Chaudhry (1994), p. 1.

154. Smith (1991), Veltmeyer (1993).

155. Clements (1994), p. 88; Esman (1991), p. 461; Pai (1994), p. 159; Stein (1994), p. 1845.

156. Smith (1991), p. 28.

157. Bello, Cunningham, and Rau (1994), p. 12; Fuhr (1994), p. 93; Young (1995), p. 166.

158. Stein (1994), p. 1834.

159. It has been found that in order to increase export and attract foreign investment under structural adjustment programs, the environmental concerns have been sacrificed in Third World countries such as India, Chile, Costa Rica, and Ghana. See Bello, Cunningham, and Rau (1994), pp. 58–61; Kumar (1993), p. 2740. Bello, Cunningham, and Rau (1994, p. 56) mention that "heightened environmental degradation and resource exploitation have often accompanied structural adjustment efforts."

160. See Blomstrom and Hettne (1984).

161. Clements (1994), p. 88.

162. Helleiner (1990).

163. Stein (1994), p. 1846.

164. In many instances, the state–centered policies achieved higher rates of economic growth, increased per capita income, reduced poverty and unemployment, eradicated various diseases, and mitigated the problem of homelessness. Bello, Cunningham, and Rau (1994); Clarke (1994).

165. See Bello, Cunningham, and Rau (1994), p. 7; ILO (1995), p. 4.

166. Veltmeyer (1993), pp. 2083–84.

167. Bello, Cunningham, and Rau (1994), p. 2; Dixon (1995), p. 203.

168. Esman (1991), p. 461; Estes (1988), pp. 143–46.

169. Clements (1994), pp. 91, 99; Huston (1995), p. 6; Rentoul (1987), p. 2.

170. During the promarket reform period 1980–92, the total external debt of India increased from $20.58 billion to $76.98 billion, Indonesia from $20.94 billion to $84.39 billion, Thailand from $8.30 billion to $39.42 billion, South Korea from $29.48 billion to $43.00 billion, Nigeria from $8.93 billion to $30.96 billion, Egypt from $20.91 billion to $40.02 billion, Brazil from $71.01 billion to $121.11 billion, Mexico from $57.38 billion to $113.38 billion, and Venezuela from $29.35 billion to $37.19 billion. See World Bank (1994), pp. 200–201.

171. Martin (1993), pp. 101–2.

172. For example, lured by the privatization and sale of telecommunications, airlines, and electricity in Latin America, various foreign companies poured $70 billion of foreign direct investment in the region between 1990 and 1994. See Miracle Unmasked (1995), p. 5.

173. Huston (1995), p. 6; Jain (1994b), p. 409; Martin (1993), p. 10.

174. Rentoul (1987), Vickers and Wright (1988).

175. See Clements (1994), Hamilton (1989).

176. Martin (1993).

177. Berthoud (1992), p. 70.

178. For instance, under the NIEO, Third World nations demanded changes in the unequal world economic order, and bargained for a new order based on the fairer distribution of global resources, mandatory transfer of technology, and restrictions on foreign investors. See Bello, Cunningham, and Rau (1994), p. 18; George (1994), p. x. On the other hand, dependency theory emphasized that the main cause of Third World underdevelopment was the world capitalist system characterized by the external dependence of peripheral nations, dominance of metropolitan nations and transnational capital, and existence of unequal international exchange. Attewell (1984), Blomstrom and Hettne (1984), Browett (1985), Ruccio and Simon (1986).

179. See Dixon, Simon, and Narman (1995), p. 1; Narman (1995), p. 55; Sarkar (1991), p. 2307.

180. Martin (1993).

181. Chaudhry (1994, p. 1) mentions that development economics became "thoroughly discredited" in the 1980s, and privatization and liberalization "became the watch–words of a new ascendancy in development policy."

182. See Esteva (1992), p. 16.

Chapter 8. Restructuring Concepts and Theories of Development

1. These trends in development thinking were noticed by Nieuwen-huijze (1982:57–60) in the early 1980s. However, it should be pointed out that more recently, development thinking has reversed toward the market centered economistic perspective. See Chaudhry (1994), Haque (1995).

2. See Steidlmeier (1987), p. 21.

3. For further analysis, see Addo (1985), pp. 40–41.

4. Shukla (1992).

5. Nieuwenhuijze (1982), pp. 53–57.

6. Haque et al. (1977), Hettne (1982).

7. See, for instance, Harrod (1982), pp. 6–19.

8. Schlegel (1977), p. 330.

9. See Cardozo (1994), MacNeill (1989), UNDP (1994), Goulet (1980).

10. Sachs (1992a), p. 4.

11. The precondition of a meaningful human existence is the negation of all the objective and subjective forces and conditions of human subjugation, including an individual's inherent physiological conditions (e.g., hunger and diseases) and the adverse natural forces (e.g., natural calamities) that often endanger his/her survival; the forces of society (e.g., the dominant groups and classes) that subjugate him/her economically and politically; and the unequal cognitive structures (e.g., dominant ideology, knowledge, and culture) that subjugate him/her intellectually, ideologically, and culturally. The negation or mitigation of these subjugating forces and conditions involves the human acts of production and exchange, social interaction and transformation, and cultural and intellectual reconstruction: all these emancipatory human activities should constitute the core of development theories and policies.

12. According to Anisuzzaman and Abdel-Malek (1983, pp. 38–88), there are structures of interclass subjugation within each nation and international subjugation between nations in the realms of culture and ideology.

13. See Anisuzzaman and Abdel-Malek (1983), Vyasulu (1977).

14. With regard to such human autonomy, although there are intellectual frameworks that emphasize emancipatory strategies, many of them have considerable shortcomings. For instance, the "liberation theology" in Latin America rejects the Western model of development, emulates a dependency framework, and equates development with the liberation of the poor and oppressed; but in their attempts to conscientize the poor about the condition of

oppression, the liberation theologians fail to consider the poor as "active agents or subjects of their own liberation" and often regard them "as objects to be manipulated." Manzo (1991), p. 25.

15. Some scholars have already identified these three forms of subjugation but in a piecemeal manner. For instance, Peet (1986) describes two forms of human subjugation or domination: the dominance of the natural forces at the early stage of development, and the dominance of the modes of production at a later stage. On the other hand, Ghosh and Kurian (1979) discuss economic and political subjugation.

16. For instance, in many Third World countries, the dimension of natural-physiological autonomy based on borrowed capital and technology has been emphasized so much that the questions of politico-economic and cultural-intellectual autonomy have been neglected or compromised. In fact, many of these countries have come under a more intensive international politico-economic and cultural-intellectual subjugation in recent years.

17. In this regard, Kappen (1994, p. 13) mentions that "judged by the standard of integral development as we have defined, the average North American is probably much less developed than any Indian villager. In the current sense of the term, we are neither developing nor underdeveloped; we are just different."

18. Mittelman (1988), p. 169; Trainer (1989), p. 49; Wasi (1984), p. 57.

19. Onyewuenyi (1977), p. 64; Tuan (1988), p. 12.

20. See Peet (1986), p. 154.

21. Nasr (1968, pp. 81–98) explains how the non-Western metaphysical traditions, including Taoism, neo-Confucianism, Shintoism, Hinduism, and Islam have unique perspectives of nature which, in common, emphasize harmony rather than competition between man and nature, and human contemplation rather than exploitation of nature. But in modern Western thinking, the strong belief is in "nature-as-object," which often encourages and legitimizes its exploitation. See Evernden (1989), p. 163.

22. However, there are purposeful human acts and processes that are common to all societies and epochs: such as the process of human adaptation with natural forces through better information and knowledge, of mutual production and reproduction between man and nature, of change in the patterns of ownership and social structure, and so on.

23. Nasr (1968), p. 20.

24. In this regard, Johnson and Ocampo (1972, p. 424) mention that development "involves the liberation of man from conditions of exploitation and oppression."

25. As Griffin (1987, p. 16) writes, "In some parts of the Third World, including parts of Asia, political power has accrued to those who control the productive sectors of the economy, namely, large landowners and industrialists."

26. See Goulet (1983), p. 616.

27. Thus, with regard to the agents of sociohistorical transformation, there is already a shift in emphasis from single agent, such as the working class in classical Marxism, to multiple subjects, including peasants, workers, women, youth, the unemployed, and so on. Zamora (1994), p. 31.

28. See Opitz (1987).

29. Galtung (1976), p. 161.

30. For instance, in Mexico, the transnationals used to have control over almost 100 percent of tobacco industry, 90 percent of patent for fertilizer manufacture, 95 percent of insecticide and pesticide industries, 93 percent of tractor and agriculture machine industry, 75 percent of oils and vegetables, 70 percent of packaged food industry, 65 percent of pulp and paper industry, and 65 percent of chocolate and sweets industry. See Mattelart (1983), p. 94.

31. Ibid., pp. 93–98.

32. See Hovart (1979), p. 673.

33. O'Manique and Pollock (1984), p. 75.

34. Usually the process of this form of human subjugation involves the reification of particular culture, ideology, and knowledge as universal, objective, and value-neutral constructs, and the claim that such constructs are true for and should be accepted by all individuals and societies. See Sachs (1979).

35. Ghosh (1989), p. 77.

36. In this regard, Ginzberg (1987, p. 3) suggests that "by the time they [students] graduate from college or university, they have had at least twenty-two years of indoctrination."

37. Garnham (1990), p. 3.

38. See Coates and Bodington (1976), p. 7.

39. Ramos (1981), p. 80.

40. For instance, in the U.S. there are nearly 1,600 daily newspapers, 7,300 weekly and semiweekly newspapers, more than 11,000 magazines, and on average, each household has more than 5 radios and 99 percent of households have television (Gilbert, 1988, p. 231).

41. Dixon (1984), p. 7.

42. Parenti (1986).

43. See Bandyopadhyaya (1988), Goonatilake (1988), Harrison (1979). In the case of India, it has been mentioned by Baber (1996, p. 8) that under the British rule, various sections of the Indian elite actively endorsed the expansion of Western education and technology which they perceived as one of the main avenues for their upward social mobility.

44. Gusdorf (1977), p. 307.

45. Sklair (1991), p. 150.

46. Garnham (1990), p. 156; Kothari (1984), p. 79.

47. David (1986), p. 177; Pred (1989), p. 217; Sklair (1991), p. 151.

48. Fossi (1977), pp. 172–74; Streeten (1975), p. 4–8; Wiarda (1981), p. 178.

49. For instance, the influence of Comte's positivism still prevails in the institutional symbols and education system in Latin America. See Arciniegas (1971), pp. 6–7; Ardao (1971), p. 13.

50. For details, see Bishop (1990), pp. 52–59.

51. Hettne (1982), p. 100.

52. Alatas (1974).

53. See Ghosh (1989), p. 82.

54. Kolland (1989), p. 59.

55. Mamadou Aw (1977, p. 273) mentions that in this epoch, the people of rich countries who constitute a minority of the world's population, have the capacity to maintain subjugation over the remaining majority by dint of their mastery of science and technology. For Western nations, such science and technology have worked not only as the means of pursuing human autonomy from the forces of nature, but also as the instruments of imposing human subjugation over other nations.

56. With regard to the cultural realm, Aina (1989, p. 123) mentions that cultural expression cannot be explained independent of power relations within and between nations.

57. See Garnham (1990), pp. 20–27.

58. Apter (1987), p. 296; James and Gutkind (1985), p. 1141.

59. Parenti (1986).

60. Babbili (1990).

61. Mattelart (1983), p. 48.

62. Keane (1991), Mattelart (1983), Parenti (1986).

63. Parenti (1986).

64. See Garnham (1990), Mattelart (1983).

65. Parenti (1986).

66. Jhally (1989), p. 68.

67. Jhally (1989), p. 67.

68. See Mattelart (1983), pp. 40–41; Peet (1986), pp. 150–51. It has been pointed out that through various cultural means, the transnational corporations are "creating new needs and desires, creating eating and living habits, and determining what foods and goods are available." Welsh and Butorin (1990), p. 472.

69. Ehrenreich et al. (1984), p. 176.

70. Weber (1994), p. 9; Sklair (1991), p. 162.

71. See Kothari (1984).

72. Demas (1975), p. 200.

73. See Helleiner (1990), p. 272.

74. Roach (1990), p. 292.

75. Frederick, Post, and Davis (1992), p. 415.

76. As Mattelart (1983, p. 32) mentions, "The film *Star Wars* gave rise to sales of more than $400 million in by-products in less than a year, whereas 160 firms have set themselves to launching 1,500 different products in the effigy of Superman."

77. According to H.I. Schiller, the current unequal international structure of information flow is maintained to perpetuate the political, military, and commercial dominance of the U.S. See Welsh and Butorin (1990), p. 716.

78. See James (1990).

79. For instance, Flavin and Lenssen (1991, p. 23) observe that the decline of oil production of some highest oil consuming countries (particularly the U.S.), an increase in the percentage of the world's known oil reserves in the Persian Gulf (from 55 percent in 1980 to 65 percent in 1989), and the threat to this huge oil supply (essential for Western countries) due to Iraq's occupation of Kuwait, led to the Gulf war.

80. In the past, many social scientists were engaged in manipulating local populations to accept the colonial rule by glorifying European superiority (Khoi, 1986, p. 37). Today, the education system has been structured in such a way as to supply a disciplined and trained work force for capitalist

market (Freeman, 1980). For Said (1983, p. 2), expert knowledge has usually served the central authority. Political scientists, for instance, play an important role in creating beliefs that are compatible with those of politicians. O'Brien (1979).

81. Hettne (1991), p. 5.

82. See Evans (1979), Cardoso and Faletto (1979).

83. For Amin (1987, pp. 1146–47), the nationalist elites who initiated national reconstruction in Third World societies, became comprador in character during the postwar period, and accepted the process of economic development that subordinated their nations to the core countries.

84. Hui (1994), p. 43.

85. Bandyopadhyaya (1988), p. 25.

86. As Mittelman (1988, p. 58) suggests, multinational corporations are both agents and results of capital accumulation process, they embody the inner logic of capitalism, and they symbolize the internationalization of capital.

87. Welsh and Butorin (1990).

88. For instance, the U.S. government has provided billions of dollars in aid to the Third World's dictatorial regimes such as those of Marcos of the Philippines, the Shah of Iran, Somoza of Nicaragua, Duvalier of Haiti, Mobutu of Zaire, Zia ul-Haq of Pakistan, and so on. Lappé, Schurman, and Danaher (1987), pp. 3–4.

89. Harrison (1979), p. 53.

90. In the cultural domain, the neocolonial culture that is externally imposed on Third World countries, is internally reinforced by Third World elites through education, media, institutions, and elitist lifestyle. See Aina (1989), pp. 123–28.

91. See Lappé, Schurman, and Danaher (1987).

92. As Griffin (1987, p. 17) suggests, through diplomatic initiatives, economic aid, and military assistance, the Western powers tend to support those Third World regimes that are often responsible for creating poverty and hunger in their own countries. Hartman and Walters (1985, pp. 432–36) also maintain that after World War II, for containing the Soviet expansion while expanding its own dominance, the U.S. provided massive military assistance that led to the emergence of repressive regimes in many peripheral states.

93. In this regard, Angus and Jhally (1989, p. 6) mention that culture is not totally dependent upon the economic realm: it has attained a significant degree of autonomy. In a more extensive analysis, Kellner (1990, p. 89) sug-

gests that "the media, information, and entertainment industries are indeed becoming more and more central to the new formation of technocapitalism."

94. See Sklair (1991), p. 76.

95. Even Third World leaders (such as those in South Africa and Palestine) who once fought for the liberation of their peoples but were rejected by the West, are getting some form of Western support today as they have increasingly come to embrace Western capitalist system, including its market ideology and transnational investment.

96. Schiller (1989), p. 318.

97. David (1986), Illich (1976), Mittelman (1988), Selwyn (1975).

98. The consumption patterns are changed by media not only through the sensational advertisements of various consumption items (e.g., foods, drinks, automobiles, electronic goods, cosmetics, and pharmaceutical products) but also through the propagation of cultural and informational products (e.g., films, television programs, newspapers, magazines, and computer networks). For Kappen (1994, p. 7), the "profit-hungry transnational companies" have established "a form of tele-colonialism" to control the patterns of consumption through cultural impact.

99. For instance, Western media has been successful in portraying the pro-American Noriega as cooperative, but anti-American Noriega as a thug; the pro-American Shah as a friend, but pro-Islamic Khomeni as a "fundamentalist"; the anti-Iranian Saddam as acceptable, but anti-Kuwaiti or anti-American Saddam as an aggressor; the pro-market Deng as progressive, but pro-state Deng as undemocratic; the social-democrat Gorbachev as unpredictable, but the authoritarian-capitalist Yeltsin as decisive and progressive.

100. In this reestablishment and expansion of Western dominance, the global cultural-intellectual means have played a significant role: for instance, Western films and news media have established a superior view of the Euro-American civilization, a virtuous and beneficial impression of colonial rule, a progressive portrayal of Western man in teaching modernity, but a distorted and racist image of Third World nations. See Falk (1987), p. 8; Hamelink (1990), p. 102; Lyman (1990), pp. 50–51; Mittelman (1988), p. 8. Such mystifying but distorted images have been quite effective in influencing Third World elites to endorse and use Western models to "modernize" their societies. In this regard, Moore (1983, p. 59) suggests that "liberation in its fullest sense means liberation from imagery that was dictated to us."

101. For example, with regard to the centrality of international information networks, Mahoney (1989, p. 42) mentions that the full–blown global expansion of transnational corporations could be almost impossible without the corresponding expansion and globalization of the "increasingly

sophisticated means of global information collection, processing, and transmission."

102. Angus and Jhally (1989), pp. 4–6.

103. Ibid., pp. 2–6.

104. For instance, it has been pointed out that the American people have been transformed into apolitical and pacified citizens through the film industry by constantly displaying to them the American military might, reinforcing their optimism in the American Dream, and assuring them of American victories. Angus and Jhally (1989), p. 1.

105. Anisuzzaman and Abdel–Malek (1983), p. 81.

106. The international structures of cultural–intellectual hegemony not only perpetuate the cultural and intellectual subordination of Third World countries (Goulet, 1983, p. 612), such structures also reinforce their economic and political dependence on advanced capitalist nations.

107. For details, see Parenti (1986).

108. Childers (1990), p. 13; Peet (1986), p. 151.

109. With regard to the hegemonic nature of the development field, Harrod (1982, p. 4) mentions that "the vocabulary of development has largely been the vocabulary of domination."

Chapter 9. Reforming Development Policies

1. For further analysis of these emerging promarket, neoliberal regimes in Third World countries, see Chaudhry (1994), Arblaster (1991), Helleiner (1990), Petras (1990), Haque (1998).

2. See Haque (1996a, 1996b).

3. Haque (1995), Sanyal (1993).

4. Welsh and Butorin (1990), p. 817.

5. In this regard, it has been mentioned by Johnston and Clark (1982, p. 2) that "the development community has failed to learn from experience, repeating the same mistakes over and over again."

6. Currently, almost 1.5 billion people are in poverty and 1.3 billion without safe drinking water, 1.5 billion people are undernourished and 770 million without adequate food, 14 million children die from hunger every year, and about 880 million adults cannot read or write. See Nafziger (1990), Welsh and Butorin (1990). For further details, also see chapter 2.

7. In the past, the interpretation of instrumental factors such as capital, technology, and skill as the most basic problems of development, encouraged Third World nations to borrow Western capital, technology, and expertise which, instead of alleviating the problems of hunger, disease, and illiteracy, worsened the conditions of external debt and technological dependence.

8. In terms of minerals, for instance, Jamaica and Guinea account for 26.7 percent of the world's bauxite; Peru and Mexico for 13 percent of its zinc; Mexico, Peru, and Chile for 33 percent of its silver; Chile, Peru, Zaire, and Zambia for 32 percent of its copper; and Brazil, China and South Africa for 56 percent of its gold. Arnold (1989), pp183–84.

9. UNDP (1994), p. 208.

10. Nafziger (1990), p. 64; UNDP (1994), p. 163.

11. See Trainer (1989), p. 23.

12. Johnston and Clark (1982), p. 38.

13. See Adelman, Bourniaux, and Waelbroeck (1989); Kaneda (1989); Nikiforov (1989).

14. Bautista (1989), p. 35; Brookfield (1979), p. 118; Nafziger (1990), pp. 146–47.

15. Segal (1993), p. 70.

16. In this regard, one may like to examine some of the principles of industrial investment in India suggested by Reddy in the early 1970s: he recommends industrial technologies that produce goods for mass consumption, that use local rather than imported materials, and that promote symbiotic rather than parasitic relationship between urban industry and rural population. See Robinson (1979).

17. Ibid., p. 132.

18. By the early 1980s, almost 80 percent of Latin American agricultural exports were accounted for by only nine products, of which six were plantation crops such as coffee, sugar, bananas, oilseeds, cocoa, and cotton; and 75 percent of African agricultural exports were accounted for by ten products, of which five were plantation crops such as tea, coffee, cocoa, cotton, and tobacco. Welsh and Butorin (1990), p. 788. Worldwide, "Latin America's share of the principal agricultural commodities is approximately as follows: coffee 66 percent, cocoa 35 percent, sugar cane 46 percent, citrus fruits 15 percent, hardwoods 15 percent, beef 25 percent, and wool 10 percent." Arnold (1989), p. 182.

19. Bodley (1982), George (1990), Grindle (1986), Redclift (1987).

20. See Nafziger (1990), p. 363.

21. Arnold (1989), p. 185.

22. Welsh and Butorin (1990), p. 789.

23. See UNDP (1994), pp. 154–55. In this regard, it is suggested that Third World countries must break away from the chain of dependence to realize self–reliance in food. Alschuler (1988), p. 19.

24. Johnston and Clark (1982), p. 254.

25. See Mittelman (1988), pp. 177–78.

26. Rice (1988), p. 36; O'Cleireacain (1990), pp. 37–42.

27. Mittelman (1988), pp. 181–82.

28. It has been mentioned by Johnston and Clark (1982, p. 72) that less capital-intensive technologies are usually less dependent on foreign exchange.

29. These labor-intensive and small-scale enterprises have favorable implications for the employment and income of the rural landless and poor. See Kinsey (1987).

30. Today, the world market is full of many harmful drugs, Which have replaced more indigenous, holistic medicines that existed in Third World countries such as India. Kappen (1994), pp. 6–7. In collaboration with Third World elites, the multinational drug companies and modern doctors have established the monopoly of medicines in Third World countries, although many of these medicines have been already proven detrimental in advanced industrial countries. Shiva (1987), pp. 256–60.

31. Welsh and Butorin (1990), p. 781.

32. Bodley (1982), Davis (1954).

33. The loss of nutrients through modern food processing can be understood from the following example: in comparison with whole–wheat bread consumed in many Third World societies, the modern white bread loses zinc by 50 percent, calcium by 60 percent, vitamin B2 by 61 percent, copper by 74 percent, potassium and magnesium by 76 percent, folic acid by 79 percent, niacin by 80 percent, manganese by 84 percent, vitamin B1 by 90 percent, and vitamin E by almost 100 percent. Davis (1954), pp. 254–55.

34. Davis (1954), p. 247.

35. Bodley (1982), pp. 150–52; Davis (1954), pp. 243–46.

36. See Davis (1954), pp. 253–61.

37. Bodley (1982), pp. 150–56; Welsh and Butorin (1990), pp. 471–72.

38. For further information, see UNDP (1994), pp. 27–28.

39. Quoted in Welsh and Butorin (1990), p. 780.

40. Ibid.

41. See Ibid., pp. 778–79.

42. Barnett (1988), pp. 138–43.

43. However, one should not forget that such changes toward a more people-oriented education system may still remain unaffordable for the landless and the underclass. They cannot even avail the opportunity of free education, because their children are income-earning members of the family. The implicit costs of education—i.e., income foregone for attending school—prevent many parents from sending children to schools. Thus, the issues of poverty and illiteracy are related.

44. Illich (1976), p. 360.

45. See Redclift (1987).

46. For example, excessive irrigation causes the salinization of soil, which has reduced the crop yielding of millions of hectares of land all over the world—about 20 million hectares in India, 7 million in China, and 3.3 million in Pakistan. See Postel (1990), p. 44. By resolving the causes of such salinization, a further decline in crop yielding could be avoided.

47. Griffin (1987), Mittelman (1988), Post (1982).

48. See Haque (1994, 1996c), Streeten (1989a).

49. Griffin (1987).

50. Cohen, Grindle, and Walker (1985).

51. Lappé, Schurman, and Danaher (1987).

52. Johnston and Clark (1982), p. 13.

53. Johnson and Ocampo (1972).

54. Nafziger (1990), p. 63.

55. For instance, Adiseshiah (1977, p. 269) suggests the eradication and transformation of all hierarchical structures in society and the introduction of genuine people's participation. These generic conclusions, which are quite common in development literature, are of minimal use to development practitioners who need more specific policy guidelines.

56. Welsh and Butorin (1990), p. 627.

57. Brown (1987), p. 31.

58. Johnston and Clark (1982), p. 115.

59. See Jayasuriya (1988), p. 44.

60. See Haque (1996c), Hays (1975), Thorsson (1983). In addition to economic cost, the expansive military establishment has also led to armed conflicts, violence against citizens, and military dictatorship in many Third World countries. See Abolfathi and Park (1975), p. 109; Renner (1989), p. 135; Sivard (1989), p. 21.

61. Haque (1996c).

62. See Haque (1997).

63. Johnston and Clark (1982), p. 198.

64. In relation to the importance of a people-centered development perspective, Johnston and Clark (1982, p. 266) mention that in the ultimate analysis, "development is about neither numbers nor solutions; rather, it is about people."

65. Blair (1985).

66. See Korten (1980), p. 482.

67. Tandon (1991), pp. 70–77.

68. Itty (1984).

69. Demas (1975), Hancock (1989), Helleiner (1990), Islam (1979), Mittelman (1988).

70. See George (1990); Helleiner (1990); Lee, Hadwiger, and Lee (1990).

71. Adiseshiah (1977), Dogra (1994), p. 25.

72. Martnelli (1975), p. 429.

73. Nafziger (1990), p. 362.

74. Frederick, Post, and Davis (1992), p. 184.

75. See Arnold (1989), p. 180. With regard to foreign control over Third World economies, one may even examine the emerging tourist industry in these countries, which has increasingly come under external control: in Asia and Africa, about 85 percent of foreign tourists are flown by foreign carriers, and more than 25 percent of all hotels are foreign owned. See Hong (1985), p. 14.

76. Galtung (1976), p. 163.

77. Helleiner (1990), Linear (1985), Mittelman (1988), Opitz (1987).

78. Dogra (1994), pp. 25–26.

79. Nafziger (1990), pp. 364–65.

80. See Islam (1979), Jennings and Weiss (1982).

81. Helleiner (1990), Mittelman (1988).

82. George (1990), Gilpin (1987), Kothari (1989), Shaw (1988), South Commission (1990).

83. It has been found that while 63 percent of Third World trade is with advanced industrial nations, only 31 percent is among Third World countries themselves. See Nafziger (1990), p. 70.

84. South Commission (1990), pp. 147–49.

85. See Mittelman (1988), Moore (1983).

86. Amin (1987), pp. 1154.

87. Amin (1987, 1993), Senghaas (1979).

88. Rice (1988), p. 37.

89. See Sachs (1987), p. 102.

90. For details, see Arnold (1989), Cole (1988), Trainer (1989).

91. Recognizing the role of various international agencies (including the United Nations) in maintaining the existing international order that serves Western interests, Schlegel (1977, pp. 253–57) concludes that a basic change is possible only through a genuine Third World unity.

92. Senghaas (1979), Abdalla (1980), Patel (1983).

93. Aw (1977), p. 277.

94. Smith and Ottaway (1995), p. 2.

95. In addition, the Western powers exercise both economic and military hegemony through their overwhelming control over the global arms trade: the top arms exporting countries that sell weapons to Third World countries and earn billions of dollars include the U.S., the U.K., and France. See UNDP (1994), pp. 54–55.

96. See Lappé, Schurman, and Danaher (1987); Nafziger (1990).

97. Dogra (1994), Martinelli (1975), Varas (1985).

98. Lappé, Schurman, and Danaher (1987), pp. 46–47.

99. Sparks and Roach (1990), p. 280.

100. As Rahman (1991, p. 23) mentions, *"there can be no development (which is endogenous) unless the people's pride in themselves as worthy human beings inferior to none is asserted or, if lost, restored* [original italic]."

101. See Golding (1985), Roach (1990).

102. For Featherstone (1990, pp. 6–7), such means of cultural-intellectual subjugation include the international flows of information (through newspapers, films, television, books, journals, and magazine); ideological images (e.g., Western views of freedom, democracy, and welfare); the people (as tourists, immigrants, refugees, and guest workers); machinery and technology (mostly produced by multinational corporations); and money (in the currency markets and stock exchanges).

103. Welsh and Butorin (1990), p. 1062.

104. According to Chambers (1987, pp. 232–33), the global structure of knowledge based on *diploma disease* (a drive for degrees or certificates) has provided tickets for jobs and upward mobility to the elites, and led to *peripheral fossilization* through the training of Third World scholars in Western ideas and orthodoxies.

105. See Bandyopadhyaya (1988), p. 77.

106. It has been pointed out that the condition of "academic dependency in which Third World scholars find themselves leaves them susceptible to the imitation and wholesale adoption of Western ideas and techniques." Alatas (1993), p. 332.

107. Frederick, Post, and Davis (1992).

108. Garnham (1990).

109. See Welsh and Butorin (1990), p. 716.

110. Mattelart (1983), p. 46.

111. In the 1970s, the imported programs occupied 84 percent of television time in Guatemala, 55 percent in Chile, 62 percent in Uruguay, 41 percent in Egypt, 64 percent in Zambia, 35 percent in Pakistan, 31 percent in Korea, and 71 percent in Malaysia. See Harrison (1979), pp. 56–57.

112. Mattelart (1983), p. 47; Roach (1990), p. 291.

113. Mattelart (1983), pp. 51–52.

114. Sabato (1977).

115. See Hong (1985), pp. 14–30.

116. Frederick, Post, and Davis (1992), p. 418; Welsh and Butorin (1990), p. 271.

117. Harris (1984), Meyer (1989), Roach (1990).

118. See "Cross-Frontier" (1992).

119. Welsh and Butorin (1990).

120. Sklair (1991), p. 78.

121. For instance, the U.S. media often create false images of women as emotional and inferior, and depict African–Americans in terms of negative behavior. Frederick, Post, and Davis (1992). On the other hand, the television networks have largely replaced the role of political parties in the conduct of American elections. Rudolph (1992), p. 1490. The U.S. media have also played a significant role in legitimating various state-sponsored policies and activities such as Roosevelt's New Deal, Kennedy's New Frontier, Johnson's Great Society programs, Nixon's Watergate defense, Carter's Middle East diplomacy, Reagan's economic policies, and so on. See Kellner (1990), pp. 97–98.

122. See Roach (1990), p. 283.

123. Harris (1984), Roach (1990).

124. Demas (1975), Mattelart (1983), Welsh and Butorin (1990).

125. The global media often provide partial and fragmented interpretations of Third World conditions. For instance, Third World famine is portrayed by the media as a matter of governmental incompetence while ignoring other major causes of famine—such as the devastating reduction in prices of Third World commodities on the world markets over which Third World countries have little control. See Welsh and Butorin (1990), p. 718.

126. Hamelink (1990), p. 102.

127. Tetzlaff (1991).

128. Dorfman and Mattelart (1980), p. 130.

129. Many of these ideas are based on Eurocentric prejudices. In this regard, Asad (1993, p. 38) mentions that it is a reexamination of the European project which may explain how the Western concepts of "justice, reason, and good life" were introduced in Third World countries.

130. Goulet (1983) suggests that the dominant Third World elites gain considerably by keeping their countries dependent on rich Western nations. This internal dimension of subjugation is crucial, although it is often neglected by those who emphasize international subjugation and demand a new international information order. Musa (1990), p. 331.

131. It has been found that in most Third World countries, the upper-class social elites prefer foreign films, while the low-income groups prefer their own national films. See Mattelart (1983), p. 42–43.

132. As Jhally (1989, p. 71) points out, the commodity form of modern culture is manufactured and sold "to divert, distract, and amuse people away from the alienation and drudgery imposed by capitalist work relations. The culture industry offers a escape through pure illusion."

133. Regarding the implications of free information exchange, Schiller (1989, p. 329) makes the following comment: "It is now blindingly apparent

that the 'free flow' [of information] principle serves the totality of transnational capital's objectives and fuses economic, political, and cultural ends."

134. It has already been pointed out by some scholars that the Western pattern of development represents only one possibility among many, and that it is quite natural and desirable to have plurality in development thinking. See Goulet (1980), Haque et al. (1977), Opitz (1987).

135. With regard to the significance of this freedom to choose their own development alternatives by different societies, this study has not only been critical of the current tendency toward deterministic universalism in development thinking, it has also attempted to overcome such a tendency by emphasizing the avenue for alternative viewpoints in its proposed restructuring of development concepts, theories, policies.

References

Abdalla, Ismail-Sabri. 1980. "What Development? A Third World Viewpoint." *IDR*. Vol. 22, Nos. 2–3. Pp. 13–16.

Abolfathi, Farid, and Tong-whan Park. 1975. "Military Spending in the Third World: The Interactions of Domestic and International Forces." In Craig Liske, William Loehr, and John McCamant (eds.), *Comparative Public Policy*, (pp. 109–25). London: John Wiley & Sons.

Adams, J. 1986. "Peasant Rationality: Individuals, Groups, Cultures." *World Development*. Vol. 14, No. 2. Pp. 273–82.

Addo, Herb. 1985. "Beyond Eurocentricity: Transformation and Transformational Responsibility." In Herb Addo et al. (eds.), *Development as Social Transformation* (pp. 12–47). Boulder, Colorado: Westview Press.

———— et al. (eds.). 1985. *Development as Social Transformation* (Introduction). Boulder, Colorado: Westview Press.

Adelman, Imra. 1975. "Growth, Income Distribution, and Equity Oriented Development Strategies." World Development. Vol. 3, Nos. 2–3. Pp. 67–76.

Adelman, Imra, J. Bourniaux, and Waelbroeck. 1989. "Agricultural Development-led Industrialisation in a Global Perspective." In J.G. Williamson and V.R. Panchamukhi (eds.), *The Balance Between Industry and Agriculture in Economic Development*. Vol. 2 (pp. 320–39). London: Macmillan Press.

Adiseshiah, S. 1977. "The Conditions for the Economic and Political Independence of the Third World." In John P. Schlegel (ed.), *Towards a Redefinition of Development* (pp. 265–70). Oxford, England: Pergamon Press.

311

Adorno, Theodor W. 1973. *Negative Dialectics*. New York: Seabury Press.

———. 1989a. "The Culture Industry Reconsidered." In Stephen E. Bronner and Douglas M. Kellner (eds.), *Critical Theory and Society: A Reader* (pp. 128–35). New York: Routledge.

———. 1989b. "Perennial Fashion—Jazz." In Stephen E. Bronner and Douglas M. Kellner (eds.), *Critical Theory and Society: A Reader* (pp. 199–209). New York: Routledge.

———. 1989c. "Society." In Stephen E. Bronner and Douglas M. Kellner (eds.), *Critical Theory and Society: A Reader* (pp. 267–75). New York: Routledge.

Agazzi, E. 1988. "Philosophical Anthropology and the Objectives of Development." In Unesco (ed.), *Goals of Development* (pp. 13–36). Paris: Unesco.

Agh, A. 1984. [review of *Emerging Development Patterns: European Contributions*]. *Development and Peace*. Vol. 5. Pp. 233–35.

Agnew, John. 1994. "Global Hegemony Versus National Economy: The United States in the New World Order." In George J. Demko and William B. Wood (eds.), *Reordering the World* (pp. 269–79). Boulder, Colorado: Westview Press.

Ahmad, Aijaz. 1992. *In Theory: Classes, Nations, Literatures*. London: Verso.

Aina, Tade Akin. 1989. "Culture in the Development Process: The Nigerian Experience." *Scandinavian Journal of Development Alternatives*, Vol. 8, No. 4. Pp. 123–37.

Alatas, Syed Farid. 1993. "On the Indigenization of Academic Discourse." *Alternatives*. Vol. 18, No. 3. Pp. 307–38.

Alatas, Syed Hussein. 1974. "The Captive Mind and Creative Development." *International Social Sciences Journal*. Vol. 16, No. 4. Pp. 691–700.

Alavi, Hamza. 1972. "The State in Post-Colonial Societies: Pakistan and Bangladesh." *New Left Review*. No. 74. Pp. 59–81.

———. 1975. "India and the Colonial Mode of Production." *Economic and Political Weekly*. Vol. 10. Pp. 1235–62.

Albelda, Randy, Christopher Gunn, and William Waller (eds.). 1987. *Alternatives to Economic Orthodoxy*. New York: M.E. Sharpe.

Alcalde, Javier Gonzalo. 1987. *The Idea of Third World Development*. New York and London: University Press of America.

Alexander, Jeffrey C., and Piotr Sztompka. 1990. "Introduction." In Jeffrey C. Alexander and Piotr Sztompka (eds.), *Rethinking Progress: Movements,*

Forces, and Ideas at the End of the 20th Century (pp. 1–12). Boston: Unwin Hyman.

Almond, Gabriel. 1970. *Political Development: Essays in Heuristic Theory.* Boston: Little Brown.

Almond, Gabriel and G. Bingham Powell. 1966. *Comparative Politics: A Developmental Approach.* Boston: Little Brown.

Alschuler, Lawrence R. 1988. *Multinationals and Maldevelopment.* New York: St. Martin's Press.

Althusser, Louis and Etienne Balibar. 1970. *Reading "Capital."* London: New Left Books.

Amariglio, Jack, Stephen Resnick, and Richard Wolff. 1990. "Division and Difference in the 'Discipline' of economics." *Critical Inquiry.* Vol. 17, No. 1. Pp. 108–37.

Amin, Samir. 1976. *Unequal Development: An Essay on Social Formations of Peripheral Capitalism.* New York: Monthly Review Press.

———. 1977. *Imperialism and Unequal Development.* Hassocks: Harvester Press.

———. 1984. "Expansion or Crisis of Capitalism?" *Contemporary Marxism.* Vol. 9 (fall). Pp. 3–17.

———. 1987. "Democracy and National Strategy in the Periphery." *Third World Quarterly.* Vol. 9, No. 4. Pp. 1129–56.

———. 1989. "Peace, National and Regional Security and Development: Some Reflections on the African Experience." *Alternatives.* Vol. 14, No. 2. Pp. 215–29.

———. 1990. *Maldevelopment: Anatomy of a Global Failure.* Tokyo:United Nations University Press.

———. 1993. "South Africa in the Global System." *Monthly Review.* Vol. 45, No. 2. Pp. 1–7.

Anderson, Thomas D. 1988. "The Socioeconomic 'Worlds' of the Caribbean Basin." In Jim Norwine and Alfonso Gonzalez (eds.), *The Third World: States of Mind and Being* (pp. 171–82). Boston: Unwin Hyman.

Angus, Ian H. and Sut Jhally. 1989. "Introduction." In Ian Angus and Sut Jhally (eds.), *Cultural Politics in Contemporary America* (pp. 1–14). New York: Routledge.

Anisuzzaman, and A. Abdel-Malek (eds.). 1983. *The Transformation of the World* (Vol. 3). London: Macmillan Press.

Antonio, Robert J. 1983. "The Origin, Development, and Contemporary Status of Critical Theory." *Sociological Quarterly.* Vol. 24. Pp. 325–51.

Appelbaum, Richard P. 1970. *Theories of Social Change*. Chicago: Markham Publishing Company.

Apter, David Ernest. 1965. *The Politics of Modernization*. Chicago: University of Chicago Press.

————. 1987. *Rethinking development*. Beverly Hills, Calif.: Sage Publications.

Arblaster, Anthony. 1991. "The Death of Socialism—Again." *Political Quarterly*. Vol. 62, No. 1. Pp. 45–51.

Archibugi, Franco and Peter Nijkamp (eds.). 1989. *Economy and Ecology: Towards Sustainable Development*. Dordrecht, Netherlands: Kluwer Academic Publishers.

Arciniegas, German. 1971. "The Search for Order and Progress in Latin America." In R.L. Woodward (ed.), *Positivism in Latin America, 1850–1900* (pp. 1–7). Lexington, Mass.: D.C. Heath & Co.

Ardao, A. 1971. "Assimilation and Transformation of Positivism in Latin America." In R.L. Woodward (ed.), *Positivism in Latin America, 1850–1900* (pp. 11–16). Lexington, Mass.: D.C. Heath & Company.

Arndt, Heinz Wolfgang. 1987. *Economic Development: The History of an Idea*. Chicago and London: University of Chicago Press.

Arnold, Guy. 1989. *The Third World Handbook*. London: Cassell Educational.

Asad, Talal. 1993. "A Commentary on Aijaz Ahmad's *In Theory*." *Public Culture*. Vol. 6, No. 1. Pp. 31–39.

Aseniero, G. 1985. "A Reflection on Developmentalism: From Development to Transformation." In Herb Addo et al. (eds.), *Development as Social Transformation* (pp. 48–85). Boulder, Colorado: Westview Press.

Attewell, Paul A. 1984. *Radical Political Economy Since the Sixties*. New Brunswick, N.J.: Rutgers University Press.

Avery, William P. 1990. "The Origins of Debt Accumulation among LDCs in the World Political Economy." *Journal of Developing Areas*. Vol. 24, No. 1. Pp. 503–22.

Aw, Mamadou. 1977. "Conceptions and Misconceptions of Development." In John P. Schlegel (ed.), *Towards a Re-definition of Development* (pp. 271–278). New York: Pergamon Press.

Ayer, A.J. and Jane O'Grady, (eds.). 1992. *A Dictionary of Philosophical Quotations*. Oxford: Basil Blackwell Ltd.

Aziz, Sartaj. 1978. "The New International Order: Search for Common Ground." *International Development Review*. Vol. 20, No. 1. Pp. 6–15.

Babai, Don. 1988. "The World Bank and the IMF: Rolling Back the State or Backing Its Role?" In Raymond Vernon (ed.), *The Promise of Privatization: A Challenge for U.S. Policy* (Pp. 254–75). New York: Council on Foreign Relations.

Babbili, Anantha Sudhaker. 1990. "Understanding International Discourse: Political Realism and the Non-aligned Nations." *Media, Culture and Society*. Vol. 12, No. 3. Pp. 309–24.

Baber, Zaheer. 1996. *The Science of Empire: Scientific Knowledge, Civilization, and Colonial Rule In India*. Albany: State University of New York Press.

Bagchi, Amiya Kumar. 1982. *The Political Economy of Underdevelopment*. Cambridge: Cambridge University Press.

Banaji, Jairus. 1972. "For a Theory of Colonial Modes of Production." *Economic and Political Weekly*. Vol. 7, No. 52. Pp. 2498–502.

———. 1979. "Gunder Frank in Retreat?" *Journal of Contemporary Asia*. Vol. 9, No. 4. Pp. 478–94.

Bandyopadhyaya, Jayantanuja. 1988. *The Poverty of Nations: A Global Perspective of Mass Poverty in the Third World*. New Delhi: Allied Publishers Private.

Baran, Paul. A. 1957. *The Political Economy of Growth*. New York: Monthly Review Press.

Baran, Paul. A. and Paul M. Sweezy. 1968. *Monopoly Capital: An Essay on the American Economic and Social Order*. Harmondsworth: Penguin Books.

Barnett, Tony. 1988. *Sociology and Development*. London: Hutchinson.

Baron, Samuel Haskell. 1989. "Plekhanov: Russian Comparativist." *International Journal of Comparative Studies*. Vol. 30, Nos. 1–2. Pp. 20–32.

Baster, Nancy (ed.). 1972. "Development Indicators: An Introduction." In Nancy Baster (ed.), *Measuring Development*. London: Frank Cass.

Bastiat, F. 1964. *Economic Harmonies*. Princeton, N.J.: Van Nostrand Company.

Bautista, Romeo M. 1989. "Domestic Terms of Trade and Agricultural Growth in Developing Countries." In N. Islam (ed.), *The Balance Between Industry and Agriculture in Economic Development*, Vol. 5. (pp. 17–38). London: Macmillan Press.

Bava, N. 1981. "Approaches to Development." *Indian Journal of Political Science*. Vol. 42, No. 2. Pp. 41–47.

Bell, Daniel. 1981. "Models and Reality in Economic Discourse." In Daniel Bell and Irving Kristol (eds.), *The Crisis in Economic Theory* (pp. 46–80). New York: Basic Books.

Bello, Walden, Shea Cunningham, and Bill Rau. 1994. *Dark Victory: The United States, Structural Adjustment and Global Poverty*. London: Pluto Press.

Benhabib, Seyla. 1986. *Critique, Norm, and Utopia: A Study of the Foundation of Critical Theory*. New York: Columbia University Press.

Benjamin, Walter. 1989. "Surrealism: The Last Snapshot of the European Intelligentsia." In Stephen E. Bronner and Douglas M. Kellner (eds.), *Critical Theory and Society: A Reader* (pp. 172–83). New York: Routledge.

Benson, J.K. 1983. "A Dialectical Method for the Study of Organizations." In Gareth Morgan (ed.), *Beyond Method: Strategies for Social Research* (pp. 331–46). Beverly Hills, Calif.: Sage Publications.

Bentham, Jeremy. 1969. *A Bentham Reader*. Edited by M.P. Mack. New York: Pegasus.

Benton, T. 1977. *Philosophical Foundations of the Three Sociologies*. London: Routledge & Kegan Paul.

Berberoglu, Berch. 1978. "The Meaning of Underdevelopment: Critique of Mainstream Theories of Development and Underdevelopment." *International Studies*. Vol. 17, No. 1. Pp. 51–73.

———. 1984. "The Controversy Over Imperialism and Capitalist Industrialization: Critical Notes on Dependency Theory." *Journal of Contemporary Asia*. Vol. 14, No. 4. Pp. 399–407.

Berger, Peter L. 1976. *Pyramids of Sacrifice*. New York: Anchor Books.

———. 1985. "Speaking to the Third World." In Peter L. Berger and M. Novak (eds.), *Speaking to the Third World* (pp. 4–20). Washington, D.C.: American Enterprise for Public Policy Research.

———. 1988. "An East Asian Development Model?" In Peter L. Berger and Hsin-Huang M. Hsiao (eds.), *In Search of an East Asian Development Model* (pp. 3–11). New Brunswick, N.J.: Transaction Books.

Bernstein, Henry. 1979. "Sociology of Underdevelopment vs. Sociology of Development?" In David Lehmann (ed.), *Development Theory: Four Critical Studies* (pp. 77–106). London: Frank Cass and Company.

———. 1988. "Development I: Variations on Capitalism." In Ben Crow et al. (eds.), *Survival and Change in the Third World* (pp. 67–82). New York: Oxford University Press.

Bernstein, Richard J. 1978. *The Restructuring of Social and Political Theory*. Philadelphia: University of Pennsylvania Press.

Berthoud, Gerald. 1992. "Market." In Wolfgang Sachs (ed.), *The Development Dictionary: A Guide to Knowledge as Power* (pp. 70–87). London: Zed Books.

Bertramsen, Rene Bugge, Jens Peter F. Thomsen, and Jacob Torfing. 1991. "From the Problems of Marxism to the Primacy of Politics." In Rene B. Bertramsen, Jens P.F. Thomsen, and Jacob Torfing (eds.), *State Economy and Society* (pp. 1–34). London: Unwin Hyman Ltd.

Besharov, D.J. 1986. "Unfounded Allegations: A New Child Abuse Problem." *The Public Interest*. No. 83 (Spring). Pp. 18–33.

Bethell, Tom. 1993. "Spreading the News." *American Studies Newsletter*. No. 30. Pp. 1–6.

Bhagwati, Jagdish. 1985. "The New International Economic Order." In Jagdish Bhagwati (eds.), *Dependence and Interdependence*, Vol. 2 (pp. 13–38). Cambridge, Mass.: The MIT Press.

———. 1986. "Ideology and North-South Relations." *World Development*. Vol. 14, No. 6. Pp. 767–74.

Binder, Leonard. 1988. *Islamic Liberalism: A Critique of Development Ideologies*. Chicago: University of Chicago Press.

Bishop, Alan J. 1990. "Western Mathematics: The Secret Weapon of Cultural Imperialism." *Race and Class*. Vol. 32, No. 2. Pp. 51–65.

Black, Philip A. 1983. "Participant Observation and Logical Positivism in the Social Sciences: A Note." *World Development*. Vol. 11, No. 4. Pp. 389–90.

Blacking, John. 1987. "Development Studies and the Reinvention of Tradition." *World Development*. Vol. 15, No. 4. Pp. 527–32.

Blair, Harry W. 1985. "Participation, Public Policy, Political Economy and Development in Rural Bangladesh, 1958–85." *World Development*. Vol. 13, No. 12. Pp. 1231–47.

Blomstrom, Magnus and Bjorn Hettne. 1984. *Development Theory in Transition*. London: Zed Books.

Bodley, John H. 1982. *Victims of Progress*. Second edition. Mountain View, Calif.: Mayfield Publishing Company.

Booth, David. 1975. "Andre Gunder Frank: An Introduction and Appreciation." In Ivar Oxaal, Tony Barnett, and David Booth (eds.), *Beyond the Sociology of Development* (pp. 50–85). London: Routledge & Kegan Paul.

———. 1985. "Marxism and Development Sociology: Interpreting the Impasse." *World Development*. Vol. 13, No. 7, Pp. 761–87.

Boulding, Elise. 1990. "Building a Global Civic Culture." *Development*. No. 2. Pp. 37–40.

Bradley, P.N. 1986. "Food Production and Distribution—and Hunger." In R.J. Johnston and P.J. Taylor (eds.), *A World in Crisis?* (pp. 89–106). New York: Basil Blackwell.

Braun, Gerald. 1990. "The Poverty of Conventional Development Concepts." *Economics*. Vol. 42. Pp. 55–66.

Brenner, R. 1977. "The Origins of Capitalist Development: A Critique of Neo-Smithian Marxism." *New Left Review*. No. 104 (July-August). Pp. 25–92.

Brewer, Anthony. 1980. *Marxist Theories of Imperialism: A Critical Survey*. London: Routledge & Kegan Paul.

Briones, Leonor M. 1985. "The Role of Government-Owned or Controlled Corporations in Development." *Philippine Journal of Public Administration*. Vol. 19, No. 4. Pp. 365–91.

Bronner, Stephen Eric and Douglas MacKay Kellner. 1989. "Introduction." In Stephen E. Bronner and Douglas M. Kellner (eds.), *Critical Theory and Society: A Reader* (pp. 1–21). New York: Routledge.

Brookfield, Harold. 1975. *Interdependent Development*. Pittsburg: University of Pittsburg Press. Methuen.

———. 1979. "Urban Bias, Rural Bias, and the Regional Dimension." In A Rothko Chapel Colloquium (ed.), *Toward a New Strategy for Development* (pp. 97–121). New York: Pergamon Press.

Browett, J. 1982. "Out of Dependency Perspectives." *Journal of Contemporary Asia*. Vol. 12, No. 2. Pp. 145–57.

———. 1985. "The Newly Industrializing Countries and Radical Theories of Development." *World Development*. Vol. 13, No. 7. Pp. 789–803.

Brown, E.K. 1984. "The Neoclassical and Post-Keynesian Research Programs: The Methodological Issues." In Bruce J. Caldwell (ed.), *Appraisal and Criticism in Economics* (pp. 438–49). Winchester, Mass.: Allen & Unwin.

Brown, Lester R. 1986. "Redefining National Security." In Worldwatch Institute (ed.), *State of the world, 1986* (pp. 195–211). New York: W.W. Norton & Company.

———. 1987. "Analyzing the Demographic Trap. " In Worldwatch Institute (ed.), *State of the World, 1987* (pp. 20–37). New York: W.W. Norton & Company.

———. 1990. "The Illusion of Progress." In Worldwatch Institute (ed.), *State of the World, 1990* (pp. 3–16). New York: W.W. Norton & Company.

———. 1991. "The New World Order." In Worldwatch Institute (ed.), *State of the World, 1991* (pp. 3–20). New York: W.W. Norton & Company.

Brown, Lester R. and Jodi Jacobson. 1987. "Assessing the Future Urbanization." In Worldwatch Institute (ed.), *State of the World, 1987* (pp. 38–56). New York: W.W. Norton & Company.

Brown, Lester R. and E.C. Wolf. 1987. "Charting a Sustainable Course." In Worldwatch Institute (ed.), *State of the World, 1987* (pp. 196–213). New York: W.W. Norton & Company.

Brown, Lester R. and J.E. Young. 1990. "Feeding the World in the Nineties." In Worldwatch Institute (ed.), *State of the World, 1990* (pp. 59–78). New York: W.W. Norton & Company.

Brown, Lester R., Christopher Flavin, and Sandra Postel. 1989. "Outlining Global Action Plan." In Worldwatch Institute (ed.), *State of the World, 1989* (pp. 174–94). New York: W.W. Norton & Company.

———. 1990. "Picturing a Sustainable Society." In Worldwatch Institute (ed.), *State of the World, 1990* (pp. 173–90). New York: W.W. Norton & Company.

Bruton, Henry J. 1985. "The Search for a Development Economics." *World Development*. Vol. 13, Nos. 10/11. Pp. 1099–124.

Bubner, Rudiger. 1988. *Essays in Hermeneutics and Critical Theory*. New York: Columbia University Press.

Buchanan, Keith. 1985. "Center and Periphery: Reflections on the Irrelevance of a Billion Human Beings." *Monthly Review*. Vol. 37, No. 3. Pp. 86–97.

Bunge, W. 1986. "Epilogue: Our Planet is Big Enough for Peace but Too Small for War." In R.J. Johnston and P.J. Taylor (eds.), *A World in Crisis?* (pp. 289–91). New York: Basil Blackwell.

Burki, S.J. and D. Beckmann. 1986. "Third World Poverty: A Reevaluation." In K. Haq and U. Kidar (eds.), *Human Development* (pp. 94–105). Islamabad, Pakistan: North South Roundtable.

Burrell, Gibson and Gareth Morgan. 1979. *Sociological Paradigms and Organizational Analysis*. Portsmouth, New Hampshire: Heineman Educational Books.

Caldwell, Bruce J. (ed.). 1984. *Appraisal and Criticism in Economics* (editor's Introduction). Winchester, Mass.: Allen & Unwin.

Cammack, Paul 1988. "Dependency and the Politics of Development." In P.F. Leeson and M.M. Minogue (eds.), *Perspectives on Development* (pp. 89–125). Manchester and New York: Manchester University Press.

Caporaso, James A. 1980. "Dependency Theory: Continuities and Discontinuities in Development Studies." *International Organization*. Vol. 34, No. 4. Pp. 605–28.

Carchedi, Guglielmo. 1994. "Privatization: East Meets West." In Thomas Clarke (ed.), *International Privatization: Strategies and Practices* (pp. 289–323). Berlin: Walter de Gruyter & Co.

Cardoso, Fernando Henrique. 1972. "Dependency and Development in Latin America." *New Left Review*. No. 74. Pp. 83–95.

———. 1979. "The Originality of the Copy: The Economic Commission for Latin America and the Idea of Development." In A Rothko Chapel Colloquium (ed.), *Toward a New Strategy for Development* (pp. 53–72). New York: Pergamon Press.

Cardoso, Fernando Henrique and Enzo Faletto. 1979. *Dependency and Development in Latin America*. Berkeley, Calif.: University of California Press.

Cardozo, Nicky C. 1994. "Transforming Disasters into Development." *Lokayan Bulletin*. Vol. 10, No. 4. Pp. 15–27.

Carson, Robert B. 1983. *Economic Issues Today: Alternative Approaches* (3rd ed.). New York: St. Martin's Press.

Chafetz, J.S. 1978. *A Primer on the Construction and Testing of Theories in Sociology*. Itasca, Illinois: F.E. Peacock Publishers.

Chakravarty, Sukhamoy. 1987. "Development Strategies in the Asian Countries." In Louis Emmerij (ed.), *Development Policies and the Crisis of the 1980s* (pp. 78–95). Paris: Development Centre of the Organisation for Economic Co-operation and Development.

Chambers, Robert. 1987. "Normal Professionalism, New Paradigms and Development." In Edward Clay and John Shaw (eds.), *Poverty, Development and Food* (pp. 229–53). London: Macmillan Press.

Chao, J. 1994. "China's Choice on Cigarettes: Public Health or Revenues." *Far Eastern Economic Review*. November 3, pp. 42–43.

Chaturvedi, T.N. 1978. "Development: The Dynamics—Thorns and Thistles." In Sudesh Kumar Sharma (ed.), *Dynamics of Development*, Vol. 2 (Pp. 693–709). Delhi: Concept Publishing Company.

Chaudhry, Kiren Aziz. 1994. "Economic Liberalization and the Lineages of the Rentier State." *Comparative Politics*. Vol. 27, No. 1. (Pp. 1–25).

Chenery, Hollis et al. 1974. *Redistribution with Growth*. London: Oxford University Press.

Chidzero, Bernard T.G. 1987. "A Comment on Professor Ghai's Paper." In Louis Emmerij (ed.), *Development Policies and the Crisis of the 1980s* (pp. 130–39). Paris: Development Centre of the Organisation for Economic Co-operation and Development.

Chilcote, Ronald H. 1980. "Theories of Dependency: The View from the Periphery." In Ingolf Vogeler and Anthony R. de Souza (eds.), *Dialectics of Third World Development* (pp. 299–309). Montclair, New Jersey: Allanheld, Osmun & Co. Publishers.

———. 1984. *Theories of Development and Underdevelopment*. Boulder, Colorado: Westview Press.

Childers, Erskine B. 1990. "The New Age of Information—What Kind of Participation?" *Development*. No. 2. Pp. 11–16.

Chodak, Szymon. 1973. *Societal Development: Five Approaches with Conclusions from Comparative Analysis*. New York: Oxford University Press.

Clarke, Thomas. 1994. "Reconstructing the Public Sector: Performance Measurement, Quality Assurance, and Social Accountability." In Thomas Clarke (ed.), *International Privatization: Strategies and Practices* (pp. 399–431). Berlin: Walter de Gruyter & Co.

Clements, Kevin P. 1980. *From Right to Left in Development Theory* (ISEAS Occasional Paper No. 61). Singapore: Institute of South-East Asian Studies.

Clements, Laurie. 1994. "Privatization American Style: The Grand Illusion." In Thomas Clarke (ed.), *International Privatization: Strategies and Practices* (pp. 87–104). Berlin: Walter de Gruyter & Co.

Coate, Roger A. and Donald J. Puchala. 1990. "Global Policies and the United Nations System: A Current Assessment." *Journal of Peace Research*. Vol. 27, No. 2. Pp. 127–40.

Coates, K. and S. Bodington. 1976. Introduction. In A. Heller (ed.), *The Theory of Need in Marx*. London: Allison and Busby.

Cohen, John M., Merilee S. Grindle, and Tjip Grindle, Grindle. 1985. "Foreign Aid and Conditions: Political and Bureaucratic Dimensions." *World Development*. Vol. 13, No. 12. Pp. 1211–1230.

Cohen, S.F. 1994. Plan Now for Yeltsin's Bitter Legacy. *International Herald Tribune*, September 26, p. 6.

Cole, J.P. 1988. "The Global Distribution of Natural Resources." In J. Norwine and A. Gonzalez (eds.), *The Third World: States of Mind and Being* (pp. 55–66). Boston: Unwin Hyman.

Commoner, Barry. 1985. "The Economic Meaning of Ecology." In Jerome H. Skolnick and Elliott Currie (eds.), *Crisis in American Institutions* (pp. 293–300). Boston: Little, Brown.

Comte, Auguste. 1973. "The Progress of Civilization Through Three States." In E. Etzioni–Halevy and A. Etzioni (eds.), *Social Change: Sources, Patterns, and Consequences* (2nd edition) (pp. 14–19). New York: Basic Books.

Cook, Paul and Colin Kirkpatrick. 1995. "Privatization Policy and Performance." In Paul Cook and Colin Kirkpatrick (eds.), *Privatization Policy and Performance: International Perspectives* (pp. 3–27). London: Prentice Hall/Harvester Wheatsheaf.

Cooper, Richard N. 1979. "Developed Country Reactions to Calls for a New International Economic Order." In Rothko Chapel Colloquium (ed.), *Toward a New Strategy for Development* (pp. 243–74). New York: Pergamon Press.

Covington, Richard. 1994. "American TV Invades the World." *International Herald Tribune*, October 19, pp. 11, 18.

Cowley, G. 1988. "The Earth is one Big System." *Newsweek*, November 7, pp. 98–99.

Cross-Frontier Broadcasting. 1992. *Economist*, May 2, pp. 21–28.

Crow, Ben et al. 1988. *Survival and Change in the Third World*. New York: Oxford University Press.

Cutter, Susan L. 1994. "Exploiting, Conserving, and Preserving Natural Resources." In George J. Demko and William B. Wood (eds.), *Reordering the World* (pp. 123–40). Boulder, Colorado: Westview Press.

Dale, Reginald. 1994. "The Race to Still Larger Trade Zones." *International Herald Tribune*, November 1, p. 11.

Dallmayr, Fred. 1991. *Life-world, Modernity and Critique: Paths Between Heidegger and the Frankfurt School*. Cambridge, U.K.: Polity Press.

Damman, E. 1979. *The Future in Our Hand*. Oxford: Pergamon Press.

Darden, Joe T. 1989. "Afro-American Inequality Within the Urban Structure of the United States, 1967–1987." *Journal of Developing Societies*. Vol. 5. Pp. 1–14.

David, Wilfred L. 1986. *Conflicting Paradigms in the Economics of Developing Nations*. New York: Praeger Publishers.

Davis, Adelle. 1954. *Let's Eat Right to Keep Fit*. New Jersey: New American Library.

De Vries, E. 1968. "A Review of Literature on Development Theory: 1957–1967." *International Development Review*. Vol. 10, No. 1. Pp. 46–51.

Demas, William G. 1975. "Economic Independence: Conceptual and Policy Issues in the Commonwealth Caribbean." In Percy Selwyn (ed.), *Development Policy in Small Countries* (pp. 191–207). London: Croom Helm.

Deutsch, Karl W. 1969. *Nationalism and Its Alternatives*. New York: Knopf.

Devine, P. 1988. *Democracy and Economic Planning*. Boulder, Colorado: Westview Press.

Dhanagare, D.N. 1990. "Relevance of Sociology—Some Determinants." *Indian Journal of Social Work*. Vol. 51, No. 1. Pp. 1–13.

Diwan, R. and M. Lutz (eds.). 1985. *Essays in Gandhian Economics* (Introduction). New Delhi: Gandhi Peace Foundation.

Dixon, Chris. 1995. "Structural Adjustment in Comparative Perspective: Lessons from Pacific Asia." In David Simon et al. (eds.), *Structurally Adjusted Africa: Poverty, Debt and Basic Needs* (pp. 202–28). London: Pluto Press.

Dixon, Chris, David Simon, and Anders Narman. 1995. "Introduction: The Nature of Structural Adjustment." In David Simon et al. (eds.), *Structurally Adjusted Africa: Poverty, Debt and Basic Needs* (pp. 1–14). London: Pluto Press.

Dixon, M. 1984. "The Suez Syndrome." *Contemporary Marxism*. Vol. 9 (Fall). Pp. 5–18.

Dogra, Bharat. 1994. "International Debt Burden: In the Interests of Interest." *Economic and Political Weekly*. Vol. 29, Nos. 1–2. Pp. 25–26.

Dopfer, Kurt. 1979. *The New Political Economy of Development*. New York: St. Martin's Press.

Dorfman, A. and A. Mattelart. 1980. "The Noble Savage: Cultural Imperialism in the Disney Comics." In Ingolf Vogeler and Anthony R. de Souza (eds.), *Dialectics of Third World Development* (pp. 122–34). Montclair, Colorado: Allanheld, Osmun.

Dos Santos, Theotonio. 1970. "The Structure of Dependence." *American Economic Review*. Vol. 60, No. 2. Pp. 231–36.

———. 1976. "The Crisis of Development Theory and the Problem of Dependence in Latin America." In Henry Bernstein (ed.), *Underdevelopment and Development* (pp. 57–80). New York: Penguin Publishers.

Drake, Christine.1994. "The United Nations and NGOs: Future Roles." In George J. Demko and William B. Wood (eds.), *Reordering the World* (pp. 243–67). Boulder, Colorado: Westview Press.

Durkheim, Emile. 1982. *The Rules of Sociological Method*. (Steven Lukes, ed.). New York: Free Press.

Durning, Alan B. 1989. "Mobilizing the Grassroots." In Worldwatch Institute (ed.), *State of the World, 1989* (pp. 154–73). New York: W.W. Norton & Company.

———. 1990. "Ending Poverty." In Worldwatch Institute (ed.), *State of the World, 1990* (pp. 135–53). New York: W.W. Norton & Company.

———. 1991. "Asking How Much is Enough." In Worldwatch Institute (ed.), *State of the World, 1991* (pp. 153–69). New York: W.W. Norton & Company.

Dwivedi, O.P. 1994. "Structural Adjustment Programmes and Administrative Reforms in Third World." In R.B. Jain and H. Bongartz (eds.), *Structural Adjustment, Public Policy and Bureaucracy in Developing Societies* (pp. 351–67). New Delhi: Har-Anand Publications.

Dwivedi, O.P. and J. Nef. 1982. "Crises and Continuities in Development Theory and Administration: First and Third World Perspectives". *Public Administration and Development*. Vol. 2, No. 1. Pp. 59–77.

Easterlin, R. 1981. "Why Isn't the Whole World Developed?" *Journal of Economic History*. Vol. 41, No. 1. Pp. 1–19.

Easton, David. 1991. "The Division, Integration, and Transfer of Knowledge." In David Easton and Corrine S. Schelling (eds.), *Divided Knowledge: Across Disciplines, Across Cultures* (pp. 7–36). Newbury Park, Calif.: Sage Publications.

Eder, Klaus. 1990. "The Cultural Code of Modernity and the Problem of Nature: A Critique of the Naturalistic Notion of Progress." In Jeffrey C. Alexander and Piotr Sztompka (eds.), *Rethinking Progress* (pp. 67–87). Boston: Unwin Hyman.

Edmonds, L.S. 1977. "The Economist's Dilemma: The Relevance of Development Economics to Public Administration." *IDS Bulletin*. Vol. 8, No. 4. Pp. 13–16.

Edwards, Michael. 1989. "The Irrelevance of Development Studies." *Third World Quarterly*. Vol. 11, No. 1. Pp. 117–35.

Ehrenreich, Barbara et al. 1984. "Women and Multinationals." In P. Ayrton, T. Engelhardt, and V. Warre (eds.), *World View 1985: An Economic and Political Yearbook* (pp. 176–81). London: Pluto Press.

El-Shagi, El-Shagi. 1990. "The Population Problem and Economic Development in the Third World." *Economics*. Vol. 42, Pp. 88–105.

Elguea, J. 1985. "Paradigms and Scientific Revolutions in Development Theories." *Development and Change*. Vol. 16. Pp. 213–33.

Elster, Jon. 1985. *Making Sense of Marx*. Cambridge: Cambridge University Press.

Emmerij, Louis. 1986. "The Future of Development Cooperation: Is There One?" In Raymond Apthrope and Andras Krahl (eds.), *Development Studies: Critique and Renewal* (pp. 1–10). Leiden: E.J. Brill.

Engels, Frederich. 1978. "Socialism: Utopian and Scientific." Reprinted in Robert C. Tucker (ed.), *The Marx-Engels Reader* (pp. 683–717). New York: W.W. Norton and Company.

Esman, Milton J. 1991. "The State, Government Bureaucracies, and Their Alternatives." In Ali Farazmand (ed.), *Handbook of Comparative and Development Public Administration* (pp. 457–65). New York: Marcel Dekker.

Estes, Richard J. 1988. *Trends in World Social Development: The Social Progress of Nations, 1970–1987*. New York: Praeger Publishers.

Esteva, Gustavo. 1992. "Development." In Wolfgang Sachs (ed.), *The Development Dictionary: A Guide to Knowledge as Power* (pp. 6–25). London: Zed Books.

Etzioni-Halevy, Eva and Amitai Etzioni (eds.). 1973. *Social Change: Sources, Patterns, and Consequences* (Editors' Introduction, 2nd Edition). New York: Basic Books.

Evans, Peter. 1979. *Dependent Development: The Alliance of Multinational, State, and Local Capital in Brazil*. Princeton, N.J.: Princeton University Press.

Evernden, Neil. 1989. "Nature in Industrial Society." In Ian Angus and Sut Jhally (eds.), *Cultural Politics in Contemporary America* (pp. 151–64). New York: Routledge.

Ewing, A. and G.V. Koch. 1977. "Some Recent Literature on Development." *Journal of Modern African Studies*. Vol. 15, No. 3. Pp. 457–80.

Fagen, M. 1994. "Third World: The Argument for More Aid Goes Beyond Altruism." *International Herald Tribune*. November 9, p. 4.

Fairhead, J. et al. 1994. "Land Rights in Rwanda." *International Herald Tribune*. August 30, p. 7.

Falk, Richard. 1987. "What is Happening to America is Happening to the World." *Scandinavian Journal of Development Alternatives*. Vol. 6, Nos. 2–3. Pp. 7–18.

Farazmand, Ali. 1989. "Crisis in the U.S. Administrative State." *Administration & Society*. Vol. 21, No. 2. Pp. 173–99.

Featherstone, Mike. 1990. "Global Culture: An Introduction." *Theory, Culture and Society*. Vol. 7, Nos. 2–3. Pp. 1–14.

Federal Bureau of Investigation. 1986. *Crime in the United States: 1985*. Washington, D.C.: U.S. Government Printing Office.

Feng, C. 1986. "A reassessment of the Subject and Status of Sociology." *Social Sciences in China*. Vol. 7, No. 3. Pp. 151–68.

Fisher, Hal. 1988. "Development in Sub-Saharan Africa: Barriers and Prospects." In Jim Norwine and Alfonso Gonzalez (eds.), *The Third World: States of Mind and Being* (pp. 231–42). Boston: Unwin Hyman.

Fitzgerald, F.T. 1983. "Sociologies of Development." In Peter Limqueco and Bruce McFarlane (eds.), *Neo-Marxist Theories of Development* (pp. 12–28). New York: St. Martin's Press.

Flavin, Christopher. 1990. "Slowing Global Warming." In Worldwatch Institute (ed.), *State of the World, 1990* (pp. 17–38). New York: W.W. Norton & Company.

Flavin, Christopher and Nicholas Lenssen. 1991. "Designing a Sustainable Energy System." In Worldwatch Institute (ed.), *State of the World, 1991* (pp. 21–38). New York: W.W. Norton & Company.

Forbes, D.K. 1984. *The Geography of Underdevelopment*. Baltimore, Maryland: Johns Hopkins University Press.

Fossi, G. 1977. "New Elements for Decision Making." In J.J. Nossin (ed.), *Surveys for Development* (pp. 169–74). Amsterdam, Netherlands: Elsevier Scientific.

Foster-Carter, Aidan. 1973. "Neo-Marxist Approaches to Development and Underdevelopment." *Journal of Contemporary Asia*. Vol. 3, No. 1. Pp. 7–33.

———. 1976. "From Rostow to Gunder Frank: Conflicting Paradigms in the Analysis of Underdevelopment." *World Development*. Vol. 4, No. 3. Pp. 167–80.

———. 1978. "The Modes of Production Controversy." *New Left Review*. No. 107 (January–February). Pp. 47–77.

Frank, Andre Gunder. 1967. *Capitalism and Underdevelopment in Latin America*. New York and London: Monthly Review Press.

———. 1969. *Latin America: Underdevelopment or Revolution*. New York: Monthly Review Press.

———. 1984. "What is the Scientific Value of the Study of the Development of Underdevelopment? None!" In Andre Gunder Frank (ed.), *Critique and Anti–critique: Essays on Dependence and Reformism* (pp. 3–5). New York: Praeger Publishers.

———. 1988. "The World Economic Crisis Today: Retrospect and Prospect." *Scandinavian Journal of Development Alternatives*. Vol. 7, Nos. 2–3. Pp. 181–215.

Frederick, William C., James E. Post, and Keith Davis. 1992. *Business and Society: Corporate Strategy, Public Policy, Ethics* (7th ed.). New York: McGraw-Hill.

Freeman, Harold. 1980. *Toward Socialism in America*. Cambridge, Mass.: Schenkman Publishing Company.

French, Hilary F. 1990. "Clearing the Air." In Worldwatch Institute (ed.), *State of the World, 1990* (pp. 98–118). New York: W.W. Norton & Company.

Friberg, Mats. 1985. "Yellow versus Green: Choosing Between Super-Industrialism and Self-Reliance." *Development*. No. 2. Pp. 4–9.

Friedman, Milton. 1962. *Capitalism and Freedom*. Chicago: University of Chicago Press.

———. 1984. "The Methodology of Positive Economics." In Bruce J. Caldwell (ed.), *Appraisal and Criticism in Economics* (pp. 138–78). Winchester, Mass.: Allen & Unwin.

Fromm, Erich. 1989a. "Psychoanalysis and Sociology." In Stephen E. Bronner and Douglas M. Kellner (eds.), *Critical Theory and Society: A Reader* (pp. 37–39). New York: Routledge.

———. 1989b. "Politics and Psychoanalysis." In Stephen E. Bronner and Douglas M. Kellner (eds.), *Critical Theory and Society: A Reader* (pp. 213–18). New York: Routledge.

Fuhr, Harald. 1994. "The Missing Link in Structural Adjustment Policies— the Politico-Institutional Dimension: Some Lessons from Latin America for Eastern European Transitions." In R.B. Jain and H. Bongartz (eds.), *Structural Adjustment, Public Policy and Bureaucracy in Developing Societies* (pp. 93–132). New Delhi: Har-Anand Publications.

Fuller, Thomas. 1994. "Looming Battle of the (Television) Bands." *International Herald Tribune*. September 19, p. ix.

Furtado, Celso. 1970. *Economic Development in Latin America*. London: Cambridge University Press.

———. 1973. "The Concept of External Dependence in the Study of Underdevelopment." In Charles K. Wilber (ed.), *The Political Economy of Development and Underdevelopment* (pp. 118–23). New York: Random House.

———. 1976. "Elements of a Theory of Underdevelopment: The Under-developed Structure." In Henry Bernstein (ed.), *Underdevelopment and Development: The Third World Today* (pp. 33–43). New York: Penguin Books.

———. 1979. "An Age of Global Reconstruction." In K.P. Jameson and Charles K. Wilber (eds.), *Directions in Economic Development* (pp. 130–82). Notre Dame, Indiana: University of Notre Dame Press.

———. 1987. "Underdevelopment: To Conform or Reform." In Theodore W. Schultz et al. (eds.), *Pioneers in Development* (pp. 205–27). New York: Oxford University Press.

Galt, A.H. and L.J. Smith. 1976. *Models and the Study of Social Change.* Cambridge, Mass.: Schenkman Publishing Company.

Galtung, Johan. 1976. "Conflict on a Global Scale: Social Imperialism and Sub-Imperialism: Continuity in the Structural Theory of Imperialism." *World Development.* Vol. 4, No. 3. Pp. 153–65.

———. 1990. "The Media World-wide: Well-being and Development." *Development.* No. 2. Pp. 17–22.

Gare, Arran. 1994. "Keeping Going [book review]." *Metascience.* No. 5. Pp. 115–18.

Gareau, Frederick. 1990. "The Political Economy of Social Science: Where the Trail Leads." *International Journal of Comparative Sociology.* Vol. 31, Nos. 1–2. Pp. 49–66.

Garnham, Nicholas. 1990. *Capitalism and Communication: Global Culture and the Economics of Information.* London: Sage Publications.

Gendzier, Irene L. 1985. *Managing Political Change: Social Scientists and the Third World.* Boulder, Colorado: Westview Press.

George, Susan. 1977. *How the Other Half Dies.* Montclair, N.J.: Allanheld, Osmun.

———. 1990. "Disarming Debt: We Could—But Will We?" *Food Policy.* Vol. 15, No. 4. Pp. 328–35.

———. 1994. "Foreword." In Walden Bellow, Shea Cunningham, and Bill Rau, *Dark Victory: The United States, Structural Adjustment and Global Poverty* (pp. x–xi). London: Pluto Press.

George, Susan and N. Paige. 1982. *Food for the Beginners.* London: Writers and Readers Publishing Cooperative Society.

Ghosh, Ratna. 1989. "Strategies in Education for Development: Technologies and Educational Innovations." In John S. Augustine (ed.), *Strategies for Third World Development* (pp. 76–96). New Delhi: Sage Publications.

Ghosh, Ratna, and Kurian George. 1979. "Some Ambiguities in the Concept of Development." *Indian Journal of Political Science*. Vol. 40, No. 2. Pp. 156–64.

Gianaris, Nicholas V. 1978. *Economic Development: Thought and Problems*. North Quincy, Mass.: Christopher Publishing House.

Giddens, Anthony. 1971. *Capitalism and Modern Social Theory: An Analysis of the Writings of Marx, Durkheim and Max Weber*. London: Cambridge University Press.

Giddens, Anthony and Jonathan H. Turner (eds.). 1987. *Social Theory Today* (Introduction). Cambridge: Polity Press.

Gilbert, Dennis A. 1988. *Compendium of American Public Opinion*. New York: Facts On File Publications.

Gilderhus, Mark T. 1992. *History and Historians: A Historiographical Introduction*. Englewood Cliffs, N.J.: Prentice Hall.

Gilpin, Robert. 1987. *The Political Economy of International Relations*. Princeton, N.J.: Princeton University Press.

Ginzberg, Eli. 1987. *The Skeptical Economist*. Boulder, Colorado: Westview Press.

Global Economy: War of the Worlds. 1994. *The Economist*. October 1, p. 3.

Golding, Peter. 1985. "The Winds of Cultural Change." *Third World Book Review*. Vol. 1, No. 3. Pp. 43–44.

Goldthorpe, John E. 1984. *The Sociology of the Third World: Disparity and Development*. Cambridge, England: Cambridge University Press.

Gonzalez, Alfonso. 1988. "South America: The Worlds of Development." In Jim Norwine and Alfonso Gonzalez (eds.), *The Third World: States of Mind and Being* (pp. 183–95). Boston: Unwin Hyman.

Goonatilake, S. 1988. "Epistemology and Ideology in Science, Technology and Development." In Atul Wad (ed.), *Science, Technology and Development* (pp. 93–114). Boulder, Colorado: Westview Press.

Gouldner, Alvin. 1980. *The Two Marxisms: Contradictions and Anomalies in the Development of Theory*. New York: Seabury Press.

Goulet, Denis. 1980. "Development Experts: The One-Eyed Giants." *World Development*. Vol. 8, Nos. 7/8. Pp. 481–89.

———. 1983. "Obstacles to World Development: An Ethical Reflection." *World Development*. Vol. 11, No. 7. Pp. 609–24.

Gramsci, Antonio. 1971. *Selections from the Prison Notebooks of Antonio Gramsci* (Q. Hoare and G. N. Smith, eds.). London: Lawrence and Wishart.

Grassi, Ricardo. 1990. "A Network for Culture and Communication." *Development*. No. 2. Pp. 105–7.

Green, R.H. 1978. "Basic Human Needs: Concepts or Slogan, Synthesis or Smokescreen?" *IDS Bulletin*. Vol. 9, No. 4. Pp. 7–11.

Gregory, Chris. 1988. "Anthropology." In David Goldsworthy (ed.), *Development Studies in Australia: Themes and Issues* (pp. 7–17). Clayton Vic., Australia: Monash Development Studies Centre.

Griffin, Keith. 1987. *World Hunger and the World Economy*. London: Macmillan Press.

Grindle, Merilee S. 1986. *State and Countryside: Development Policy and Agrarian Politics in Latin America*. Baltimore: Johns Hopkins University Press.

Gulalp, H. 1983. "Frank and Wallerstein Revisited: A Contribution to Brenner's Critique." In Peter Limqueco and Bruce McFarlane (eds.), *Neo-Marxist Theories of Development* (pp. 114–36). New York: St. Martin's Press.

———. 1987. "Dependency and World-System Theories: Varying Political Implications." *Journal of Contemporary Asia*. Vol. 17, No. 2. Pp. 131–39.

Guocang, Huan. 1994. "China's Inflation Threat." *Far Eastern Economic Review*. October 20, p. 30.

Gurley, J.G. 1979. "Economic Development: A Marxist View." In K.P. Jameson and C. K. Wilber (eds.), *Directions in Economic Development* (pp. 183–251). Notre Dame, Indiana: University of Notre Dame Press.

Gusdorf, G. 1977. "The Language of the Question." In John P. Schlegel (ed.), *Towards a Re-definition of Development* (pp. 306–8). New York: Pergamon Press.

Habermas, Jürgen. 1970. *Toward a Rational Society*. Boston: Beacon Press.

———. 1971. *Knowledge and Human Interests*. Boston: Beacon Press.

———. 1973. *Theory and Practice*. Boston: Beacon Press.

———. 1975. *Legitimation Crisis*. Boston: Beacon Press.

———. 1979. *Communication and Evolution of Society*. Boston: Beacon Press.

———. 1989a. "The Public Sphere: An Encyclopedia Article." In Stephen E. Bronner and Douglas M. Kellner (eds.), *Critical Theory and Society: A Reader* (pp. 136–42). New York: Routledge.

———. 1989b. "The Tasks of a Critical Theory of Society." In Stephen E. Bronner and Douglas M. Kellner (eds.), *Critical Theory and Society: A Reader* (pp. 292–312). New York: Routledge.

Hagen, Everett E. 1962. *On the Theory of Social Change: How Economic Growth Begins*. Homewood, Ill: Dorsey Press.

Halachmi, Arie and Marc Holzer. 1993. "Towards a Competitive Public Administration." *International Review of Administrative Sciences*. Vol. 59, No. 1. Pp. 29–45.

Hamelink, Cees J. 1990. "Democratizing Communications: A Human Rights Issue." *Development*. No. 2. Pp. 101–4.

Hamilton, Clive. 1989. "The Irrelevance of Economic Liberalization in the Third World." *World Development*. Vol. 17, No. 10. Pp. 1523–30.

Hancock, Graham. 1989. *Lords of Poverty*. London: Macmillan.

Hansen, Craig C. 1989. "Are We Doing Theory Ethnocentrically? A Comparison of Modernization Theory and Kemalism." *Journal of Developing Societies*. Vol. 5, No. 2. Pp. 175–87.

Haque, M. Shamsul. 1994. "The Emerging Challenges to Bureaucratic Accountability: A Critical Perspective." In Ali Farazmand (ed.), *Handbook of Bureaucracy* (pp. 265–86). New York: Marcel Dekker.

———. 1995. "Globalization of Market Ideology and Its Impact on Third World Development." Paper presented at the Twenty-Third International Congress of Administrative Sciences, 1–5 July 1995, Dubai, United Arab Emirates.

———. 1996a. "The Intellectual Crisis in Public Administration in the Current Epoch of Privatization." *Administration & Society*. Vol. 27, No. 4. Pp. 510–36.

———. 1996b. "Public Service Under Challenge in the Age of Privatization." *Governance: An International Journal of Policy and Administration*. Vol. 9, No. 2. Pp. 186–216.

———. 1996c. "The Contextless Nature of Public Administration in Third World Countries." *International Review of Administrative Sciences*. Vol. 62, No. 3. Pp. 315–29.

———. 1997. "Local Governance in Developing Nations: Reexamining the Question of Accountability." *Regional Development Dialogue*. Vol. 18, No. 2. Pp. iii–xxiii.

———. 1999. "The Fate of Sustainable Development Under Neoliberal Regimes in Developing Countries." *International Political Science Review*. Vol. 20, No. 2. Pp. 199–222.

Haque, Wahidul et al. 1977. "Towards a Theory of Rural Development [editorial]." *Development Dialogue*. No. 2. Pp. 3–6.

Harbison, Frederick H. 1973. *Human Resources as the Wealth of Nations*. New York: Oxford University Press.

Harris, Phil. 1984. "The Battle for UNESCO." *Third World Book Review.* Vol. 1, No. 2. Pp. 56–60.

Harrison, David. (1988). *The Sociology of Modernization and Development.* London: Unwin Hyman.

Harrison, Paul. 1979. *Inside the Third World: The Anatomy of Poverty.* Sussex: Harvester Press.

Harrod, Jeffrey. 1982. "Development Studies: From Change to Stabilization." In B. de Gaay Fortman (ed.), *Rethinking Development* (pp. 1–19). The Hague: Institute of Social Studies.

Hartman, John and Pamela B. Walters. 1985. "Dependence, Military Assistance and Development: A Cross-National Study." *Politics and Society.* Vol. 14, No. 3. Pp. 431–58.

Hays, Margaret Daly. 1975. "Policy Consequences of Military Participation in Politics: An Analysis of Tradeoffs in Brazilian Federal Expenditures." In Craig Liske, William Loehr, and John McCamant (eds.), *Comparative Public Policy* (pp. 21–52). London: John Wiley & Sons.

Heald, David. 1990. "The Relevance of Privatization to Developing Economies." *Public Administration and Development.* Vol. 10, No. 1. Pp. 3–18.

Healey, J. and C. Clift. 1980. "The Development Rationale for Aid Reexamined." *ODI Review.* No. 2. Pp. 14–34.

Helleiner, Gerald K. 1990. *The New Global Economy and the Developing Countries: Essays in International Economics and Development.* Aldershot, England: Edward Elgar Publishing Company.

Hellinger, Stephen, Douglas Hellinger, and Fred M. O'Regan. 1988. *Aid for Just Development: Report on the Future of Foreign Assistance.* Boulder, Colorado: Lynne Rienner Publishers.

Henig, Jeffrey R., Chris Hamnett, and Harvey B. Feigenbaum. 1988. "The Politics of Privatization: A Comparative Perspective." *Governance.* Vol. 1, No. 4. Pp. 442–68.

Henry, J.S. 1986. "Third World Debt: Where the Money Went." *New Republic.* April 14, pp. 20–23.

Hershlag, Z.Y. 1984. *The Philosophy of Development Revisited.* Laiden, Netherlands: E.J. Brill.

Hettne, Bjorn. 1982. *Development Theory and the Third World.* Stockholm: Swedish Agency for Research Cooperation with Developing Countries.

———. 1990. *Development Theory and the Three Worlds.* Essex, England: Longman Scientific & Technical.

————. 1991. *The Voice of the Third World: Currents in Development Thinking*. Budapest: Institute for World Economics of the Hungarian Academy of Sciences.

Hexing, Wang. 1991. "A Forecast for the North-South Relationship in the 1990s." *Foreign Affairs Journal*. No. 19. Pp. 42–53.

Hicks, J.R. 1981. *Wealth and Welfare*. Vol. 1. Oxford: Basil Blackwell.

Hilferding, Rudolf. 1981. *Finance Capital: A Study of the Latest Phase of Capitalist Development* (Tom Bottomore edited). London: Routledge & Kegan Paul.

Hirschman, Albert O. 1958. *The Strategy of Economic Development*. New Haven: Yale University Press.

Hoagland, J. 1994. "U.S.-Russian Summitry: Oil and Gas Fields Loom Large." *International Herald Tribune*. September 26, p. 6.

Holm, Hans-Henrik. 1990. "The End of the Third World?" *Journal of Peace Research*. Vol. 27, No. 1. Pp. 1–7.

Holton, Robert. 1990. "Problems of Crisis and Normalcy in the Contemporary World." In Jeffrey C. Alexander and Piotr Sztompka (eds.), *Rethinking Progress* (pp. 39–52). Boston: Unwin Hyman.

Hong, Evelyne. 1985. *See the Third World While It Lasts*. Penang, Malaysia: Consumers' Association of Penang.

Honneth, Axel. 1987. "Critical Theory." In Anthony Giddens and Jonathan H. Turner (eds.), *Social Theory Today* (pp. 347–82). Cambridge: Polity Press.

Hoogvelt, Ankie M.M. 1982. *The Third World in Global Development*. London: Macmillan Education.

Horkheimer, Max. 1972. *Critical Theory: Selected Essays*. New York: Seabury Press.

————. 1989. "The State of Contemporary Social Philosophy and the Tasks of an Institute for Social Research." In Stephen E. Bronner and Douglas M. Kellner (eds.), *Critical Theory and Society: A Reader* (pp. 25–36). New York: Routledge.

Horkheimer, Max and Theodor W. Adorno. 1972. *Dialectic of Enlightenment*. New York: Seabury Press.

"Housing: Poverty's Foundation." 1992. *Economist*. April 11, Pp. 32–34.

Hovart, B. 1979. "A Note on the World Economic Development from the Socialist Viewpoint." *Development and Change*. Vol. 10. Pp. 673–77.

Hui, P.K. 1994. "East Asian NICs—the Other View." *Lokayan Bulletin*. Vol. 10, No. 4. Pp. 37–45.

Hulme, David and Mark M. Turner. 1990. *Sociology and Development: Theories, Policies and Practices*. New York: Harvester Wheatsheaf.

"Human Environment." 1982. *New Internationalist*. August, Pp. 10–11.

Hunt, E.K. 1979. *History of Economic Thought: A Critical Perspective*. Belmont, Calif.: Wadsworth Publishing Company.

Huntington, Samuel P. 1965. "Political Development and Political Decay." *World Politics*. Vol. 17, No. 3. Pp. 386–430.

———. 1968. *Political Order in Changing Societies*. New Haven, Conn.: Yale University Press.

———. 1993. "The Clash of Civilizations?" *Foreign Affairs*. Vol. 72, No. 3. Pp. 22–49.

Huston, Perdita. 1995. "Social Development with Band-Aids?" *International Herald Tribune*. March 10, p. 6.

Hutchful, Eboe. 1985. "Disarmament and Development: An African View." *IDS Bulletin*. Vol. 16, No. 4. Pp. 61–67.

Hutchison, Terence W. 1981. *The Politics and Philosophy of Economics*. Oxford: Blackwell Publishers.

Illich, Ivan. 1976. "Outwitting the 'Developed' Countries." In Henry Bernstein (ed.), *Underdevelopment and Development* (pp. 357–68). New York: Penguin Publishers.

ILO (International Labour Organization). 1976. *Employment, Growth and Basic Needs: A One-World Problem*. Geneva: International Labour Office.

———. 1995. *Impact of Structural Adjustment in the Public Services*. Geneva: International Labour Office.

Inequality: For Richer, for Poorer. 1994. *Economist*. November 5, pp. 19–23.

Ingalls, Gerald L. and Walter E. Martin. 1988. "Defining and Identifying NICs." In Jim Norwine and Alfonso Gonzalez (eds.), *The Third World: States of Mind and Being* (pp. 82–98). Boston: Unwin Hyman.

InterAction Council. 1990. "Ecology and the Global Economy." *Development*. Nos. 3/4. Pp. 23–27.

International Herald Tribune. 1994. 7 August.

Irvin, George. 1991. "New Perspective for Modernization in Central America." *Development and Change*. Vol. 22, No. 1. Pp. 93–115.

Islam, Nurul. 1979. "Revolt of the Periphery." In A Rothko Chapel Colloquium (ed.), *Toward a New Strategy for Development* (pp. 171–97). New York: Pergamon Press.

Itty, C.I. 1984. "Development Goals and Values." In C.I. Itty (ed.), *Searching for Asian Paradigms* (pp. 15–28). Bangkok: Asian Cultural Forum on Development.

Jacobson, Jodi. 1988. "Planning the Global Family." In Worldwatch Institute (ed.), *State of the World, 1988* (pp. 151–69). New York: W.W. Norton & Company.

———. 1989. "Abandoning Homelands." In Worldwatch Institute (ed.), *State of the World, 1989* (pp. 59–76). New York: W.W. Norton & Company.

Jaffee, David. 1990. *Levels of Socio-economic Development Theory.* New York: Praeger Publishers.

Jaguaribe, Helio. 1990. "Latin America in the 1990s." *Development.* Nos. 3/4. Pp. 159–65.

Jain, R.B. 1994a. "Nature and Problems of Structural Adjustment: Emerging Critical Issues in Developing Societies." In R.B. Jain and H. Bongartz (eds.), *Structural Adjustment, Public Policy and Bureaucracy in Developing Societies* (pp. 37–55). New Delhi: Har-Anand Publications.

———. 1994b. "Structural Adjustment: Perspective for Future." In R.B. Jain and H. Bongartz (eds.), *Structural Adjustment, Public Policy and Bureaucracy in Developing Societies* (pp. 408–15). New Delhi: Har-Anand Publications.

James, Jeffrey and Efraim Gutkind. 1985. "Attitude Change Revisited: Cognitive Dissonance Theory and Development Policy." *World Development.* Vol. 13, Nos. 10/11. Pp. 1139–49.

James, Joy. 1990. "US Policy in Panama." *Race & Class.* Vol. 32, No. 1. Pp. 17–32.

Jayasuriya, Sisira. 1988. "Economics Research and Agriculture." In David Goldsworthy (ed.), *Development Studies in Australia: Themes and Issues* (pp. 44–52). Clayton Vic., Australia: Monash Development Studies Centre.

Jennings, Anthony and Thomas G. Weiss. 1982. "Summary and Conclusions." In A. Jennings and T.G Weiss (eds.), *The Challenge of Development in the Eighties* (pp. 115–22). Oxford, England: Pergamon Press.

Jessop, Bob. 1982. *The Capitalist State.* New York: New York University Press.

Jhally, Sut. 1989. "The Political Economy of Culture." In Ian Angus and Sut Jhally (eds.), *Cultural Politics in Contemporary America* (pp. 65–81). New York: Routledge.

Johnson, D.L. and J.F. Ocampo. 1972. "The Concept of Political Development." In James D. Cockcroft, Andre Gunder Frank, and Dale L. Johnson (eds.), *Dependence and Underdevelopment: Latin America's Political Economy* (pp. 399–424). New York: Anchor Books.

Johnston, Bruce F. and William C. Clark. 1982. *Redesigning Rural Development: A Strategic Perspective*. Baltimore: Johns Hopkins University Press.

Jolly, Richard. 1977. "Changing Views on Development." In J. J. Nossin (ed.), *Surveys for Development: A Multidisciplinary Approach* (pp. 19–35). Amsterdam: Elsevier Scientific Publishing Company.

———. 1987. "Adjustment with a Human Face: A Broader Approach to Adjustment Policy." In Edward Clay and John Shaw (eds.), *Poverty, Development and Food* (pp. 61–77). London: Macmillan Press.

Jones, G.S. 1973. "Engels and the End of Classical German Philosophy." *New Left Review*. No. 79 (May–June). Pp. 17–36

Jose, J. 1987. "Review of Marxian Theory and the Third World." *Journal of Contemporary Asia*. Vol. 17, No. 4. Pp. 495–500.

Kamal, Raja and Hal Fisher. 1988. "Change and Development in the Arab World—Advance amid Diversity: An Economic and Social Analysis." In Jim Norwine and Alfonso Gonzalez (eds.), *The Third World: States of Mind and Being* (pp. 196–208). Boston: Unwin Hyman.

Kaneda, Hiromitsu. 1989. "Rural Resource Mobility and Intersectoral Balance in Early Modern Growth." In J.G. Williamson and V.R. Panchamukhi (eds.), *The Balance Between Industry and Agriculture in Economic Development*. Vol. 2 (pp. 367–89). London: Macmillan Press.

Kapoor, R. and M. Kohli. 1994. "Campaign Against World Bank and Destructive International Aid." *Lokayan Bulletin*. Vol. 10, No. 4. pp. 57–66.

Kappen, S. 1994. "Towards an Alternative Cultural Paradigm of Development." *Lokayan Bulletin*. Vol. 10, No. 4. Pp. 5–14.

Kassiola, Joel Jay. 1990. *The Death of Industrial Civilization: The Limits of Economic Growth and the Repoliticization of Advanced Industrial Society*. Albany: State University of New York Press.

Katouzian, Homa. 1980. *Ideology and Method in Economics*. New York: New York University Press.

Kautsky, John H. 1989. "Classical Marxism and Its Social Science: An Introduction." *International Journal of Comparative Sociology*. Vol. 30, Nos. 1–2. Pp. 1–4.

Kay, Cristobal. 1991. "Reflections on the Latin American Contribution to Development Theory." *Development and Change*. Vol. 22, No. 1. Pp. 31–68.

Keane, John. 1991. *The Media and Democracy*. Cambridge: Polity Press.

Keller, Bill. 1988. "Big Soviet Budgets Are Disclosed by Kremlin: Wasteful Subsidies Blamed." *New York Times*. October 28, pp. A1, A11.

Kellner, Douglas. 1989. *Critical Theory, Marxism, and Modernity*. Baltimore: Johns Hopkins University Press.

———. 1990. *Television and the Crisis of Democracy*. Boulder, Colorado: Westview Press.

Kemp's Commission on the Prevention of Drug and Alcohol Abuse. 1986. *Final Report*. Office of the Attorney General, California Department of Justice.

Keynes, John Maynard. 1936. *The General Theory of Employment, Interest and Money*. New York: Harcourt, Brace and World.

Khoi, Le Thanh. 1986. "Science and Technology: Options for Endogenous Development." In Huynh Cao Tri et al. (eds.), *Strategies for Endogenous Development* (pp. 19–75). New Delhi: Oxford & IBH Publishing.

Kim, D.H. 1984. *Development Theories and Strategies: Critical Perspectives*. Seoul, Korea: Sung Kyun Kwan University Press.

Kinsey, B.H. 1987. *Agribusiness and Rural Enterprise*. London: Croom Helm.

Klompe, M.A.M. 1977. "Closing Address: Science, Technology and Humanity." In J.J. Nossin (ed.), *Surveys for Development* (pp. 175–82). Amsterdam: Elsevier Scientific Publishing Company.

Kolland, Franz. 1989. "The Perception of Culture and Cultural Influence: Their Role in Technology Transfer." *Scandinavian Journal of Development Alternatives*. Vol. 8, No. 2. Pp. 59–73.

Kono, Shigemi. 1989. "Population Structure." *Population Bulletin of the United Nations*. No. 27. Pp. 108–24.

Korb, Lawrence J. 1990. "The End of the Cold War and Declining Military Expenditures." *Disarmament*. Vol. 13, No. 3. Pp. 1–8.

Korten, David C. 1980. "Community Organization and Rural Development: A Learning Process Approach." *Public Administration Review*. Vol. 40, No. 5. Pp. 480–511.

———. 1990. *Getting to the 21st Century*. West Hartford, Conn.: Kumarian Press.

Kothari, Rajni. 1984. "Communications for Alternative Development: Towards a Paradigm." *Development Dialogue*. Nos. 1–2. Pp. 13–82.

————. 1989. "The New Détente: Some Reflections from the South." *Alternatives*. Vol. 14, No. 3. Pp. 289–99.

Koven, Steven G. 1989. "Fighting the Drug Wars: Rhetoric and Reality." *Public Administration Review*. Vol. 49, No. 6. Pp. 580–83.

Kumar, Arun. 1993. "New Economic Policies: An Assessment." *Economic and Political Weekly*, 11 December, pp. 2735–43.

Kurspahic, Kemal. 1994. "Stop Dickering with Serbs and Help Bosnia Survive." *International Herald Tribune*. August 29, p. 8.

Kuttner, R. 1988. "Getting Lifeline from Foreign Creditors." *Los Angeles Times*. December 25.

Laclau, Ernesto. 1971. "Feudalism and Capitalism in Latin America." *New Left Review*. No. 67. Pp. 19–38.

————. 1977. *Politics and Ideology in Marxist* Theory. London: New Left Books.

Laite, F. 1988. "The Sociology of Development." In P.F. Leeson and M.M. Minogue (eds.), *Perspectives on Development* (pp. 160–93). Manchester and New York: Manchester University Press.

Lal, D. 1985. *The Poverty of Development Economics* (Appendix 2). Cambridge, Mass.: Harvard University Press.

Lall, S. 1975. "Is 'Dependence' a Useful Concept in Analysing Underdevelopment?" *World Development*. Vol. 3, Nos. 11–12. Pp. 799–810.

————. 1976. "Conflicts of Concepts: Welfare Economics and Developing Countries." *World Development*. Vol. 4, No. 3. Pp. 181–95.

Lamar, Jacob V. 1988. "The Homeless: Brick by Brick." *Time*. October 24, pp. 34–38.

Lamm, Leonard J. 1993. *The Idea of the Past*. New York: New York University Press.

Landau, Saul. 1990. "A New World to Exploit: The East Joins the South." *Monthly Review*. Vol. 42, No. 5. Pp. 29–37.

Langley, Winston. 1990. "What Happened to the New International Economic Order?" *Socialist Review*. Vol. 20, No. 3. Pp. 47–62.

Lappé, Frances M., Rachel Schurman, and Kevin Danaher. 1987. *Betraying the National Interest*. New York: Grove Press.

Larrain, Jorge. 1989. *Theories of Development: Capitalism, Colonialism and Dependency*. Cambridge, UK: Polity Press.

Lauer, Robert H. 1973. *Perspectives on Social Change*. Boston: Allyn and Bacon.

Leaver, R. 1977. "The Debate on Underdevelopment: 'On Situating Gunder Frank'." *Journal of Contemporary Asia*. Vol. 7, No. 1. Pp. 108–15.

———. 1979. "Samir Amin on Underdevelopment." *Journal of Contemporary Asia*. Vol. 9, No. 3. Pp. 325–36.

Lee, Yong S., Don F. Hadwiger, and Lee Chong-Bum. 1990. "Agricultural Policy Making Under International Pressure." *Food Policy*. Vol. 15, No. 5. Pp. 418–33.

Leeson, P.F. 1988. "Development Economics and the Study of Development." In P.F. Leeson and M.M. Minogue (eds.), *Perspectives on Development* (pp. 1–55). Manchester and New York: Manchester University Press.

Leftwich, A. 1993. "States of Underdevelopment: The Third World State in Theoretical Perspective." *Journal of Theoretical Politics*. Vol. 6, No. 1. Pp. 55–74.

Leibenstein, Harvey. 1957. *Economic Backwardness and Economic Growth*. New York: John Wiley & Sons.

Lewis, Anthony. 1994. "The UN Effort in Bosnia Was Wrong from the Start." *International Herald Tribune*. October 25, p. 4.

Lewis, W. Arthur. 1955. *The Theory of Economic Growth*. London: Allen & Unwin.

Leys, Colin. 1977. "Underdevelopment and Dependency: Critical Notes." *Journal of Contemporary Asia*. Vol. 7, No. 1. Pp. 92–107.

Lieske, Joel. 1988. "The United States as a Third World Country: Race, Education, Culture, and the Quality of American Life." In Jim Norwine and Alfonso Gonzalez (eds.), *The Third World: States of Mind and Being* (pp. 253–64). Boston: Unwin Hyman.

Linear, Marcus. 1985. *Zapping the Third World: The Disaster of Development Aid*. London: Pluto Press.

Linnemann, Hans, and Atul Sarma. 1991. "Economic Transformation in Eastern Europe: Its Genesis, Adjustment Process, and Impact on Developing Countries." *Development and Change*. Vol. 22, No. 1. Pp. 69–92.

Lipset, Seymour Martin. 1963. *The First New Nations: America in Comparative and Historical Perspective*. New York: Basic Books.

———. 1978. "Growth, Affluence, and the Limits of Futurology." In Sudesh Kumar Sharma (ed.), *Dynamics of Development*. Vol. 1 (pp. 49–78). Delhi: Concept Publishing Company.

Livingstone, I. 1981. "The Development of Development Economics." *ODI Review*. No. 2. Pp. 1–19.

Lowe, Marcia D. 1990. "Cycling into the Future." In Worldwatch Institute (ed.), *State of the World, 1990* (119–34). New York: W.W. Norton & Company.

Lowenthal, Leo. 1989a. On Sociology of Literature." In Stephen E. Bronner and Douglas M. Kellner (eds.), *Critical Theory and Society: A Reader* (pp. 40–51). New York: Routledge.

————. 1989b. "Historical Perspectives on Popular Culture." In Stephen E. Bronner and Douglas M. Kellner (eds.), *Critical Theory and Society: A Reader* (pp. 184–98). New York: Routledge.

Lukacs, Georg. 1971. *History and Class Consciousness: Studies in Marxist Dialectics*. London: Merlin Press.

Luxemburg, Rosa. 1951. *The Accumulation of Capital*. London: Routledge & Kegan Paul.

Luxemburg, Rosa, and N.I. Bukharin. 1972. *Imperialism and the Accumulation of Capital*. London: Allen Lane.

Lyman, Stanford M. 1990. "Race, Sex, and Servitude: Images of Blacks in American Cinema." *International Journal of Politics, Culture and Society*. Vol. 4, No. 1. Pp. 49–77.

Machan, Tibor R. 1977. *Introduction to Philosophical Inquiries*. Boston, Mass.: Allyn and Bacon.

MacNeill, Jim. 1989. "'Our Common Future,' Sustaining the Momentum." In F. Archibugi and P. Nijkamp (eds.), *Economy and Ecology: Towards Sustainable Development*. Dordrecht, Netherlands: Kluwer Academic Publishers.

Macpherson, C.B. 1972. "Reflections on the Sources of Development Theory." In Manfred Stanley (ed.), *Social Development: Critical Perspectives* (pp. 206–20). New York: Basic Books.

Mafeje, Archie. 1978. *Science, Ideology and Development: Three Essays on Development Theory*. Uppsala: Scandinavian Institute of African Studies.

Magdoff, Harry. 1986. "Third World Debt: Past and Present." *Monthly Review*. Vol. 37, No. 9. Pp. 1–10.

Mahoney, Eileen. 1989. "American Empire and Global Communication." In Ian Angus and Sut Jhally (eds.), *Cultural Politics in Contemporary America* (pp. 37–50). New York: Routledge.

Malloy, James M. 1989. "Policy Analysis, Public Policy and Regime Structure in Latin America." *Governance*. Vo.2, No. 3.

Malthus, Thomas Robert. 1989. *The Principles of Political Economy*. Vols. I and II. Cambridge: Cambridge University Press.

Mannheim, Karl. 1991 [1936]. *Ideology and Utopia: An Introduction to the Sociology of Knowledge*. London: Routledge.

Manzo, Kate. 1991. "Modernist Discourse and the Crisis of Development Theory." *Studies in Comparative International Development*. Vol. 26, No. 2. Pp. 3–36.

Marcuse, Herbert. 1989a. "Philosophy and Critical Theory." In Stephen E. Bronner and Douglas M. Kellner (eds.), *Critical Theory and Society: A Reader* (pp. 58–74). New York: Routledge.

————. 1989b. "The Obsolescence of the Freudian Concept of Man." In Stephen E. Bronner and Douglas M. Kellner (eds.), *Critical Theory and Society: A Reader* (pp. 233–46). New York: Routledge.

————. 1989c. "Liberation from the Affluent Society." In Stephen E. Bronner and Douglas M. Kellner (eds.), *Critical Theory and Society: A Reader* (pp. 276–87). New York: Routledge.

————. 1989d. "The Reification of the Proletariat." In Stephen E. Bronner and Douglas M. Kellner (eds.), *Critical Theory and Society: A Reader* (pp. 288–91). New York: Routledge.

Marlowe, L. 1994. "Destroying Souls." *Time*. 144(6), pp. 40–44.

Marsh, Sue. 1990. "Our Lasting Shame: Homelessness in the United States." *The New Renaissance*, Vol. 8, No. 1, Pp. 41–61.

Martin, Brendan. 1993. *In the Public Interest: Privatization and Public Sector Reform*. London: Zed Books.

Martinelli, A. 1975. "Multinational Corporations, National Economic Policies, and Labor Unions." In Leon N. Lindberg et al. (eds.), *Stress and Contradiction in Modern Capitalism* (pp. 425–43). Lexington, Mass.: Lexington Books.

Marx, Karl. 1978a [1859]. "Preface to *A Contribution to the Critique of Political Economy*." Reprinted in Robert C. Tucker (ed.), *The Marx-Engels Reader* (pp. 3–6). New York: W.W. Norton & Company.

————. 1978b [1843]. "Critique of Hegel's Philosophy of Right." Reprinted in Robert C. Tucker (ed.), *The Marx-Engels Reader* (pp. 16–25). New York: W.W. Norton & Company.

————. 1978c [1853]. "On Imperialism in India." Reprinted in Robert C. Tucker (ed.), *The Marx-Engels Reader* (pp. 653–58). New York: W.W. Norton & Company.

————. 1978d [1853]. "The Future of British Rule in India." Reprinted in Robert C. Tucker (ed.), *The Marx-Engels Reader* (pp. 659–64). New York: W.W. Norton & Company.

————. 1978e [1867]. *Capital* (Vols. 1 & 3). Reprinted in Robert C. Tucker (ed.), *The Marx-Engels Reader* (pp. 294–442). New York: W.W. Norton & Company.

Marx, Karl and Frederich Engels. 1978. *Manifesto of the Communist Party*. Reprinted in Robert C. Tucker (ed.), *The Marx Engels Reader* (pp. 469–500). New York: W.W. Norton & Company.

Mathieu, H. and Gottschalk. 1992. "UNCED II and Beyond: The Politics of the Global Environment." *Problems of International Cooperation* (Vierteljahres Berichte), No. 128, pp. 110–18.

Mathur, G.B. 1989. "The Current Impasse in Development Thinking: The Metaphysics of Power." *Alternatives*. Vol. 14, No. 4, Pp. 463–79.

Mattelart, Armand. 1983. *Transnationals and the Third World: Struggle for the Culture*. Boston: Bergin & Garvey Publishers.

McCarthy, Thomas. 1978. *The Critical Theory of Jürgen Habermas*. Cambridge, Mass.: MIT Press.

McCaughan, Edward J. 1993. "Race, Ethnicity, Nation, and Class Within Theories of Structure and Agency." *Social Justice*. Vol. 20, Nos. 1–2. Pp. 82–103.

McClelland, David C. 1961. *The Achieving Society*. Princeton, N.J.: Van Nostrand.

McCloskey, Donald N. 1984. "The Rhetoric of Economics." In Bruce J. Caldwell (ed.), *Appraisal and Criticism in Economics* (pp. 320–56). Winchester, Mass.: Allen & Unwin.

McGowan, Francis. 1994. "The Internationalisation of Privatization." In Thomas Clarke (ed.), *International Privatization: Strategies and Practices* (pp. 25–42). Berlin: Walter de Gruyter & Co.

McKenzie, Richard B. and Gordon Tullock. 1975. *The New World of Economics: Explorations into Human Experience*. Homewood, Ill: Richard D. Irwin.

Meier, Gerald M. 1984. *Emerging from Poverty: The Economics That Really Matters*. New York, Oxford University Press.

Mellor, John. W. 1966. *The Economics of Agricultural Development*. Ithaca, N.Y.: Cornell University Press.

Merriam, Allen H. 1988. "What Does 'Third World' Mean?" In Jim Norwine and Alfonso Gonzalez (eds.), *The Third World: States of Mind and Being* (pp. 15–22). Boston: Unwin Hyman.

Meyer, William H. 1989. "Global News Flows: Dependency and Neoimperialism." *Comparative Political Studies*. Vol. 22, No. 3. Pp. 243–64.

Mill, John Stuart. 1909. *Principles of Political Economy*. London: Longmans, Green and Co.

Miller, Richard W. 1984. *Analysing Marx: Morality, Power and History*. Princeton, N.J.: Princeton University Press.

Mills, Charles W. 1990. "Getting Out of the Cave: Tension Between Democracy and Elitism in Marx's Theory of Cognitive Liberation." *Social and Economic Studies*. Vol. 39, No. 1. Pp. 1–50.

Minhas, Bagicha S. 1979. "The Current Development Debate." In A Rothko Chapel Colloquium (ed.), *Toward a New Strategy for Development* (pp. 75–96). New York: Pergamon Press.

Miracle Unmasked. 1995. *The Economist*. 9 December, pp. 4–6.

Miszlivetz, Ferenc and Mary Kaldor. 1985. "Civilizational Crisis." *IDS Bulletin*. Vol. 16, No. 1. Pp. 56–61.

Mitsuo, O. 1982. "The Sociology of Development and Issues Surrounding Late Development." *International Studies Quarterly*. Vol. 24, No. 4. Pp. 596–622.

Mittelman, James H. 1988. *Out from Underdevelopment*. London: Macmillan Press.

Mkandawire, P.Thandika. 1983. "Accumulation on a World Scale." In Peter Limqueco and Bruce McFarlane (eds.), *Neo-Marxist Theories of Development*. New York: St. Martin's Press.

Montgomery, John D. 1976. "Toward a Value Theory of Modernization." In Harold Lasswell, Daniel Lerner and John D. Montgomery (eds.), *Values and Development: Appraising Asian Experience* (pp. 1–19). Cambridge, Mass.: MIT Press.

Moore, M. 1980. "Public Bureaucracy in the Post-Colonial State: Some Questions on 'Autonomy' and 'Dominance' in South Asia." *Development and Change*. Vol. 11, No. 1. Pp. 137–48.

Moore, M. 1994. "India Awakes to Kellog: U.S. firm Targets a Vast Middle Class." *International Herald Tribune*. October 28, p. 15.

Moore, Robert. 1983. "How to Produce a Possible Balance of Equations in North-South Relations." In Ann Mattis (ed.), *A Society for International Development: Prospectus, 1984* (pp. 59–70). Durham, N.C.: Duke University Press.

Moore, Wilbert E. 1963. *Social Change*. Englewood Cliffs, N.J.: Prentice-Hall.

Morgan, Gareth. 1983. "Toward a More Reflective Social Science." In Gareth Morgan (ed.), *Beyond Method: Strategies for Social Research* (pp. 368–76). Beverly Hills, Calif.: Sage Publications.

Morrow, Lance 1991a. "Starting at Year Zero." *Time*. September 9, pp. 8–20.

Morrow, Raymond A. 1991b. "Toward a Critical Theory of Methodology: Habermas and the Theory Argumentation." *Current Perspectives in Social Theory*. Vol. 11. Pp. 197–228.

Munch, Richard. 1991. "American and European Social Theory: Cultural Identities and Social Forms in Theory Production." *Sociological Perspectives*. Vol. 34, No. 3. Pp. 313–35.

Murphy, Craig N. 1990. "Freezing the North–South Bloc(k) After the East-West Thaw." *Socialist Review*. Vol. 20, No. 3. Pp. 25–45.

Murray, R. 1971. "The Internationalization of Capital and the Nation State." *New Left Review*. No. 67 (May–June). Pp. 84–109.

Musa, Mohammed. 1990. "News Agencies, Transnationalization and the New Order." *Media, Culture and Society*. Vol. 12, No. 3. Pp. 325–42.

Nafziger, E. Wayne. 1979. "A Critique of Development Economics in the U.S." In David Lehmann (ed.), *Development Theory: Four Critical Studies* (pp. 32–48). London: Frank Cass and Company.

———. 1990. *The Economics of Developing Countries* (2nd ed.). Englewood Cliffs, N.J.: Prentice-Hall.

Nandy, Ashis. 1989. "The Idea of Development: The Experience of Modern Psychology as a Cautionary Tale and as an Allegory." In John S. Augustine (ed.), *Strategies for Third World Development* (pp. 34–46). New Delhi: Sage Publications.

Narman, Anders. 1995. "Fighting Fire with Petrol: Counter Social Ills in Africa with Economic Structural Adjustment." In David Simon et al. (eds.), *Structurally Adjusted Africa: Poverty, Debt and Basic Needs* (pp. 45–56). London: Pluto Press.

Nash, N.C. 1994. "Latin Recovery Passes the Poor By." *International Herald Tribune*. September 8, p. 1, 3.

Nasr, Seyyed Hossein. 1968. *Man and Nature: The Spiritual Crisis of Modern Man*. Kuala Lumpur, Malaysia: Foundation for Traditional Studies.

Nelson, B. 1972. "Communities, Societies, Civilizations: Postmillennial Views on the Masks and Faces of Change." In Manfred Stanley (ed.), *Social Development: Critical Perspectives* (pp. 105–33). New York: Basic Books.

New Internationalist. 1982. "The Shape of Things to Come—Facts on a Changing World." No. 113 (July). Pp. 10–11,

New World Order. 1991. *Economist*. September 28, pp. 21–26.

Nguyen, T.Q. 1989. *Third-World Development*. London and Toronto: Associated University Presses.

Nicholson, Norman K. and E.F. Connerley. 1989. "The Impending Crisis in Development Administration." *International Journal of Public Administration*. Vol. 12, No. 3. Pp. 385–425.

Nieuwenhuijze, C.A.O. van. 1982. *Development Begins at Home: Problems and Prospects of the Sociology of Development*. Oxford: Pergamon Press.

Nikiforov, L.V. 1989. "The Development of the Agro-Industrial Complex in the USSR." In J.G. Williamson and V.R. Panchamukhi (eds.), *The Balance Between Industry and Agriculture in Economic Development*. Vol. 2 (pp. 253–63). London: Macmillan Press.

Nisbet, Robert. 1969. *Social Change and History: Aspects of the Western Theory of Development*. New York: Oxford University Press.

———. 1980. *History of the Idea of Progress*, New York: Basic Books.

Noble, J.B. 1982. "Social Structure and Paradigm Synthesis: Theoretical Commensurability and the Problem of Mannheim's Paradox." In W.T. Bluhm (ed.), *The Paradigm Problem in Political Science* (pp. 65–109), Durham, N.C: Carolina Academic Press.

Nohlen, D. 1980. "Modernization and Dependence: An Outline and Critique of Competing Theories." *Intereconomics*. No. 2 (March/April), Pp. 81–86.

Norwine, Jim. 1988. "Afterword." In Jim Norwine and Alfonso Gonzalez (eds.), *The Third World: States of Mind and Being* (pp. 265–70). Boston: Unwin Hyman.

Nurkse, Ragner. 1964. *Problems of Capital Formation in Underdeveloped Countries*. New York: Oxford University Press.

Nuscheler, Franz. 1988. "Learning from Experience or Preaching Ideologies?: Rethinking Development Theory." *Law and State*. Vol. 38. Pp. 104–25.

O'Brien, D.C. 1979. "Modernization, Order, and Erosion of a Democratic Ideal: American Political Science 1960–70." In David Lehmann (ed.), *Development Theory: Four Critical Studies* (pp. 49–76). London: Frank Cass and Company.

O'Brien, P.J. 1975. "A Critique of Latin American Theories of Dependency." In Ivar Oxaal, Tony Barnett and David Booth (eds.). *Beyond the Sociology of Development* (pp. 7–27). London: Routledge & Kegan Paul.

O'Cleireacain, Seamus. 1990. *Third World Debt and International Public Policy*. New York: Praeger Publishers.

O'Manique, J. and D.H. Pollock. 1984. "Human Values and Planning: A View from the North." *Managing International Development*. Vol. 1, No. 1. Pp. 70–77.

Olson, Guy E. 1993. "America's Cable News Network." *American Studies Newsletter*. No. 30. Pp. 38–42.

Onyewuenyi, Innocent C. 1977. "The Concept of Man in the Philosophy of Karl Marx." *African Review*. Vol. 7, Nos. 3–4. Pp. 59–69

Opitz, P.J. 1987. "The United Nations and the Emancipation of the Third World." *Law and State*. Vol. 35. Pp. 7–21.

Ottaway, Richard N. 1983. "The Change Agent: A Taxonomy in Relation to the Change Process." *Human Relations*. Vol. 36, No. 4. Pp. 361–92.

Pai, Sudha. 1994. "Transition from Command to Market Economy: Privatization in Brazil and Argentina." In R.B. Jain and H. Bongartz (eds.), *Structural Adjustment, Public Policy and Bureaucracy in Developing Societies* (pp. 158–82). New Delhi: Har-Anand Publications.

Palma, G. 1978. "Dependency: The Formal Theory of Underdevelopment or a Methodology for the Analysis of Concrete Situations of Underdevelopment?" *World Development*. Vol. 6, Nos. 7/8. Pp. 881–924.

Palmer, N.D. 1978. "Development: The Need for an Effective Dialogue." In Sudesh Kumar Sharma (ed.), *Dynamics of Development*. Vol. 1 (pp. 95–101). Delhi: Concept Publishing Company.

Parenti, Michael. 1986. *Inventing Reality: The Politics of Mass Media*. New York: St. Martin's Press.

———. 1988. *Democracy for the Few*. New York: St. Martin's Press.

Parsons, Talcott and Edward Shils (eds.). (1951). *Toward a General Theory of Action*. Cambridge: Harvard University Press.

Parsons, Talcott and Neil J. Smelser. 1965. *Economy and Society*. New York: Free Press.

Patel, Surendra J. 1983. "The Age of the Third World." *Third World Quarterly*. Vol. 5, No. 1. Pp. 58–71.

Patterson, John G., and Nanda R. Shrestha. 1988. "Population Growth and Development in the Third World: The Neocolonial Context." *Studies in Comparative International Development*. Vol. 23, No. 2. Pp. 3–32.

Pear, R. 1988. "Soviets Understate Deficit, U.S. Specialists Say." *New York Times*. October 30, p. L14.

Peck, Jim. 1984. "US Foreign Policy." In Pete Ayrton, Tom Engelhardt, and Vron Ware (eds.). *World View 1985: An Economic and Political Yearbook* (pp. 51–56). London: Pluto Press.

Peet, Richard. 1986. "The Destruction of Regional Cultures." In R.J. Johnston and P.J. Taylor (eds.), *A World in Crisis?* (pp. 152–72). New York: Basil Blackwell.

Perlez, J. 1994. "From Bad to Worse for Health Care in Eastern Europe." *International Herald Tribune.* November 25, p. 2.

Peters, Evelyn. 1988. "World (Third?) within a World (First): Canadian Indian People." In Jim Norwine and Alfonso Gonzalez (eds.), *The Third World: States of Mind and Being* (pp. 243–52). Boston: Unwin Hyman.

Petras, James F. 1970. *Politics and Social Structure in Latin America.* New York: Monthly Review Press.

———. 1978. *Critical Perspectives on Imperialism and Social Class in the Third World.* New York: Monthly Review Press.

———. 1983. "New Perspectives on Imperialism and Social Classes in the Periphery." In Peter Limqueco and Bruce McFarlane (eds.), *Neo-Marxist Theories of Development* (pp. 198–220). New York: St. Martin's Press.

———. 1990. "The World Market: Battleground for the 1990s." *Journal of Contemporary Asia.* Vol. 20, No. 2. Pp. 145–76.

Petrazzini, Ben A. 1995. *The Political Economy of Telecommunications Reform in Developing Countries.* Westport, Conn.: Praeger Publishers.

Phillips, Paul. 1990. "The Debt Crisis and Change in Eastern Europe." *Monthly Review.* Vol. 41, No. 9. Pp. 19–27.

Pieterse, Jan Nederveen. 1988. "Counterpoint and Emancipation." *Development and Change.* Vol. 19, No. 2. Pp. 327–41.

———. 1991a. "Dilemmas of Development Discourse: The Crisis of Developmentalism and the Comparative Method." *Development and Change.* Vol. 22, No. 1. Pp. 5–29.

———. 1991b. "Fictions of Europe." *Race and Class.* Vol. 32, No. 3. Pp. 3–10.

Pollock, Frederick. 1989. "State Capitalism: Its Possibilities and Limitations." In Stephen E. Bronner and Douglas M. Kellner (eds.), *Critical Theory and Society: A Reader* (pp. 95–118). New York: Routledge.

Pomfret, John. 1994. "The Reasons Behind the Fall from Grace of East Europe's Dissidents." *International Herald Tribune.* October 25, pp. 1, 8.

Pope, Whitney. 1976. *Durkheim's Suicide*. Chicago: University of Chicago Press.

Post, K. 1982. "The Politics of Developing Areas and the 'Son of a Bitch' Factor." In B. de Gaay Fortman (ed.), *Rethinking Development* (pp. 49–64). The Hague: Institute of Social Studies.

Postel, Sandra. 1987. "Stabilizing Chemical Cycles." In Worldwatch Institute (ed.), *State of the World, 1987* (pp. 157–76). New York: W.W. Norton & Company.

———. 1989. "Halting Land Degradation." In Worldwatch Institute (ed.), *State of the World, 1989* (pp. 21–40). New York: W.W. Norton & Company.

———. 1990. "Saving Water for Agriculture." In Worldwatch Institute (ed.), *State of the World, 1990* (pp. 39–58). New York: W.W. Norton & Company.

Poverty Figures. 1988. *Washington Post*. September 1, p. A22.

Prebisch, R. 1963. *Towards a Dynamic of Development Policy for Latin America*. New York: United Nations.

Pred, A. 1989. "Survey 14: The Locally Spoken Word and Local Struggles." *Society and Space*. Vol. 7, No. 2. Pp. 216–23.

Preston, Peter W. 1985. *New Trends in Development Theory*. London: Routledge & Kegan Paul.

———. 1986. *Making Sense of Development*. London: Routledge & Kegan Paul.

———. 1987. *Rethinking Development: Essays on Development and Southeast Asia*. London: Routledge & Kegan Paul.

Pye, Lucian W. 1966. *Aspects of Political Development*. Boston: Little, Brown.

———. 1978. "Confrontation Between the Social Sciences and Area Studies." In Sudesh Kumar Sharma (ed.), *Dynamics of Development*. Vol. 1 (pp. 79–93). Delhi: Concept Publishing Company.

Rademaekers, W. 1994. "Those Foreign Legions: How Paris Uses Military Muscle to Maintain Its Global Influence." *Time*. September 5, pp. 28–29.

Raghaviah, Y. 1987. "Post–Positivist Bureaucratic Theory and the Third World Predicament." *Indian Journal of Public Administration*. Vol. 33, No. 1. Pp. 1–13.

Rahman, Md. Anisur. 1991. "Towards an Alternative Development Paradigm." *Ifda Dossier*. April/June. Pp. 18–27.

Ramirez-Faria, Carlos. 1991. *The Origins of Economic Inequality Between Nations: A Critique of Western Theories on Development and Underdeveloment*. London: Unwin Hyman.

Ramos, Alberto Guerreiro. 1981. *The New Science of Organizations: A Reconceptualization of the Wealth of Nation*. Toronto: University of Toronto Press.

Ramphal, Shridath. 1992. "In a North-South Gap, Seeds of Environment Discord." *International Herald Tribune*. January 24, p. 4.

Randall, Vicky and Robin Theobald. 1985. *Political Change and Underdevelopment*. Durham, N.C.: Duke University Press.

Rapaczynski, Andrzej. 1987. *Nature and Politics: Liberalism in Philosophies of Hobbes, Locke, and Rousseau*. Ithaca, N.Y.: Cornell University Press.

Redclift, Michael. 1987. *Sustainable Development: Exploring the Contradictions*. London, Methuen & Co.

Reglar, Stephen. 1987. "Mao Zedong as a Marxist Political Economist: A Critique." *Journal of Contemporary Asia*. Vol. 17, No. 2. Pp. 208–33.

Renner, Michael. 1989. "Enhancing Global Security." In Worldwatch Institute (ed.), *State of the World, 1989* (pp. 132–53). New York: W.W. Norton & Company.

———. 1991. "Assessing the Military's War on the Environment." In Worldwatch Institute (ed.), *State of the World, 1991* (pp. 132–52). New York: W.W. Norton & Company.

Rensberger, B. 1994. "In Cairo, a Chance to Slow the Population Express Train." *International Herald Tribune*. September 5, pp. 1, 4.

Rentoul, John. 1987. "Privatization: The Case Against." In Julia Neurberger (ed.), *Privatization: Fair Shares for All or Selling the Family Silver?* (pp. 1–35). London: Macmillan.

Reuters. 1995. "Poverty Gnaws at a Russia in Transition." *International Herald Tribune*. April 18, p. 15.

Reuveny, J. 1979. "Development Theory: Marxist Challenge and Non-Marxist Response." *International Problems*. Vol. 18, Nos. 1–2. Pp. 47–57.

Ricardo, David. 1957. *The Principles of Political Economy and Taxation*. London: J.M. Dent & Sons.

Rice, Robert. 1988. "Economics." In David Goldsworthy (ed.), *Development Studies in Australia: Themes and Issues* (pp. 36–43). Clayton Vic., Australia: Monash Development Studies Centre.

Riggs, Fred W. 1964. *Administration in Developing Countries: The Theory of Prismatic Society*. Boston: Houghton Mifflin.

—. 1987. *A New Paradigm for 'Comparative Government'*. Unpublished paper, University of Hawaii.

Rist, Gilbert. 1978. "The Not-So-New International Order." *International Development Review*. Vol. 20, Nos. 3–4. Pp. 48–51.

—. 1990. "'Development' as a Part of the Modern Myth: The Western 'Socio-Cultural Dimension' of 'Development'." *European Journal of Development Research*. Vol. 2, No. 1. Pp. 10–21.

Ritzer, George. 1991. "Reflections on the Rise of Metatheorizing in Sociology." *Sociological Perspectives*. Vol. 34, No. 3. Pp. 237–48.

Rivera-Batiz, L.A. and P.M. Romer. 1991. "Economic Integration and Endogenous Growth." *Quarterly Journal of Economics*. Vol. 106, No. 2. Pp. 531–55.

Roach, Colleen. 1990. "The Movement for a New World Information and Communication Order: A Second Wave?" *Media, Culture and Society*. Vol. 12, No. 3. Pp. 283–307.

Robinson, Joan. 1979. *Aspects of Development and Underdevelopment*. Cambridge: Cambridge University Press.

Romer, Paul M. 1986. "Increasing Returns and Long Run Growth." *Journal of Political Economy*. Vol. 94, No. 5. Pp. 1002–37.

—. 1990. "Endogenous Technological Change." *Journal of Political Economy*. Vol. 98, No. 5, Pp. S71–S102.

—. 1993. "Economic Growth." In David R. Henderson (ed.), The Fortune Encyclopedia of Economics (pp. 183–89). New York: Time Warner.

Rondinelli, Dennis A. 1987. *Development Administration and U.S. Foreign Policy*. Boulder, Colorado: Lynne Rienner Publishers.

Rosenau, Pauline M. 1988. "Philosophy, Methodology, and Research: Marxist Assumptions About Inquiry." *Comparative Political Studies*. Vol. 20, No. 4. Pp. 423–54.

—. 1992. *Post-modernism and the Social Sciences: Insights, Inroads, and Intrusions*. Princeton: Princeton University Press.

Rosenstein-Rodan, Paul N. 1957. *Notes on the Theory of the "Big Push."* Cambridge, Mass.: Center for International Studies, MIT.

Rosh, Robert M. 1990. "Third World Arms Production and the Evolving Interstate System." *Journal of Conflict Resolution*. Vol. 34, No. 1. Pp. 57–73.

Rostow, W.W. 1962. *The Process of Economic Growth* (2nd edition). New York: W.W. Norton & Co.

——. 1973. "The Takeoff into Self-sustained Growth." In Amitai Etzioni and Eva Etzioni-Halevy (eds.), *Social change* (2nd ed.) (pp. 285–300). New York: Basic Books.

Rourke, John T. 1986. *International Politics on the World Stage*. Monterey, Calif.: Brooks/Cole Publishing Company.

Routh, Guy. 1975. *The Origin of Economic Ideas*. New York: International Arts and Sciences Press.

Roy, K.C. and R.K. Sen. 1989. "LDC's Borrowing Debt Trap, and Development." *Journal of Developing Areas*. Vol. 5. Pp. 254–68.

Ruccio, D.F. and L.H. Simon. 1986. "Methodological Aspects of a Marxian Approach to Development: An Analysis of the Modes of Production School." *World Development*. Vol. 14, No. 2. Pp. 211–22.

——. 1988. "Radical Theories of Development: Frank, the Modes of Production School, and Amin." In Charles K. Wilber (ed.), *The Political Economy of Development and Underdevelopment* (4th edition) (pp. 122–73). New York: Random House Business Division.

Rudolph, Lloyd I. 1992. "The Media and Cultural Politics." *Economic and Political Weakly*. Vol. 27 (July 11). Pp. 1489–96.

Sabato, E. 1977. "What Development? And Why?" In John P. Schlegel (ed.), *Towards a Re-definition of Development* (pp. 315–19). New York: Pergamon Press.

Sachs, Ignacy. 1979. "Development, Maldevelopment and Industrialization of Third World Countries." *Development and Underdevelopment*. Vol. 10, Pp. 635–46.

——. 1987. "A Comment on Professor Chakravarty's Paper." In Louis Emmerij (ed.), *Development Policies and the Crisis of the 1980s* (pp. 101–4). Paris: Development Centre of the OECD.

Sachs, Jeffrey. 1994. "Beyond Bretton Woods: A New Blueprint." *Economist*. October 1, pp. 23–29.

Sachs, Wolfgang. 1992a. "Introduction." In Wolfgang Sachs (ed.), *The Development Dictionary: A Guide to Knowledge as Power* (pp. 1–5). London: Zed Books.

——. 1992b. "One World." In Wolfgang Sachs (ed.), *The Development Dictionary: A Guide to Knowledge as Power* (pp. 102–15), London: Zed Books.

Sage, Colin. 1988. "Coca, Cocaine and the Subterranean 'Boom': The Consequences for Development in Bolivia." In Altap Gauhar (ed.), *Third World Affairs, 1988* (pp. 150–60). London: Third World Foundation for Social and Economic Studies.

Said, Edward W. 1978. *Orientalism*. London: Routledge & Kegan Paul.

———. 1983. *The World, the Text, and the Critic*. Cambridge, Mass.: Harvard University Press.

Samuelson, Paul A. 1976. *Economics* (10th ed.). New York: McGraw-Hill.

Sanction, T.A. 1989. "What on Earth Are We Doing." *Time*. January 2, pp. 26–30.

Sanger, D. 1994. "Washington Turns Away from Japan Trade Fight." *International Herald Tribune*. November 5–6, pp. 1, 4.

Sanyal, Kalyan K. 1993. "Paradox of Competitiveness and Globalisation of Underdevelopment." *Economic and Political Weekly*. Vol. 28 (June). Pp. 1326–30.

Sarkar, Prabirjit. 1991. "IMF/World Bank Stabilisation Programme: A Critical Assessment." *Economic and Political Weekly*. Vol. 26 (5 October). Pp. 2307–10.

Saul, John S. 1974. "The State in Post-Colonial Societies: Tanzania." In Ralph Miliband and John Saville (eds.), *The Socialist Register*. New York: Monthly Review Press.

———. 1979. *The State and Revolution in Eastern Africa*. New York: Monthly Review Press.

Saunders, Norman C. 1990. "Defense Spending in the 1990s—the Effect of Deeper Cuts." *Monthly Labor Review*. Vol. 113, No. 10. Pp. 3–15.

Sawer, M. 1978–79. "The Politics of Historiography: Russian Socialism and the Question of the Asiatic Mode Production, 1906–1931." *Critique*. Vols.10–11. Pp. 15–35.

Schiller, Herbert I. 1989. "The Privatization and Transnationalization of Culture." In Ian Angus and Sut Jhally (eds.), *Cultural Politics in Contemporary America* (pp. 317–32). New York: Routledge.

Schlegel, John P. (ed.). 1977. *Towards a Re-definition of Development*. New York: Pergamon Press.

Schultz, T.W. 1971. *Investment in Human Capital: The Role of Education and Research*. New York: Free Press.

Schultz, T.W. 1980. "Nobel Lecture: The Economics of Being Poor." *Journal of Political Economy*. Vol. 88, No. 4. Pp. 639–51.

Schumacher, E. Friedrich. 1973. *Small is Beautiful*. New York: Harper and Row.

Schumpeter, Joseph. 1951. *The Theory of Economic Development*. Cambridge, Mass.: Harvard University Press.

Seers, Dudley. 1979a. "The Congruence of Marxism and Other Neoclassical Doctrines." In A Rothko Chapel Colloquium (ed.), *Toward a New Strategy for Development* (pp. 1–17). New York: Pergamon Press.

———. 1979b. "The Meaning of Development." In David Lehmann (ed.), *Development Theory: Four Critical Studies* (pp. 9–24). London: Frank Cass and Company.

Segal, Gerald. 1993. *The World Affairs Companion* (rev. ed.). London: Simon & Schuster.

Selwyn, Percy. 1975. "Introduction: Room for Manoeuvre?" In Percy Selwyn (Ed), *Development Policy in Small Countries* (pp. 8–24). London: Croom Helm.

Senghaas, Dieter. 1979. "Dissociation and Autocentric Development: An Alternative Development Policy for the Third World." *Applied Sciences and Development*. Vol. 14. Pp. 43–55.

Shamuyarira, Nathan M. 1976. "Political Development in New African states." In Rajni Kothari (ed.), *State and Nation Building*. New Delhi: Allied Publishers.

Sharma, Keshav C. 1994. "Africa's Economic Crisis, Public Policies of Structural Adjustment Programmes, Considerations for Political Restructuring and Role of Public Service Bureaucracies." In R.B. Jain and H. Bongartz (eds.), *Structural Adjustment, Public Policy and Bureaucracy in Developing Societies* (pp. 201–16). New Delhi: Har-Anand Publications, New Delhi.

Shaw, T.M. 1988. "Africa's Conjuncture: From Structural Adjustment to Self-Reliance." In Altap Gauhar (ed.), *Third World Affairs, 1988* (pp. 318–36). London: Third World Foundation for Social and Economic Studies.

Shea, Cynthia Pollock. 1989. "Protecting the Ozone Layer." In Worldwatch Institute (ed.), *State of the World, 1989* (pp. 77–96). New York: W.W. Norton & Company.

Sheth, D.L. 1987. "Alternative Development as Political Practice." *Alternatives*. Vol. 12, No. 2. Pp. 155–71.

Shils, Edward. 1965. *Political Development in the New States*. London: Mouton & Company.

————. 1989. "The Limits on the Capacities of Government." *Government and Opposition.* Vol. 24, No. 4. Pp. 441–57.

Shiva, Vandana. 1987. "The Violence of Reductionist Science." *Alternatives.* Vol. 12, No. 2. Pp. 243–61.

Shivji, Issa G. 1976. *Class Struggles in Tanzania.* New York: Monthly Review Press.

Shukla, Vibhooti. 1992. "Rethinking Development." *Economic and Political Weekly.* Vol. 27 (August). Pp. 1797–99.

Simon, L.H., and D.F. Ruccio. 1986. "A Methodological Analysis of Dependency Theory: Explanation in Andre Gunder Frank." *World Development.* Vol. 14, No. 2. Pp. 195–209.

Simons, M. 1994. "In the New Eastern Europe, Old Pollution Problems Worsen." *International Herald Tribune.* November 4, pp. 1, 6.

Sinaceur, M.A. 1983. "Foreword: Development—to What End?" In F. Perroux, *A New Concept of Development* (pp. 1–19). London & Canberra: Croom Helm.

Singer, Hans W. 1975. *The Strategy of International Development: Essays in the Economics of Backwardness.* London: Macmillan.

Singh, Rahul. 1994. "Too Many People Can Hamper Development." *Far Eastern Economic Review.* September 22, pp. 21–22.

Sivard, Ruth Leger. 1986. *World Military and Social Expenditure.* Washington, D.C.: World Priorities.

————. 1988. *World Military and Social Expenditures: 1987–88.* Washington, D.C.: World Priorities.

————. 1989. *World Military and Social Expenditures: 1989.* Washington, D.C.: World Priorities.

————. 1991. *World Military and Social Expenditures: 1991.* Washington, D.C.: World Priorities.

Skinner, Curtis. 1988. "Population Myth and the Third World." *Social Policy.* Vol. 19, No. 1. Pp. 57–62.

Sklair, Leslie. 1991. *Sociology of the Global System.* New York: Harvester Wheatsheaf.

Skolnick, Jerome H., and Elliott Currie. 1985. Inequality." In Jerome H. Skolnick and Elliott Currie (ed.), *Crisis in American Institutions* (pp. 91–93). Boston: Little, Brown.

Smelser, Neil J. 1973. "Toward a Theory of Modernization." In Amitai Etzioni and Eva Etzioni-Halevy (eds.), *Social Change* (pp. 268–84). New York: Basic Books.

Smith, Adam. 1930. *An Inquiry into the Nature and Causes of the Wealth of Nations* (Vols. 1–2) (edited with an introduction by E. Cannan). New York: Random House.

Smith, Anthony D. 1973, *The Concept of Social Change: A Critique of the Functionalist Theory of Social Change*. London: Routledge & Kegan Paul.

Smith, Brian C. 1991. "The Changing Role of Government in Comparative Perspective." In Brian C. Smith (ed.), *The Changing Role of Government: Management of Social and Economic Activities* (pp. 27–43). London: Management Development Programme, Commonwealth Secretariat.

Smith, J.R. and D.B. Ottaway. 1995. "Developing Nations Threaten to Sabotage Nuclear Treaty." *International Herald Tribune*. March 2, p. 2.

Smith, S. 1983. "Class Analysis versus World System: Critique of Samir Amin's Typology of Underdevelopment." In Peter Limqueco and Bruce McFarlane (eds.), *Neo-Marxist Theories of Development* (pp. 73–86). New York: St. Martin's Press.

Smith, Steven B. 1984. *Reading Althusser: An Essay on Structural Marxism*. Ithaca, N.Y.: Cornell University Press.

Smith, Tony. 1979. "The Underdevelopment of Development Literature: The Case of Dependency Theory." *World Politics*. Vol. 31, No. 2. Pp. 247–88.

———. 1981. "The Logic of Dependency Theory Revisited." *International Organization*. Vol. 35, No. 4. Pp. 755–61.

So, Alvin Y. 1990. *Social Change and Development: Modernization, Dependency, and World-System Theories*. Newbury Park, Calif.: Sage Publications.

Soldatenko, M. 1982. "An Overview of Development Theories." *South Asia Bulletin*. Vol. 2, No. 2. Pp. 35–47.

Solo, Robert A. 1975. "The Economist and the Economic Roles of the Political Authority in Advanced Industrial Societies." In Leon N. Lindberg et al. (eds.), *Stress and Contradiction in Modern Capitalism* (pp. 99–113). Lexington, Mass.: Lexington Books.

South Commission. 1990. *The Challenge to the South*. New York: Oxford University Press.

Southall, A. 1972. "Community, Society, and the World in Emergent Africa." In Manfred Stanley (ed.), *Social Development: Critical Perspectives*. New York: Basic Books.

Sparks, Colin and Colleen Roach. 1990. "Editorial." *Media, Culture and Society.* Vol. 12, No. 3. Pp. 275–81.

Spencer, Herbert. 1973. "The Evolution of Societies." In Amitai Etzioni and Eva Etzioni-Halevy (eds.), *Social Change* (2nd edition) (pp. 9–13). New York: Basic Books.

Srinivasan, T.N. 1988. "Introduction to Part I." In Hollis Chenery and T.N. Srinivasan (eds.), *Handbook of Development Economics* (Vol. I). Amsterdam, Netherlands: Elsevier Science Publishers.

Srisang, Koson. 1984. "Ethics and Politics: Youth in National Development." In C.I. Itty (ed.), *Searching for Asian Paradigms* (pp. 43–53). Bangkok: Asian Cultural Forum on Development.

Stanley, Manfred. 1972. "Technicism, Liberalism, and Development: A Study in Irony as Social Theory." In Manfred Stanley (ed.), *Social Development: Critical Perspectives* (pp. 274–325). New York: Basic Books.

Steidlmeier, Paul. 1987. *The Paradox of Poverty: A Reappraisal of Economic Development Policy.* Cambridge, Mass.: Ballinger Publishing Company.

Stein, Howard. 1994. "Theories of Institutions and Economic Reform in Africa." *World Development.* Vol. 22, No. 12. Pp. 1833–49.

Straubhaar, T. 1986. "The Economics of Third World Arms Imports." *Intereconomics.* Vol. 21, No. 3. Pp. 137–41.

Streeten, Paul. 1975. *The Limits of Development Research.* Oxford: Pergamon Press.

———. 1979. "A Basic-Needs Approach to Economic Development." In K.P. Jameson and Charles K. Wilber (eds.)., *Directions in Economic Development.* Notre Dame, Indiana: University of Notre Dame Press.

———. 1983. *Development Dichotomies* [discussion paper]. England: IDS Publications.

———. 1989a. "The Politics of Food Prices." In N. Islam (ed.), *The Balance Between Industry and Agriculture in Economic Development.* Vol. 5 (pp. 61–71). London, Macmillan Press.

———. 1989b. "Global Institutions for an Independent World." *World Development.* Vol. 17, No. 9. Pp. 1349–59.

Sukhwal, B.L. 1988. "South Asia: A Region of Conflicts and Contradictions." In Jim Norwine and Alfonso Gonzalez (eds.), *The Third World: States of Mind and Being* (pp. 209–21). Boston: Unwin Hyman.

Sunkel, Osvaldo. 1969. "National Development Policy and External Dependence." *Journal of Development Studies.* Vol. 6, No. 1. Pp. 23–48.

Szeftel, Morris. 1987. "The Crisis in the Third World." In Ray Bush, Gordon Johnston, and David Coates (eds.), *The World Order: Socialist Perspectives* (pp. 87–140). Cambridge: Polity Press.

Tagliabue, J. 1994. "Pizza Hut's Last Frontier: Italy." *International Herald Tribune*. September 2, p. 8.

Talbott, Strobe. 1991. "And Now for the Sequels." *Time*. September 9, p. 30.

Tandon, Yash. 1991. "Foreign NGOs, Uses and Abuses: An African Perspective." *Ifda Dossier*. April/June. Pp. 67–78.

Targetti, Ferdinando and Anthony P. Thirlwall. 1989. "Introduction." In Ferdinando Targetti and Anthony P. Thirlwall (eds.), *The Essential Kaldor* (pp. 1–23). London: Gerald Duckworth.

Taylor, Alwyn B. 1989. "The Debt Problem of Sub-Saharan Africa." *European Journal of Development Research*. Vol. 1, No. 2. Pp. 10–31.

Taylor, John. 1974. "Neo-Marxism and Underdevelopment: A Sociological Fantasy." *Journal of Contemporary Asia*. Vol. 4, No. 1. Pp. 5–23.

Taylor, John G. 1979. *From Modernization to Modes of Production: A Critique of Sociologies of Development and Underdevelopment*. London: Macmillan Press.

Taylor, P. 1995. "South Africa Confronts Its New Realities." *International Herald Tribune*. April 24, p. 2.

Tetzlaff, David. 1991. "Divide and Conquer: Popular Culture and Social Control in Late Capitalism." *Media, Culture and Society*. Vol. 13, No. 1. Pp. 9–33.

Thorsson, Inga. 1983. "Relationships between Disarmament and Development: How Disarmament Would Promote Development and Security." In Ann Mattis (ed.), *A Society for International Development: Prospectus, 1984* (pp. 30–41). Durham, N.C.: Duke University Press.

Thrift, Nigel. 1986. "The Geography of International Economic Order." In R.J. Johnston and P.J. Taylor (eds.), *A World in Crisis?* (pp. 12–67). New York: Basil Blackwell.

Tice, Terrence N. and Thomas P. Slavens. 1983. *Research Guide to Philosophy*. Chicago: American Library Association.

Time. 1993. December 6, p. 10.

Tokei, F. 1982. "Some Contentious Issues in the Interpretation of the Asiatic Mode of Production." *Journal of Contemporary Asia*. Vol. 12, No. 3. Pp. 294–303.

Toye, John. 1987." Development Theory and the Experience of Development: Issues for the Future." In Louis Emmerij (ed.), *Development Policies and the Crisis of the 1980s* (pp. 18–41). Paris: Development Centre of the OECD.

Trainer, Ted. 1989. *Developed to Death: Rethinking Third World Development*. London: Green Print.

Tri, Huynh Cao. 1986. "Cultural Identity and Development: Scope and Significance." In Huynh Cao Tri et al. (eds.), *Strategies for Endogenous Development* (pp. 1–17). New Delhi: Oxford & IBH Publishing Co.

Tuan, Yi-Fu. 1988. "On the Rewarding Human Life." In Jim Norwine and Alfonso Gonzalez (eds.), *The Third World: States of Mind and Being* (pp. 9–14). Boston: Unwin Hyman.

Tucker, Robert C. (ed.). 1978. "Introduction." In Robert C. Tucker (ed.), *The Marx-Engels Reader* (pp. xix–xxxviii). New York: W.W. Norton & Company.

Ullrich, Otto. 1992. "Technology." In Wolfgang Sachs (ed.), *The Development Dictionary: A Guide to Knowledge as Power* (pp. 275–87). London: Zed Books.

UNDP (United Nations Development Programme). 1994. *Human Development Report 1994*. New York: Oxford University Press.

Urmson, J.O. and Jonathan Ree (eds.). 1989. *The Concise Encyclopedia of Western Philosophy and Philosophers*. London: Unwin Hyman.

Urquidi, V.L. 1988. "Ideal and Attainable Goals for Development." In Unesco (ed.), *Goals of Development* (pp. 85–101). Paris: Unesco.

Valenzuela, J. Samuel and Arturo Valenzuela. 1978. "Modernization and Dependency: Alternative Perspectives in the Study of Latin American Underdevelopment." *Comparative Politics*. Vol. 10, No. 4. Pp. 535–57.

Van Leeuwen, A.T. 1970. *Development Through Revolution*. New York: Charles Scribner's Sons.

Varas, Augusto. 1985. *Militarization and the International Arms Race in Latin America*. Boulder, Colorado: Westview Press.

Veltmeyer, Henry. 1993. "Liberalisation and Structural Adjustment in Latin America: In Search of an Alternative." *Economic and Political Weekly*. Vol. 28 (25 September). Pp. 2080–86.

Vengroff, R. 1977. "Dependency and Underdevelopment in Black Africa: An Empirical Test." *Journal of Modern African Studies*. Vol. 15, No. 4. Pp. 613–30.

Vickers, J. and V. Wright. 1988. "The Politics of Privatization in Western Europe: An Overview." *West European Politics*. Vol. 11, No. 4. Pp. 1–30.

Villamil, J.J. 1977. "Development Planning and Dependence." *IDS Bulletin*. Vol. 9, No. 1. Pp. 57–61.

Vogeler, Ingolf and Anthony R. De Souza. 1980. "Dialectics of Understanding the Third World." In Ingolf Vogeler and Anthony R. De Souza (eds.), *Dialectics of Third World Development* (pp. 3–27). Montclair, N.J.: Allanheld, Osmun & Co.

Vyasulu, V. 1977. *The Paradox of Static Change*. New Delhi: Sterling Publishers Pvt. Ltd.

Wallerstein, Immanuel. 1974. "Rise and Future Demise of the World Capitalist System: Concepts and Comparative Analysis." *Comparative Studies in Society and History*. Vol. 16, No. 4. Pp. 387–415.

———. 1980. "The State in the Institutional Vortex of the Capitalist World Economy." *International Social Science Journal*. Vol. 32, No. 4. Pp. 743–51.

———. 1984a. "Patterns and Prospectives of the Capitalist World-Economy." *Contemporary Marxism*. No. 9 (Fall). Pp. 59–95.

———. 1984b. *The Capitalist World Economy: Essays*. Cambridge: Cambridge University Press.

———. 1989. "The Capitalist World Economy: Middle-run Prospects." *Alternatives*. Vol. 14, No. 3. Pp. 279–88.

Walras, Leon. 1954. *Elements of Pure Economics or the Theory of Social Wealth*. London: George Allen and Unwin.

Ward, Benjamin. 1988. "Trade and Development in the Pacific Rim's Third World." In Altap Gauhar (ed.), *Third World Affairs, 1988* (pp. 339–48). London: Third World Foundation for Social and Economic Studies.

Wasi, Prawase. 1984. "Buddhism and Social Problems in Thailand." In C.I. Itty (ed.) *Searching for Asian Paradigms* (pp. 57–63). Bangkok: Asian Cultural Forum on Development.

Weaver, James H. (ed.). 1973. *Modern Political Economy*. Boston: Allyn and Bacon.

Weaver, James H., and Kenneth P. Jameson. 1978. *Economic Development: Competing Paradigms—Competing Parables*, DSP Occasional Paper No. 3. Washington, D.C.: Agency for International Development.

Weber, B. 1994. "McDonald's Launches McDelivery." *International Herald Tribune*. November 7, p. 9.

Weber, Max. 1947. *The Theory of Social and Economic Organization* (edited with T. Parsons' Introduction). New York: Free Press.

——. 1958. *The Protestant Ethic and the Spirit of Capitalism* (with a Foreword by R. H. Tawney). New York: Charles Scribner's Sons.

Weigel, Van B. 1989. *A Unified Theory of Global Development*. New York: Praeger Publishers.

Weiss, S.A. 1994. "Middle East: Investment Attraction or Arms Bazaar?" *International Herald Tribune*. October 28, p. 6.

Weiss, Thomas G. 1982. "The Third World Views of the New International Development Strategy for the Third United Nations Development Decade." In Anthony Jennings and Thomas G. Weiss (eds.), *The Challenge of Development in the Eighties* (pp. 31–46). Oxford: Pergamon Press.

Welsh, Brian W.W. and Pavel Butorin. 1990. *Dictionary of Development: Third World Economy, Environment, Society* (Vols.I & II). New York and London: Garland Publishing.

Werker, S. 1985. "Beyond the Dependency Paradigm." *Journal of Contemporary Asia*. Vol. 15, No. 1. Pp. 79–95.

Wesson, Robert. 1990. "Wrapping Up the Debt Problem." *Political Science and Politics*. Vol. 23, No. 3. Pp. 419–24.

Westergaard, Kirsten. 1985. *State and Rural Society in Bangladesh: A Study in Relationship*. London: Curzon Press.

White, Michael. 1977. "Kalecki's Theories of Economic Growth and 'Development'." *Journal of Contemporary Asia*. Vol. 7, No. 3. Pp. 298–331.

Whitney, C.R. 1994. "Cold War Radios Feel Pinch: Free Europe and Liberty Reel from Big Cuts." *International Herald Tribune*. August 22, p. 2.

Wiarda, Howard J. 1981. "The Ethnocentrism of the Social Science Implications for Research and Policy." *The Review of Politics*. Vol. 43, No. 2. Pp. 163–97.

——. 1989–90. "Rethinking Political Development: A Look Backward Over Thirty Years, and a Look Ahead." *Studies in Comparative International Development*. Vol. 24, No. 4. Pp. 65–82.

——. 1990. "The Politics of Third World Debt." *Political Science and Politics*. Vol. 23, No. 3. Pp. 411–18.

Wilber, Charles K. and Kenneth P. Jameson (eds.). 1979. "Paradigms of Economic Development and Beyond." In Kenneth P. Jameson and Charles K. Wilber (eds.), *Directions in Economic Development* (pp. 1–41). Notre Dame, Indiana: University of Notre Dame Press.

Wilson, V. 1988. "A Fate Worse Than Debt." *News Week*. November 7, p. 87.

Winik, L.W. and D. Mehic. 1994. "Bosnia: Culture Offers the Seeds of Survival." *International Herald Tribune*. September 14, p. 4.

Wionczek, M. 1979. "The New International Economic Order: Past Failures and Future Prospects." *Development and Change*. Vol. 10, No. 4. Pp. 647–71.

Witton, Ron. 1988. "Rural Sociology." In David Goldsworthy (ed.), *Development Studies in Australia: Themes and Issues* (pp. 18–24). Clayton Vic., Australia: Monash Development Studies Centre.

Wolf, Laurence Grambow. 1988. "The Poorest of Us All." In Jim Norwine and Alfonso Gonzalez (eds.), *The Third World: States of Mind and Being* (pp. 99–111). Boston: Unwin Hyman.

Wood, Geof. 1977. "Rural Development and the Post-Colonial State: Administration and the Peasantry in the Kosi Region of North-East Bihar, India." *Development and Change*. Vol. 8, No. 3. Pp. 307–23.

———. 1980. "Bureaucracy and the Post-Colonial State in South Asia: A Reply." *Development and Change*. Vol. 11, No. 1. Pp. 149–56.

World Bank. 1987. *World Debt Tables: External Debt of Developing Countries*. Washington, D.C.: World Bank.

———. 1988. *World Development Report, 1988*. New York: Oxford University Press.

———. 1990. *World Debt Tables, 1990–91: External Debt of Developing Countries*. Washington, D.C.: World Bank.

———. 1991. *World Development Report, 1991: The Challenge of Development*. New York: Oxford University Press.

———. 1994. *World Development Report 1994: Infrastructure for Development*. New York: Oxford University Press.

World Economy: Fear of Finance. 1992. *The Economist*. September 19.

Worsley, Peter. 1984. *The Three Worlds: Culture and World Development*. Chicago: University of Chicago Press.

Yeltsin's Economic Tinkering. 1992. *The Economist*. April 11, pp. 19–20.

Young, Ralph A. 1995. "Privatization: African Perspectives." In Paul Cook and Colin Kirkpatrick (eds.), *Privatization Policy and Performance: International Perspectives* (pp. 162–77). London: Prentice Hall/Harvester Wheatsheaf.

Zack-Williams, A.B. 1982. "Crisis of Marxist Theory of Imperialism and Underdevelopment." *African Review*. Vol. 9, No. 1. Pp. 125–31.

Zagorin, Adam. 1994. "Damning the World Bank." *Time*. July 25, pp. 30–32.

Zamora, Ruben. 1994. "Five Propositions and Three Reorientations for the Popular Movement." *Lokayan Bulletin*. Vol. 10, No. 4. Pp. 29–35.

Name Index

Addo, Herb, 147
Adelman, Irma, 83, 85, 86
Adorno, Theodor, 83, 97, 99
Aghion, Philippe, 64
Alatas, Syed Hussein, 173
Alavi, Hamza, 104, 118, 123, 124, 125, 126
Almond, Gabriel, 75, 142, 148
Alpert, Paul, 55, 70
Althusser, Louis, 116
Amin, Samir, 104, 119, 120, 121, 227, 234
Anber, Paul, 76
Angus, Ian, 35
Appelbaum, Richard, 44
Apter, David, 142
Arndt, Heinz, 92

Balibar, Etienne, 116
Banaji, Jairus, 115, 118
Baran, Paul, 104, 112
Barnett, Tony, 214
Barro, Robert, 55, 64
Barros de Castro, Antonio, 92
Bastiat, Frederic, 55, 60, 68, 108, 133, 141
Bendix, Reinhard, 76
Benjamin, Walter, 83, 97, 99
Bentham, Jeremy, 60, 90, 108, 141
Berger, Peter, 46
Bernstein, Henry, 112
Berthoud, Gerald, 157
Boeke, J.H., 71

Bohm-Bawerk, Eugen von, 60, 61
Booth, David, 93
Boulding, Elise, 135
Bradley, P.N., 17
Braun, Gerald, 3
Brewer, Anthony, 24, 131
Bronner, Stephen, 97
Brown, Lester, 28
Buchanan, Keith, 104
Bukharin, Nikolai, 107, 110, 139
Bunge, W., 17

Caldwell, Bruce, 104, 131
Cardoso, Henrique, 83, 91, 94, 95, 96, 184
Casanova, Pablo, 83, 91, 94, 96
Chattopadhyay, P., 118
Chodak, Szymon, 45, 75
Clark, John Bates, 60, 61, 68
Clements, Kevin, 46, 63, 155
Cliffe, Lionel, 122
Comte, Auguste, 55, 73, 131

Davis, Adelle, 211
Deutsch, Karl, 142
Dixon, M., 171
Dogra, Bharat, 225
Dopfer, K., 5
Dos Santos, Theotonio, 111, 112, 113, 115
Durkheim, Emile, 55, 73, 74, 131, 136, 139, 141
Durning, Alan, 20

Easterlin, Richard, 83, 85, 86
Easton, David, 75
Emmanuel, Arghiri, 104, 119, 120, 121
Engels, Frederich, 50, 105, 116, 142, 147
Esteva, Gustavo, 158
Evans, Peter, 184

Fagen, M., 16
Faletto, Enzo, 83, 91, 95, 96, 184
Fanon, Franz, 104
Ferres, Aldo, 92
Foster-Carter, Aidan, 46, 104, 118
Frank, Andre Gunder, 104, 111, 112, 113,
   114, 115, 118, 131
Friedman, Milton, 55, 61, 133, 136, 141
Fromm, Erich, 83, 97, 98
Furtado, Celso, 83, 91, 92, 93, 94, 96

Gadamer, Hans Georg, 133
Galtung, Johan, 170
Gareau, Frederick, 143
Garnham, Nicholas, 171
Gendzier, Irene, 148
Ghosh, Ratna, 171
Goldthorpe, John, 72
Goulet, Denis, 5, 145, 152
Gramsci, Antonio, 97
Grant, James, 84
Gregory, Chris, 152
Gulalp, H., 104
Gusdorf, G., 172
Gusfield, Joseph, 76

Habermas, Jurgen, 83, 97, 98, 99, 100,
   101
Hagen, Everett, 55, 76, 78, 134
Hamelink, Cees, 234
Hancock, Graham, 152
Hansen, Craig, 139
Haq, Mahbub ul, 84
Harbison, Frederick, 83, 85, 86
Harrod, Jeffrey, 146
Helleiner, Gerald, 155
Hettne, Bjorn, 41, 172
Hicks, J.R., 63
Hilferding, Rudolf, 107, 110
Hirschman, Albert, 45, 55, 70
Hodgskin, Thomas, 83, 90, 91

Horkheimer, Max, 83, 97, 98, 99, 100
Howitt, Peter, 55, 64
Hunt, E.K., 68
Huntington, Samuel, 55, 76, 148

Illich, Ivan, 215
Itty, C.I., 223

Jaffee, David, 40, 45
Jaguaribe, Helio, 76
Jevons, Williams, 55, 60, 61
Jhally, Sut, 180
Johnson, D.L., 76
Johnston, Bruce, 217, 219
Jolly, Richard, 46

Kaldor, N., 63
Katouzian, Homa, 131
Kautsky, John, 139
Kay, Cristobal, 104
Kellner, Douglas, 35
Keynes, John Maynard, 55, 66
Kim, D.H., 44
Korten, David, 143, 151

Laclau, Ernesto, 116, 118
Laite, F., 45
Lall, S., 104
Landau, Saul, 22
Lanzendorfer, M., 118, 124, 125
Larrain, Jorge, 45
Leeson, P.F., 44
Leibenstein, Harvey, 70
Lenin, V.I., 107, 110, 116, 139
Lewis, W. Arthur, 55, 70, 71
Leys, Colin, 125, 126
Lipset, Martin, 142
Lowenthal, Leo, 97, 99
Lukacs, George, 97
Luxemburg, Rosa, 107, 110, 139

McClelland, David, 55, 76, 77, 134
McCloskey, Donald, 131
McEachern, D., 118
McKenzie, Richard, 133
Macpherson, C.B., 134

Maine, Henry Sumner, 73
Malthus, Thomas, 53, 55, 57, 108, 138, 141
Manzo, Kate, 140
Marcuse, Herbert, 83, 97, 98, 99, 100
Marini, Ruy Mauro, 111, 112, 113, 114, 115
Marshall, Alfred, 60, 61, 66, 74
Martin, Brendan, 157
Marx, Karl, 50, 105, 116, 118, 120, 132, 134, 137, 139, 142, 147, 148
Mathur, G.B., 5
Mellor, John, 83, 86
Menger, Carl, 55, 60, 61, 133, 141
Michalet, C., 119
Mill, J.S., 53, 55, 57, 58, 59, 108, 138, 141
Mittelman, James, 210
Moore, Wilbert, 44, 55, 74, 75, 124, 145
Morgan, Lewis Henry, 73, 133
Murphy, Craig, 147
Murray, Robin, 119

Nafziger, E. Wayne, 218, 225
Nandy, Ashis, 146
Nasr, Seyyed, 167
Negt, Oskar, 97
Nieuwenhuijze, C.A.O. van, 45, 161
Nurske, Ragnar, 55, 69

O'Brien, P.J., 94, 104
Offe, Claus, 97
O'Manique, J., 171
Owen, Robert, 90

Parenti, Michael, 36, 179
Pareto, Vilfred, 63, 74
Parsons, Talcott, 55, 74, 75, 131, 139, 142
Patnaik, U., 118
Petras, James, 23, 122, 126, 127
Pieterse, Jan, xiii, 3
Pollock, Friedrich, 97, 98, 99
Prebisch, Raul, 83, 91, 92, 93, 96
Preston, Peter, 46, 72, 88, 139
Pye, Lucien, 55, 75, 76, 148

Ramirez-Faria, Carlos, 147
Ramos, Alberto, 171
Ramphal, Shridath, 150
Randall, Vickey, 105
Reuveny, Jacob, 6
Rey, Pierre-Philippe, 116, 117
Ricardo, David, 53, 55, 57, 58, 107, 108, 138, 141
Rice, Robert, 210
Rivera-Batiz, Luis, 55, 63-64
Robinson, Joan, 55
Romer, Paul, 55, 63, 64, 65
Rosenstein-Rodan, Paul, 55, 69, 91
Rostow, W.W., 69, 71, 138, 139, 140
Roxborough, I., 122
Ruccio, D.F., 119
Rudolph, Lloyd, 76
Rudolph, Suzanne, 76
Rudra, A., 118

Sachs, Wolfgang, ix, 149, 163
Samuelson, Paul, 55, 67, 68
Saul, John, 125
Sauvant, Karl, 89
Say, Jean-Baptiste, 55, 60, 68, 108
Schiller, Herbert, 196
Schmidt, Alfred, 97
Schultz, Theodore, 83, 85
Schumacher, E. Friedrich, 83, 85
Schumpeter, Joseph, 55, 76, 77, 78
Seers, Dudley, 84
Senghaas, Dieter, 230
Senior, Nassau, 55, 60, 68, 108, 133
Shils, Edward, 76, 142, 148
Shivji, Issa, 125, 126
Simon, L.H., 119
Singer, Hans, 55, 70
Sivard, Ruth, 24
Smelser, Neil, 74
Smith, Adam, 53, 55, 57, 107, 108, 138, 141, 154
Sparks, Colin, 232
Spencer, Herbert, 55, 73
Srinivasan, T.N., 44
Stavenhagen, Rodolfo, 83, 91, 94, 96
Steidlmeier, Paul, 16, 46
Stein, Howard, 155
Streeten, Paul, 83, 87, 140
Sunkel, Osvaldo, 83, 91, 92, 93, 94, 96
Sussman, Gerald, 234

Tandon, Yash, 222
Taylor, Alwyn, 25–26
Taylor, John, 117
Thompson, William, 83, 90, 91
Toye, John, 46

Valenzuela, J. Samuel, 44
Vengroff, R., 44

Wallerstein, Immanuel, 111, 112, 113, 114, 131

Walras, Leon, 55, 60, 61, 133, 141
Waterston, A., 86
Weber, Max, 55, 74, 76, 77, 136, 139
Weigel, Van, 88
Wellmer, Albrecht, 97
Wilber, Charles, 46
Witton, Ron, 146
Wood, Geof, 123, 124, 125

Ziemann, W., 118, 124, 125

Subject Index

Africa, 170; economic growth, 14; external debt in, 15; landholding in, 15; living standards, 255n7; mineral resources, 229; poverty in, xi, 2

Agriculture, 219; capitalist, 113; cash crops, 17, 209; commercial, 75; control of, 2; employment in, 86; environmental threats to, 28; expansion of, 54; income from, 70; investment in, 70; labor-capital ratio, 70; plantation, 209; production, 208, 230; subsistence, 75; surplus in, 54

Asia, 170; landholding in, 15; migration from, 18; poverty in, 2, 14–15

Austrian School, 55fig, 61

Authoritarianism, 84, 163, 185, 186, 201

Authority: charismatic, 77; rational legal, 77

Autonomy, 164; internal, 218–223; international, 223-233; preconditions for, 198–199; relative, 199; struggles for, 185

Balanced growth theory, 55fig, 69–70

Balance of payments, 92, 93, 182, 272n30

Basic needs approach, 47–48, 84, 87–88, 131, 271n13

Big-push theory, 55fig, 69

Bosnia, ethnic conflict, 26

Bourgeoisie: absence of, 125; bureaucratic, 125; indigenous, 123, 124, 125; metropolitan, 123; petty, 125

Brain-drain, 2, 18–19, 214

Capital: accumulation, 57, 58, 59, 69, 71, 92, 95, 96, 108, 109, 125, 127, 166, 206, 266n6; agrarian, 121; analysis of, 132; concentration of, 108, 109, 119; corporate, 194; export of, 110, 119; finance, 110; fixed, 267n17; flight, 16, 241; human, 56, 64, 65; indivisibility of, 69; industrial, 110; investment, 54, 70; lack of, 68, 69, 207, 268n39; merchant, 121; mobility of, 120; ownership of, 90; reproducible, 71; state, 95; transnational, xi, 7, 30, 93, 194, 195, 197; variable, 108, 279n20

Capitalism: colonialism and, 107, 114; corporate, 65, 100; creative destruction of, 78; crises of, 108; critique of, 98-99; dynamics of, 101; emergence of, 77, 107, 110; expansion of, 39, 119; exploitation of, 90; global, 228, 250n3; imperial, 110, 126; industrial, 39, 53, 56, 57, 108, 263n2; international structure of, 137, 195; metropolitan, 113; monopoly, 95, 98, 126; oligopolistic, 65; peripheral, 114, 121, 273n42; postliberal, 98; stages of, 98

367

Capitalist development, 45, 48, 76, 109, 115, 121, 227, 284n117

Capitalist nations: economic growth in, 59; Keynesian theory in, 66-68; political economy in, 98; radical reform in, 90-91; relations with, 88-89; sociocultural disorders in, 3

Chicago School, 55fig, 61

Class: alliances, 123, 126; articulation, 122; conflict, 136; defining, 283n97; exploitation, 145, 163; formation, 168; identity, 168; interactions, 126; landed, 123, 124, 218; radicalization, 194; struggle, 100, 108, 109, 137

Class analysis perspective: Africa, 125–126; Asia, 123–125; Latin America, 126–127

Class structure, 47, 51, 104, 115, 121–124, 135, 136, 137, 154, 155

Classical theory, ix, 48, 55fig, 56-59, 57–59

Colonialism, 4, 25, 39, 123, 139, 141, 166, 198, 263n3, 280n39, 282n77; capitalism and, 107, 114; cultural-intellectual subjugation and, 172; indigenous culture and, 2; labor displacement in, 17; phases of, 114; progressive effect of, 109

Conflict: class, 136; economic, 262n140; ethno-religious, ix; ideological, 187; international, 33; racial, 24–26, 36; religious, 22; resolution, 226–227

Conservative development theories, ix–x, 48–49, 53–79, 55fig; economic primacy in, 53

Consumption, 267n33; excessive, 150; foreign goods, 18; guidelines, 99; income and, 58, 93; as indicator of development, 150; patterns, 18, 93, 167, 181; propensity for, 66–67; subsistence, 278n19; Western patterns of, 197

Corruption, 9, 21, 23, 221, 241

Crime, 3, 9, 19, 36, 236

Critical reformist theories, 48–49, 97–102, 265n35

Critical theory, 50, 97–102, 265n35

Cultural: bias, 237; confusion, 149; differences, 22; diversity, 141; ethnocentrism, xiii; exchange, 236; formation, 2–3; heritage, 236–238;

identity, xii, 1, 6, 148-150, 237; indoctrination, 149; interventions, 184; products, 182, 191, 234; recolonization, 149; sovereignty, 138; traditions, 236

Cultural-intellectual autonomy, 170–173, 176, 177, 179, 180, 181, 196, 197, 198–204, 233–243

Culture: capitalist, 4; disappearance of, 149; erosion of, 148–150; industry, x, xii, 4, 99, 172, 181, 196, 201; mass, 98, 199; transformation of, 220–221

Deforestation, 27, 28, 150

Democracy: bourgeois, 94, 96; rhetoric of, 197

Dependency, 2, 15, 152; as cause of underdevelopment, 89; causes of, 113; colonial, 24, 113; effects of, 115; food import, 209; historical periods of, 113; military, 229, 262n131; nature of, 113; political, 16; structural, 274n55; technological, 1, 181; Third World, 152

Dependency theories, x, 2, 8, 45, 50, 91, 104, 105, 111–115, 274n9, 289n84; empiricism in, 131, 132; normative indifference in, 135; universalism in, 143

Deregulation, xi, xii, 8, 36, 153, 154, 162

Development: alternative perspectives, 161–204; authentic, 163; autocentric, 121; capitalist, 45, 48, 76, 109, 115, 121, 227, 284n117; as concept, 162–173; conceptual plurality of, 162; criteria for, 74–75, 75; deconstruction of, xiii; dependent, 50, 83fig, 91, 95–97; disorders, 13–27; distorted, 151–153, 164; Eurocentric view of, 3; market-centered, xii, 153; partial, 164, 165; political, 45, 75, 131, 270n68; priorities, xii, 8; self-reliant, 82; state-centered, 153; subjugation and, 164; sustainable, 163, 228, 255n4

Development crises: in capitalist nations, 20–21; environmental, 27–29; global, 23–36; in socialist nations, 21–23; in Third World countries, 14–20

Development policies, 63; agricultural, 2, 208–209; communications, 214–217; priorities in, 207; education, 213–214; flaws in, 5–6; global context, 4–5;

health services and, 211–213; need-based production, 209–210; reformulation of, 205–248; rural-agricultural perspective, 208–209; transportation, 214–217; urban-centered, 2; urban-industrial perspective, 208–209
Development theories: controversial terminology, 45–46; adverse implications of, 144–153; categories of, 42; challenges to, 153–157; classification of, 39–51; conservative, 252n27; critique of, 129–159; economic empiricism in, 6; environment and, 150–151; epistemological empiricism, 130–133; exclusion of cultural values, 130; failures of, ix, 10, 36, 151–153; historical contexts of, 45; inadequacies in, x, 10, 13–27, 130–143; intellectual hegemony and, 144–146; limitations of, 6; normative indifference in, 6, 133–135, 252n42; politico-economic dominance and, 146–148; practical relevance of, 6, 130; reductionism in, 135–138; restructuring of, 161–204
Dualism theory, 48, 55fig, 70–71

Economic growth, xi, xii, 8, 14, 56, 59, 64, 66, 68, 85, 86, 87, 92, 136, 154, 163, 206, 228, 225n4, 265n34; Africa, 14; capitalist nations, 59; China, 23; Hong Kong, 14; Indonesia, 19; Latin America, 14; Philippines, 19; Singapore, 14; South Korea, 14, Taiwan, 14
Economic growth theories, ix–x, 44, 46, 47, 48, 53–79, 55fig, 252n27; analytical reductionism in, 135–138; empiricism in, 132; epistemological empiricism in, 130–133; ethnocentrism in, 138; intellectual hegemony and, 144–146; interventionist theories, 65–72; noninterventionist theories, 56–65; normative indifference in, 133–135; universalism in, 141–143
Education, xi; contextless, 213–214; expansion of, 207; globalization of, 234; inappropriate, 2, 18; indigenization of, 234–236; investment in, 64, 140; need-based, 213–214; shortcomings in, 213;

Western model, 149, 172, 182, 193, 202, 213, 234–236
Entrepreneurship, 77–78, 85
Environment(al), 4–5; adaptation to, 73; catastrophes, xii, 27–29, 36; control over, 269n60; crises, 1; degradation of, 5; desertification, 28; disasters, 150–151; movements, xi; pollution, ix; problems, 65, 260n107
Ethnic conflict, 1, 22, 24–26, 36, 226, 258n62; in Angola, 25; Bosnia, 26; Estonia, 26; Latvia, 26; Mozambique, 25; Rwanda, 26; South Africa, 25; Sri Lanka, 25; Turkey, 25; Ukraine, 26
Eurocentrism, 3, 5–6, 6, 39, 138–141, 146, 147, 148, 263n2, 287n47, 288n52, 289n66
Export-led: agriculture, 70, 113; capitalism, 121; growth, 209–210; policies, 2; production, 192, 209–210, 241
External debt, xi, 1, 2, 7, 15, 16, 23, 36, 146, 147, 152, 192, 195, 210, 224; expansion of, 146, 147; in African countries, 15–16; in Asian countries, 15–16; in Latin America, 15–16, 19; in socialist countries, 22; relief of, 88–89
External Dependence, ix, xii, 8, 16, 20, 22, 24, 32, 36, 92, 96, 154, 182, 195, 225; expansion of, 146, 147

Feudalism, 54, 116, 142, 175
Financial crises in: capitalist nations, 20–22; China, 23; Estonia, 22; Indonesia, 228; Malaysia, 228; South Korea, 228; Thailand, 228
Foreign investment, 8, 31, 36, 64, 113, 162, 194, 206, 225, 226
Frankfurt School, 48–49, 97, 271n1, 281n64, 285n2
Functionalism: ahistorical, 73; structural, 73–74

Globalization of: capital, 95, 116, 118–119, 184, 194; culture, x, 172; education, 234; information, x–xi; media, 172, 196, 197, 201
Greenhouse effect, 27, 28, 29, 150, 177, 259n90

Hegemony: class, 116, 124, 137, 169, 171, 176, 179; cultural, xii, 7, 8, 172, 181, 235, 236; economic, 222; intellectual, 144–146, 235; political, 222; state, 125

Imperialism, 45, 46, 110, 111, 184
Import substitution, 93, 96, 210, 273n42
Income distribution, xi, 15, 58, 82, 84, 85, 86, 87, 136, 152, 154, 217
Indigenous: capital, 121; class, 123; consumption, 34; culture, 2, 4, 148–150, 201, 236–238; knowledge, 178, 234–236, 240; production, 197, 210; resources, 207; technology, 178; values, 2
Individualism, 53, 134, 154, 155, 236, 269n53
Industrialization, 255n4; agriculture and, 86; capital accumulation and, 92; conditions of, 75; consequences of, 75; costs of, 4–5; environmental crises and, 29; import substitution and, 93
Industrial Revolution, 39, 54, 57
Inequality: class, 65, 192; economic, 3, 8, 15, 23–24, 86, 136, 155, 156, 195, 271n2; international, 23–24; social, ix, xii, 37, 121, 191
Inflation, 1, 22, 258n58
Information: authentic, 37; as commodity, 34; distorted, 35; media, 196; misleading, 196; networks, x, 234; structure, 34
Institutions: capitalist, 90; democratic, 220; educational, 171, 172, 192; effective, 229–232; international, 195, 250n3; participative, 220; people-centered, 221–223; political, 72, 221–223; sociocultural, 99; for solidarity, 229–232
Internal colonialism, 48–49, 83fig, 91, 94–95, 168
International agencies/laws, 7, 15, 16, 29, 30, 31, 32, 33, 84, 87, 88, 91, 170, 195, 203, 210, 225, 226, 230, 231, 240, 252n23, 261n129
International Monetary Fund, 8, 29, 30, 88, 195, 203, 224, 225, 226, 230, 252n23

Keynesian-neoclassical synthesis, 67–69
Keynesian theory, ix, 48, 53, 55fig; in capitalism, 66–68; empiricism in, 131; normative indifference in, 134; reductionism in, 136; universalism in, 141

Labor: agricultural, 54; aristocracy, 122; capital and, 100; commodification of, 108; displacement, 17; international division of, 92, 114, 120; organized, 184; sexual division of, 90; social division of, 95, 278n17; source of surplus value, 108; superexploitation of, 114; surplus, 66, 68, 69, 71; theory of value, 60, 90, 109, 120
Land: degradation, 27; desertification, 28; diminishing returns from, 58; distribution, 219; ownership, 15, 217; plunder of, 94; reform, 140; rent on, 58
Latin America, 170; colonial hegemony in, 172–173; doctrine of market failure in, 91; economic condition in, 112; economic growth, 14; external debt in, 15, 19; industrial development in, 115; landholding in, 15; poverty in, xi, 2, 14, 151; privatization in, 156; radical development theory in, 106fig; socialism in, 95; underdevelopment in, 92
Liberalization, xi, 8, 156, 162; trade, 88–89, 206
Living standards, xi, 23, 39, 84, 208, 255n7, 260n107

Maldevelopment, 9, 163, 164–165, 170
Market: black, 254n49, 254n51; capitalism, 98; competition, 8, 54, 56, 57, 65, 91; crises, 19–20, 67; distortion, 121; failures, 66, 91; foreign, 209–210; free, 53, 57, 60, 67, 153, 154; ideology, xi, 8; local, 85, 209–210; principles, xii; regional, 261n124; relations, 96
Marxist theories, x, 2, 44, 46, 107–111, 111, 112, 264n15, 286n14; classical, 50, 104, 105–111, 106fig, 111, 142, 274n10, 274n11; critical, 97, 105, 274n10, 274n60; critique of, 99–100; empiricism in, 131; ethnocentrism in,

139; normative indifference in, 134; orthodox, 100, 274*n11*, 274*n61*; reductionism in, 137; universalism in, 142, 143

Mass Media: construction of opinion through, 35; consumerism and, 191; control of, 4; culture and, 99, 236–238; global, 4, 7, 33, 172, 196, 197, 201, 239, 254*n44*, 262*n147*; independent, 238–240; information order and, 4; manipulation by, 196, 197, 201; marketing and, 34–35; ownership, 196; propaganda by, 196; transnational corporations and, 35; Western control of, 34, 172, 179–180

Metropoles, 92; dominance of, 94; links with, 115

Migration, 2, 18–19, 25, 150; rural-urban, 85

Military: asistance, 200, 201; dependence, 229, 262*n131*; expenditures, 16, 26–27, 32, 71, 217, 220, 255*n16*; interventions, 76, 84, 184, 195, 197, 225; oligarchy, 123, 124; research, 225; weaponry, 225; world order, 32–33

Modernization theories, ix, 8, 44, 45, 46, 47, 49, 55*fig*, 72–79, 252*n27*, 263*n3*; empiricism in, 131, 132; ethnocentrism in, 139; normative indifference in, 134; political, 49, 55*fig*, 72, 75–76; production side, 62; psycho-cultural, 49, 55*fig*, 72, 76–79, 134; reductionism in, 136; sociological, 49, 55*fig*, 72, 73–75; universalism in, 142

Modes-of-production, 19, 45, 51, 94, 108, 109, 111, 112, 116, 117, 118, 120, 121, 122, 123, 142, 166, 282*n66*; articulation of, 116–117; Asiatic, 109; feudal, 54; peripheral, 117–118; schools of, 116–119

Monopolies, 34, 95, 98, 110, 113, 119, 120, 126

Natural-physiological autonomy, 165–167, 174, 177, 180, 206–217

Neoclassical theory, ix, xii, 8, 44, 48, 53, 55*fig*, 59–63, 153, 154; components of, 62–63; consumption side, 62; dominance of, 6; empiricism in, 131;

methodological grounds, 61–62; reductionism in, 136; universalism in, 141

Neo-colonialism, 284*n117*; dependent, 126

Neo-evolutionary revival, 73–74

Neo-Marxist theories, x, 2, 8, 44, 46, 47, 51, 104, 105, 106*fig*, 115–127, 281*n64*, 281*n65*, 286*n14*; empiricism in, 131; normative indifference in, 134; reductionism in, 137; universalism in, 142

New growth theory, ix, 53, 55*fig*, 56, 63–65, 131; empiricism in, 131; normative indifference in, 133–134; technology in, 64; universalism in, 141

New International Economic Order, 30, 83*fig*, 84, 87, 88–89, 89, 134, 136–137, 271*n2*; ethnocentrism in, 140

Newly Industrialized Countries, 112, 208, 255*n4*; development model, 19, 20; economic growth in, 14

Newspapers. *See* Mass Media

Non-Aligned Movement, 30, 229, 240

Non-Government Organizations (NGOs), 222–223

Ownership: of assets, xi, 22, 156; of capital, 90; of culture industry, 196; land, 15, 217; of means of production, 168; media, 196; unequal, 169, 175, 177, 180

Ozone-layer depletion, 27, 28, 150, 177, 260*n96*

Periphery, 114, 120; capital flow in, 126; development of, 95; economic structures, 118, 124, 125; exports from, 113, 272*n34*; liberation of, 163; precapitalist mode of production in, 117; superexploitation of, 114, 120; underdevelopment of, 121

Policy reforms: for cultural-intellectual autonomy, 233–243; for natural-physiological autonomy, 206–217; for politico-economic autonomy, 81, 217–233; in landownership, 140, 218–219; prioritization in, 241–243

Political: anarchy, 22; consciousness, 222; dependence, 16; development, 45, 131; diversity, 141; dominance, 218; elections, 4; institutions, 72, 221–223; power, 125, 169; repression, 8, 151, 195; stability, ix, 3, 23, 75, 131, 163, 258n73; systems, 72, 75, 194; unrest, 21, 37,195

Political economy, 45, 46, 98, 133, 223–226, 227

Politico-economic autonomy, 167–170, 175, 177, 178, 179, 180, 181, 196, 197, 200, 217–233

Population, 59, 256n24, 262n134; consumption and, 24; growth, 70; theories of, 57; Third World, 16–18; uncontrolled growth, 57

Postcolonial societies: Bangladesh, 123; Pakistan, 123; Tanzania, 125

Post-Keynesian theory, 48, 53, 55fig; normative indifference in, 134; reductionism in, 136; universalism in, 141

Poverty, ix, xi, 1, 2, 4, 6, 8, 14–15, 37, 57, 66, 69, 84, 94, 151, 152, 155, 192, 202, 250n7; in Africa, xi; in Asia, 2, 14–15; in Eastern Europe, 22; in Latin America, xi, 14, 151; in Soviet Union, 22; in United States, 20

Privatization, xi, xii, 8, 153, 154, 156, 162, 206, 258n58

Production: agricultural, 70, 208, 230; capital-intensive, 192; capitalist, 3, 53, 57, 109; commodity, 108, 109, 114, 278n17; factors of, 61, 62, 272n30; food, 17, 28, 177, 207, 228; forces of, 76, 103, 108, 274n16; hierarchies in, 94, 108; industrial, 5–6, 58, 150; labor-intensive, 87, 219; means of, 168, 175, 176, 179, 274n16; need-based, 209–210; relations of, 94, 96, 103, 108, 115, 119, 137, 138, 163, 274n16, 282n77; surplus, 54, 70

Radical development theories, x, 48–49, 50–51, 103–127, 106fig, 252n27, 265n36; articulation of mode of production, 106fig, 116–117; class analysis, 121–127, 135, 139; contributions of Marx and Engels, 107–110; depen-

dency theories, x; empiricism in, 132; internationalization of capital, 116, 118–119; Marxist theories, x; mode of production school, 116–119; neo-Marxist theories, x, 115–127; peripheral mode of production, 117–118; universalism in, 142

Rationality: capitalism and, 77; economic, 136; instrumental, 151

Reductionism, 186; analytical, xiii, 130, 135–138, 144; methodological, 286n30

Reform: agrarian, 93, 96; antidevelopmental, 36; in developed countries, 83fig; economic, 22, 81; international, 49, 83fig, 84, 88–89; in landownership, 140, 218–219; market-centered, ix, xi; as means of development, 81; national level, 49, 83fig, 85–87; promarket, 8, 9, 22, 155, 195; social, 81; socioeconomic, 48–49, 82

Reformist development theories, x, 49–50, 81–102, 252n27; conservative, 82, 83fig, 84–89; critical, 83fig, 97–102; ethnocentrism in, 140; radical, 82, 83fig, 89–97; redistribution with growth, 48–49, 83fig, 85–86; redistribution with/without growth, 83fig, 84, 87–88; reductionism in, 136

Regionalism (regional blocs), 30, 31, 32, 33, 89, 170, 225, 260n112, 261n129

Resources: allocation of, 59, 67; depletion of, 56; diversion of, 181, 192; employment of, 77–78; human, 83fig, 85–86, 131, 136, 150, 207; local, 85, 87, 182, 207, 225; nonrenewable, 177; reverse flow, 16; transfer of, 156

Restructuring: development concept, 162–173; development policies, 205–248; development theories, 161–204

Rights: civil, 73; human, 195, 197; in South Africa, 25

Rural development, 46, 84, 85, 86, 131, 136, 143

Self-reliance, xii, 8, 9, 86, 189; in production, 228; Third World, 82, 86

Slavery, 109, 142, 175, 209, 258n71

Social: action, 77, 134, 270n72; change, 44, 48, 49, 72, 73, 74, 81, 89, 95, 96,

100, 104, 107, 108, 142, 145, 148, 265n36; class, 104, 122, 123; contradictions, 48; differentiation, 73–74, 163; dualism, 71; elites, 214; formations, 99, 121, 122, 125, 142, 183; inequality, ix, xii, 37, 121, 191; integration, 101, 163, 269n53; pathologies, ix; power, 193; progress, 73, 90, 138, 147; relations, 53, 133; repression, 97; security, 72, 156; structures, 71, 72; subjugation, 170, 191; transformation, 50, 81, 82, 97, 99, 100, 103, 111, 137, 164

Socialism, 142; emergence of, 110; establishment of, 103, 104, 109; proletarian route, 95; reemergence of, 252n19; through revolution, 103, 121, 122; transitions to, 95, 96, 109

Socialist nations: collapse of, 2; crises in, 21–23; current problems, 3; external debt in, 22; regime legitimacy in, 3; "Third Worldization of," 3

Stages-of-growth theory, 55fig, 69, 71–72; ethnocentrism in, 138

State: administrative, 65; autonomy, 124, 125; capitalism, 98, 99; centrality of, 125; civil society and, 107; class relations and, 122, 123; composition of, 51, 142; control, 37, 98, 99, 179; expanion of, 65; intervention, 48, 54, 61, 66, 67, 70, 94, 123; nature of, 122; overdeveloped, 125, 284n114; planning, 70, 99; policies, 45, 222, 228; role of, xi, 110, 126, 142, 154

Structural adjustment programs, xi, xii, 8, 15, 30, 153, 154, 156, 255n10

Structuralism, 112, 116, 279n38

Sub-imperialism, 113

Subjugation: acceptance of, 194; autonomy from, 164, 165; colonial, 192, 193, 198, 206; cultural-intellectual, 25, 170–173, 174, 176, 177, 179, 180, 181, 191, 193, 196, 197, 198–204, 234; external, 189, 190, 191; interclass, 168, 192, 218; internal, 168, 183–186, 187, 189, 190, 191, 194, 196; international, 172, 183–186, 190, 191, 194, 226; levels of, 184, 185, 186–191, 193, 196–198; modes of, 196–198; natural-physiological, 165–167, 174, 177, 180, 191; neocolonial, 198, 206; politico-economic, 167–170, 174, 175, 176, 177, 178, 179,

180, 181, 182, 185, 192–193, 196, 197, 217–233; racial, 190; social, 170, 191; structural basis for, 175

Surplus value, 61, 108, 109, 278n19, 279n20

Taxonomy of development, 39–51, 250n8; adequacy of categories, 41–42; categorical exclusiveness, 42–43; current limitations, 44–47; logic of hierarchy, 42; principles of, 41–44; restructured, 47–51; selection of terms, 43–44

Technology: agricultural, 86; alternative, 239; appropriate, 83fig, 85, 87; capital-intensive, 93; communication, 33; high-cost, 192; inappropriate, 192; innovations in, 56; labor-intensive, 84, 86, 87, 219

Television. See Mass Media

Third World: capitalist interventions in, 109; change-agents for, 232–233; decolonization of, 39, 72, 73, 185, 190; dependency in, 32, 92, 152, 262n131; division within, 226–227; external debt in, 15–16; fertility in, 17, 87, 256n24; imperialist intervention in, 110, 111; imports, 31, 114, 176, 210; indigenous culture and, 2, 4; international structures and, 227–229; literacy in, 145, 207, 208; migration from, 18–19; Most Favored Nation status for, 31; population, 16–18; poverty in, 1, 2, 4, 6, 8, 14–15; radical reform in, 91–97; relations with West, 88–89; solidarity, 229–232; urbanization in, 19–20

Trade: balances, 92; deficits, ix, 21, 31, 36; dependence, 92; free, 8, 31, 36, 58; international, 30, 63, 64, 92, 96, 188, 217, 224; liberalization, 88-89, 206; monopoly, 113; terms of, 16, 30, 209, 224; unequal, 96

Trade blocs, 29, 30, 31, 88, 170, 260n112

Transnational capital, xi, 2, 7, 9, 30, 93, 156, 192, 194, 195, 197, 200

Transnational corporations: agriculture and, 2; control by, 170, 210, 224, 225; expansion of, 225; media and, 35; monopolistic status of, 114; ownership of assets by, 22, 156; regulation of, 88–89; Third World exploitation by, 185

Unbalanced growth theory, ix, 48, 55*fig,*
　69, 70
Underdevelopment, ix, x, 48–49, 50, 66,
　83*fig,* 89, 91, 92–94, 96, 111, 112, 115,
　138, 170, 178, 273*n42*
Unemployment, 1, 3, 19, 22, 23, 85, 192
Unequal exchanges, 65, 111, 113, 114,
　119, 121, 131, 154
United Nations, 230; Children's Fund,
　16; Development Programme, 15;
　Economic Commission for Latin
　America, 91, 94, 112, 120; Educational,
　Scientific and Cultural Organization,
　240; Environmental Programme, 87;
　as instrument of United States policy,
　33; Security Council, 7, 32, 33, 195,
　203, 225, 226, 252*n23*
United States: budget deficits, 21, 31;
　economic inequality in, 20; exports, 31,
　261*n121;* interventions, 33, 182;
　migration to, 18; military dominance,
　32–33; military expenditures in,
　26–27; poverty in, 20; socioeconomic
　problems in, 21
Universalism, 145, 289*n73;* unfounded,
　130

Urbanization, 2, 19–20, 71
Utilitarianism, 90, 134; hedonistic, 151

Vicious circle theory, 55*fig,* 69

Western: bias, 2; capitalism, 77;
　consumption, 197; education, 149, 172,
　182, 213–214, 234–236; film imports,
　236; ideology, 72; influence, 181;
　information, 33; interference, 88;
　knowledge, 145, 146, 148; media, 35,
　179–180, 239; production patterns,
　197; superiority, 147; trade
　domination, 30; values, 197
Working class, 82, 97, 100, 145, 185, 192,
　194, 219
World Bank, 8, 29, 30, 84, 87, 88–89, 154,
　155, 195, 203, 224, 225, 226, 230
World order: cultural-informational,
　33–36; economic, 29–32; legal
　structures, 32; liberalization of, 89;
　politico-military, 32–33; unequal,
　29–36, 200